THE
CYGNUS KEY

"*The Cygnus Key* is the new astronomical paradigm that shines light on the primal awakening of human consciousness, sparked by the discovery of precession cycles, sound acoustics, and number cosmology. Andrew Collins had already decoded the alignments to the Cygnus star system at Göbekli Tepe and the Giza pyramid complex in his book *Göbekli Tepe: Genesis of the Gods.* Now, going back even further to 45,000 years ago, he explores how our ancestors first discovered the Cygnus connection, the pathway of souls through the constellation of the swan. This brilliant book is the sign I've been waiting for! We *are* recovering from our species trauma from the great cataclysms 12,000 years ago. *The Cygnus Key* is a must-read for all students of ancient timelines, star alignments, and cosmology."

BARBARA HAND CLOW, AUTHOR OF
AWAKENING THE PLANETARY MIND AND
REVELATIONS OF THE AQUARIAN AGE

"*The Cygnus Key* is a monumental work bringing numerous ancient mysteries into focus. It provides a lucid and well-reasoned understanding for readers who make the effort to digest it all. Starting with the amazing site of Göbekli Tepe, Collins leads the reader to Egypt and various other ancient civilizations. He shows how both Orion and Cygnus were key astronomical elements in the ancient world's understanding of the soul's journey to the stars and the probable source of these beliefs."

GREGORY L. LITTLE, PH.D., AUTHOR OF
*THE ILLUSTRATED ENCYCLOPEDIA OF NATIVE AMERICAN
INDIAN MOUNDS & EARTHWORKS*

"A dynamic quest to discover the cosmology of our earliest ancestors and its relevance today. Collins takes us on a convincing journey following the lore of the constellation of Cygnus. From Göbekli Tepe to the pyramids of Egypt and the archaic myths of Greece, we are led to humanity's ultimate psycho-spiritual roots in the Paleolithic world of Russian Siberia and the realm of the Denisovans. A triumph."

CAROLINE WISE, EDITOR OF
FINDING ELEN: THE QUEST FOR ELEN OF THE WAYS
AND COEDITOR OF *THE SECRET LORE OF LONDON*

THE
CYGNUS KEY

The Denisovan Legacy, Göbekli Tepe, and the Birth of Egypt

ANDREW COLLINS

with additional research by Rodney Hale

Bear & Company
Rochester, Vermont

Bear & Company
One Park Street
Rochester, Vermont 05767
www.BearandCompanyBooks.com

Bear & Company is a division of Inner Traditions International

Library of Congress Cataloging-in-Publication Data

Names: Collins, Andrew, 1957- author.
Title: The Cygnus key : the Denisovan legacy, Göbekli Tepe, and the birth of
  Egypt / Andrew Collins ; with additional research by Rodney Hale.
Description: Rochester, Vermont : Bear & Company, 2018. | Includes
  bibliographical references and index.
Identifiers: LCCN 2017041918 (print) | LCCN 2017061775 (e-book) |
  ISBN 9781591432999 (paperback) | ISBN 9781591433002 (e-book)
Subjects: LCSH: Denisovans. | Cygnus A. | Göbekli Tepe (Turkey) | Pyramids
  of Giza (Egypt) | BISAC: BODY, MIND & SPIRIT / Mythical Civilizations. |
  BODY, MIND & SPIRIT / Unexplained Phenomena. | BODY, MIND & SPIRIT /
  Occultism.
Classification: LCC GN285.2 .C65 2018 (print) | LCC GN285.2 (e-book) |
  DDC 569.9/8—dc23
LC record available at https://lccn.loc.gov/2017041918

Printed and bound in the United States by P. A. Hutchison Company

10 9 8 7 6 5 4 3 2 1

Text design and layout by Debbie Glogover
This book was typeset in Garamond Premier Pro with Guardi LT Std, Gill Sans MT Pro,
and Museo Sans used as display typefaces

Image Credits
Hugh Newman, 1.1a, 3.1, 3.3, plate 2; Rodney Hale, 1.1b, 2.1, 2.2, 2.3, 2.4, 3.4, 3.5,
4.1, 13.1, 13.4, 14.1, 14.2, 14.3, 17.1, 17.2, 18.1, 18.2, 18.3, 18.4, 19.1b, 25.2, 25.3, 25.4,
26.1, 27.1, 40.1; Nick Burton, 3.2, 6.1, 18.6 a and b, 19.1a, 19.2, 21.1, 29.1, 35.2, 35.5,
plate 24; Billy Walker John, 4.2, 17.4; Google Earth/Digital Globe, 27.1, 36.2; Yuri Leitch,
35.1; Russell M. Hossain, 3.4, plates 7, 22; Wiki Commons Agreement, plate 23;
Daniel Kordan, plate 25. All other illustrations and plate pictures are from the author's
personal collection and are copyright Andrew Collins. Every attempt has been made by
the author to clarify the ownership of illustrations used in this book. Any oversights or
omissions will be corrected in future editions.

To send correspondence to the author of this book, mail a first-class letter to the author
c/o Inner Traditions • Bear & Company, One Park Street, Rochester, VT 05767, and we will
forward the communication, or contact the author directly at **www.andrewcollins.com**.

For
Geoffrey Ashe,
A true pioneer in the quest of discovery,
And Rodney Hale,
Without whom this book might never have happened

CONTENTS

PART THREE

SECRETS OF THE PYRAMIDS

PART FOUR

COSMIC CODE

PART FIVE

GENESIS POINT

PART SIX

STARRY WISDOM

ACKNOWLEDGMENTS

I would like first to thank Debbie Cartwright and Richard Ward, whose intuitive thoughts and guidance have been essential in the book's creation. I would also like to thank Rodney Hale, for his unerring support and critical observations in every technical aspect of this project, as well for his hard work in the creation of so many essential illustrations; Greg and Lora Little, for their continued friendship, support, and belief in my work; Catherine Hale, Caroline Wise, and Bob Trubshaw, for line reading and suggestions; Jan Summers Duffy, Kira Van Deusen, Juan Antonio Belmonte, and Uzi Avner, for their scholarly advice and help; Russell M. Hossain, for the cover artwork and illustrations; Daniel Kordan, for use of the image of Ergaki; Nick Burton, for his illustrations and comments; Hugh Newman, for his partnership in our various explorations and ventures around the world; Rob Macbeth, for recording everything that comes out of my head on an intuitive level; and Geoffrey Ashe, for being a pioneer in this field, and for recognizing the importance of the Altai-Baikal seedbed long before I ventured down this same road.

In addition to this, I would like to thank the following people for their friendship and support: Abbie and Buster Todd; my goddaughter, Darcie; Leela Bunce; my godson, Eden; Renée Goulet; Paul Weston; Joan Hale; Robert Bauval; Jay Druce; Matthew Smith; Maria Smith, Yuri Leitch; Michael Staley; Yvan Cartwright; Graham Phillips; Eileen Buchanan; Roma Harding; Gordon Service; Ramon Zürcher; Brent Raynes; Patricia Awyan; Adam Crowl; Rowan Campbell Miller; Marion Briggs; Graham Hancock; Brien and Irene Foerster; Jim Vieira; Brian Wilkes; Nigel Skinner Simpson; Storm

Constantine; Jim Hibbert; and everyone at Gaia TV and also at Prometheus Productions, the makers of History Channel's *Ancient Aliens*. Finally, I would like to thank Jon Graham; John Hays; Manzanita Carpenter; Patricia Rydle; Mindy Branstetter; Erica B. Robinson; Kelly Bowen; and all the staff at Inner Traditions for their patience and support for this project, which has been five years in the making.

LAST OF THE DENISOVANS

The date is approximately 45,000 years ago; the location, a mountain pass somewhere in the Altai-Sayan region of southern Siberia. From a rocky vantage point, four tall, darkened forms emerge into view from behind a patch of cold early-morning mist. They stand a few meters apart, gazing toward the only path permitting access to the mountain's central plateau.

Each figure is of extraordinary size, being as much as 7 feet (2.15 meters) in height. Their stature is that of giant wrestlers, their enormous frames accentuated by broad shoulders and streams of furs that immerse their bodies from head to feet. Their heads also are of incredible size, being both long and broad, with large, powerful jaws. What little can be seen of their exposed skin suggests it is brown; their long, matted hair either dark or the color of straw. Adding to the almost alien appearance of these strange individuals are their extremely large noses and unusual eyes, which have striking black pupils and irises so pale they seem almost white. Completing the picture are the long, dark feathers attached to their furs, which blow about in the gentle breeze that has followed the first light of day.

They are Denisovans, members of an archaic human population whose very existence had gone unrecognized until the first decade of the twenty-first century, when oversized fossil remains were discovered in a large cave in the Altai Mountains of southern Siberia.

The purpose of these four figures at the head of this rocky pass is to await the arrival of others—a new people from a distant land located in the direction of the setting sun. In small groups these people have been approaching ever nearer to the Denisovans' mountain retreats, and now, finally, they were within sight, moving slowly toward the Denisovans's elevated position. These intruders were shorter and more slightly built, their heads smaller and more elongated. Furthermore, their approach to life seemed quite different. They enter new territories, assume control of them, and exploit their natural resources before dispatching some of their growing number in pursuit of even more suitable places of occupation. They have been advancing in this manner for several thousand years, encountering and even interbreeding with the Old People of the West, who will one day become known as Neanderthals. For countless millennia the Old People have occupied vast swaths of the western Eurasian continent, while the Denisovans have been content to remain in the eastern part of the continent.

Now, finally, the New People had arrived in the Altai-Sayan region and were about to encounter a small group of Denisovans for the very first time. Their advance party was perhaps ten to twelve in number. They too wore furs to combat the colder climate found at these higher altitudes, and in the hands of some of them were long wooden spears. One, the leader of the group, was brandishing his weapon in a provocative manner, as if ready to attack at the first sign of aggression from the tall strangers.

Yet the Denisovans say and do nothing. They simply stand their ground, gazing down at the intruders, who are now shuffling to a halt no more than 15 meters away.

The leader of the New People seems unsure what to do. Should they advance farther and strike out at these people who look like tree trunks? Why did they not attack? More pressingly, why did they not carry weapons? What strange magic was this? Were they powerful shamans who did not need weapons? Could they kill simply by making eye contact? Could they send out spirits to torment the families of intruders?

The Denisovans were indeed powerful shamans. They knew that any confusion or uncertainty in the minds of the New People would cause them to question their actions. What is more, the plan was working. They approached no farther. A few final thrusts into the air of the leader's spear did nothing to prompt a response from the Denisovans, who simply stood their ground, unfazed by what was unfolding in front of them.

Unnerved and fearful of their enemy's powerful magic, the New People all at once turn around and retreat back down the mountain pass and out of sight. The Denisovans have won the day. Yet they know full well that eventually the New People will return, this time in much greater numbers. Eventually the intruders will overrun the Denisovans' world, spelling an end to their population. It might take a few decades, a few centuries, or even a few millennia, but it will happen.

In the future the preservation of the Denisovans' profound ancient wisdom, accumulated across hundreds of generations, will become the property of the New People. It will be through them that the Denisovans will continue to exist. Yet this will not happen through conquest or submission, but through interbreeding. The last of the Denisovans will give way to hybrid descendants, who with an entirely revitalized mind-set will continue to thrive, not just in the Old World, but also in the far-off American continent. Sadly, however, the Denisovans were aware also that for many millennia knowledge of their very existence will be suppressed, belittled, and finally forgotten. Yet one day, as the prophecies determine, they will rise again, their contribution to the genesis of civilization laid bare for all to see. Then, finally, everyone will know the legacy of the Denisovans.

This is an imagined first meeting between anatomically modern humans (*Homo sapiens*) and the last of the Denisovans (tentatively *Homo sapiens altaiensis*). It is based on what meager evidence we have regarding their physiognomy, behavior, genetics, and technological achievements, along with local folklore, which perhaps preserves a memory of their former existence in the region.

Whatever the accuracy behind this all-important encounter between our own ancestors and the Denisovans, the chances are it occurred around 45,000 years ago, either in the Altai Mountains, where their fossil remains have been found in the Denisova Cave, the type site of the Denisovans, or a little further north in the western Sayan Mountains. (A type site is a site that is considered to be the model of a particular archaeological culture.) These straddle the republics of Khakassia and Tuva, between which is a narrow strip of land constituting the most southerly part of the Russian province of Krasnoyarsk Krai. Here age-old folk stories speak of the former presence of a giant population that inhabited the nearby Yenisei and Abakan River basins. They recall how these giants—referred to in Khakassia as the 'Akh Kharakh, the "white-eyed people"—created the first stone fortresses (*kurgans*), the first irrigation channels, the first dams and bridges, and even the first divine melodies played on musical instruments.

The description of these legendary giants best fits what we know about the Denisovans who occupied southern Siberia for hundreds of thousands of years before their disappearance around 40,000 years ago. DNA analysis of many modern populations in East Asia, South Asia, Indonesia, Australia, and even Melanesia and Micronesia, tells us that Denisovans interbred with the earliest modern humans who passed through their territories. More significantly, there is every reason to link the Denisovans with the sudden acceleration in human behavior known to have occurred in southern Siberia between 20,000 and 45,000 years ago. This included the making of some of the first bird-bone flutes anywhere in the world, along with the creation of settled habitation sites, the employment of advanced hunting techniques, the formalizing of tool kits, including the use of microblade technology, and the first sustained appearance of a specialized form of stone-tool production known as pressure flaking.

In addition to this, there is compelling evidence that the earliest human societies to occupy the Altai-Sayan region possessed an extraordinary knowledge of long-term eclipse cycles. Evidence suggests they used a knowledge of these cycles to develop complex, numerically based calendrical systems that would go on to permeate religious cosmologies in many parts of the ancient world. All the indications are that this grand calendrical system, as we shall call it, had its inception in southern Siberia and might well have been inherited from the lost world of the Denisovans. There are also tantalizing clues that the principal creative influence seen as responsible for long-term time cycles and the inaudible sounds once thought to be emitted by the sun, moon, and stars was identified with a cosmic bird symbolized in the night sky by the stars of Cygnus, the celestial swan. Through this association the constellation went on to become guardian of the entrance to the sky world, through which human souls had to pass either to achieve incarnation or enter the afterlife.

In time many of the technological, cultural, and cosmological achievements that appear first in southern Siberia circa 20,000–45,000 years ago, reach the Pre-Pottery Neolithic world of southeast Anatolia and begin to flourish at key cult centers such as Göbekli Tepe. From here they are carried southward through the Levant to northern Egypt. On the banks of the Nile River, as early as 8500–8000 BCE, they find a new home at a site named Helwan, which is today a thriving industrial city immediately south of Cairo. Yet it was here, almost certainly, that the predynastic world of ancient Egypt would begin in earnest, and it would be just across the river, on the plateau at Giza, that the fruits of the Denisovan legacy would finally find manifestation in the greatest and most enigmatic architectural accomplishment of the ancient world—the Great Pyramid, built for the pharaoh Khufu circa 2550 BCE. As we shall see, its underlying geometry, which underpins the entire pyramid field at Giza, displays a profound knowledge of long-term time cycles, numeric systems, and sound acoustics, as well as a polarcentric cosmology featuring the stars of Cygnus. All of this might well have had its origins in southern Siberia as much as 45,000 years ago. Piecing this story together will require some patience. Yet those who persevere will discover not only tantalizing evidence of a lost civilization, but also the true founders of our own.

PART ONE

GÖBEKLI TEPE

1

AN ARTIST'S WORK

I t was found during routine excavations at the site of Göbekli Tepe, the most extraordinary megalithic temple complex in the world. Yet no one could have quite realized just how important the tiny bone plaque would be to our knowledge of the beliefs, practices, and sophistication of the Pre-Pottery Neolithic world of southeast Anatolia some 11,000 years ago.

Archaeologists and other specialized teams of scientists have been investigating Göbekli Tepe since 1995 (see plate 1). What they have found has changed the way we view the emergence of high culture and even of civilization itself. So far several major enclosures containing rings of T-shaped standing stones, set up like spokes of a wheel around a pair of much larger monoliths, have been uncovered at the site. Each one is magnificent in its style and design, with exquisite carved decorations on many of the stones that speak volumes about the level of sophistication and technological advancement of their builders, who emerged on the scene as if out of nowhere.

END OF THE ICE AGE

The oldest enclosures at Göbekli Tepe are around 11,500 years old. Indeed, construction at the site probably began within a generation or so of the end of the last ice age, which had given way to a sudden increase in temperature about 15,000 years ago. This had lasted for around 2000 years until approximately

10,800 BCE, when there was a rapid resurgence of the ice sheets, which had been withdrawing gradually before this time. This had brought back severe Arctic conditions across large areas of the Northern Hemisphere, creating a mini–ice age that lasted around 1200 years and then abruptly halted circa 9600 BCE. This is known to palaeoclimatologists as the Younger Dryas event. It was shortly after this time that the first colossal stone structures were built on this remote mountaintop in southeast Anatolia.

The earliest monuments at Göbekli Tepe were constructed by an advanced prehistoric society officially classified as hunter-gatherers, since there was no animal husbandry or wide-scale cultivation of cereal crops at this time. Both came only after Göbekli Tepe had been up and running for at least half a millennium. During this time further stone enclosures were being built either alongside or on top of their predecessors, until finally, around 8000 BCE, Göbekli Tepe was abandoned. All remaining enclosures were buried beneath thousands of tons of earth, rubble, stone chippings, and human refuse. Thereafter the communities brought together to take part in this mammoth building project, which had lasted approximately 1500 years, dispersed into other parts of the ancient world, carrying with them new ideas in domesticated agriculture, stone technologies, engineering, and arguably even the brewing of beer and making of wine.

The achievements of the Göbekli builders remained hidden beneath the occupational mound or *tepe* (Turkish for "hill," usually a former occupational mound) until 1994, when the late Professor Klaus Schmidt (1962–2014), a German archaeologist with the University of Heidelberg and the German Archaeological Institute, arrived at the site. He saw the tops of stones peaking out of the fertile earth, as well as fragments of carved stone scattered about the surface of the mound, used today for cultivation purposes. Their great age was made clear by the presence of countless stone tools and projectile points across a wide area. These could accurately be dated to the Pre-Pottery Neolithic age, meaning that many of them were as much as 10,000–11,000 years old.

The following year, 1995, excavations began at the site. These have continued through till the present day, with new discoveries being made every year. In addition to the stone enclosures, archaeologists have uncovered a number of portable objects, including carved statues of animals and human figures, as well as a whole series of smaller items fashioned from hard stone. They include perforated beads and buttons, along with various holed pendants bearing abstract images of snakes, birds, and other creatures of the natural world.

DISCOVERY OF THE BONE PLAQUE

Among the portable items found at Göbekli Tepe in 2011 was the afore-mentioned bone plaque, which is just 6 centimeters in length, 2.5 centimeters in width, and 3–4 millimeters in thickness (see plate 2). Its smooth surface, which appears highly polished, bears etched carvings, although only on one side; the other side is blank. After discovery, the object was cleaned, recorded, and placed in storage. With the opening of a new archaeological museum in Şanlıurfa, Turkey, in May 2015, the tiny bone plaque was displayed for the first time. Although experts had obviously noticed that it bears some minute etchings, no consensus opinion had been reached on what they might represent.[1]

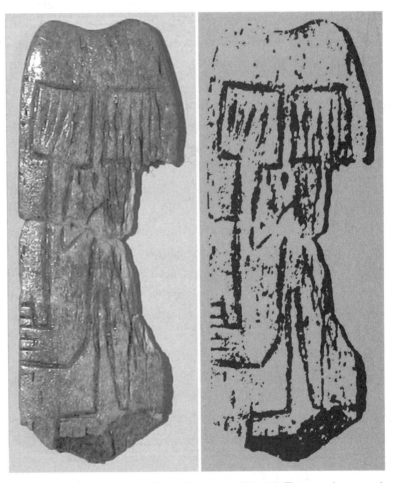

Figure 1.1. Left, the bone plaque found at Göbekli Tepe and currently on display at the Şanlıurfa archaeological museum, and, right, the plaque's unique imagery highlighted.

This task was left to Matthew Smith, a British expat telephone engineer then living in Turkey. During a tour of the museum organized by my colleague Hugh Newman and myself, Matthew—who had recently undergone lazer eye surgery in Istanbul—noticed three tiny bone pieces in a display cabinet. All had been found at Göbekli Tepe, and so were likely to be as much as 11,000 years old. Yet it was the one on the left that drew his attention. His keen eyes picked out the fact that its minuscule etching, done with an extremely sharp instrument, a flint or obsidian graver or awl most likely, showed a pair of T-pillars (see fig. 1.1). The fact that they were more or less identical to each other probably meant they represented the twin monoliths that had once stood at the center of all the main enclosures at Göbekli Tepe. Some of these twin monoliths, such as those in the installations known as Enclosures C and D (see plate 3), originally stood around 5.5 meters in height and weighed as much as 15–20 metric tons apiece.

Although the twin central pillars seen at Göbekli Tepe are usually positioned parallel to each other, in this plaque their narrow front edges are turned toward the entrant. Thus the artist would appear to have twisted the pillars 90 degrees so that they could be viewed sideways on, most likely to ensure that the viewer knew exactly what was being shown.

THE RANGE OF GÖBEKLI TEPE

Precisely which enclosure is depicted on the bone plaque will probably never be known. Nine major installations have so far been investigated at Göbekli Tepe. They are Enclosures A, B, C, D, E, F, G, H, and the Lion Pillars Building. Yet a ground-sensing radar survey carried out at the site in 2004 indicated that as much as twenty more structures of a similar size and complexity probably await discovery. Any one of these might be illustrated on the bone plaque, which was found in an excavation area in the northwest part of the mound.

Another important question posed by the existence of the bone plaque was how did it come to be made and what exactly was its purpose? Even though it bears no holes indicating use as a pendant and is officially classified as the end of a prehistoric spatula, it probably functioned as an amulet or talisman.[2] The likeness of the twin central monoliths in one of the enclosures at Göbekli Tepe was perhaps thought to connect the plaque with the creative potency of the site, imbuing it with some kind of magical quality.

MULTI-LAYERED IMAGERY

Yet the plaque's importance as the first recorded pictorial representation of Göbekli Tepe's famous T-shaped pillars was just the beginning. A more detailed examination of its carved imagery reveals various other remarkable features, including its artist's use of three-dimensional perspective. This is apparent about halfway down the right-hand edge of the left-hand T-pillar. Here a line rises at an angle from the stone toward the center of the image. It appears to portray a retaining wall linking the pillar with an inner area of the enclosure. At Göbekli Tepe the pillars making up the stone circles that surround the twin central monoliths are set within what are known as ringwalls, original retaining walls made of layers of rock held together by a hardened clay mortar. Centrally placed, below the plaque's twin pillars, is what appears to be a pedestal, from which rise two lines that converge at its center. Visually, these convey the impression of a walkway leading into the enclosure. The converging lines utilize the concept of parallax, whereby parallel lines appear to get closer the farther they are away from the viewer.

Just as intriguing is the fact that the converging lines between the T-pillars give the impression of a long-legged, abstract stick person standing either between or in front of the stones. This trick of the eye does not appear to be coincidence.

DEEP PECK MARK

Something additionally noted when the plaque was first inspected in the Şanlıurfa museum in September 2015 was the manner that its converging lines focus the eye on a deep peck mark positioned centrally beneath the heads of the twin pillars. On either side of it is a vertical line, creating the likeness of a porthole stone similar to the example seen at the rear of Göbekli Tepe's Enclosure D (see fig. 1.2). This stone is unique because it is the only example in the installation that has one of its wide faces turned toward the twin central monoliths; the rest have one of their narrow edges turned in this direction. Indeed, a person standing between the two pillars would originally have been able to peer through the porthole stone's circular opening—around 25–30 centimeters in diameter—toward the local skyline.

A similar porthole stone is to be seen in the outer ringwall of Enclosure C at exactly the same position as the one in Enclosure D. Yet this example

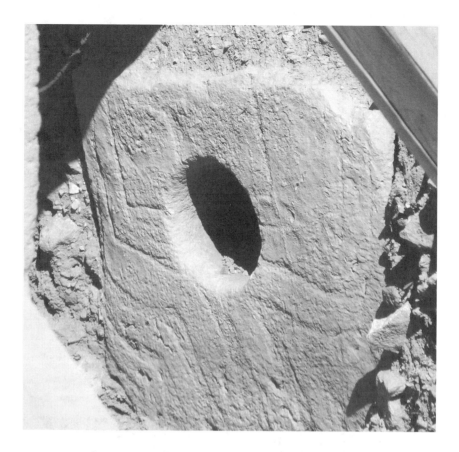

Figure 1.2. The porthole stones to be seen in two key enclosures at Göbekli Tepe. Top, the example in Enclosure D, and, bottom, the one in Enclosure C, which is today broken and on its side.

(officially designated Pillar 59) has toppled onto its side and is fractured across its circular aperture, perhaps because of the weight of the infill and rubble bearing down on it prior to excavation (see fig. 1.2). An inner ring of stones, set within another retaining wall, was added to Enclosure C after its original construction.[3] This would have effectively blocked the line of sight between the twin central pillars and the holed stone. Yet before this time a person would, as in the case of Enclosure D, have been able to stand between its twin central monoliths and gaze out through the stone toward the local horizon.

Both holed stones, in Enclosures C and D, were originally positioned to reflect the mean azimuth bearings of their corresponding twin central pillars, suggesting that they played a key role in the religious beliefs and practices of the Göbekli builders. Indeed, their very specific placement indicates that they acted in the same capacity as the stone niches built into the walls of later Pre-Pottery Neolithic cult buildings in southeast Anatolia. One such example was found during the early 1980s within the rear wall of a 10,500-year-old, rectangular cult building at a site named Nevalı Çori in the extreme north of Şanlıurfa province. Such areas of special sanctity were unquestionably the forerunners of the sacred altars that would eventually become an integral feature in religious buildings all over the world.

SOUL HOLES

Professor Klaus Schmidt, who headed excavations at Göbekli Tepe between 1995 and his untimely death in 2014, never passed comment on the site's porthole stones, which appear in the two most accomplished enclosures discovered to date. He did, however, have something to say about the fragments of stone rings his team found scattered about the site—one of which has been pieced together and is on display at Şanlıurfa's archaeological museum (see plate 4). These are around half a meter in diameter and were positioned originally either in the ringwalls of now-lost enclosures or in overhead ceilings. As to their function, Schmidt proposed they were *Seelenlöcher,* a word in his native German language meaning "soul holes."[4] So what exactly are soul holes?

A large number of megalithic (that is, large stone) chambered tombs, or dolmens, from Ireland in the west to India in the east, have circular apertures cut into their entrance facades. Like the porthole stones at Göbekli Tepe, these bored holes are usually between 25 and 40 centimeters in diameter, too small for a grown person to pass through. The porthole stones seen in Neolithic and later Bronze Age dolmens, which generally date to circa 3000–2000 BCE, could have functioned as a means of offering food and gifts to the spirits of human remains interred within the structures. Alternately, the apertures might have enabled further burials to be added, or original interments to be removed.

Such ideas, however, are inadequate to fully explain the widespread use of circular apertures in a funerary context. For example, in India circular apertures appear in stone slabs used as entrances to cist burials, which were generally sealed beneath the earth following construction.[5] Deliberately bored holes are seen also in ceramic urn jars found in cemeteries across Europe and Southwest Asia. These date to the Iron Age and later Roman times.[6] The purpose of these holes was to provide a means for the release of the soul, the presence of dirt or any other constrictions not being seen as a hindrance to the soul's ability to leave its place of interment.

In a like manner, small doors or windows known as *armen Seelenlöcher* ("poor soul holes") were once incorporated into the walls of houses in the Austrian Tyrol. A number survive today, and there seems little question that their primary function was to allow the exit of a soul following death, since these miniature doors were opened only when a death occurred in the household.[7] The function of the *armen Seelenlöcher* has been linked with the porthole stones of megalithic monuments located in the same region, suggesting a continuity of ideas from the Neolithic age through to the present day.[8]

Almost certainly related to the *armen Seelenlöcher* tradition of western Europe is the fact that members of the Ojibwa tribe, an indigenous people of Canada and the northern United States, would bore a hole in a coffin so as "to let the soul go out and in at pleasure."[9] In a similar manner, hospital nurses in southern England upon the death of a patient would open the window nearest to the feet of a body so that the soul might escape. (This tradition is known to have prevailed in the south of England and also in London and the Home Counties through till the 1950s, and arguably even later.[10]) Very likely at least some of the porthole stones at Göbekli Tepe served a similar function, although here it was probably the soul or spirit of the shaman,* rather than that of the deceased, that was thought to exit this world through these circular apertures.

---

*The term *shaman* is used gender-free, and thus applies to both male and female practitioners of shamanism. However, when a female shaman is specifically meant, the term *shamaness* appears.

SHAMANISTIC PRACTICES

Shamanistic practices in various parts of the world—particularly those in Siberia—incorporate the use of a symbolic hole, either in a rock, in the ground, in a tree, or in the roof of a yurt or tent. Their presence enables the spirit of the shaman, or that of the deceased, to leave its physical environment and enter invisible realms described in terms as the Upper and Lower World.[11] The Upper World was thought to exist in the sky; the Lower World beneath the earth.

Siberian shamans are known also to have employed the use of bones with holes at their center to begin to "see all, and to know all." This "is when one becomes a shaman."[12] In other words, pierced bones were used in ritual practices whereby participants achieved an ecstatic or altered state of consciousness. They would then project their thoughts through the hole to "enter" unseen realms. Here they would attain otherworldly knowledge and enlightenment not normally accessible to the living.

So the pecked hole on the carved bone plaque very likely indicates that during rites and ceremonies, a person entering the site's enclosures approached between the twin central monoliths and focused their eyes on the porthole stone. The stone would form a bridge or portal between the liminal realm created by the enclosure's circular interiors and the otherworldly environments thought to exist beyond the physical plane.

This was an important realization, for it helped confirm the axial orientation of Enclosures C and D, which in both cases is toward the north-northwest, where both portholes stones are located. Yet why were both the twin central pillars and the holed stones oriented toward the north-northwest? Was there something of interest in this direction? The answer to this question is, of course, yes. Those who created the megalithic enclosures as well as the tiny bone plaque believed that there was something of extreme importance in this direction—the entrance to the sky world.

2

MYSTERY
OF THE NORTH

It was in June 2004 that I first set eyes on Göbekli Tepe, having wanted to go there ever since I had first read about its discovery in a German magazine four years earlier.* I was lucky enough to be invited to a festival of Kurdish culture at Diyarbakır, in southeastern Turkey, and as part of the agreement I was given a driver and interpreter for a week so that I could explore some of the archaeological sites I had written about in my earlier books on the Pre-Pottery Neolithic world of southeast Anatolia.[1]

On my return from Turkey I found it impossible to get out of my mind the strange carvings on the mysterious stone monoliths of Göbekli Tepe. They haunted me at night, especially since I had no real idea what to think about the beliefs and practices of those who created these strange megalithic structures as much as 11,500 years ago. The one thing I *was* convinced about from the outset, however, was the importance of their orientation, which was toward the north.

---

*The feature in question appeared in *Bild der Wissenschaft* (Michael Zick, 2000, and Sperlich, 2000), and was the first to bring Göbekli Tepe to the public's attention. Prior to this time, it had featured only in obscure academic publications.

aning of the orientation of these stone installations
.1at the star-worshipping Sabians of the ancient city of
, which lies on the Harran Plain around 45 kilometers to
.ast of Göbekli Tepe, venerated the North under the name
1 simply means "the North"[2]). He was their greatest and oldest
god,   as seen as the visible manifestation of heaven, where human souls
came from prior to incarnation and returned to in death.[4] The North was seen
as the source of light and power,[5] as well as the Primal Cause, which was eternal.[6] From the North emanated the "cosmic existences."[7] These were thought
to manifest through the seven planets,[8] which were seen as individual deities
under the rule of the North.

The Sabians, whose name was said to derive from *saba,* meaning "star
rising,"[9] celebrated Shamal during annual celebrations known as the Mystery
of the North.[10] These would include the release of cockerels to the North,[11] further confirming the significance of this direction in their religious traditions.
In 1926 Sabian expert Bayard Dodge wrote that the Harranians most likely
inherited their beliefs and practices regarding the North from a much earlier
culture.[12] The Sabians, who were known also as the Chaldeans, the inhabitants
of Chaldea, that is, southeastern and eastern Anatolia (and later confused with
southern Iraq), originally possessed a profound knowledge of astronomy, astrology and mathematics, and even used an early form of astrolabe.[13]

TELL IDRIS

Recent archaeological excavations at an occupational mound immediately to
the south of Harran called Tell Idris (the "mound of Idris," Arabic for the antediluvian patriarch Enoch, as well as for the Greek Hermes) have revealed that
the earliest inhabitants arrived in the area during the Pre-Pottery Neolithic B
period, some 10,000 years ago.[14] This was around the same time that building
construction ceased at Göbekli Tepe. After Tell Idris was abandoned, the center of focus would appear to have shifted to the city itself. Here evidence has
been found of a Pottery Neolithic settlement belonging to the so-called Halaf
culture, which thrived circa 6000–4500 BCE.[15] Thereafter Harran (Akkadian
Harrânu, "intersecting roads," Latin *Carrhae*) emerged as a cosmopolitan city
known throughout the ancient world. It was thus reasonable to conclude that

some semblance of the beliefs and practices of the Pre-Pottery Neolithic peoples of Göbekli Tepe had somehow been absorbed into the religious traditions of the earliest Harranians, the precursors of the Sabians or Chaldeans, who occupied the region through till medieval times.

Shortly after visiting both Harran and Göbekli Tepe for the first time, I had asked British chartered engineer Rodney Hale—who has worked for the past twenty years in the field of archaeoastronomy, the study of the archaeology of ancient astronomies—to examine the orientations of the latter's stone enclosures. I wanted to see whether any kind of pattern of orientation might emerge. Back then Enclosures C and D were still under excavation, with only the upper halves of their T-shaped pillars exposed above the surrounding infill. Despite this, Hale used available plans of the site to determine within a fair degree of accuracy the mean azimuth bearings of the twin central pillars in Enclosures B, C, D, and E, all of which were found to be oriented approximately north-northwest to south-southeast.

Checking this data against a suitable astronomical software program, Hale was able to establish that all four enclosures were aligned north-northwest toward the setting of Deneb (α Cygni) (see fig. 2.1), the brightest star in the constellation of Cygnus, the celestial bird, during the epoch of construction at Göbekli Tepe. In two cases, Enclosures C and D (and also in Enclosure H, see figs. 2.3 and 2.4), there is additional evidence of this alignment toward the local horizon through the presence of the porthole stones, their apertures corresponding almost perfectly with the setting of the star as viewed from between the twin central monoliths. Since then, this data has been confirmed and refined, demonstrating the following correlations between the mean azimuths of the enclosures' twin central monoliths and the setting of Deneb.

THE EFFECTS OF PRECESSION

Not only do these dates fit very well the assumed construction dates of these enclosures, but they also help determine the order in which the installations were constructed. This is because precession, the slow wobble of the earth's axis across a cycle of around 26,000 years, very slowly shifts the position a star rises and sets on the local horizon. From a latitude corresponding to Göbekli Tepe, circa 9600–8000 BCE, Deneb was setting ever more west of north, something clearly seen in the orientation of the twin pillars in the various enclosures. In this knowledge, it implies that Enclosure D, with its

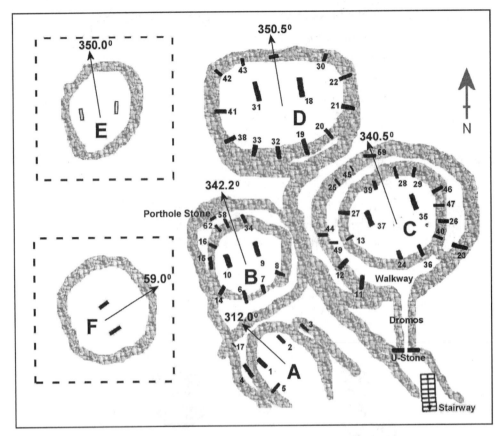

Figure 2.1. Plan showing the main enclosures in the southeastern depression
of Göbekli Tepe with their mean azimuths marked.

Enclosure D @ 350.5° = 9580 BCE

Enclosure E @ 350.0° = 9550 BCE

Enclosure C @ 340.5° = 8950 BCE

Enclosure B @ 342.2° = 8980 BCE*

*Calculations generated using the Carte du Ciel astronomical software program, and based on an extinction height for Deneb of 2 degrees.

twin pillars oriented closest to north, is the oldest structure uncovered so far.

It is difficult to know to what level of accuracy the Göbekli builders might have incorporated astronomical alignments in the construction of the enclosures. Nonetheless, the dates offered by the azimuth bearings of their twin central pillars very closely match the radiocarbon dates obtained from organic materials found inside the installations. For example, loam taken from wall plaster in Göbekli Tepe's Enclosure D has provided calibrated radiocarbon dates in the range of 9745 to 9314 BCE.[16] These correspond perfectly with a

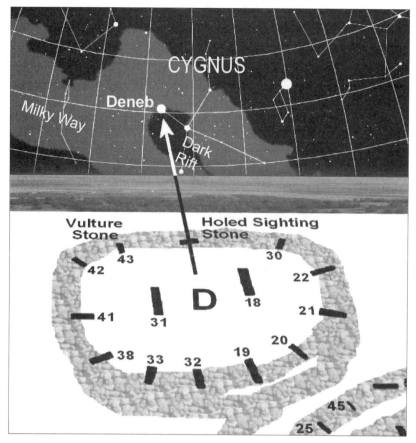

Figure 2.2. Artist's impression of the alignment between
Göbekli Tepe's Enclosure D and the Cygnus star Deneb. Not to scale.

date of circa 9580 BCE for the installation's construction based on the alignment of its twin pillars with the setting of the star Deneb at this time (see
fig. 2.2).

Bone samples from a burial taken from Enclosure B's ringwall have provided a calibrated radiocarbon age of 8306–8236 BCE.[17] Since this burial is
likely to have taken place around the time of the installation's closure following
a long period of use, a proposed construction date of circa 8980 BCE based on
the alignment of its twin central pillars toward Deneb makes sense.

A NEW PORTHOLE STONE

Possibly connected to this surmise is the fact that in 2011 an in-situ porthole
stone was found during exploration work immediately to the northwest of

Enclosure B.[18] Resembling the outward shape of a Victorian fireplace, it has a rectangular aperture around 70 centimeters in height and 60 centimeters in width, on each side of which is a relief of a climbing fox, an animal seen on the inner faces of various central pillars at the site. It is located in a boundary wall just outside of the installation and, oddly, is positioned immediately behind Enclosure B's Pillar 62. This makes no practical sense and suggests either that the porthole stone had a symbolic function, or that it predates the erection of the pillar in front of it. Although located slightly west of the enclosure's central axis, the porthole stone's aperture is oriented at approximately 341 degrees, within a degree or so of the axial orientation of Enclosure B, based on the mean azimuth of its twin pillars. Whatever the original function of this stone, its existence lends weight to the proposal that all the key enclosures excavated so far at Göbekli Tepe are oriented toward the north-northwest.

Enclosure E is simply an oval-shaped area cut into the bedrock with two raised pedestals at its center that once supported twin central pillars. These, along with the rest of the enclosure, vanished in antiquity, meaning that any proposed dating of the installation can only be a matter of conjecture.

THE DATING OF ENCLOSURE C

In the case of Enclosure C (see plate 6) organic material taken from an area close to its outer ringwall has offered calibrated radiocarbon dates in the range of circa 9261 to 9139 BCE, slightly more recent than those of nearby Enclosure D.[19] Oliver Dietrich, an expert on radiocarbon dating at Göbekli Tepe, admits this suggests that "the outer ringwall of Enclosure C could be younger than Enclosure D,"[20] adding that construction of this installation was perhaps under way even as the backfilling of Enclosure D was still taking place.[21]

The radiocarbon dates for Enclosure C, that is, circa 9261–9139 BCE, are a little earlier than the date proposed based on the alignment of its twin pillars toward the setting of Deneb circa 8950 BCE. At first sight this might seem a problem. However, as I have pointed out elsewhere,[22] the carved slots within the rock-cut pedestals into which the twin pillars of Enclosure C were placed are aligned slightly more toward north than are the actual pillars. It almost seems as if the angles of the pillars were changed after the carving of the pedestals.

What might this mean? The most likely answer is that the twin pillars were deliberately realigned to continue tracking Deneb as it set farther and farther west of north. This process continued until the pillars could be moved no farther and thus could no longer target the star's setting. Could this have been a signal that the installation had completed its purpose and needed now to be decommissioned or revamped? Perhaps this was why an inner ringwall was then added, effectively changing the entire nature of the structure by blocking the view through the porthole stone to the northern horizon. If all this is correct, the original construction date of the installation was closer to the range of dates obtained through radiocarbon testing, while the current position of the pillars reflects their final use as astronomical markers a few centuries after their original placement.

STELLAR TARGETS

No other stars in either the northern or the southern night skies were found to match the mean azimuth bearings of the twin pillars at the centers of the enclosures at Göbekli Tepe during the epoch of their construction. This means that the setting of Deneb almost certainly helped determine the axial orientation of these enclosures, which in the case of Enclosures C and D was emphasized still further by the presence of porthole stones in the north-northwestern sections of their original ringwalls.

More significantly, in a paper published in the journal *Archaeological Discovery,* Italian academics Alessandro De Lorenzis and Vincenzo Orofino of the University of Salento in Lecce confirm that the setting of Deneb was indeed responsible for the axial orientation of Enclosures B, C, D, and E.[23] In their words: "These orientations [of the main enclosures at Göbekli Tepe toward the setting of Deneb] and the relative dating proposed by Collins [and Hale] . . . have been verified."[24]

ALTERNATIVE IDEAS

Despite this very solid evidence for the astronomical interests of the Göbekli builders, others have offered alternative theories regarding the possible orientation of the main enclosures. It has been proposed, for instance, that they were oriented, not north toward Cygnus, but south, toward the rising of either the stars of Orion[25] or the bright star Sirius (α Canis Majoris).[26] Rodney Hale examined both of these proposals and found them to be completely unworkable from the latitude of Göbekli Tepe during the time frame in question, circa 9600–8000 BCE.[27]

THE DISCOVERY OF ENCLOSURE H

In addition to this there is yet further evidence that the main enclosures at Göbekli Tepe were oriented north-northwest, and not south-southeast. Recently, a new ellipsoid-shaped enclosure has been unearthed in an area of the occupational mound known today as the northwestern depression. It lies around 250 meters northwest of its southeastern counterpart, where all the other excavated enclosures can be seen. The new installation has been designated the title Enclosure H and to date a number of carved pillars have been uncovered, some unique to the site. This includes Pillar 66 (see fig. 2.3), a T-shaped stone that stands in the ringwall with one of its wide faces directed toward the center of

Figure 2.3. Pillar 66 in Göbekli Tepe's Enclosure H.

the installation. This is important because, like the porthole stones seen in Enclosures C and D, which also face toward the center of the installations, Pillar 66 has a circular aperture. It is centrally positioned beneath the pillar's T-shaped head and is approximately 20 centimeters in diameter.

Using an overhead image of Enclosure H,[28] Rodney Hale calculated the orientation of Enclosure H's Pillar 66, along with that of Pillar 51, the installation's one remaining central pillar. Both the aperture of Pillar 66 and the long axis of Pillar 51 were found to display an azimuth bearing of approximately 341 degrees (see fig. 2.4). Using this information, he determined that the enclosure would therefore have been aligned to the setting of Deneb in

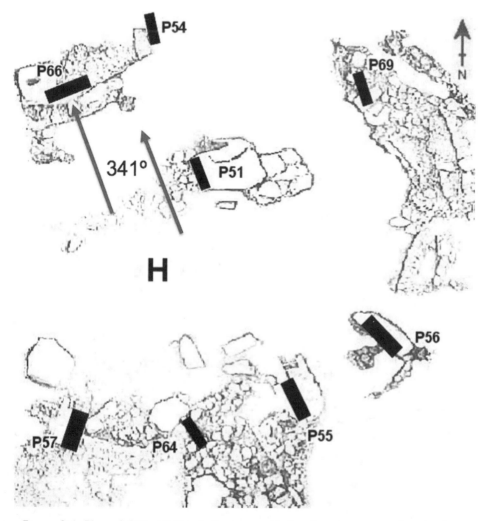

Figure 2.4. Plan of Göbekli Tepe's Enclosure H showing the mean azimuth of its remaining central pillar (Pillar 51) and the alignment of its porthole stone (Pillar 66).

around 8900 BCE. (The extinction height for the setting of Deneb was set at 2 degrees.) It is a date that conforms pretty well with the installation's currently proposed epoch of construction, which is thought to have been sometime around the transition from the Pre-Pottery Neolithic A period into the Pre-Pottery Neolithic B period circa 8800 BCE.*[29]

LEAPING PANTHERS

On the western face of Enclosure H's Pillar 51 is the relief of a large leaping feline, most likely a panther. It faces south, and replaces the leaping foxes seen on the inner faces of various twin central pillars found in the main enclosures of the southeastern depression. The pillar's southerly orientation tells us that entry to Enclosure H was probably from the south, a fact recently confirmed by the discovery of a rock-cut staircase on the structure's southern side.[30] Celebrants, initiates, and shamans could then have stood or sat between its central monoliths and gazed through Pillar 66's circular aperture toward the north-northwestern horizon. Thus there is every reason to conclude that, like the porthole stones in Enclosures C and D, Enclosure H's Pillar 66 was the structure's central focus—its prehistoric altar or holy of holies. Also in similar with its counterparts in the southeastern depression, Enclosure H was most likely aligned to the setting of Deneb during the epoch of its construction.

A CHANGE IN DIRECTION

There seems little question that the point of entry into all the older so-called Layer III enclosures uncovered at Göbekli Tepe—that is, those found at its greatest depth and dating to circa 9600–8800 BCE—was from the south (with the possible exception of Enclosure E, which remains an enigma). Yet much

---

*German archaeologist Nico Becker and his colleagues at Göbekli Tepe have suggested that the structure dates to the last quarter of the tenth millennium BCE (Becker et al, 2014). However, two carbon-14 dates taken from charcoal found within the infill covering the structure have offered calibrated dates of 8650 ± 50 and 8680 ± 80 BCE. A third date obtained from clay mortar removed from the installation produced a date of 8520 ± 60 BCE. These provide a date for the last building activities within the enclosure. This strongly suggests the enclosure was constructed around the termination of the Pre-Pottery Neolithic A period and the start of the Pre-Pottery Neolithic B period, circa 8800 BCE.

younger installations, such as Enclosure F and the Lion Pillars Building, both belonging to Layer II, circa 8800–8000 BCE, seem to have been entered from the west. (Layer I refers solely to surface finds dating from the prehistoric age to the present day.) This is probably because they were oriented not toward the stars, but toward the rising sun. Indeed, the twin pillars of Enclosure F are oriented within a degree or so of the rising sun at the time of the summer solstice, while the Lion Pillars Building is aligned almost precisely east-west. At its eastern end are twin pillars, one on each side of the room, on the inner faces of which are carved reliefs of large felines, arguably panthers, which face toward the west.

So in the Lion Pillars Building, the entrant enters the structure from the west and is greeted by large felines rearing up out of the east. This, of course, is the direction of the rising sun at the time of the equinoxes. In contrast, the entrants entering the much larger and far older installations in both the south-eastern and northwestern depressions enter from the south and are greeted by rearing animals (foxes in Enclosures A, B, C, and D, and large felines in Enclosure H) that approach out of the north-northwest.* This, of course, is the direction of the setting of the Cygnus star Deneb.

NORTHERN NIGHT SKY

During the construction of the earliest enclosures at Göbekli Tepe, circa 9600–8800 BCE, the stars of Cygnus would have been perfect examples of so-called grazing stars. These are stars that rise on the north-northeastern horizon, make their journey around the northern celestial pole—the perceived turning point of the starry heavens—and then set briefly in the north-northwest before rising again shortly afterward. Perhaps the rising and setting of Cygnus enabled its stars to be used as markers in some kind of primitive time calendar. More likely is that their presence enabled the Göbekli builders to focus their attention on the Milky Way, the starry stream signifying the edge of our own galaxy, for it is on this that the stars of Cygnus appear to be placed. Indeed, most often they are identified as a celestial bird, its wings outstretched, flying along this glittering band of stars.

---

*As an aside, Enclosure A is an anomaly, with a rearing fox facing south on one central pillar, but with anthropomorphic features facing north on the other. Enclosure G is the designation given to an area in the northern part of the northwestern depression, where some quite strange architectural features were found during the 2000s. However, no further information is available at this time.

Since prehistoric times the Milky Way has been seen as a shining pathway, usually a road or river, linking the land of the living with the realm of the dead. This was an invisible world synonymous with the Upper World or sky world of shamanic tradition. Certainly in the case of Enclosures C, D, and H this unseen realm was likely to have been reached via the perceived soul holes found in their astronomically aligned porthole stones. How and why Cygnus might have become important to the Göbekli builders will be dealt with in due course. For the moment, though, we must return to the bone plaque, for its minute etchings were about to reveal what exactly the artist had seen when this unique piece of prehistoric art was carved around 11,000 years ago.

3

CELESTIAL SIGNS

Just two weeks after Hugh Newman and I returned to the United Kingdom following our eventful visit to southeast Turkey in September 2015, news of the discovery of Göbekli Tepe's tiny bone plaque was released online.[1] I wrote various articles on its amazing carved imagery, while Hugh created a video featuring actual footage from Şanlıurfa's archaeological museum showing my initial reactions to Matthew Smith's realization of the bone plaque's extraordinary significance.[2]

Obviously there was considerable interest in this plaque, and within just a few days of the announcement of its importance, the story had gone viral, with many hundreds of news items, blogs, and forums featuring the discovery. Yet even as the excitement was still rising, engineer Rodney Hale was finding out new things about this unique artifact.

Using up to twenty high-resolution images of the plaque supplied by Hugh Newman and myself, Hale set about examining its polished surface in the minutest detail. Where possible, he used two consecutive frames to look at the artifact in stereo. The results of this investigation were remarkable indeed.

Hale noted minor fractures and fissures in the surface of the plaque, some of which are longitudinal, with others more like furrows. Some were fairly big, while others were much smaller. Yet all of them seemed quite natural and simply the product of aging processes caused by exposure to the elements or contact with abrasive materials. However, he did note three more distinct peck marks,

Figure 3.1. The three peck marks above the twin pillars on the Göbekli Tepe bone plaque.

their presence made even more striking by the fact that they were positioned in a line immediately above the plaque's T-shaped pillars. Although the central mark seemed to be a natural fissure that might have been slightly enhanced, those on either side of it appeared to have been deliberately fashioned using a sharp instrument (see fig. 3.1). No other holes on the surface of the plaque bore the same hollow definition, leading Hale to single out these examples as unique.

On the premise that the three peck marks might represent celestial objects, Hale examined various combinations of three stars. He came up with just one possible solution: that they exactly matched the astronomical positions of the three Cygnus "wing" stars. These are Gienah (ε Cygni), Sadr (γ Cygni), and Rukh (δ Cygni), which, together with Deneb, form an asterism known as the Triangles.[3]

CELESTIAL HORIZON

No similar peck mark on the plaque corresponded to the position of the bright star Deneb. However, a concave indentation along its top edge began to take our interest since it bore a distinct likeness to the Egyptian hieroglyph known as the *djew,* meaning "mountain" (see fig. 3.2). Its presence made Hale and me wonder whether the purpose of this tiny portable object was to hold it up in front of the eye so that a celestial object, most likely the star Deneb, could be lined up with the saddleback indentation. It was a thought that, although easily dismissed as fantasy, started to make more sense as the days went by.

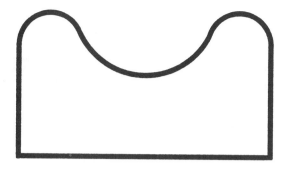

Figure 3.2. The ancient hieroglyph *djew*, symbolizi... "mountain." Compare this wi... the saddleback indentation at the top of the Göbekli Tepe bone plaque.

The possible presence of the three Cygnus wing stars on the bone plaque raised the question of exactly what these stars might have meant to the Göbekli Tepe community some 11,000 years ago. Whatever the answer, the plaque's artist would appear to have felt it necessary to include the stars alongside representations of twin T-shaped pillars, between which was a well-defined pecked *Seelenlöch,* or "soul hole," and an abstract human figure standing in the foreground. There seemed to be a meaningful connection between these individual components. In other words, there was a clear relationship between the positioning of the artist, which perhaps mimicked the role played by the human figure etched on the plaque, and the apparent direction of focus of the tiny object's etched imagery.

MODERN RECONSTRUCTION

The time was now mid-October, and I was preparing to present my findings on the bone plaque at Origins 2015, the annual Origins of Civilization conference, which I coproduced with Hugh Newman. I wanted the audience to see the view that might have been on offer to the artist when he or she inscribed the bone plaque. With this in mind I asked London graphic artist Russell M. Hossain (who has done the cover artwork for this book) to prepare a representation of the scene. It was to show a shamanlike figure standing before a pair of T-shaped pillars located inside a typical Göbekli Tepe–style enclosure, with a porthole stone in between them and the Cygnus wing stars in the sky above.

For this, I quickly prepared a mock-up, which I sent off to Russell. Within just a few days he had made a detailed preliminary sketch. What this showed was so lifelike that it made me realize something potentially very important. Was it possible that the perspective of the three Cygnus wing stars shown on the plaque reflected their *true astronomical positions in the night sky*? If correct,

ZERO DEGREES SKYLINE

Once again, I asked Rodney Hale to investigate the matter. He determined that the angle of the three peck marks on the plaque very closely matched the position of the Cygnus wing stars as the middle star, Sadr, reached an altitude of 45 degrees above the northwest horizon. Having placed an overlay of the area of night sky in question over an image of the bone plaque, with the Cygnus wing stars accurately aligned to the three indentations, Hale observed something quite extraordinary. Since a sky program can show celestial lines of altitude and azimuth, he now saw that the T-shaped pillars as etched on the bone plaque occupied a position whereby their tops would have corresponded with an altitude of precisely 30 degrees. Even more striking was the fact that, with the star Sadr located at 45 degrees and the top of the stone pillars at 30 degrees, the deeply incised peck mark representing the soul hole in the center of the porthole stone *lay at exactly 0 degrees altitude* (see fig. 3.3). In other words, the position of the porthole stone's aperture corresponded with an assumed line of sight from the eye of the artist through the soul hole to the local horizon.

These new findings appeared to confirm that the three peck marks seen above the plaque's T-shaped pillars were indeed representations of the Cygnus wing stars. What is more, they demonstrated that the artist had very accurately translated exactly what he or she could see when the striking imagery on the plaque was created. What this meant is that, first, its tiny etchings were a virtual photograph of the setting visible to the artist at the time, and, second, there could now be little question that the perspective of the artist, along with the orientation of the enclosure pictured, was toward the northwest, where the Cygnus constellation can be seen in the night sky immediately before it sets in the north-northwest.

The reason why the descent of the three Cygnus wing stars, instead of the bright star Deneb, was etched onto the plaque is quite simple. Depicting just one star could never have singled out its identity. So capturing the exact astronomical relationship of the three wing stars as they descended toward the

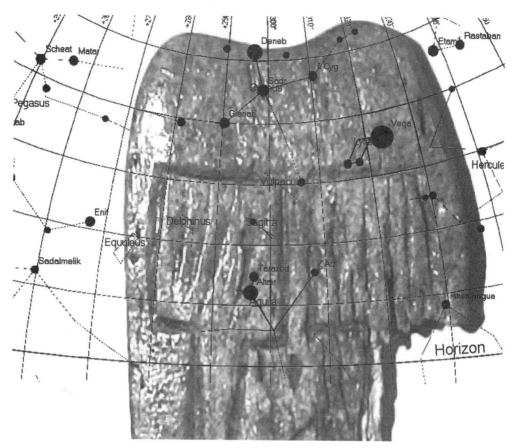

Figure 3.3. The Göbekli Tepe bone plaque with the stars of the northern skyline overlaid. Note the 30-degree height of the top of the twin pillars, and the 0-degree horizon coinciding with the aperture of the porthole stone.

horizon made it clear that this was the area of sky being depicted—the same general direction toward which the earliest enclosures were orientated.

Yet Hale was not finished with his assessment of this extraordinary new data. In assuming that the artist was accurately portraying what could be seen from their perspective, Hale realized that a measurement could be made for what he took to be the baseline of the twin pillars. Using all the angles outlined so far—the 45-degree altitude of Sadr, the 30-degree elevation of the tops of the stone pillars, the 0-degree altitude of the soul hole, and the baseline angle of the pillars, which was calculated to be −25 degrees—he produced a scaled diagram showing the artist's viewing perspective. This required one additional piece of information to provide a true scale to the picture—the heights of the stone pillars shown on the plaque. For this he used the measurements of the twin central monoliths seen in Enclosure D, which stand at around 5.5 meters above the installation's rock-cut floor surface.[4]

Hale's resulting diagram (see fig. 3.4) offers a unique perspective on what the artist might have seen when the plaque was created some 11,000 years ago. It shows an imaginary observer looking across the site with the Cygnus wing stars as a backdrop low in the northwest sky. This same message is re-created in Russell M. Hossain's painting of the bone plaque's etched imagery, revealed

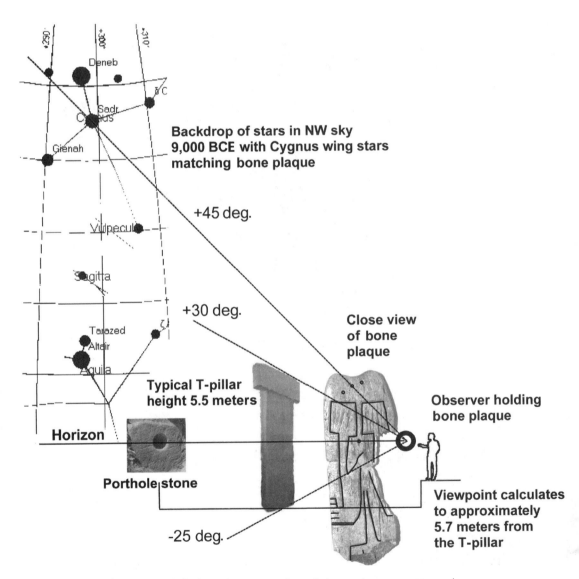

Figure 3.4. Artist's perspective of the enclosure portrayed
on the bone plaque by Rodney Hale.

for the first time at the Origins of Civilization event in November 2015 (see plate 7).

These conclusions are, of course, just one interpretation of the plaque's carved imagery. Others are, indeed, possible. For instance, in March 2017, an article on the subject by Oliver Dietrich, one of the German archaeologists currently working at Göbekli Tepe, appeared online.[5] It draws attention to the clear likeness between the plaque's carved imagery and Göbekli Tepe's T-shaped pillars. Yet Dietrich concludes either that the whole thing is an ad hoc series of doodlings without real meaning, or that it shows the forelegs of a lizard-like creature.

Yet in the opinion of Rodney Hale and the author, the Pre-Pottery Neolithic peoples of southeast Anatolia would appear to have held a deep fascination with the stars of Cygnus, and not just at Göbekli Tepe. It is seen at other sites as well. For instance, at the 10,000-year-old site of Çayönü, which lies around 130 kilometers northeast of Göbekli Tepe, close to the city of Diyarbakır (see fig. 3.5), all three of its cult buildings would appear to have been oriented toward the setting of Deneb during the time frame of their construction.[6] Moreover, at the 10,500-year-old hilltop site of Karahan Tepe,[7] located in the Tektek Mountains some 37 kilometers east of Göbekli Tepe,

Figure 3.5. Map of Anatolia showing Neolithic and Chalcolithic (Copper Age) sites featured in this book.

further alignments toward the setting of Cygnus have been recorded.[8] If these alignments are meaningful, why might Cygnus have played such an important role in the mind-set of these people? The key to unraveling this mystery is Göbekli Tepe's Pillar 43, known also as the Vulture Stone. It is to this that we must now turn to better understand the most ancient beliefs and practices of our Neolithic ancestors.

THE ENIGMA OF PILLAR 43

Göbekli Tepe's Pillar 43, otherwise known as the Vulture Stone, is very possibly the key to understanding the cosmological beliefs and practices of the Pre-Pottery Neolithic world of southeast Anatolia. It was one of twelve T-shaped pillars that stood in Enclosure D's ringwall, eleven of which remain in place today. Positioned like spokes of a wheel, they face the two colossal monoliths standing at the center of the installation.

A FUNNY-LOOKING VULTURE

The principal carved relief found on Pillar 43 (see fig. 4.1, and plate 8), which stands in the north-northwestern section of the enclosure's ringwall, immediately to the west of the enclosure's porthole stone, is a funny-looking vulture, its wings slightly retracted in the likeness of the letter *W*. It seems also to have either knock-knees or a stomach swollen with pregnancy. It is impossible to say which, because the back half of the pillar remains obscured by the boundary wall into which it was placed. Below this unusual bulge, the vulture's normal feet are replaced by what looks like oversized clown shoes.

Below the funny-looking vulture is the carved relief of a scorpion, its claws reaching up toward the bird. It is placed in a lower register, below a

a   b

Figure 4.1. Pillar 43 (left), otherwise known as the Vulture Stone,
which stands in Göbekli Tepe's Enclosure D.

well-defined horizontal line corresponding to the division between the stone's
T-shaped head and stem. Archaeoastronomer Juan Antonio Belmonte was perhaps the first to propose that this scorpion is a representation of Scorpius (also
known as Scorpio), the zodiacal constellation signified by a scorpion in both
ancient Greek and Mesopotamian sky lore.[1] If Belmonte is correct, other creatures shown on the pillar might also be abstract representations of either stars
or constellations.

VULTURE SYMBOLISM

In Greek Hellenic sky lore, no less than three constellations were identified with the symbol of a vulture. These were Cygnus, Lyra, and Aquila. All
three constellations are found in the same area of sky, their brightest stars—
Deneb (α Cygni), Vega (α Lyrae), and Altair (α Aquilae)—forming what is
known as the Summer Triangle, a familiar sight in the northern night sky
throughout the summer months.

THE STYMPHALIAN BIRDS

Greek mythology equated these three constellations with, among other things, the three Stymphalian birds that were sent against Hercules in his Sixth Labor.[2] This association is confirmed by the fact that all three asterisms are located in the vicinity of the constellation of Hercules. In Mesopotamian star lore, three similar birds attack the god Marduk, and these too were personified in the night sky as the constellations of Cygnus, Lyra, and Aquila.[3] With the knowledge that the Greeks identified Marduk with Heracles,[4] it becomes clear that the myth of the Stymphalian birds originated in Mesopotamia, where all three constellations were identified as winged creatures as early as the third millennium BCE.

The Stymphalian birds, collectively known as the Stymphalides or Harpies, are said to have been winged monsters with "the faces of women, the bodies of vultures, and claws upon their hands."[5] The fact that they were thought to be monstrous vultures confirms their link with the constellations in question, which are all identified as vultures—*Vultur cadens* ("the falling vulture") in the case of Cygnus and Lyra, and *Vultur volans* ("the flying vulture") in the case of Aquila.[6]

So if the vulture on Pillar 43 does represent one of the Stymphalian birds (and, interestingly, there are six birds of various species and sizes carved on the stone), then most likely it is Cygnus. Not only did the twin central pillars in Enclosure D (and also those in Enclosures B, C, E, and H) accurately target the setting of Deneb, Cygnus's brightest star, but we know also that its porthole stone, which stands just a few meters to the east of the Vulture Stone, was positioned so that this astronomical spectacle could be witnessed each night on the local skyline. In other words, the imagery on the Vulture Stone was in some way related to the purpose behind the axial orientation of the installation. What is more, the funny-looking vulture on Pillar 43 almost perfectly matches the outline of the main stars of Cygnus during the suspected time frame of the construction of Enclosure D (see fig. 4.1).

CYGNUS IN ARMENIA

Another piece of information linking Cygnus with the vulture comes from neighboring Armenia. In the past, the influence of Armenia and its ruling dynasty extended as far south as Edessa, modern-day Şanlıurfa. This embraced the area around Göbekli Tepe. Indeed, many Armenians still inhabited the

Şanlıurfa region until the horrific atrocities of the Armenian Genocide of 1915–17. It is thus significant that Armenian star lore refers to Cygnus as Angegh, a word meaning "vulture."[7] Of direct relevance here is the fact that an Armenian village named Angeghakot, close to the megalithic complex of Karahunj, is thought to reflect the importance of the Cygnus constellation.[8] Karahunj is made up of hundreds of standing stones that together create the likeness of Cygnus in its guise as a bird,[9] while the circular aperture in one prominently placed stone is said to target the transit of Deneb as it crosses the meridian.[10] Karahunj as a whole is attributed to the Bronze Age, circa 2500 BCE, although the alignment toward Deneb argues for a much earlier date of construction, perhaps circa 5500–5000 BCE.[11]

Since *angegh* in the Armenian language can also mean "angel," Cygnus is seen in Armenia as a heavenly angel, as well as the celestial home of the angels.[12] Yet prior to the rise of Christianity, Cygnus in Armenia was quite simply a vulture, just as it would seem to have been in Mesopotamian sky lore.

JOURNEY OF THE SOUL

Cygnus sits astride the Milky Way, which, as we shall see, was once imagined as a road, river, or pathway along which souls in the guise of birds were able to reach the sky world. Furthermore, stellar dust and debris cause the Milky Way to bifurcate, or fork, into two separate streams in the area of Cygnus. The dark region between the two arms of the Milky Way stretches between the star Deneb all the way down to the constellations of Sagittarius and Scorpio, where the sun crosses the Milky Way in one of only two places (the other being in the vicinity of Taurus, Gemini, and Orion on the opposite side of the sky). This extended area of darkness, known as the Great Rift, Dark Rift, or Cygnus Rift has long been recognized as having very specific mythological associations. For instance, among the K'iche'- or Quiché-speaking Maya of Central America it was the Black Road that led from the world of the living to Xibalba, the realm of the dead,[13] accessed most likely via the Dark Rift's northern entrance in the vicinity of the star Deneb. Native Americans recognized the northern opening to the Dark Rift as the entrance to the afterlife.[14] They believed that this gateway or portal was guarded by a supernatural raptor bird that acted as judge of the dead. Known as Brain Smasher to some tribes, it has been identified with the star Deneb.[15]

In ancient Mesopotamia a terrifying winged creature also guarded the northern opening of the Dark Rift. It was constructed of various stars belonging both to Cygnus and to its closest neighbor, Cepheus. These were seen to create a winged griffin called [mul]UD.KA.DUH.A ("constellation [MUL] of the storm demon with the gaping mouth"). This sky creature, also known by the Akkadian name *nimru*, "panther,"[16] was composed of the head and body of a panther or leopard and the wings and feet of a raptor bird, either a vulture or eagle.[17] Rising around midwinter, a traditional time of the dead, [mul]UD.KA.DUH.A was seen as a place of reception of dead souls entering the afterlife.[18]

CULT OF THE SKULL

Yet Cygnus on Göbekli Tepe's Pillar 43 would appear to be represented by a somewhat odd-looking vulture. Very likely it signified the soul's entrance to the afterlife, equated perhaps with the northern opening of the Dark Rift. Confirmation of the vulture's association with the afterlife comes from the presence of a curious filled circle above the bird's left wing. Professor Klaus Schmidt identified this object as a rather abstract human head being tossed around by the vulture as part of some macabre ball game.[19] Although Schmidt's hypothesis makes sense, I doubt that such a gruesome interpretation of the scene is necessary. More likely is that this abstract human head signifies the soul of a dead person, shaman, or initiate that has reached the realm of the dead under the guardianship of a supernatural vulture personified as Cygnus.

In the prehistoric rock art of southeast Anatolia, carved images of ball-like heads drawn as filled circles have long been recognized as symbols of the human soul, as Anatolian rock-art expert Muvaffak Uyanik explains:

> In the Mesolithic age [i.e., in the epoch of the Göbekli builders], it was realized that man had a soul, apart from his body and, as it was accepted that the soul inhabited the head, only the skull of the human body was buried. We also know that the human soul was symbolized as a circle and that this symbol was later used, in a traditional manner, on tombstones without inscriptions.[20]

As Uyanik proposes, the use of the circle to represent the human soul came about because the spirit of a living person was thought to reside in the head. Even after death, the connection with the deceased's soul was through the skull, which acted as a gateway or window to the realm of the dead. It was for this reason that, during the Early Neolithic, human skulls were used for oracular purposes. This is something thought to have occurred at the Pre-Pottery Neolithic urban center of Jericho (Tell es-Sultan), located on the west side of the Jordan Valley in the Palestinian West Bank. Here, and at other similarly aged sites in the region, excavations have unearthed plastered human skulls, dating to circa 7500–6000 BCE. Almost certainly they featured in cultic practices in which they acted as portals for communication with ancestral spirits, including, we must assume, the former owner of the skull.

A number of carved human heads shown clutched in the claws of vulture-like birds have been unearthed at both Göbekli Tepe and Nevalı Çori (see plate 9). They form fragments of much larger stone objects similar to the wooden totem poles of Native American tradition. These carved stone pillars would have stood within installations, showing the intimate relationship between the human soul and the vulture in its role as a *psychopomp,* from ψυχοπομπός (*psukhopompós*), a Greek expression meaning something like "soul carrier," "soul accompanier," and even "guide of souls."[21]

If the sunlike disk above the wing of the funny-looking vulture on Pillar 43 represents the human soul released from its physical body, then where is the body? This we see below the scorpion as a headless figure with an erect penis that seems to be on the nape or neck of a large bird with a hooked beak, arguably another vulture.

THE ACT OF EXCARNATION

The fact that the human figure is headless is a sign that the soul, in the form of a head, is no longer present, having left the body. Headlessness may also reflect the idea that the body has been subjected, perhaps symbolically, to a process known as sky burial. This is where scavenger birds, primarily vultures, are allowed to deflesh human corpses left out in the open for the purposes of excarnation (removing flesh from the bones of the deceased). Afterward the remaining bones are collected up and interred in what is known to archaeologists as a disarticulated or secondary burial. In other words, the bones are interred together as a group. Under certain circumstances the skull may have been removed and used for cultic practices; hence the image of the headless body.

Sky burial was used extensively across Europe and the Near East throughout the Neolithic and was almost certainly a practice inherited from the Upper Paleolithic, circa 43,000–9,600 BCE.[22] Simply googling "excarnation" and "sky burial" will bring up some gruesome images of this very ancient, but highly efficient, way of disposing of the dead, which is still carried out today on the Tibetan plateau by Buddhist monks.

VULTURES AT ÇATALHÖYÜK

Evidence of excarnation can be found at Çatalhöyük, the 9,000-year-old Neolithic urban center situated on the Konya plain in southern central Anatolia. Here a faded wall fresco uncovered at the beginning of the 1960s by British archaeologist James Mellaart and his team showed two vultures at the top of what appears to be a wooden tower set aside for exposure of the dead. The birds are represented in the act of defleshing a human corpse (see fig. 4.2), which, as on Pillar 43, is shown as a headless individual, almost like a matchstick figure without a head (see fig. 4.1 on page 38). Next to this is a second tower showing two more vultures. But here they appear to be taking

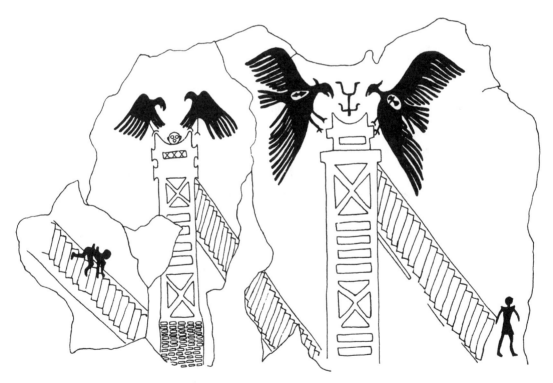

Figure 4.2. Reconstructed mural from Çatalhöyük, showing, on the right, wooden excarnation towers and vultures devouring a human body, and, on the left, vultures taking under their wing a soul in the form of a human head (after James Mellaart).

under their wing a ball-like head like the one above the wing of the vulture on Pillar 43. This ball-like head, however, has three small circles inside it, clearly indicating eyes and a mouth.

This strange wall fresco portrays not only the act of excarnation, but also, and more significantly, vultures taking the soul of the deceased into their care in preparation for its entry to the afterlife. If this is correct, it raises the question of whether something similar is being conveyed by the carved imagery on Pillar 43, which also has a headless figure (the body of the deceased), a ball-like head (the soul of the deceased), and at least two, and possibly three, carved images of vultures.

Another fresco uncovered within one of the so-called cult shrines at Çatalhöyük shows vultures swooping down to attack a headless human figure, once again suggesting excarnation. Interestingly, this particular fresco was found to be located on the north wall of the shrine in question.[23] Scenes at Çatalhöyük showing either vultures or subjects relating to death were displayed either on the north or east walls of shrines, usually the former. From this fact, Mellaart concluded that the north and east were the directions most strongly connected with death at Çatalhöyük, with the south and west walls being reserved for themes relating to life.[24]

Curiously, the above-mentioned mural in which vultures attack a headless person shows the birds with articulated legs. This suggested to Mellaart that in some manner these birds might actually be "human beings disguised in vulture garb performing what is evidently a funerary rite."[25] The shrine in question was also found to contain four human skulls,[26] supporting the idea that the vulture fresco relates in some manner to rites associated with the transmigration of the soul.

VULTURE SHAMANISM

Vulture shamanism is thought to have been a major feature of religious rites across the Neolithic world of Anatolia and the northern Levant between the tenth and sixth millennia BCE.[27] The griffon vulture (*Gyps fulvus*) in particular was singled out for special attention. For instance, excavations carried out at the Pre-Pottery Neolithic site of Jerf el-Ahmar in northern Syria between 1995 and 1999 under the leadership of Danielle Stordeur, director of research at the French National Center for Scientific Research (CNRS), uncovered an inordinate number of bones belonging to the griffon vulture.[28] An examination of the remains indicated the wholesale removal of feathers and feet, and even the scalping of skulls.[29] This was not done simply for their consumption as food, suggesting the use of vulture bones and feathers for cultic practices, most obviously the creation of ritual garments and other paraphernalia.

The wings of vultures, many still in an articulated state, were found during excavations in the 1950s at a site named Zawi Chemi Shanidar on the Great Zab River in the Zagros Mountains of northern Iraq. A team led by American archaeologists Rose and Ralph Solecki uncovered the wings of seventeen large predatory birds, together with the skulls of at least fifteen goats and wild sheep. The bearded vulture (*Gyptaeus barbatus*) and griffon vulture were among the bird species represented, along with various species of eagle. They had been buried, almost certainly on purpose, next to the wall of a stone structure that probably functioned as a cult building.[30] The Soleckis noted that the wings had been removed from the birds at death and appropriated for use as part of ritual costumes.[31]

The age of the remains was determined through radiocarbon dating to be circa 8870 BCE (±300 years).[32] However, modern recalibration of carbon-14 dates would suggest that the Zawi Chemi Shanidar community thrived at the beginning of the Pre-Pottery Neolithic A period, circa 9600 BCE. This makes it contemporary with the emergence of Göbekli Tepe, which lay just 450 kilometers away to the west.

VULTURE GODDESS

In addition to the evidence of vulture shamanism discovered at Jerf el-Ahmar (which, like Göbekli Tepe 115 kilometers away, is dated to the Pre-Pottery Neolithic A period, circa 9600–8800 BCE), excavators unearthed a grooved stone showing various pictograms, including one that was identified as a raptor or vulture. They also came across two limestone pillars, their tops carved into the likeness of accipitrids, the name given to various species of raptor birds, including eagles, hawks, kites, ospreys, and, tellingly, Old World vultures.[33] The pillars, which stand about 1 meter high, possess anthropomorphic stems, including what appear to be abstract human breasts.[34] Are they feminized forms of the vulture? At Çatalhöyük the beaks of vultures protruding like teats from sculpted plaster breasts were found on some walls, while a statue of an old woman showed her "accompanied by a bird of prey, probably a vulture."[35]

So are the bird pillars of Jerf el-Ahmar crude representations of a primeval mother in the form of a vulture? It is interesting that in ancient Egypt thousands of years later, the vulture would become the chief totemic form of various mother goddesses, including Mut, Nekhbet, and Nut, a matter we return to in chapter 15.

Aside from the extraordinary number of vulture carvings both in reliefs and in sculptures found at both Göbekli Tepe and Nevalı Çori, along with the ritual use of vulture feathers, feet, wings and skulls at places like Jerf el-Ahmar and Zawi Chemi Shanidar, several other similarly aged sites, including Nemrik in northern Iraq, have shown clear indications of the unique significance of the vulture in Pre-Pottery Neolithic and later Pottery Neolithic society.[36] This was the conclusion also of archaeozoologist Lionel Gourichon of CNRS, who, in an important study on the subject, stated: "Taken as a whole, archaeozoological and archaeological evidence indicates that the vulture was of particular importance in the symbolic systems of Early Neolithic societies."[37]

The clear relationship between vulture shamanism, sky burials, and the Pre-Pottery Neolithic world of Anatolia and the Near East is something I have attempted to demonstrate elsewhere.[38] The direct involvement of vultures in the act of excarnation enables us to see how the bird might have come to be associated with early Neolithic beliefs and practices concerning the transmigration of the soul and entry into the afterlife. In this manner the vulture becomes an obvious symbol of the soul's death journey, not only as its protector and psychopomp, but also as its guide and guardian between this world and the next. It is worth recalling also that the Sabians of Harran saw the North (Shamal) not only as the Primal Cause, but also the direction of heaven, where souls came from prior to incarnation and returned to in death.[39] Although they offered up cockerels as sacrifices, birds of prey with talons were seen as special and not sacrificed.[40]

PILLAR 66'S
DEAD BOVINE AND BIRD RELIEF

Enclosure H's porthole stone, Pillar 66, has some highly symbolic reliefs of animals on its front face that now become relevant to this debate. Immediately above its proposed soul-hole aperture, on the T-shaped head section, is a large bovine with its tongue hanging out (see fig. 2.3. on page 24). Archaeologist Oliver Dietrich argues that the exposed tongue and the awkward stance of the animal indicate that it is dead, having been killed in some manner. (Other examples of killed animals with their tongues exposed have been recorded at Çatalhöyük.)[41] This is interesting considering the north-northwesterly positioning of the stone and the fact that the pillar's circular aperture targets the setting of Deneb and thus the northern opening of the Dark Rift, seen in terms of an entrance to the realm of the dead.

Yet it is what is on the bovine's back that is important, for we see the outline of a bird with outstretched wings that seems to be attempting to balance itself on the animal's spine.[42] It is difficult to make out the bird's species, although the shape of the head and apparent hooked beak is consistent with its being a vulture. If this is correct, it suggests that the bird is feeding off the dead carcass, a significant fact since vultures often balance themselves on the backs of dead carcasses when removing flesh. Once again we see evidence of a relationship between scavenger birds, excarnation, the act of death, and the north-northwest as the direction associated with death and the dead. The presence of the soul-hole aperture targeting the setting of the star Deneb helps to confirm this supposition.

One final point of interest about Pillar 66 is that when it was found, it was covered with the fragment of a limestone pillar with an oval aperture.[43] The purpose of this detail is open to speculation. Oliver Dietrich suggests it was done to preserve the pillar from damage or destruction when the installation was buried beneath hundreds of tons of rock debris at the end of its useful life.[44] Only one other pillar was given the same protection. This was Pillar 69, uncovered recently in the northeast corner of Enclosure H. It too was found to have a large piece of broken pillar protecting its head. Like the installation's only remaining central monolith, Pillar 51 (see plate 10), the stem of Pillar 69 is decorated with the carved relief of a large feline, which leaps out of the northwest. Like the porthole stone, its wide, decorated face is uncharacteristically directed toward the center of the enclosure, providing it with a special function of some kind, perhaps the reason that it too was spared destruction.

Returning to the porthole stone, Pillar 66, it is possible that it was given special status because it was seen as the entrance to the spirit world. Was it felt that due respect had to be given to the stone to avoid offending the spirits of the dead? If so, then perhaps Pillar 69 also had a directional connection with the afterlife, its large feline, like that of the enclosure's remaining central pillar, being seen as a guardian of the realm of the dead.

THE WORLD'S FIRST PICTOGRAPH

These interrelated themes help provide the key to understanding the carved imagery of Göbekli Tepe's Vulture Stone, Pillar 43. I was thus heartened when in July 2015 Müslüm Ercan—the then-director of Şanlıurfa's archaeological museum and head of excavations at Göbekli Tepe on behalf of the museum—independently voiced similar opinions on the function of the stone. In an article published in Turkey's *Hurriyet Daily News,* Ercan stated: "The scene on the obelisk unearthed in Göbeklitepe [Enclosure D's Pillar 43] could be construed as the first pictograph because it depicts an event thematically. It depicts a human head in the wing of a vulture and a headless human body under the stela.

"There were no graves 12,000 years ago," he went on. "The dead bodies were left outdoors and raptors [that is, vultures] ate them. In this way, people believed the soul goes to the sky." This process, he explained, was called "burial in the sky," adding, "We see this type of thing portrayal [*sic*] on the walls in 6,000–5,000 B.C. in Çatalhöyük."[45]

So, like me, Ercan proposes that the overall theme conveyed by Pillar 43 is one of the soul's transmigration, its funny-looking vulture acting as a psychopomp because of its role in excarnation. Moreover, he too sees the sunlike disk above the vulture's right wing as symbolic of the soul of the deceased, while the headless man on the neck of the great bird beneath the scorpion represents his corporeal body. These are extraordinary realizations. Yet we cannot leave the story here, as we have additional evidence that the carved imagery of Pillar 43 not only preserves a memory of the route taken by the soul to enter the afterlife, but also how and when this was to take place.

5

SCORPIONIC GATEWAY

xamine the skies for the epoch of 9600–8800 BCE—the Pre-Pottery Neolithic A period in Anatolia and the Near East—and the close interplay between Cygnus and Scorpius, the two constellations featured on the Vulture Stone, becomes obvious. As Cygnus crossed the meridian on its upper transit high in the northern night sky, the stars of Scorpius lay immediately above the western horizon, just about to set. Moreover, as Cygnus rose in the north-northeast, the stars of Scorpius were themselves transiting the meridian. Linking the two constellations was, of course, the Milky Way, and in particular the Dark Rift, which ran from the vicinity of the Cygnus star Deneb all the way down to the area of sky just above Scorpius.

Ancient populations who spent time studying the heavens are likely to have noted such interplays between these two very distinctive constellations. Knowledge of the movements of stars, when and where they rose, when they crossed the meridian, and where and when they set, would have been crucial to understanding their own relationship to the celestial realms.

Synchronizations between the sun and the Milky Way would have taken on an even greater significance when they occurred either at the solstices (the most northerly and southerly rising and setting points of the sun, marking the longest and shortest days of the year) or at the equinoxes (when the sun rises and sets exactly east and west, marking the two days in the year when night and day are of equal length). Most likely it would have been at such times that the soul was expected to make its journey along the Milky Way to the place of the afterlife.

THE CYGNUS SHORTCUT

Yet as we have seen in connection with the porthole stones and axial alignments of the main enclosures at Göbekli Tepe, it would appear that here the builders incorporated an architectural shortcut into the design of the monuments in order to target a specific location in the Milky Way, one presumably seen as a direct point of access to the realm of the dead. That location was, of course, Cygnus, which marks the northern entrance to the Milky Way's Dark Rift. Not only does this imply a special relationship with the constellation, but it also suggests that the souls of shamans and initiates were able to bypass the normal points of access onto the starry stream, in other words the twin horizonal gateways of Scorpius and Sagittarius on one side of the sky and Taurus, Gemini, and Orion on the other. They, as we saw in chapter 4, are the two areas where the ecliptic, the sun's path, crosses the Milky Way, a connection emphasized on equinoxes and solstices, when the starry stream can be seen towering into the sky in the hours immediately before dawn or after sunset.

WARNING SIGN

Pillar 43's carved art suggests also that a route to Cygnus and the sky world was thought possible via a portal in the vicinity of Scorpius. If so, then it implies that the strange vulture with the *W*-shaped wings was seen to protect the soul—shown as a sunlike disk on the bird's right wing—from the threat of Scorpius in its guise as the underworld scorpion that lurks immediately below the line of the ecliptic. Since the scorpion is one of the most deadly creatures known to humankind, the imagery on Pillar 43 implies that it was considered just as deadly in its supernatural form.

So is the Vulture Stone in actuality a warning sign to make it clear that any rites and rituals involving the transition of the soul from the land of the living to the realm of the dead should take place only after Scorpius has disappeared into the underworld, in other words, well below the horizon? Arguably this fact is emphasized by the scorpion's position on the pillar, well below the deeply cut horizontal line dividing the stone's T-shaped head from its broad stem. This line forms a noticeable partition between the scorpion and the vulture directly above it. In this manner the scorpion is shown immediately beneath the local horizon, its claws reaching up toward the vulture located firmly in the sky world above.

WHEN THE TIME IS RIGHT

In astronomical terms, Göbekli Tepe's Vulture Stone appears to be telling us that the correct time to make the death journey from the earthly plane to the sky world is after Cygnus has crossed the meridian high in the sky. Only afterward will the influence of Scorpius begin to fade as its stars sink slowly beneath the horizon. Once this has happened, Cygnus, the celestial vulture, will be in full control of the Milky Way's Dark Rift, the role it will play until its own setting just a few hours later. Most likely it was believed that it was during this window of opportunity, between Cygnus's culmination on the meridian through its setting on the north-northwestern horizon, that the soul's journey between the earthly plane and the sky world could take place. Whether this journey had to pass through the Scorpius-Sagittarius portal, or whether a more direct route to the sky world was achieved via the soul-hole stones remains unclear. Arguably, both routes were used depending on the time of year and the exact purpose behind the death journey.

If these surmises are correct, they tell us why Göbekli Tepe's Vulture Stone so obviously features celestial creatures representing the constellations of Scorpius and Cygnus. They also explain why its main enclosures are aligned north-northwest, toward the setting of Cygnus, and not toward the constellation's rising, when Scorpius would have been high in the sky. At such times the influence of the latter would presumably have been too strong and too dangerous for death journeys to take place. This scenario also explains why the tiny bone plaque found at Göbekli Tepe shows the Cygnus wing stars at the halfway point between their culmination on the meridian and their setting on the north-northwestern horizon. Its imagery clearly displays the Cygnus stars during their time of superiority, when those of Scorpius were firmly beneath the horizon.

PILLAR 43: A COSMIC SIGNBOARD

The image of a scorpion guarding the entrance to the underworld was, it seems, universal.[1] It was related to the role played by Scorpius in granting the soul access to the Milky Way via one of the two horizonal gates where this was possible (the other, as previously explained, being in the vicinity of Taurus, Gemini, and Orion on the other side of the sky). Very likely similar concepts were behind the creation of the carved imagery on Göbekli Tepe's Pillar 43. If this is correct, then the imagery can be seen as a signboard showing the cosmic geography required for the soul to embark on its death journey. This information was available not only to the newly dead, but also to the shaman, initiate, and celebrant during altered states of consciousness.

The ritual practices associated with Göbekli Tepe, as well as the various other Pre-Pottery Neolithic sites of the region, were most likely highly abstract expressions of more archaic beliefs that were once more widespread, not only across Eurasia, but also in the Americas. This shared cosmography can be seen from the beliefs and practices intimately bound up with the Native American death journey, where Scorpius was seen as the Water Panther or Great Snake that threatened the soul as it attempted to reach the afterlife via the Milky Way, known to countless tribes as the Path of Souls. Here too Scorpius had to be below the horizon before the soul's hazardous journey could take place.[2] Yet although the Water Panther was a dangerous creature to be avoided on the Native American death journey, among the peoples of southeast Anatolia's Pre-Pottery Neolithic age, the panther-leopard will, as we see next, go on to become the ultimate symbol of the soul's transition from this world to the next.

Plate I. General view of Göbekli Tepe's southeastern depression from the northwest, showing Enclosure D in the foreground.

Plate 2. The small bone plaque found at Göbekli Tepe, showing etched relief of twin pillars like those seen in the center of the site's key installations. The plaque can be seen in Şanlıurfa's archaeological museum.

Plate 3. The twin central monoliths at the center of Göbekli Tepe's Enclosure D. Note the porthole stone at the rear of the installation.

Plate 4. Reconstructed stone porthole found at Göbekli Tepe and today on display in Şanlıurfa's archaeological museum.

Plate 5. Old photo of the ancient city of Harran showing its beehive houses and remaining astronomical tower. This was once a center for Chaldean and Sabaean astronomers and astrologers, some of whom might have been descendants of those who built nearby Göbekli Tepe many thousands of years earlier.

Plate 6. The inner ringwall of T-pillars in Göbekli Tepe's Enclosure C. New radiocarbon dates suggest the installation was built after its nearest neighbor, Enclosure D.

Plate 7. Artist Russell M. Hossain's reconstruction of the carved imagery on the bone plaque found at Göbekli Tepe based on all available architectural and astronomical information. The three stars are Gienah, Sadr, and Rukh, the three wing stars of Cygnus, which appear as peck marks above the plaque's twin pillars.

Plate 8. Pillar 43, also known as the Vulture Stone, in Göbekli Tepe's Enclosure D. Is its carved relief the key to understanding the cosmology of the Pre-Pottery Neolithic world of Anatolia and the Near East?

Plate 9. Section of a stone totem pole found at Göbekli Tepe showing a vulture with its talons clutching a human head, a Neolithic symbol of the human soul. It is currently on display in Şanlıurfa's archaeological museum.

Plate 10. Pillar 51 in Göbekli Tepe's Enclosure H. Its panther relief, along with a similar feline on newly uncovered Pillar 69 in the same installation, are clear indications that, like the vulture, the panther-leopard was one of the principal totems of the Pre-Pottery Neolithic world of Anatolia and the Near East.

Plate 11. The northern twin pillar in Göbekli Tepe's Lion Pillars Building, built circa 8800–8000 BCE. Its carved relief most likely shows not a lion but a panther-leopard, like those seen on two pillars in Enclosure H.

Plate 12. Ceramic seated female figure, perhaps an ancestress, known today as the Ana Tanriça ("Mother Goddess"). It was found at Çatalhöyük by James Mellaart and his team in 1961. Her arms rest on panther-leopards and between her legs is a human head, a symbol of the soul's rebirth in the next world. It can be viewed in Ankara's Museum of Anatolian Civilizations.

Plate 13. Figurine of a woman seated on a leopard and wearing a leopard shawl like those worn by the Maenads, the followers of Bacchus-Dionysus. The piece was found at Çatalhöyük in the early 1960s and can be seen today in Ankara's Museum of Anatolian Civilizations.

Plate 14. Stone beer vat in the corner of one of the Level II enclosures at Göbekli Tepe, built circa 8500–8000 BCE. Evidence suggests that both beer brewing and wine fermentation were the invention by the Pre-Pottery Neolithic peoples of southeast Anatolia. The widespread use of beer and wine went hand in hand with the emergence of the panther-leopard as a symbol of supernatural strength and otherworldly communication.

Plate 15. Pebble mosaic of Dionysus holding the thyrsus staff and riding a leopard from Pella, Greece, circa 400 BCE. Very likely his cult emerged from that of the panther-leopard, which thrived among the Pre-Pottery and later Pottery Neolithic peoples of Anatolia.

Plate 16. Life-size human statue known today as the Urfa Man. It was found during urban development in Şanlıurfa's Yeni Yol Street in the heart of the old city. It dates to the end of the Pre-Pottery Neolithic A, circa 9000–8800 BCE. Excavations at the site led to the discovery of a Helwan point exactly like those found at Helwan in northern Egypt.

Plate 17. The main three pyramids of Giza, built for the Fourth Dynasty kings Khufu, Khafre, and Menkaure, circa 2550–2479 BCE. Like the main enclosures at Göbekli Tepe they are aligned to the setting of key stars in the constellation of Cygnus.

Plate 18. The head of the Great Sphinx at Giza, carved from the natural bedrock. Although it is attributed to the age of Khafre, the builder of the Second Pyramid, its true age is today a matter of fierce debate. However, as a natural promontory or knoll, the site was revered as a place of the dead as early as the fourth millennium BCE.

Plate 19. Heit el-Ghurab, the "Wall of the Crow," located at the southeastern edge of the Giza plateau. It may have provided the division between the Giza pyramid field as the realm of the dead to the north and the City of the Pyramids, representing the realm of the living, to the south. Its huge cyclopean gateway, pictured here, was very likely the plateau's southern entrance.

Plate 20. Roman mosaic from Şanlıurfa, southeast Anatolia, showing the poet and musician Orpheus charming the animals with his fabled lyre. In the sky he is represented by the constellation of Cygnus, his lyre becoming the nearby constellation of Lyra. The many writings attributed to Orpheus influenced the rise of Pythagoreanism in the Greek Hellenic world.

Plate 21. A red-figure bell krater showing Apollo, the Greek god of music and poetry. He is shown seated on a swan playing his lyre. Two Muses are seen nearby, one playing a lyre and the other dancing.

Plate 22. Artist Russell M. Hossain's reconstruction of the primeval enclosure described in the Edfu building texts. All the indications are that this structure was located in the vicinity of Helwan in northern Egypt.

Plate 23. The Denisova Cave in the Altai Krai region of southern Siberia. Here over the last decade archaeologists have uncovered anatomical evidence of a previously unknown hominin today known as the Denisovans. Insets: left, one of the two huge Denisovan molars found in the cave's layer 11 and, right, one of the pierced ostrich-eggshell beads along with the fragment of choritolite bracelet found in the same archaeological layer.

Plate 24. Reconstruction of the choritolite bracelet found in the Denisova Cave's layer 11, and thought to have been made by Denisovans. If this is correct, it shows their advanced level of behavior as much as 60,000–70,000 years ago.

Plate 25. The Milky Way's Dark Rift setting between the twin peaks known as the Brothers in the Ergaki National Park, located in the western Sayan Mountains of southern Siberia. Was this gigantic natural amphitheater used by the Denisovans and their hybrid descendants as an astronomical observatory?

6

CULT OF THE LEOPARD

By far the most impressive stone enclosure of Göbekli Tepe's later phase of building construction is the Lion Pillars Building. Built sometime circa 8800–8000 BCE, it is situated around 12 meters above the bedrock enclosures of the site's southeastern depression. Indeed the massive wall of stone rubble and debris left behind by the excavation of Enclosure D looks at first glance to be a natural cliff face that rises up to where the Lion Pillars Building sits close to the summit of the mound. However, the *entire* tepe is artificial, with at least two, possibly even three, distinct layers of construction beginning on the bedrock and rising to the height of the Lion Pillars Building.

This Layer II structure has a rectilinear form, with an internal size of approximately 8.5 meters by 5.5 meters and interior walls standing around 2 meters in height. Two standing pillars with human features, both with their T-shaped heads now missing, are seen opposite each other about halfway along the building's north and south walls. Two more undecorated T-pillars, both of them damaged, stand side by side immediately to the west of the pillars in the retaining walls.

LION RELIEFS

The most interesting features of the Lion Pillars Building, however, are the two T-pillars standing at its eastern end. They sit flush against the east wall with their narrow front edges facing the center of the installation. Between them is a bench made up of two stone slabs supported by underlying stone blocks. Decorating the inner face of each pillar is the carved relief of a fierce-looking quadruped, unquestionably a large feline of some kind. They rear up toward the entrant, who approaches from a westerly direction. Their open jaws reveal mouths full of sharp teeth, while long curving tails arch over their backs. The striking pose created by these carved reliefs actually mimics the shape of the pillar's nail-like termination, something that appears to have been deliberate to accentuate the animated stance adopted by these predators (see plate 11).

PANTHER SHRINE

The feline carvings in the Lion Pillars Building very probably represent the speckled panther or leopard (*Panthera pardus*). What is more, several other notable felines are found in the carved art at Göbekli Tepe. Some of these are almost certainly panthers or leopards, a fact confirmed by Professor Joris Peters, an archaeozoologist at the Ludwig Maximilian University of Munich in Germany. He has made a detailed study of the zoomorphic imagery at Göbekli Tepe and, in an important paper coauthored with Klaus Schmidt, concluded that a large number of the carved representations of quadruped predators found at the site are almost certainly leopards, and not lions, as some might think.[1]

DISCOVERING ENCLOSURE H

This realization can help us better understand the importance of other examples of feline imagery at Göbekli Tepe. As mentioned in chapters 2 and 4, in Enclosure H there are leaping pantherlike creatures on two stones—its remaining central pillar, Pillar 51, and also Pillar 69, located in the northeast section of the installation's ringwall. In each case the animal is huge, and with its bulky body, exposed teeth, and menacing stance, it is meant to be seen as an advancing predator.

Using the azimuthal orientation of Pillar 51, along with that of the circular aperture of the installation's porthole stone, Pillar 66, Rodney Hale was able to determine that both were aligned toward the setting of Deneb at a date of approximately 8900 BCE, well within the structure's proposed time frame of construction.[2]

THE MESOPOTAMIAN SKY PANTHER

Seemingly, on entering Enclosure H, the shaman, initiate, or celebrant would have approached between its twin central pillars, where, on the eastern example at least, the carved relief of a pantherlike beast would have been seen to rear up at them. Standing here they would have been able to project their mind through the circular aperture of the porthole stone toward the direction of the realm of the dead, which was presumably guarded by just such a creature. If so, then the pantherlike creatures of Enclosure H are almost certainly proto-forms of [mul]UD.KA.DUH.A (Akkadian Ukaduhha or Kadduhha),[3] the Mesopotamian sky panther or panther-griffin, whose name, as we have already seen, means "constellation [MUL] of the storm demon with the gaping mouth."[4] It was an asterism made up of key stars of Cygnus, along with others from the neighboring constellation of Cepheus.

Figure 6.1. This drawing, adapted from the MUL.APIN text, shows the Mesopotamian constellation [mul]UD.KA.DUH.A, the panther-griffin, from which emerges Nergal's forked staff, its twin prongs ending in panther heads.

The Babylonian astronomical text known as the MUL.APIN identifies the sky panther with Nergal, the Mesopotamian god of the underworld. Under the influence of Nergal, the sky panther is represented by the polelike staff the god carries, which has a U-shaped top with the heads of twin panthers facing away from each other (see fig. 6.1).

ENCLOSURE C'S INVERTED GATEWAY

Among the feline carvings that Joris Peters undoubtedly considered when assessing the feline imagery of the carved art at Göbekli Tepe are the twin predators that sat atop the inverted stone doorway in the shape of the letter *U*. This doorway originally stood at the entrance to the southerly positioned *dromos,* or passageway, leading into Enclosure C's outer ringwall. At the top of its twin prongs are a pair of beautifully carved felines, shown in a crouched position facing away from each other. These uncannily mimic the panther heads at the top of the strange *U*-shaped termination of Nergal's staff in the MUL.APIN image, implying that both signify the manner in which a sky panther was thought to guard the entrance to the realm of the dead. Enclosure C's axial alignment, determined by the mean azimuth bearing of its twin central pillars and the presence of its porthole stone, targets the setting of Deneb and thus the northern opening of the Milky Way's Dark Rift, making this theory seem plausible indeed.

ORIGINS OF THE GRIFFIN

When the panther-griffin ^{mul}UD.KA.DUH.A is shown in Mesopotamian art, most obviously on cylinder seals, the creature appears to have the head and body of a panther-leopard and the wings and feet of a raptor. Although this raptor is usually identified as an eagle, it was originally most likely a vulture.[5]

The ancient Greeks regarded the vulture as the offspring of the griffin,[6] which, although simply a myth, does show the clear relationship between the two beasts, both of which were important in the beliefs and practices of the Neolithic peoples of Anatolia. In fact it is more likely that the connection is the other way around—the vulture combining with the panther, or leopard, to create the mythical griffin, which in its celestial form was personified in Mesopotamian tradition as ^{mul}UD.KA.DUH.A. This frightening sky creature was seen to rise around midwinter, exactly when the souls of the deceased were thought to enter the realm of the dead.[7]

As the personification of the god Nergal, the ruler of the dead, the sky panther [mul]UD.KA.DUH.A was identified with Shamal, the god venerated by the Harranians during special celebrations known as the Mystery of the North. Like Nergal, Shamal was a god of darkness, demons, and death, just as much as he was the Primal Cause, the source of all life and the origin point of human souls. Indeed, Nergal's identification with Shamal was noted by Near Eastern scholar Tamara Green in her important work on the religious traditions of Harran titled *The City of the Moon God* (1992).[8]

LEOPARDS AT ÇATALHÖYÜK

Perhaps the greatest evidence of a panther-leopard cult existing among the Neolithic peoples of ancient Anatolia comes from Çatalhöyük in south-central Anatolia. The site's connection with the symbol of the vulture has already been noted (see chapter 4). Nevertheless, the prolificacy of panther- and leopard-related art at Çatalhöyük is crucial in determining the ultimate fate of the beliefs and practices that thrived in Anatolia and the Near East during the Neolithic age.

One painted mural at Çatalhöyük, for instance, depicts warriors either wearing or holding leopard skins as they hunt a gigantic bovine creature, most likely an aurochs. Just like the carved relief of the large bull-like creature on Enclosure H's porthole stone, the fresco shows the animal with its tongue protruding, suggesting that it is either dead or dying, a victim of the hunt. Other large felines are shown in sculpted relief, their legs outstretched in a birthing position. Sometimes the head of a large bovine with curved horns, or that of a caprid, is seen directly beneath the assumed position of the leopard's vulva, perhaps indicating that the feline is giving birth to this animal.

ANA TANRIÇA

Then there is the striking baked-clay statue of a nude, full-bodied woman unearthed at Çatalhöyük in 1961 and thought to date to around the start of the Ceramic Neolithic age in Anatolia, circa 6000 BCE (see plate 12). She is seated with her arms resting on a pair of front-facing leopards that stand on either side of her. A small head protrudes from between her legs, which has been interpreted as that of a newborn child (although see below). Known in Turkish as Ana Tanrıça ("Mother Goddess"), this unique statue can be seen in Ankara's Museum of Anatolian Civilizations.

In addition to this, a blue limestone statue of a woman, perhaps a priestess or shamaness, was also found at Çatalhöyük. It shows her seated sidesaddle on what is quite clearly a leopard, complete with spots. Her head is missing, as are her lower arms, although around her neck we see what appears to be a shawl or scarf made of leopard's skin, exactly the manner in which the Maenads, the frenzied followers of the Greek and Roman god Bacchus-Dionysus are depicted in classical Greek and Roman art (see plate 13). Various other portable figurines of women either in brown or blue limestone also show them wearing leopard-skin shawls. In one example, the woman holds what appears to be a pair of leopard cubs. Similar stone figurines from the Pottery Neolithic and later Chalcolithic site of Hacilar in the Taurus Mountains of southwest Anatolia, which thrived circa 5500–4500 BCE, also show women seated on leopards.

THE LEOPARD'S TALE

Both James Mellaart, who excavated Çatalhöyük during the 1960s and Hacilar in the 1950s, and more recently Ian Hodder of Stanford University, who was director of the Çatalhöyük Research Project from 1993 to 2014, have recognized the importance of the leopard to the Neolithic peoples of Anatolia.[9] Mellaart saw the figurines and statues of women with leopards as "mother goddesses" or "birthing goddesses," forerunners of Cybele, the Magna Mater ("Great Mother") of Anatolian tradition.[10]

Hodder, on the other hand, has proposed that the carved images of women with leopards are connected more with what he calls "ancestry," since they are also often linked with the proximity of human skulls. In his book *The Leopard's Tale* (2006), named in honor of this all-important beast, Hodder cites the discovery of a perforated leopard claw inside one of the houses. It was found in association with a plastered human skull held in the hands of a female burial.[11] This was the first leopard bone identified from an estimated 650,000 bone fragments found at the site. Before its discovery Hodder had even come to believe that it might have been taboo to bring leopard bones into the settlement.[12] In their study of the zoomorphic imagery at Göbekli Tepe, Joris Peters and Klaus Schmidt reported that just one leopard bone had been found among a total of 38,704 mammalian specimens recorded at the site.[13] Here, as much as

2,000 years before the foundation of Çatalhöyük, the animal must have held a similar importance among the local population.

Strengthening this proposed connection between leopards and ancestry, Hodder says, is the Ana Tanrıça, the baked-clay statue of the seated woman with standing felines on either side of her. As previously mentioned, a small headlike bulge emerges from between her legs, something that Mellaart interpreted as the head of a child being born.[14] Hodder on the other hand proposes that this protrusion is the top of a human skull (a clear symbol, of course, of the human soul). This, he feels, shows the relationship between large felines and ancestry, something conveyed also by the presence of the leopard-claw pendant found alongside the aforementioned female burial.

> Once again in the burial or *northern part of a house* we have the focus on the sharp pointed part of a wild animal. And the bone is associated with a woman holding a plastered skull that seems to have been replastered several times, handed down through time. The prowess or spiritual power of the claw is associated with ancestry. The pendant was worn and may have been associated with specific memories and histories.[15]

According to Hodder, leopards thus formed a psychic connection, a liminal bridge, between the activities of the living and the realm of the ancestors. Note also where this all-important burial was found—in the "northern part of a house," one of the two directions, the other being east, connected at Çatalhöyük with death and the afterlife, according to Mellaart. Hodder makes it clear that the northern part of a building was invariably reserved for decoration and burial, leaving the "dirty" area of the house in the south for hearths, ovens, human debris, and general occupation.[16]

THE GREAT MOTHER

So what became of this apparently powerful and prominent cult of death, transformation, and rebirth among the Neolithic and later Chalcolithic peoples of central and southeast Anatolia? The first clue comes from the full-bodied female statues and figurines found at both Çatalhöyük and Hacilar, which, as Mellart pointed out, bear striking resemblances to the iconography and symbolism attached to Cybele, the Anatolian mother goddess.[17] Although venerated in Anatolia perhaps as early as the Late Bronze Age, circa 2000–1200 BCE,

Cybele does not appear in her more recognizable form until the rise of the kingdoms of Phrygia and Lydia during the later Iron Age, 1200-6th century BCE.
Thereafter the cult of the Magna Mater, as the goddess became known, was
adopted by incoming Greek colonists, who had started to colonize Asia Minor
by around 700 BCE. They in turn transported it to mainland Greece, where
Cybele became fused with the cult of another great goddess, that of Rhea, the
Magna Mater of Crete.

MEADOW OF THE BLESSED

Although Ian Hodder associates the Ana Tanriça statue found at Çatalhöyük
with the veneration of family "ancestry," it is perhaps more appropriate to identify her as an embodiment of the mother of life. This was not life in a physical
sense, but one experienced on entering the afterlife. In other words, she was a
mother of rebirth in the next world, as is emphasized by the emergence from
between her legs of a human skull as a symbol of the soul. The idea of being
born anew in the afterlife is a religious concept known to have been present
among the Bronze Age peoples of Anatolia at the same time as the emergence
of the cult of Cybele in the west of the region. They believed that the soul utilized subterranean springs and lakes to reach a place of the afterlife called the
"Meadow of the Blessed."[18]

The Bronze Age peoples of central Anatolia understood death to be a kind
of second birth, conceived of as a change in state of being, a straightforward
transition from the land of the living to the realm of the dead. This was known
as "the day of (one's) mother," a reference to an imagined primeval mother giving birth to the soul in the next world.[19] Once in the Meadow of the Blessed,
the newly reborn soul lived out its second life in an environment that was,
presumably, little different from our own. Furthermore, it was able to return
to the land of the living through entrances to otherworldly domains.[20] Food
would be left at such locations to encourage communication between the living
and the dead. Once a month the link between the two worlds was strengthened by leaving a more substantial meal at the place of burial.[21] This was done
between the old moon and new moon, when the lunar orb made its passage
through the underworld.[22]

These ideas are further supported by the female human burial found
at Çatalhöyük and presented in such detail by Ian Hodder in his book
The Leopard's Tale. The fact that the woman holds in her hand a decorated

human skull, near to which was found a leopard claw, tells us that the latter was being used as a point of contact between this world and the next. Moreover, the plastered skull arguably formed a link with her own ancestors. Is it possible that the feline spirit presumably thought to be attached to the leopard's claw accompanied the woman into the afterlife as a psychopomp, or did she herself adopt the guise of a leopard to make this treacherous journey?

Whatever the answer, in ancient Anatolian tradition the symbol of the panther-leopard would appear to have been integrally bound up with beliefs and practices attached to the soul's death journey. Moreover, statues of full-bodied women like the Ana Tanrıça should not be seen as givers of life in this world; they were the means for the soul to begin its second life in the realm of the dead. Yet by the Bronze Age the purpose of the Anatolian goddess of rebirth would appear to have transformed into something quite different, for she was now the great mother of the gods. Thereafter the clearest line of diffusion from the Neolithic and Chalcolithic urban centers of Anatolia to the classical age were the Greek mystery religions associated with Bacchus-Dionysus, the Greek and Roman god of wine, fertility, vitality, madness, ecstasy, and agriculture. These, I suspect, derived at least in part from ecstatic rites originally performed at Pre-Pottery Neolithic sites in southeast Anatolia, where the earliest known evidence for the production of wine and beer has been found.

THE GENESIS OF WINE AND BEER

Swiss botanist and grape DNA analyst José Vouillamoz, working alongside American biomolecular archaeologist Patrick McGovern, conducted a comprehensive project to examine wild and cultivated grapevines from various countries of the Near East, including Anatolia, Armenia, and Georgia. Its aim was "to see in which place the wild grape was, genetically speaking, linked the closest to the cultivated variety."[23] Comparing the DNA of wild grapes from various localities against organic residues associated with winemaking vessels from the prehistoric age, Vouillamoz and McGovern were able to determine that the genesis point of grape domestication and wine production was southeast Anatolia, and in particular the area around Diyarbakır.[24]

Vouillamoz and McGovern's extraordinary findings show that the original center of wine production in the Near East coincided almost precisely with the heartland of southeast Anatolia's Pre-Pottery Neolithic culture. Indeed, Göbekli Tepe is located just 150 kilometers from Diyarbakır, while Çayönü, where emmer wheat domestication is attested as early as 7000 BCE, is just 40 kilometers away. More significantly, these findings eerily echo the extraordinary discovery that sixty-eight modern strains of wheat, used today for everything from making bread to brewing beer, derive from a wild variety of the plant called einkorn, which grows to this day on the slopes of an extinct volcano named Karaca Dağ, just 45 kilometers away from Diyarbakır.[25]

Beer storage and consumption has long been suspected at Göbekli Tepe. This comes from the discovery in certain of its Layer II structures of large stone vats (see plate 14). When organic residue found at the base of these stone vessels was tested it was found to contain chemicals consistent with beer manufacture.[26] Thus both wine and beer production may have originated in the very same area of the ancient world.

CHILDREN OF THE STARRY SKY

If correct then it can be no coincidence that in the frenzied rites of Bacchus-Dionysus, whose own animistic form was the panther-leopard (see plate 15), the Maenads are said to have consumed large amounts of wine before tearing part animals, having first assumed the guise of leopards.[27] The fact that they also wore leopard shawls like the stone figurines of women from both Çatalhöyük and Hacilar tells us that the origins of these ecstatic rites go back several thousand years. What is more they were not simply an excuse for licentiousness and orgiastic behavior. The mysteries of Bacchus-Dionysus contained important information concerning death and resurrection, and the journey the soul must take to reach the afterlife. They are themes found in writings attributed to the legendary founder of his cult, the divine poet Orpheus,[28] and include the fact that the souls of initiates or bacchoi called "children of the starry sky"[29] are required to choose between a left-hand and right-hand path located on a "mystic road" identified with the Milky Way.[30] If the correct path was taken the righteous would enter a celestial Isle of the Blessed and unite with their origins and became as stars themselves.[31]

Almost certainly the location of the fork in the heavenly path, beyond which access to the afterlife was achieved, was the northern entrance to the Milky Way's Dark Rift. This, of course, is marked by the stars of the Cygnus constellation, identified with the vulture and sky panther as early as the age of Göbekli Tepe, circa 9600–8000 BCE, and with the divine poet Orpheus during the classical age (see chapters 21 and 22).

SUMMARY

There can be little doubt that many of the cosmological beliefs and practices that had their inception at sites like Göbekli Tepe continued to exist for many thousands of years, influencing the emergence of complex religious and mythogical ideas that remain strong in the minds of humankind even today. In the wake of the Neolithic revolution these cosmological notions would seem to have been carried across the Eurasian continent. We will explore another strand next, as there is now compelling evidence to suggest that what began at sites in Anatolia's Pre-Pottery Neolithic world would go on to find a new home in Egypt's Nile Valley, the future land of the pharaohs.

PART TWO

THE BIRTH OF EGYPT

7

THE LOST OASIS

Helwan in northern Egypt lies directly opposite the ruins of the ancient city of Memphis, the capital of Upper and Lower Egypt from the beginning of dynastic history, circa 3120 BCE.[1] It sits on a rocky plateau located just beyond the eastern edge of the Nile floodplain, around 25 kilometers to the south of modern-day Cairo. Today it is a large industrial city with its own steel mills, assembly plants, cement factories, and university. Yet in the 1800s, during the pioneering years of Egyptology, it was little more than a desert oasis around a series of mineral springs that have attracted people to the area for at least 20,000 years.

Lying within sight of the Giza pyramid field,[2] close to the entrances to various wadis (dry river channels) that connect Egypt's eastern desert with the Red Sea coast, Helwan appears to have become important as a settlement site toward the end of the Pleistocene epoch. This was the geological age that had run the entire length of the ice age and, following a 2000-year period of warming circa 13,000–11,000 BCE, had culminated in the so-called Younger Dryas event, a mini–ice age that had struck the Northern Hemisphere suddenly for a period of 1200 years circa 10,800–9600 BCE. In southeast Anatolia and the Levant (modern Syria, Lebanon, Jordan, Palestine, Israel, and the Egyptian Sinai) the post–ice age period had coincided with the beginning of the Pre-Pottery Neolithic. In Egypt, as in Europe, the transitional stage between the end of the Paleolithic, circa 9600 BCE, and the emergence of the first Pottery

Neolithic settlements in the Nile Valley is often called the Mesolithic age. It is a term used, somewhat erroneously, to describe Helwan's earliest settlements. (Indeed, today the term "Mesolithic" is used only to define the transitional stage between the Upper Paleolithic and Neolithic periods in Europe, circa 9600–5000 BCE.)

What occurred at Helwan during this period will help forge a bridge between everything that happened at places like Göbekli Tepe in southeast Anatolia in the wake of the Younger Dryas event and the appearance in the Nile Valley of a high culture that culminated with the great achievements of the Pyramid Age some 5,000 years later. This is why it will be necessary to dissect Helwan's history in the minutest detail in advance of the extraordinary revelations that emerged during the writing of this book that confirm just how important this settlement site was to the eventual foundation of the nearby Giza pyramid field. So please bear with me in this endeavor, as everything within these pages will come together and make sense in the end.

HELWAN'S THERAPEUTIC SPRINGS

The original discoverer of Helwan's previously unknown "Mesolithic" past was Dr. Wilhelm Reil (1820–1880),[3] a homeopath and art historian from Germany who became director of the town's sanitorium, a medical facility for the treatment of long-term illnesses such as tuberculosis.[4] This was founded to make use of the oasis's unique series of springs, which were of three distinct types. There were hot thermal springs with a sulfurous content, which were said to reach 33 degrees centigrade (91 degrees Fahrenheit) in temperature.[5] There were also quite bitter saline springs, and also chalybeate springs,[6] whose iron-rich content leaves behind a distinctive rustlike stain.

These springs led to the area becoming known as Ain Helwan ("Helwan spring"), and also Kabrittaj, from the Arabic root *kibrīt,* "sulfur."[7] Indeed, the Anglicized name Helwan (French *Heluan* and German *Hilwan*) is thought to derive from the Arabic *helw,* or *halw,* meaning "sweet, pleasant (to the eye, mind, or taste),"[8] although the brackish nature of the saline springs,[9] along with the "peculiarly offensive"[10] nature of its sulfur baths, appears at odds with this explanation.

There seems little doubt that Helwan's three distinct types of spring would have been important from the very beginning, which, even without their claimed therapeutic properties, would always have offered a plentiful supply of drinking water. Unquestionably the ancient Egyptians knew the springs, especially since Memphis (the modern town of Mit Rahina) was located immediately opposite Helwan on the other side of the Nile.

It was in 690 CE that ʿAbd al-ʿAzīz ibn Marwān, the governor (*walī*) of Egypt, retreated to Helwan following a skirmish with an enemy that was laying waste to Fustát (Old Cairo). Here Marwān established a royal residence with extensive gardens watered by the nearby springs, which were diverted for this purpose.[11] Around this time a hospice and a monastery dedicated to Saint Gregorius were founded at Helwan. This served as a hostelry for pilgrims visiting the area.[12] Yet Helwan's therapeutic waters must have been popular at an even earlier date as its famous *hammam* (bathhouse) was built on the foundations of a former Roman building.[13]

MIRACLE CURES

After the monastery of Saint Gregorius had fallen into disuse, arguably during the medieval period, Helwan's popularity rapidly declined, leaving only its bathhouse as the focus of its oasislike village close to the water's edge. Then, in the mid-nineteenth century, soldiers sent to Helwan for recuperation reported being cured of skin diseases and rheumatism after bathing in its medicinal waters.[14] Khedive Abbas Hilmi I, the ruler of Egypt between 1848 and 1854, learned of these cures and ordered chemists from Cairo's School of Medicine to analyze the mineral waters. This led to the establishment of Helwan's Al Hayat sanitorium (in Arabic *al-hayat* means "the life"), which turned the area into a major spa resort, with its own hotel, railway line from Cairo, golf course, and royal palace founded by Abbas I's grandson Mohammed Tewfik Pasha. Thereafter Helwan was promoted under the name Heluán-les-Bains to liken it to the highly popular spa resort of Aix-les-Bains in France.[15] Soon rich Europeans from France, Germany, Britain, and Italy flocked to the area to spend extended vacations, sampling its bathhouse and mineral waters, playing golf in the local hotel grounds, and taking picnics in the nearby Arabian desert, whose mild climate, due to its high elevation, was suitable for curing respiratory ailments.

HELWAN'S SILEX WORKS

This was the situation when in 1871 the German Wilhelm Reil, while exploring the sandy ground around the mineral springs outside the old

Arab village of Helwan, began noticing large scatterings of prehistoric stone tools.[16] He collected these and later donated them to the Boulak Museum,[17] the predecessor to Cairo's Museum of Egyptian Antiquities. The tools were the product of a prehistoric population that had once occupied the area and made use of its therapeutic waters.[18] Fortunately, Reil compiled a list of the ten different "silex [silica] works" he came across in 1871–1872.[19] Other European collectors did the same, leaving us with at least a basic record of the thousands of finds made in Helwan during the second half of the nineteenth century.[20]

MOOK'S EXCAVATIONS

Excavations were carried out in the vicinity of the springs on just one occasion during those early days, in 1877–1878, under the leadership of a German pre-historian, theologian, and writer named Friedrich Mook, PhD, (1844–1880).[21] At one location he uncovered three separate levels of occupation, interspersed with layers of sterile sand.[22] Each level was packed with animal bones, evidence of burning, and enormous numbers of flint implements.[23] Among the bones and teeth unearthed were those of the zebra, camel, hyena, hippopotamus, donkey, and large antelope.[24] Mook also found a large number of bird bones, including those of the ostrich.[25]

In addition to faunal remains, Mook found traces of the "red rotted roots" of trees, showing that the springs were once the center of a thriving oasis with abundant tree cover. Mook realized that he was looking at evidence of a time when Egypt enjoyed a climate like that of equatorial Africa today and was peopled by a human population quite different from the ancient Egyptians of the dynastic age.[26]

These prehistoric communities, Mook found, manufactured knives, saws, scrapers, and borers, as well as spearheads and arrowheads. Mook reported that his collection of over 15,000 artifacts[27] was so extensive that it would fill a large room.[28] Moreover, almost all the flint and "jasper" (i.e., chert) tools that Mook collected in 1877–1878 came from just a few specific locations, all of which were connected with springs. One of the most important sites was in the vicinity of a noted palm tree and spring to the east of Helwan village and south of the spa resort,[29] with another by a second palm tree and spring located near the railway station of Al Ma'sarah,[30] a little to the north of Helwan (see fig. 7.1).[31]

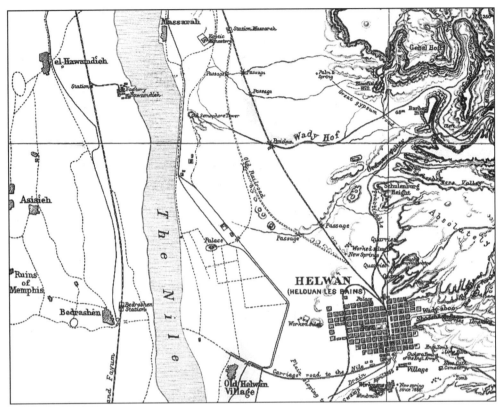

Figure 7.1. Section of map of the Helwan-Ma'sarah area
drawn by Georg A. Schweinfurth in 1895–1896 for the book *Helwan and the
Egyptian Desert: A Guide to the Health Resort of Egypt* (1901). Note Wadi Hôf
and also Gebel Hôf, the historical Mons Troicus. Note also the groups of crosses
to the west of Helwan marked "worked silex." They denote sites where
prehistoric stone tools and projectile points were found.

PROLONGED OCCUPATION

No signs of any pottery were found either on the surface or during excavations,[32] making it clear that the settlement predated the first appearance of ceramics in Egypt circa 6000–5000 BCE. It also seems clear from pictures of the tools and points shown in the tables appended to Mook's book that they reflect an interest in the area by prehistoric peoples across a prolonged period of time, spanning many thousands of years.[33]

Most of the stone tools found at Helwan were of basic appearance, although among them were various examples of beautifully crafted projectile points (spearheads and arrowheads), some made from exotic materials such as rock crystal.[34] Yet Mook was puzzled as to why these were present only in small numbers. Was it because the need for such high-status items was low, or was it because there were simply not enough people in the community with the technical skills to make them? Or was it because those who possessed these finely worked arrowheads were few in number and were only occasionally present in the Helwan area?[35] In other words, were they the product of a nomadic elite who visited the area infrequently?

APATHY AND SUSPICION

Despite Mook's findings, leading Egyptologists of the day were simply not interested in the Helwan artifacts. Great men like Auguste Mariette,[36] Karl Richard Lepsius,[37] and many more besides simply refused to accept the archaic nature of these finds.[38] Those of the highest quality were seen as too advanced for predynastic Egyptians to have made.[39] Indeed, because some of the tools came from the proximity of "Arab ruins," it was concluded that they dated to "l'époque des sultans [the epoch of the sultans]," in other words the age of the Mamluk Sultanate, circa 1250–1517 CE.[40] Other tools were attributed to the dynastic age, while less accomplished examples were dismissed by Lepsius as "natural fragments splintered by the action of the sun and by excessive alternations of temperature."[41] If they were the "produce of industry," he asked, why should "hundreds and thousands of perfect and serviceable instruments" have been left neglected on the ground, as if unworthy to be picked up?"[42]

THE WORK OF FERNAND DEBONO

Clearly this somewhat baffling attitude toward Egypt's prehistoric past thwarted any proper investigation of Helwan's Mesolithic settlements, a situation that was never really rectified prior to their destruction in the modern age. Just one person, an Italian scholar named Fernand Debono (1914–1997), examined the silex work stations before they vanished forever, first beneath a military airfield, and then later beneath the rapid transformation of Helwan into an industrial metropolis under the Nasser regime of the 1950s and 1960s.

During preliminary surveys of the area, first in 1936 and then again in 1941, Debono was able to amass a huge collection of around 3000 artifacts from no less than twenty-three sites in and around the spa resort. His book, *El Omari: A Neolithic Settlement and Other Sites in the Vicinity of Wadi Hof,*

Helwan (1990, coauthored with Bodil Mortensen), includes useful entries on all the known private collections of Helwan prehistoric artifacts. This has proved invaluable to modern-day researchers, who are only now realizing the true potential of Helwan's emergence as northern Egypt's premiere settlement during the Epipaleolithic age, circa 18,000–9600 BCE. Yet what did the collections contain, and how might they be of value to our knowledge of Göbekli Tepe and of the dissemination of its sky religion in the wake of the Neolithic revolution? These are the questions we must now begin to examine.

8

EGYPTIAN
GENESIS

The many thousands of prehistoric artifacts found at Helwan in the late nineteenth century, along with those collected by Fernand Debono during his investigations in 1936 and 1941, paint a very clear picture of what was happening in northern Egypt toward the end of the last ice age. What is more, they tell us who made them, where they came from, and what level of sophistication their manufacturers achieved.

The many thousands of stone tools found in the vicinity of Helwan are almost all made of either flint or chert. We see distinctive geometrical shapes including triangles, trapezes, and lunates (see fig. 8.1). These last mentioned are slim crescents with blunted backs and curved cutting edges that in the Near East are known to have been used to harvest wild grasses.[1] We see also many beautifully finished miniature graving tools known as microburins, which, although familiar to many sites in the Near East, are considered "extremely rare" in Egypt.[2] Additionally, we find an inordinate number of sickle blades with one long edge serrated and the other blunt. These were inserted along their flat edges into bone sickles, which were also used to harvest grasses.

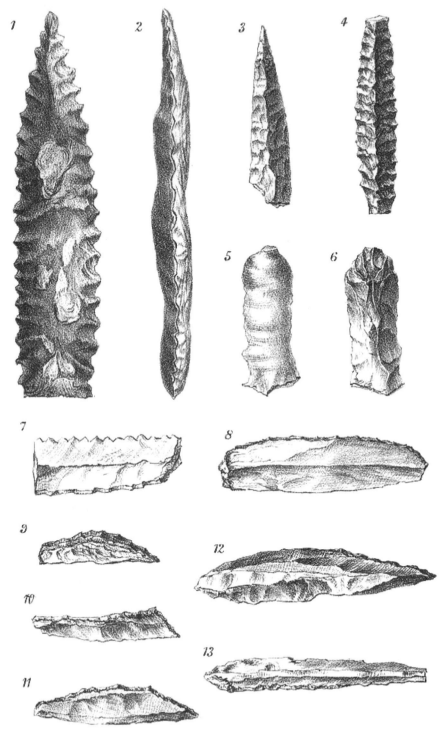

Figure 8.1. Page of stone tools found at Helwan and Al Ma'sarah from an 1878 article by A. J. Jukes Browne (see Browne, 1878a, pl. I).

HELWAN SICKLE BLADES

Similar sickle blades have been found at an early settlement site in the Faiyum Oasis, around 100 kilometers southwest of Cairo, as well as at Merimde Beni-Salame in the western Nile Delta, and also at El Omari, a huge occupational site complete with two separate cemeteries located at the mouth of Wadi Hôf, 4 kilometers north of Helwan. Yet all three sites date to the Chalcolithic period, circa 5500–4500 BCE, which followed the introduction of agriculture into northeast Africa from the Near East.[3] In contrast, the sickle blades found at Helwan belong to a much earlier age. Indeed, "Helwan sickle blades," as they are known, have been found at several so-called Natufian settlement sites, which thrived in the Levant toward the end of the Epipaleolithic age, circa 13,500–9600 BCE.[4]

Natufian sickle blades often show evidence of what is known as sickle-gloss, a type of shine thought to have come from cutting down the sugar-rich stems of cultivated cereal crops, thus indicating the presence of agriculture. A knowledge of whether or not the tools found at Helwan showed any sign of sickle-gloss is crucial in establishing whether they too were used in the cultivation of wild cereal crops. If this could be established, it would indicate not only that they were of Natufian origin, but also that cereal cultivation took place at Helwan at this time.

EVIDENCE
OF PROTO-AGRICULTURE

One vital clue to this enigma comes from an important paper on the stone implements found at Helwan by British geologist and prehistorian A. J. Jukes Browne, published in 1878.[5] He writes about the discovery of various types of stone tools in the vicinity of approximately eleven to twelve thermal springs stretching from Wadi Karafish in the north to Wadi Rashid in the south (with several others in the so-called valley of the palm trees located in the central area of Helwan, close to the bathhouse).[6] He refers to one type as a saw, between "two and four inches" (5–10 centimeters) in length, with its ends squared and a series of "teeth, wide or narrow" along one side.[7] It is very likely a form of sickle blade. This fact is highly significant because of what he goes on to say about the examples of this tool found at Helwan:

In many instances the teeth are much polished, and more or less broken, as if by dint of hard service, while, in some of them, both sides are worked into serrations, one edge being more broken than the other, as if it had been used up and the other side had been chipped out, in order to refit the instrument for service.[8]

Very likely the polish displayed on the teeth of the sickle blades is indeed sickle-gloss, while their broken nature is yet further evidence of their heavy usage in the harvesting of wild grasses. Should this surmise prove correct, it would make Helwan one of the oldest sites of proto-agriculture anywhere in the world. Clearly, something quite amazing was going on here even before the end of the last ice age. Possibly related to this discovery is the fact that a form of proto-agriculture is known to have been present among advanced communities belonging to the Isnan and Qadan cultures that thrived on the Upper Nile, in southern Egypt, between 13,000 and 10,500 BCE.

Various occupational sites of the Qadan and Isnan have revealed the presence of well-used grinding stones, as well as sickle blades that show evidence of sickle-gloss, suggesting that they were used to cut and reap wild grasses, including wheat and barley. Backing this up is evidence from pollen analysis, which has indicated the presence of cereal grains among these communities.[9]

THE HELWAN RETOUCH

Further evidence for the highly advanced nature of Helwan's Epipaleolithic settlement can be seen from the lunates and sickle blades, many of which display what is known as the "Helwan retouch." In basic terms, this relates to the unique bifacial, that is, double-sided, retouching technique applied to these tools. It is a style that was first identified at Helwan and has since been recorded in connection with lunates and sickle blades found at a number of Natufian sites in the Levant, providing evidence of a common origin in style and manufacture. What is important here is that the Helwan retouch largely disappears around the beginning of the Younger Dryas period, circa 10,800 BCE,[10] once again suggesting that Helwan's earliest settlements were not just contemporary with the Natufian tradition of the Levant, circa 13,500–9600 BCE, but that they were very closely related to one another.

Throwing a spanner in the works of this tidy scenario is the fact that radiocarbon testing of ostrich eggshells found by Fernand Debono at one of the campsites at Helwan has produced dates in the region of circa 19,931–19,415 BCE. If this is correct—and there is no reason to question these results—it shows that occupation around Helwan's sulfur and mineral springs began around the same time that large parts of the Eurasian and North American continents were experiencing the Last Glacial Maximum, the coldest phase of the last ice age, circa 20,000–18,000 BCE.[11] Ostrich-eggshell containers, like those found at Helwan, have also been found among Natufian settlements in the Negev region of Israel.[12]

Completing the picture is the discovery at Helwan of long tubular or horn-like seashells called Dentalium, or tooth shell, used to create jewelry, necklaces in particular.[13] Pierced Dentalium shells have frequently been found at Natufian sites, where they were used to create necklaces. As William C. Hayes states in his important summary of Helwan's Epipaleolithic settlements: "Like their Natufian contemporaries the Helwan people wore jewelry made up of strings of marine shells, pierced or trimmed for the purpose, the favorite type being the tubular Dentalium, or tooth-shell."[14]

THE HARIFIAN TRADITION

Detailed studies of the private collections of Helwan stone tools have shown that the closest match to many of them are localized forms of the Natufian tradition that thrived in the Sinai Peninsula and Negev region circa 13,500–9600 BCE.[15] These populations not only used lunates with the distinctive Helwan retouch,[16] but they are also thought to owe their origins to indigenous cultures of the Nile Valley and Red Sea Basin.[17] Yet, after this time, as the climate grew more arid with the onset of the Younger Dryas, circa 10,800 BCE, there would appear to have been a hiatus in occupation at Helwan.[18] Its settlements focused around the thermal springs were abandoned until the arrival much later of a new people who had links with the so-called Harifian tradition, named after Ramat Harif, its type site in the Negev Highlands of southern Israel (see fig. 8.2).[19]

The Harifians thrived in the Negev, and also in neighboring Sinai, during the Younger Dryas, circa 10,800 to 9600 BCE.[20] However, as A. Nigel Goring-Morris, a leading expert on Epipaleolithic cultures of the Levant, has noted, the pronounced semiarid and arid zones created during the Younger Dryas "sounded the death knoll" for the Final Natufian/Harifian peoples of Sinai and the Negev.[21] As a consequence, they were forced to relocate, leaving the region unoccupied through till the Early Pre-Pottery Neolithic B period, circa 8800–7600 BCE. Sinai and the Negev were then repopulated by groups

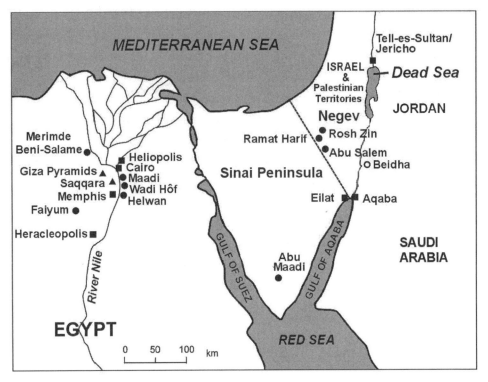

Figure 8.2. Map of Egypt, Israel, and the Palestinian territories showing Epipaleolithic, Neolithic, Chalcolithic, and Predynastic sites mentioned in this book.

of mobile foragers, who took over earlier Harifian sites and continued their tradition in certain ways.[22] It would also seem that they continued their journey into northern Egypt and reestablished settlements around the thermal springs at Helwan.[23]

THE FIRST MONOLITHS

The Harifians and their Post-Harifian descendants are known to have achieved a fairly advanced level of society, with their own hamlets consisting of clusters of circular huts with stone foundations.[24] Some of these structures were reserved for cultic activity, and occasionally they would contain standing pillars referred to by Israeli archaeologists as *masseboth* (*massebah* in the singular).

At the Harifian site of Abu Salem in the central Negev, for instance, a single-room structure of circular design known as Locus 1 was found to contain a single unhewn pillar.[25] It was positioned in the room's ringwall, directly opposite a southerly entrance doorway. In the middle of the room, excavations revealed the presence of a large, flat table slab, its surface containing around fif-teen cupules, or cuplike indentations. Further groupings of cupules were found at Abu Salem either on stone slabs or, as at Göbekli Tepe and also on the sum-mit of Karahan Tepe, on exposed bedrock. Israeli archaeologist Uzi Avner, a specialist in Israel's masseboth tradition, suspects that the pillar inside Abu Salem's Locus 1 is an early example of a massebah sacred stone,*[26] although this opinion is not shared by all his colleagues.[27]

What isn't in dispute is the massebah, or standing stone, located at the Epipaleolithic settlement of Rosh Zin, also in the central Negev.[28] Here in the early 1970s archaeologist Donald O. Henry uncovered the remains of a whole series of stone-built structures, among which was a special room, known as Locus 4. This was found to contain a unique slab-lined floor and a stand-ing pillar with a rounded stem. Henry saw the structure as possibly cultic in nature and wrote that the pillar had "phallic connotations."[29] Close by, excava-tors found a series of cupules cut into the bedrock, like those found at Abu Salem and also at the Harifian type site of Ramat Harif in the Negev high-lands. Pierced Dentalium shells and beads made of ostrich eggshells, like those recorded at Helwan, were also found at the site.[30]

Rosh Zin is attributed to the Late Natufian period, circa 11,000–9600 BCE, although the monolithic pillar, the style of the settlement, and the presence of the cupules all hint at links with the Harifian tradition.[31] Rosh Zin is located on the summit of a low hill (520 meters above sea level) overlooking the Divshon Plain, in which is located a prominent spring called Ein Avdat. Its standing pillar—which was fractured when found, but was later restored—remains in place today. It is arguably one of the oldest menhirs or standing stones in the world.

If the connection between Helwan's Epipaleolithic community and the Harifian tradition of Sinai and the Negev is valid, then do very similar stone structures await discovery at Helwan? If so, then they would unquestionably have included special rooms, in other words cult buildings, like Locus 1 at Abu Salem and Locus 4 at Rosh Zin, both of which were found to contain mono-lithic pillars.

Uzi Avner suspects the masseboth tradition that spread eventually through-out the Negev from the Pottery Neolithic, circa 6000 BCE, down to the end

---

*Avner proposes that Locus 1's isolation at the southern end of the settlement at Abu Salem sug-gests that it was a place of cultic significance, the northerly positioned stone pillar supporting this assertion.

of the Middle Bronze Age, circa 1550 BCE, might owe its existence to the Harifian tradition, which thrived in the same region during the Late Natufian period, circa 11,000–9600 BCE.[32] So there is every chance that it entered northern Egypt via settlement sites like Helwan in a similar way.

ONWARD TO HELWAN

The above information suggests that nomadic peoples associated with the Post-Harifian peoples of Sinai and the Negev established a settlement around Helwan's sulfurous, saltine, and chalybeate springs during the Early Pre-Pottery Neolithic B period, circa 8800–7600 BCE. Hot thermal waters emerging from the bowels of the earth might have been seen as possessing a magical, nourishing quality, encouraging cultic activity in the vicinity of the springs. Indeed, the springs' therapeutic qualities almost certainly caused Helwan to become a major religious center from a very early date, a connection that no doubt persisted through to the emergence of dynastic Egypt, circa 3120 BCE. Thereafter, as we shall find out in chapter 27, its sacred waters were seen, symbolically at least, as nourishing the dead on their journey into the afterlife.[33]

Further back in time, Helwan's Epipaleolithic community would seem to have had direct connections with the Natufian tradition of the southern Levant, particularly its localized forms in Sinai and the Negev. Yet, as we have seen, there appears to have been a gap in occupation at Helwan sometime between the onset of the Younger Dryas event, circa 10,800 BCE, and the Early Pre-Pottery Neolithic B period, circa 8800–7600 BCE.

CATASTROPHIC EVENTS

One cannot help but speculate that the hiatus in occupation at Helwan might have been due to severe climate changes known to have taken place in the Nile Valley soon after the onset of the Younger Dryas. For instance, "truly massive Nile floods" are said to have taken place in Egypt sometime around 10,500 BCE, causing "a prolonged series of natural disasters" that brought about "catastrophic events,"[34] whose effect would have been disastrous for those living on the edge of the Nile floodplain. Around the same time, the Isnan and Qadan communities of southern Egypt, who as we saw earlier practiced a form of proto-agriculture, also suddenly vanish from the archaeological record.[35]

Is it possible that Helwan's Mesolithic community was linked in some manner with the Qadan and Isnan peoples of southern Egypt? Both would appear to have practiced early forms of agriculture, even though one was clearly African in origin and the other might well have been related to the Natufians of the Levant. It is even possible that the Qadan and Isnan introduced agriculture to the Helwan community, which in turn communicated this knowledge to the Levant. Since it has been proposed that agriculture first reached the Levant from the Nile Valley,[36] this becomes a very real possibility, which, if correct, would make Helwan one of the key genesis points of early agriculture in northeast Africa.

Arguably the severe climate changes that would appear to have wiped out the Qadan and Isnan communities of southern Egypt also brought about the decline of Helwan's Epipaleolithic community. Yet sometime around the beginning of the Early Pre-Pottery Neolithic B period, circa 8800–7600 BCE, a new population emerges in Helwan. As we see next, there is tantalizing evidence that it had links with Göbekli Tepe, Nevalı Çori, and even Şanlıurfa. This information comes from the discovery at Helwan of a highly significant type of projectile point known to archaeologists as the Helwan point.

9

MYSTERY OF
THE HELWAN POINT

ashioned on a blade of flint, obsidian, or rock crystal removed from a prepared core, the Helwan point is easily recognizable. It has a pair, sometimes even two pairs, of parallel, or bilateral, notches cut into the sides of its
long, narrow, delta-shaped body. It also has a distinct "tang" or "shoulder"
at its base, achieved through careful retouching. This tang is created so that
the projectile point can more easily be affixed to the shaft of an arrow; the
notches being used to bind the two together using a cord of sinew or rawhide.
Occasionally the Helwan point is found to have barbs, or corner notches immediately above the tang. This is a feature more commonly associated with flint
arrowheads produced in Europe and the Near East during the Bronze Age,
circa 2500–800 BCE, or on the North American continent from the Early
Archaic period through to the Mississippi period, circa 8000 BCE–1520 CE.

Arrowheads themselves were certainly nothing new to the indigenous peoples of Africa when the highly efficient Helwan point first appears in Egypt's
Nile Valley sometime around the end of the last ice age. They were used as
long as 64,000 years ago during the Middle Stone Age (or Middle Paleolithic),
as crude examples have been found at a site named Sibudu Cave in northern
KwaZulu-Natal, South Africa.[1] Another Middle Stone Age stone-tool industry known to have used arrowheads was the Aterian, which thrived between

110,000 and 40,000 BCE in what is today the Sahara Desert of Morocco, Algeria, and Libya.[2] Aterian peoples produced tanged projectile points with a triangular profile for hafting onto arrows or spears by 40,000 BCE, by which time they had entered areas of Egypt's Libyan Desert.[3]

Other than a brief appearance among the peoples responsible for the Khormusan industry of Sudanese Nubia circa 40,000–30,000 BCE, who might well have been the descendants of the Aterians, the use of the bow and arrow on the African continent then seems to disappear, and is only reintroduced to Egypt with the invention of the Helwan point. Maybe it was introduced from Sinai or the Negev by Harifian-linked peoples, whose presence at Helwan is tantalizingly apparent. This is indeed possible, although the picture, as we shall see, is by no means clear, and will bring us to the very door of southeast Anatolia's Pre-Pottery Neolithic world.

OLD ILLUSTRATIONS

Our earliest knowledge of the Helwan point comes from collections of stone artifacts found at Helwan during the late nineteenth century by European visitors to the area's spa resort. Two examples appear among the illustrations accompanying Friedrich Mook's book *Aegyptens vormettalische Zeit* ("Egyptians before the Metal Age"), published in 1880.[4] Both are long, slender examples, one with damage to its left-hand tang.

Two further examples of the Helwan point can be seen in a book by French geologist and archaeologist Jean-Jacques de Morgan titled *Recherches sur les origines de l'Égypte: l'age de la pierre et les métaux* ("Research on the Origin of Egypt: the Stone and Metal Ages"), published in 1896.[5] These also are long and slim, and very finely finished. They apparently belonged to a large private collection of Helwan finds put together by M. A. Lombard,[6] proprietor of the Helwan Hotel.[7]

Fernand Debono also found two examples of the Helwan point during his investigation of the area in 1936 and 1941.[8] Although those illustrated by Mook and de Morgan in their books have now been lost to the world of archaeology, Debono's collection of at least 3000 artifacts found at Helwan existed as recently as 1992,[9] and may still be available for scrutiny today.

Completing the picture are two final examples of the Helwan point listed in A. J. Jukes Browne's studies of the stone implements found at Helwan during the 1870s.[10]

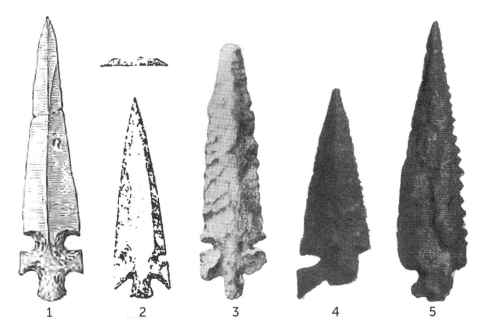

Figure 9.1. Examples of Helwan points found in the area of
Helwan and Ma'sarah in the second half of the nineteenth century:
(1 and 2) after de Morgan, 1896: figs. 226, 228; (3) Puglisi, pl. 1
(after Browne, 1878b); (4 and 5) Puglisi, pl. 5, nos. 6, 8.

In all, eight complete Helwan points (see fig. 9.1), and at least two damaged examples,[11] have been recorded in connection with Helwan's Pre-Pottery
Neolithic settlement sites. Arguably many more were once to be found in private collections that today no longer exist.

THE HARIFIAN CONNECTION

Nowhere else in Egypt is the Helwan point found during this epoch (although
it does reappear much later in time—see below). It has, however, been found
with some frequency at settlement sites in the Negev Highlands connected
with the Harifian tradition,[12] adding weight to the link between these communities and Helwan in Egypt. Yet in no way did the Helwan point originate
in this region.

British archaeologist Kathleen Kenyon found examples of the Helwan
point among the Pre-Pottery Neolithic ruins of Jericho in the Jordan Valley of
the Palestinian West Bank.[13] They have been found also at other sites in the
Levant, their suspected place of origin being somewhere to the north on the

Middle Euphrates. This is according to Israeli archeaologist Avi Gopher of the University of Tel Aviv, a leading expert on Epipaleolithic and Neolithic projectile points in the Levant (see below).[14] Indeed, there is every reason to conclude that the Helwan point's initial place of development was even farther north, in southeast Anatolia, as examples have been found at Pre-Pottery Neolithic sites in the region, including Nevalı Çori in the north of Şanlıurfa province[15] and Göbekli Tepe near Şanlıurfa itself.[16]

YENI YOL STREET, ŞANLIURFA

In addition to this, Turkish archaeologist Bahattin Çelik of Harran University found a perfect example of a Helwan point during his excavation of a Pre-Pottery Neolithic site uncovered in Yeni Yol Street in the heart of Şanlıurfa's old city in 1997.[17] It was the discovery here four years earlier of a life-sized human statue in limestone, and known today as Urfa Man (see plate 16), that had prompted Çelik's investigation of the Yeni Yol Street site.

Before the excavation area was finally lost to urban development, Çelik's team uncovered terrazzo floors, like those found at Nevalı Çori, Çayönü, and Göbekli Tepe, as well as a basalt grinding stone, all of which suggested that at least one "special building" had existed at the site.[18] Çelik dated the settlement to the Pre-Pottery Neolithic A period, circa 9000 BCE, and wrote that the Helwan point may date from this same period,[19] although there was no evidence to corroborate this conclusion. If proved correct, this means that the trail of the Helwan point leads from Helwan in Egypt all the way to the cult centers of the Pre-Pottery Neolithic A culture that thrived in southeast Anatolia, circa 9600–8800 BCE.

In 1989 Avi Gopher wrote a major paper on the diffusion of the Helwan point, the first to focus on its widespread distribution from the extreme north all the way down to Helwan in northern Egypt. He proposed that it originated among Early Pre-Pottery Neolithic sites on the Middle Euphrates in northern Syria.[20] It then spread southward through the Levant, eventually reaching Sinai and the Negev in the eighth millennium BCE, and, finally, Helwan in Egypt shortly after that. Yet when Gopher wrote his paper, neither the Yeni Yol Street site in Şanlıurfa nor Göbekli Tepe had been discovered. If he *had* known about them, he would probably have seen the Helwan point's place of origin as further north in southeast Anatolia. So is it really possible that highly sophisticated projectile points that originated at Pre-Pottery Neolithic sites in southeast Anatolia found their way to Helwan in northern Egypt? If so, what impact might the one have had on the other? Moreover, how much of the influence of Göbekli Tepe ended up entering Egypt's Nile Valley, or indeed vice versa?

Perhaps we should recall now the speculations of Friedrich Mook. He was amazed by the contrast between the thousands of quite functional stone tools, found either among surface scatterings or during his excavations at Helwan in 1877–78, and the beautifully finished arrowheads he would occasionally come across at the same sites. He concluded that these were not manufactured locally, or if they were, then they must have been the workmanship of an advanced, specialized group, a power elite perhaps, who were only occasionally present in the area.[21] Who might this power elite have been, and where exactly did they come from?

Some idea of the highly advanced nature of the Helwan stone tools can be found in the plate accompanying a paper on the subject written by A. J. Jukes Browne and published in 1878. The quality and retouching style of some of the examples illustrated is quite remarkable, showing a level of sophistication of the highest order. More importantly, some show signs of having been manufactured using a specialized technique known as pressure flaking, a process that has been linked very specifically with the production of the Helwan point.[22]

THE PRESSURE-FLAKING TECHNIQUE

Pressure flaking is a highly skilled process whereby an experienced toolmaker takes a sticklike tool, usually of wood, bone, or horn, and uses it to apply pressure to the edge of the tool or point being worked on. This causes small flakes to be prised off in a regular manner. If done correctly, this creates neat overlapping "scars" or furrows, some of which can reach the center of the tool's convex face. Another use of pressure flaking is the removal from prepared cores of long, thin flakes known as blades or bladelets.

This style of tool manufacture is unique and extremely difficult to achieve without tutoring from someone already versed in stone-tool manufacture. It involved knowledge passed on from one generation to the next, leading to a diffusion through education, and not simply through copying or chance discovery. Thus the presence of pressure flaking in any culture is important, for it probably shows links with forerunners who must have used this same process themselves.

The origins of pressure flaking in southeast Anatolia and the Levant remain obscure. Unquestionably the technique was present at key sites in the former during the Early Pre-Pottery Neolithic B period, circa 8800–7600 BCE.[23] Arguably it was present even earlier. So where exactly did it come from?

POST-SWIDERIAN CULTURES

Although known from a few isolated sites in southern Africa during the Middle Stone Age, circa 75,000–70,000 years ago, pressure-flaking technique did not become established until the Upper Paleolithic age, circa 40,000–9600 BCE. For instance, it was used by ice age cultures of Central Mongolia in East Asia circa 20,000–30,000 years ago, a fact that will become important later on in this book.[24] The technique was thereafter used by the Solutrean peoples of Western Europe circa 20,000–15,000 BCE. They created exquisite lance points, bifaces (generally oval- or pear-shaped tools retouched on two surfaces), and tanged or shouldered arrowheads. Yet immediately prior to the emergence of the Pre-Pottery Neolithic complexes of southeast Anatolia, the only groups known to have employed the use of pressure-flaking were the Clovis culture of North America (who might well have had links to the Solutreans of Europe, a matter outside the scope of this present book), and the post-Swiderian cultures of northern, eastern, and central Europe (who were also distant cousins of the Solutreans). Post-Swiderian populations included the Butovo culture from the area north of the Black Sea in what is today western Russia and Ukraine,[25] and the Kunda culture of Scandinavia, Poland, and the Baltic region.[26] Both cultures thrived circa 9,500–5000 BCE,[27] and thus in their earliest stages were contemporary with the emergence of the Pre-Pottery Neolithic populations of southeast Anatolia and the Levant.

As their name suggests, these post-Swiderian cultures were linked to the earlier Swiderians. They were Epipaleolithic reindeer hunters, miners of exotic flint, long-distance traders, and stone-tool specialists who occupied large areas of the central and eastern European plain before, during, and immediately after the Younger Dryas event.[28]

Elsewhere I argue that the earliest installations at Göbekli Tepe were built under the influence of Swiderian groups who had crossed the Caucasus Mountains and entered eastern Anatolia circa 10,800–9600 BCE.[29] German archaeologist Klaus Schmidt compared the hunting techniques of southeast

Anatolia's Pre-Pottery Neolithic communities with those of the Swiderians,[30] and suggested also that clues regarding the origins of Göbekli Tepe might be looked for among the Epipaleolithic peoples north of the Black Sea,[31] where the post-Swiderian Butovo culture thrived.

If such speculations prove correct, then those responsible for introducing the pressure-flaking technique into southeast Anatolia and the Levant came from the north, most likely Russia and Ukraine. Whether or not the Swiderians might have introduced the original design for the Helwan point is unclear. What is more certain, however, is that the technology *behind* the manufacture of these beautiful stone arrowheads came originally from the north, the direction of southeast Anatolia.

Could it be that in addition to a mixture of Nilotic peoples, perhaps related to the Qadan and Isnan traditions, which date to the late Epipalcolithic age, circa 13,500–10,500 BCE, along with descendants of the Harifian peoples from Sinai and the Negev, there was an additional third component that was occasionally present at Helwan? Could these individuals have come from much farther afield, bringing with them examples of the Helwan point, which we know was occasionally manufactured using exotic materials such as rock crystal[32] and obsidian?[33] Might they have come from sites in southeast Anatolia like Göbekli Tepe, Nevalı Çori, and even the Yeni Yol Street settlement in the city of Şanlıurfa? Incredibly, answers to these questions were provided as far back as 1996 by someone already familiar to us from his remarkable work at Göbekli Tepe—Klaus Schmidt.

10

VISIONS OF HELWAN

While writing the section of this book on the prehistory of Helwan and the origins of the Helwan point, I was stunned to find that Klaus Schmidt, who was responsible for the rediscovery of Göbekli Tepe in 1994, had written a paper titled "Helwan in Egypt: A PPN site?"[1] The paper helped catapult Helwan's Epipaleolithic past back into the minds of archaeologists who were attempting to understand the diffusion of the Helwan point and the impact of the Pre-Pottery Neolithic world on the birth of ancient Egypt.

Although Avi Gopher had as far back as 1989 drawn attention to the vast area of distribution of the Helwan point, which stretched from the Middle Euphrates region of northern Syria all the way down into Egypt, it was Klaus Schmidt who was the first to highlight the significance of its presence at Helwan itself. The opening lines of Schmidt's paper, published in an obscure academic monograph in 1996, make for compelling reading:

> Once Helwan was a famous site. It has been known for more than a hundred years for its microlithic industries dominated by lunates and other bladelet tools. The sites [where stone tools are found] are located around several thermal springs on the right bank of the Nile some kilometers south of Cairo. . . . In spite of its previous importance, today Helwan has been nearly forgotten or is viewed with suspicion, expressed for example by doubts regarding the providence of Helwan points from Helwan.[2]

Not only did Schmidt collect together information on all the various private collections of stone tools and artifacts found at Helwan during the late nineteenth century, but he was also able to examine the collection of over 3000 artifacts found there in 1936 and 1941 by Fernand Debono. Vitally, Schmidt's paper included line drawings of all eight Helwan points found at Helwan, as well as four other fragments he also came across during his investigations.[3]

In order to better understand the history of Helwan's Epipaleolithic and later Pre-Pottery Neolithic community, Schmidt undertook a diagnostic analysis of many of the flint and chert tools in the Debono collection. He conclued that Helwan had been a major settlement site during the Epipaleolithic age, with links to the Natufian tradition of Sinai and the Negev.[4] Yet crucially, as the title of his paper suggests, he found clear evidence that Helwan had been occupied again during the Early Pre-Pottery Neolithic B period, circa 8800–7600 BCE, most likely by post-Harifian peoples, who also came from Sinai and the Negev.[5]

Frustratingly, Schmidt did not write any more on the subject, his interests now fully focused on his work at Göbekli Tepe. Yet there is a subtext to be gained from reading his extremely important paper. It was published in 1996, the first full year of exploration at Göbekli Tepe. Back then the occupational mound, as well as the surrounding hillsides and gullies, were littered with many thousands of stone tools and projectile points, including examples of the Helwan point.

Schmidt would have been aware also that aside from the Helwan points found at Göbekli Tepe,[6] others had already been found both at the Yeni Yol Street settlement site in Şanlıurfa and at Nevalı Çori.[7] This he would have known firsthand, as he had worked at the latter site alongside Professor Harald Hauptmann from the University of Heidelberg prior to the site's submersion beneath the rising waters of the Euphrates in 1992, two years after the completion of the Atatürk Dam.

BEYOND SCHMIDT

There seems little question that before his death in 2014, Klaus Schmidt pondered over the possible relationship, indirect as it might seem, between Helwan's Epipaleolithic settlement and the proto-Neolithic cult centers of Göbekli Tepe and Nevalı Çori in southeast Anatolia. We can only imagine what went through his mind as he was writing his paper proposing that Helwan was itself a Pre-Pottery Neolithic site. All we can say is that by bringing this topic back into the minds of scholars, he encouraged others to look into the possible significance of the Helwan point. One such person was Noriyuki Shirai, who as a PhD student at Waseda Univeristy in Japan in 2002 wrote an important paper titled "Helwan Points in the Egyptian Neolithic."[8]

Acknowledging Schmidt's contribution, Shirai reproduces pictures of all eight known Helwan points found at Helwan. He also shows images of further examples found at two other Neolithic centers in Egypt—Merimde Beni-Salame on the western edge of the Nile Delta, and a site in the Faiyum Oasis, around 100 kilometers southwest of Cairo. The points from Merimde Beni-Salame come from an occupational layer corresponding to a radiocarbon date of 4800 BCE, while those from the Faiyum settlement derive from layers dating to circa 5200–4500 BCE.[9]

Having categorized all the known Egyptian examples of Helwan points, Shirai was able to confirm that those found at Helwan were much older than those discovered at Merimde Beni-Salame and in the Faiyum Oasis.[10] Crucially, he added that six of the examples from Helwan bear striking similarities to those found at two sites in the southern Levant. The first is Abu Maadi, a settlement in the southern Sinai with links to the Harifian tradition,[11] where a large number of tools and points from the Pre-Pottery Neolithic B period have been found.[12]

The second site was Beidha, an extensive Pre-Pottery Neolithic B complex situated immediately to the north of the Nabatean city of Petra in southern Jordan.[13] Like the Pre-Pottery Neolithic world of Jericho, some 320 kilometers to the north, Beidha was an incredibly advanced urban center with sophisticated masonry architecture, including communal rooms 6 by 9 meters in size, with raised circular hearths at their center and wide seats on the south side.[14] Beidha was located on a trade route that stretched from the main sources of the Jordan River in the Ante-Lebanon range in the north all the way down to the head of the Gulf of Aqaba in the south. It was this same route, which extended through the Sinai Peninsula to Egypt's Nile Valley, that was exploited by the Nabatean traders of Petra many thousands of years later.

Adding to the likelihood that the Helwan point originated as far north as southeast Anatolia and reached as far south as Beidha in Jordan and Helwan in Egypt, is the fact that obsidian from a known source near Çiftlik, a town and province in central Anatolia, was found during excavations at Beidha.[15] Although its presence is easily explained as the result of a trading network utilizing a series of urban centers, including Jericho, there is no reason why individuals from these distant places could not have visited Beidha. Possibly when this happened, some of these individuals continued the journey into northern Egypt, carrying with them examples of the Helwan point.

THE DESTRUCTION OF BEIDHA

Beidha was destroyed by fire sometime around 7090 BCE, according to radiocarbon dating evidence obtained in the 1960s.[16] With modern recalibration, this date should rise to somewhere in the region of circa 8000 BCE, making Beidha's destruction roughly contemporary with the abandonment of Göbekli Tepe in southeast Anatolia.

So if the presence of the Helwan point indicates a connection between Beidha and Helwan, this must have been prior to the former's destruction by fire. Certainly this is the conclusion of Noriyuki Shirai, who is today an archaeologist with the UCL Institute of Archaeology in London. In *The Archaeology of the First Farmer-Herders in Egypt* (2010) he argues that the point's first appearance at Helwan was almost synchronous with its spread southward through the Levant.[17] This must have begun soon after circa 9000 BCE, the age of the Yeni Yol Street settlement site at Şanlıurfa.

So if we take everything into account, it seems reasonable to suggest that the Helwan point entered Helwan during the Early Pre-Pottery Neolithic B period, circa 8800–7600 BCE. What is more, an examination of the stone tools and projectile points found at Helwan makes it clear that members of its Pre-Pottery Neolithic community possessed a sophisticated understanding of the pressure-flaking technique,[18] something that came, most likely, from places like Göbekli Tepe and Nevalı Çori in southeast Anatolia.

PLACE OF THE ANCESTORS

So what exactly might the impact of Helwan's Pre-Pottery Neolithic peoples have been on the rise of dynastic Egypt? Did they introduce masonry architecture, like that seen at Harifian-linked sites in Sinai and the Negev, and also at Beidha? Or could they have brought with them an understanding of monumental architecture similar to that found at places like Jericho and Göbekli Tepe? More importantly, did they carry with them a preexistent knowledge concerning the human soul's origin among the stars?

In part 3 we shall see how compelling evidence suggests that the cosmological beliefs and practices present among the Pre-Pottery Neolithic peoples of southeast Anatolia helped forge the ancient Egyptian death journey as preserved in the important corpus of religious literature known as the Pyramid Texts. These appear fully formed sometime around 2350 BCE inside pyramids built within clear sight of Helwan. What is more, these same cosmological ideas, which probably inspired the construction of the oldest stone enclosures at Göbekli Tepe, can be shown to have determined the design, structure, function, and geographical placement of the main monuments of the Giza pyramid field, a realization that will only help further clarify Helwan's role in the birth of ancient Egypt.

PART THREE

SECRETS OF THE PYRAMIDS

11

A GRAND DESIGN
AT GIZA

In 1838 British engineer H. C. Agnew proposed that "the *three great pyramids of Gizeh were component parts of one immense system,* members of a vast united triad, each in itself admirable, but all three so connected with the first principle of the system as to form but one perfect whole."[1]

Proposals for the existence of a grand design at Giza have generally focused on the plateau's three main pyramids—the Great Pyramid, Second Pyramid, and Third Pyramid (see plate 17), built by the pharaohs Khufu, Khafre, and Menkaure, respectively, during the Fourth Dynasty of Egypt's Old Kingdom period, which is dated circa 2613–2479 BCE.[2] Theories have ranged from the suggestion of a rigorous common geometry[3] to that of coordinated alignments toward the city of Heliopolis, the center for the cult of the sun god Re, located to the northeast of modern-day Cairo.[4] Still others have proposed that Giza's three main pyramids were positioned to reflect the rising and setting positions of the sun at key moments in the year, such as the equinoxes and solstices.[5] Other suggestions have been proposed, with basic geometry and potential astronomical targets being the most commonly offered solutions.

As far back as 2008 British engineer Rodney Hale had started to discern an underlying pattern in the placement of monuments at Giza.[6] However, for reasons outlined below, in 2015 he reexamined the layout of the pyramids in order to reevaluate their potential connection to the stars.[7]

METHODOLOGY

Positioning the major monuments on the Giza pyramid field requires finding an accurate map, which is actually no easy matter. The survey of the Giza plateau undertaken by Sir William Flinders Petrie in 1880–82[8] has frequently been employed for such purposes.[9] Some recent attempts to compare the geographical positioning of the Giza monuments against potential astronomical targets have relied on diagrams based on GPS data offered by Google Earth.[10]

More accurate data is now available courtesy of the Giza Plateau Mapping Project (GPMP) initiated in 1984 by Mark Lehner, PhD, of the Oriental Institute at the University of Chicago, and David Goodman, a surveyor with Ancient Egypt Research Associates (AERA). Using trigonometric points generated by the survey, a calculated route of 6 kilometers around the plateau arrived back at the starting point with an error of less than 2 centimeters.[11] The full set of data amassed by the GPMP has yet to be released, although digitally generated grid maps using a geographic information system (GIS) are available to the public. The best of these offer a resolution of nearly 1 pixel per square meter, adequate for any basic survey of the placement of monuments on the plateau.[12]

HILL OF THE SOUTH

The primary piece of triangulation discernable in connection with the Giza pyramid field employs an equilateral triangle. If two of its corners are correlated with the peaks of the Great Pyramid and Third Pyramid, its third corner falls on the heights of Gebel el-Qibli (see fig. 11.1). This is a prominent rocky knoll rising to a height of 59 meters above sea level and belonging to the Maadi Formation, a geological outcrop running east-west along the entire southern edge of the plateau. Gebel el-Qibli, which means "hill of the south," takes its name from the Arabic *qiblah,* or direction of prayer, since it is located to the southeast of the Giza plateau in the approximate direction of Mecca. Occasionally referred to as the "fourth pyramid" because of its distinctive profile when viewed from the pyramid field, the summit of Gebel el-Qibli is positioned approximately 430 meters south of the Sphinx (see fig. 11.2).[13]

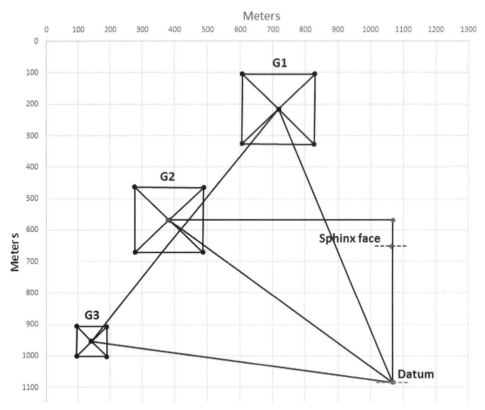

Figure 11.1. The Giza pyramid field, showing an equilateral triangle embracing the peaks of the Great Pyramid, Third Pyramid, and the datum on Gebel el-Qibli. Also shown are the north-south datum line and the 3-4-5 triangle embracing Gebel el-Qibli and the peak of the Second Pyramid. NB: All plans of the Giza plateau in this book have been generated in Excel spreadsheets using geographical coordinates offered by the GPMP.

This basic triangle defines the positions of both the Great Pyramid and Third Pyramid in coordination with the heights of Gebel el-Qibli, something that might explain why the latter was anciently known as Tarfiya, meaning, apparently, "the place of beginning."[14] Indeed, during the construction of the three main pyramids at Giza, circa 2550–2479 BCE, Gebel el-Qibli almost certainly acted as the pyramid field's datum, its primary survey point. Adding weight to this idea is the fact that in the 1980s Gebel el-Qibli was the starting point for the GPMP's own survey of the pyramid field.[15]

Gebel el-Qibli's role in the emergence of the pyramid field is shown again with the introduction of a right-angled triangle with sides that have ratios of length equaling 3, 4, and 5 units. This can be seen by projecting a line from

Figure 11.2. Nineteenth-century illustration of the
Giza pyramid field from the heights of Gebel el-Qibli.

Gebel el-Qibli due north to create the side of 3 units. Then project a line due
west of this line until it hits the peak of the Second Pyramid to create the
side of 4 units. To complete the triangle, extend a line from the peak of the
Second Pyramid back to the start point on Gebel el-Qibli; this creates the side
of 5 units, in other words the hypotenuse (see fig. 11.1).

MYSTERY OF THE SPHINX

If the north-south datum line from Gebel el-Qibli is then extended northward until it meets the east-west line marking the latitude defining the peak
of the Great Pyramid, the head of the Great Sphinx can be seen to fall almost
exactly halfway along its course (there is a small error of around 3 meters). The
Sphinx, as we know, is one of Egypt's most iconic images—a huge recumbent
lion with the head of a man and the headdress of a pharaoh (see plate 18).
Around 73.5 meters in length, 19.5 meters in width, and 20 meters in height,
it was carved from an outcrop of hard limestone that had protruded above the

softer bedrock of the underlying Mokattam Formation for anything up to several hundred thousand years before its appropriation for use in dynastic times.[16]

Egyptologists believe that the Sphinx forms part of the funerary or mortuary complex attached to the Second Pyramid. This is attributed to the pharaoh Khafre, circa 2520 BCE, because his name is mentioned in connection with the Sphinx on the so-called Dream Stela standing between its paws. What is more, the leonine monument is located at the end of a stone causeway linking the Second Pyramid's mortuary temple to its so-called valley temple, located immediately to the southeast of the Sphinx. Although there are no inscriptions mentioning the Sphinx until the New Kingdom, circa 1550–1069 BCE, it is thereafter identified with Re-horakhti, a form of the sun god Re combined with the hawk or falcon god Horus. This attribution makes sense since we know that the three pharaohs responsible for the construction of the Giza pyramid field—Khufu, Khafre, and Menkaure—were among the first kings to embrace the cult of Re.

SPHINX KNOLL

Yet the presence of this conspicuous rocky knoll exactly halfway between Gebel el-Qibli and the east-west line created by the peak of the Great Pyramid is again unlikely to be without meaning. It suggests that the latitudinal positioning of the Great Pyramid conforms to an underlying geometry featuring both the Sphinx and Gebel el-Qibli. If so, then the Sphinx knoll must have had some importance even before the construction of the pyramid field, which, aside from a few scattered tombs and monuments, is generally considered to have been a virtual blank canvas before Egypt's Fourth Dynasty.

Serena Love of the University of Queensland in Australia is an expert on symbolic landscapes in the prehistoric age. She has made a detailed study of what she calls the Sphinx promontory and has concluded that in its original, unaltered form it must have been a focus for local communities long before the age of the pharaohs. It could even, she suspects, have "influenced people's later choice in settling and burying their dead [on the plateau]."[17] This we know was happening as early as circa 3900–3200 BCE, because burials belonging to the so-called Maadi culture, which thrived at this time, have been found in the proximity of the Sphinx.[18]

The Maadi culture takes its name from its principal settlement at Maadi, a suburb of Cairo located on the east bank of the Nile around 15 kilometers

Figure 11.3. Old print of the Sphinx before excavation work began in the nineteenth century. It gives some idea of what might have been visible of the Sphinx knoll prior to the carving of the monument.

north of Helwan (see fig. 8.2 on page 78). Their presence at Giza as early as the mid–fourth millennium BCE makes it clear that by this time the area around the Sphinx was being used as a necropolis. Yet Love goes further in suggesting that with the advent of the dynastic age, the former use of the Sphinx knoll as the marker for a predynastic cemetery allowed it to be seen as a "monumental relic" of a former age, associated with the earliest ancestors of the ancient Egyptians.[19]

The idea that the Sphinx monument is older than conventional thinking has been proposed on many occasions.[20] Yet Serena Love suspects that the knoll's predynastic usage does not have to have involved the wholesale sculpting of the leonine monument and its accompanying enclosure, simply the veneration of the promontory from which it was fashioned (see fig. 11.3). Arguably it bore some kind of natural simulacrum, perhaps anthropomorphic or zoomorphic in nature. It is even possible, and in fact likely, that this simulacrum resembled the head of a large feline or canine of some kind.

A CHTHONIC REALM

Such an identification might have determined the nature of the plateau's *genius loci,* which came to be seen as a large feline, either a lion, panther, or leopard, or alternately a wolf, guarding the entrance to a chthonic realm of the dead. The fact that the Sphinx promontory is oriented east-west would only have emphasized this connection, since this would have aligned it with the passage of the sun at the time of the equinoxes (when it would have risen due east in line with the Sphinx's face and set due west behind its back). To local communities, this might have suggested that this strange monument guarded the entrance to a tunnel-like domain through which the equinoctial sun entered at night in the west and exited at sunrise the following morning in the east. Very likely this cave underworld was thought to pass directly beneath the plateau.

This surmise seems borne out by the fact that the entrance and indeed exit to this chthonic realm, known in ancient Egyptian mythology as the Duat, was in dynastic times considered to be guarded either by a wolf god named Wepwawet (Upuaut, Wep-wawet), meaning "opener of the ways," who acted as a guide to the dead as they passed through the underworld, or by a double-headed lion named Akeru. Adding weight to this idea is the fact that Giza's ancient name was Rostau, which translates as "mouth of the passages," an allusion, seemingly, to its role as the entrance to an imagined cave tunnel, symbolizing a physical opening into the Duat.

Interestingly, just such a cave complex does exist at Giza. It was rediscovered by British Egyptological researcher Nigel Skinner-Simpson and the author in April 2008 after 200 years of obscurity. Its entrance is located within a little-known tomb designated NC2 (North Cliff 2) by American Egyptologist George Reisner. Today it is more popularly known as the Tomb of the Birds, because of its use in late dynastic times as a bird cemetery. It is a natural cave system tens of thousands of years old stretching for some distance beneath the western part of the plateau. Its full extent has yet to be determined, although there is every reason to conclude that it heads toward the Second Pyramid, following the path of natural fissures conforming to the northwest-southeast trend of the plateau.[21]

The rocky knoll from which the Sphinx monument was later carved was important hundreds, if not thousands, of years before the arrival of the dynastic Egyptians. This claim is supported by the very basic geometry outlined above. It strongly suggests that the Sphinx knoll was used in conjunction with Gebel el-Qibli to define the extent of the Giza pyramid field through the establishment of the datum on Gebel el-Qibli and the north-south datum line.

THE PYRAMID ARC CIRCLE

Building on the employment of the equilateral and right-angled triangles at Giza is the simple fact that the peaks of the three main pyramids form an arc, showing that they are positioned on the perimeter of an invisible circle. Rodney Hale was able to determine that the center of this circle fell around 2384 meters southeast of the peak of the Second Pyramid (see fig. 11.4) on the edge of the village of Kafr el-Gebel (29°57′47″ N, 31°09′01″ E), an extension today of the much larger village of Nazlet el-Batran. Here evidence of an important dynastic settlement dating to the New Kingdom period has been found, including a temple from the reign of Rameses II, circa 1290–1224 BCE, and a stone stela bearing the name of the king's son Khaemweset. Cut-and-dressed stone blocks,

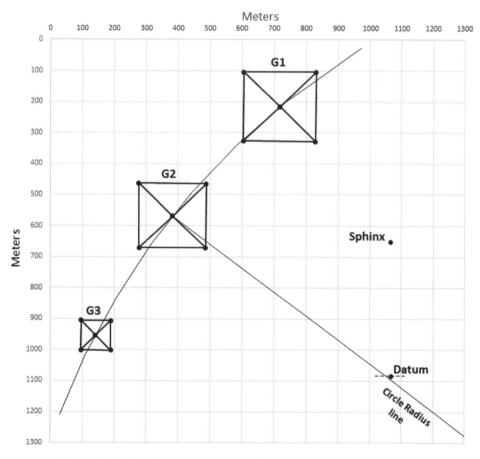

Figure 11.4. The Giza pyramid field showing the arc embracing the three main pyramids with its center point 2384 meters southeast of the peak of the Second Pyramid.

probably from the same temple, are also to be seen in the walls of several modern tombs in a local cemetery.[22]

The immediate significance of this extraordinary discovery is that a straight line drawn between the peak of the Second Pyramid and the center of the pyramid arc circle passes through Gebel el-Qibli, close to the datum point. This is unlikely to be coincidence, and will prove to be important as we now move on to examine whether or not star alignments and the positions of stars might have featured in the genesis of the Giza pyramid field.

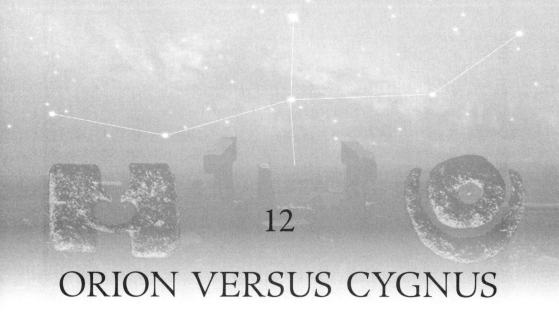

12

ORION VERSUS CYGNUS

M any theories have been proposed in support of a connection between the Giza pyramids and asterisms known to have been important to the dynastic Egyptians. Despite this, only two groups of stars have been seriously considered in this respect. These are the three "belt" stars of Orion, the great hunter, and the three "wing" stars of Cygnus, the celestial bird. The latter are the same three stars—Rukh (δ Cygni), Sadr (γ Cygni), and Gienah (ε Cygni)— that appear as peck marks on the tiny bone plaque found at Göbekli Tepe (see chapter 3). Yet the story of how each set of stars came to be associated with the Giza pyramid field is an interesting one.

THE ORION CORRELATION THEORY

In the case of Orion, the story begins in 1983. At the time Egyptian-born Belgian engineer Robert Bauval (1948–) was working in Saudi Arabia. During a visit to Alexandria in Egypt he entered the Egyptian Museum in Cairo, where he became transfixed by a large aerial photo of the Giza Pyramids. This highlighted the noticeable offset between the Second Pyramid and its two neighbors. After returning to Saudi Arabia he found himself reading the so-called Pyramid Texts, which are found in Old Kingdom pyramids from around 2350 BCE onward. On several occasions these speak about the pharaoh's spirit departing in death to Orion. The next evening he was talking to a friend about how to find east and was told that this is where Orion rose into the sky. It was then that Bauval noticed that the three belt stars of Orion, which had already risen, seemed to mimic the geographical arrangement of the three Giza Pyramids. Indeed, the middle star, Alnilam (ε Orionis), was slightly askew of its two companions—Alnitak (ζ Orionis) and Mintaka (δ Orionis)—exactly like the pyramids on the ground.

The close match between the Orion belt stars and the pyramids of Giza led Bauval to propose that the pyramid builders had deliberately positioned these monuments to reflect the celestial influence of Orion. This was in order to lock the pyramids into a grand design reflecting the final destination of the king's spirit among the stars. Orion, he pointed out, could be identified with Osiris, the mummiform god of death and the underworld that every pharaoh became in death.

This was the basic premise originally outlined by Bauval in an article published in the journal *Discussions in Egyptology* in 1989.[1] The idea was later expanded into a major book, coauthored with ancient mysteries writer Adrian Gilbert, titled *The Orion Mystery* (1994).[2] Despite the book's groundbreaking theories, which presented a completely new vision of the ancient Egyptian death journey, some were not fully convinced by its claims. Among them was British engineer Rodney Hale. He attempted to superimpose a high resolution image of Orion's belt stars onto a suitable overhead plan of the Giza pyramids.

Synchronizing the first two stars—Alnitak and Alnilam—with the peaks of the Great Pyramid and Second Pyramid, respectively, was easily done. Yet it revealed that there was no match between the third star, Mintaka, and the peak of the Third Pyramid. Indeed, when overlaid in this manner, with all the offset placed on the Third Pyramid, Mintaka did not even hit the pyramid, but instead fell slightly beyond its west side. The results of this simple exercise disappointed Hale. He felt that if the ancient Egyptians could accurately align the Great Pyramid toward true north (it is aligned to within 6 minutes of a degree of arc),[3] then surely they would have done a better job of replicating the astronomical positions of the Orion belt stars, especially if this was the destination of the soul of the pharaoh in death.

A MOMENT OF INSIGHT

The gross mismatch between the Orion belt stars and the Giza pyramids troubled Hale. Yet eventually the matter was put aside and did not rear its head again until one eventful night in January 2005. Aware that, following my visit to Göbekli Tepe in June the previous year, I was now investigating the importance of Cygnus in the ancient mind-set, Hale, unable to sleep, had a sudden insight. What would happen if he synchronized the three "wing" stars of Cygnus—Rukh, Sadr, and Gienah—with the peaks of the three main pyramids of Giza, exactly as Robert Bauval had done with the belt stars of Orion?

On rising, Hale obtained a high-resolution image of the Cygnus wing stars and used a computer program to match them against the peaks of the three main pyramids of Giza. His intuition paid off. There was a good match between the astronomical positions of the Cygnus wing stars and the peaks of the Giza pyramids. He had no idea what this meant or whether it would make sense in terms of what was known about the beliefs of the ancient Egyptians. He just knew it was something he had to do for his own satisfaction.

LITERARY DILEMMA

Later that day I received an email from Hale outlining his intriguing discovery. Seeing the correlation between the Cygnus wing stars and the Giza pyramids for the first time was an exciting moment. Yet it also sent my mind into a spin. Knowing that the match was that much more accurate than the Orion correlation theory, or OCT, as it had become known, was troubling, for although it offered a fresh insight into the cosmological views of the pyramid builders, promoting the discovery would bring me into conflict with Robert Bauval and his supporters. I would need to thoroughly investigate ancient Egyptian astronomy, complete with its proposed relationship to the funerary beliefs and practices of the Pyramid Age, to explain why the three main pyramids at Giza might have been laid out to mimic the positions of key stars in Cygnus instead of those of Orion.

THE CYGNUS MYSTERY

The results of this study were published in my book *The Cygnus Mystery* (2006).[4] As predicted, its allegiance to Cygnus instead of Orion at Giza was soon challenged by Bauval. In various online posts he expressed the opinion that context was crucial for making such claims, and since there was no evidence that Cygnus ever played a role in ancient Egyptian astronomy, proposing that three of its stars matched the layout of the Giza pyramids was, in essence, meaningless. I welcomed the criticism, and responded by providing ample evidence that Cygnus had indeed been important to the ancient Egyptians, particularly during the Pyramid Age (see chapter 15).[5]

Eventually the barrage of criticism died down, and a kind of stalemate was reached. In the years that followed, I wrote various articles on Cygnus at Giza and featured the topic again in a book titled *Beneath the Pyramids* (2009).[6] Here I demonstrated that the Cygnus-Giza correlation, as it was now known, had proved invaluable in locating the entrance to the lost cave complex rediscovered in 2008 by Nigel Skinner-Simpson and myself just 750 meters west of the Great Pyramid.[7]

WE ARE THE CHAMPIONS

Thereafter the Cygnus-Giza correlation was put to one side until the fall of 2015, when Robert Bauval announced on his Facebook page that the Orion correlation theory had finally been vindicated. No details were offered, other than the fact that a soon-to-be-published academic paper, written independently of Bauval's influence, would demonstrate once and for all that the stars of Orion did indeed match the peaks of the three main pyramids at Giza. At the same time, he said, the paper would show that no correlation existed between the Giza pyramids and the constellation of Cygnus, Orion's only rival in this debate. To celebrate this victory, Bauval linked his Facebook post to Queen's "We Are the Champions," something that in the opinions of Rodney Hale and myself seemed a little premature!

For several weeks, Hale and I attempted to obtain a copy of this upcoming paper without success. All we could ascertain was that it had been written by Italian academics Vincenzo Orofino and Paolo Bernardini of the University of Salento at Lecce.[8] Ironically, it had been one of these authors, Orofino, who had coauthored the paper published in 2015 vindicating Göbekli Tepe's alignments toward Cygnus (at the expense of Orion).[9]

STATISTICAL PROBABILITY

It was not until Hale and I finally got the chance to read Orofino and Bernardini's paper, posted online in December 2015,[10] that we finally understood how the Italian academics had achieved their results. Since the angle of arc made in the sky by the Cygnus wing stars is approximately 16 degrees, while that of Orion's belt is just 3 degrees, any results favoring Cygnus should, in their opinion, be *six times* more accurate than those of Orion for them to be valid. Since this was always going to be a sheer impossibility, the authors of the paper felt justified in dismissing any correlation between the stars of Cygnus and the three main pyramids at Giza, leaving Orion as the sole contender to take the crown; hence "We Are the Champions"!

As unrealistic as this situation might seem, Orofino and Bernardini were simply invoking standard statistical practice to make their case. If one wanted to accept this view, then the Orion correlation theory would indeed be more accurate than the Cygnus-Giza correlation. Yet both Rodney Hale and I realized the matter was not that simple. Statistics alone cannot decide which set of stars might have been important to the pyramid builders during the age of Khufu, and to this end we decided to initiate a new study of the Giza pyramids and their possible relationship to the stars. Our joint findings were published during the spring of 2016 in *Archaeological Discovery*,[11] the same peer-reviewed journal in which Orofino and Bernardini's own paper on Giza had appeared a few months earlier.[12]

GROUND-SKY CORRELATIONS

Hale began his study by entering the tracks of any relevant star at the beginning of Khufu's reign, circa 2550 BCE, to an existing spreadsheet containing the coordinates of the three main pyramids at Giza. This was the same date used by Orofino and Bernardini in their own study. The stars chosen were also the same as those used by Orofino and Bernardini: the belt stars of Orion— Alnitak, Alnilam, and Mintaka—and the wing stars of Cygnus—Rukh, Sadr, and Gienah. In this same order they would be matched against the peaks of the Great Pyramid, Second Pyramid, and Third Pyramid, with any offset displayed in meters.

Having said all this, Hale realized that simply overlaying stars on pyramid peaks to determine their accuracy should not be a primary concern, for even if this *had* been achieved by the pyramid builders, it could only ever have existed as a symbolic gesture; it could never have been observable from any location on the ground. More important was to explore whether or not star-to-peak correlations might have existed at Giza in the horizontal plane, for these alone would have been observable at ground level.

STAR-TO-PEAK CORRELATIONS
IN THE HORIZONTAL PLANE

With these thoughts in mind, Hale used the spreadsheet data to examine how exactly stars might have been perceived in relationship to the Giza pyramids, and was able to determine that from a position 2940 meters southeast of the peak of the Second Pyramid (2082 meters from the datum on Gebel el-Qibli), an observer could have watched the three Cygnus wing stars—Gienah, Sadr, and Rukh—set into the peaks of, respectively, the Third Pyramid, Second Pyramid, and Great Pyramid (see fig. 12.1). The accuracy of this star-to-peak correlation was remarkable, with an overall error of just 9 arc minutes. What is more, the *height* of each pyramid could be visually linked to a star, meaning that each peak appeared deliberately placed to receive its respective star close to its point of extinction.

Even more significant is the position from which this celestial spectacle could have been observed circa 2550–2479 BCE—a site we shall refer to as the convergence point.[13] It falls on the existing line connecting the peak of the Second Pyramid with the heights of Gebel el-Qibli and the center of the pyramid arc circle. All four points are in near perfect alignment (see fig. 12.2).

Here are the facts regarding this extraordinary alignment:

The Second Pyramid as seen from the datum point = 306.95 degrees
The Second Pyramid as seen from the center of the pyramid arc = 307.65 degrees
The Second Pyramid as seen from the convergence point = 307.55 degrees
The Second Pyramid as seen along the hypotenuse of the 3-4-5 triangle = 306.87 degrees

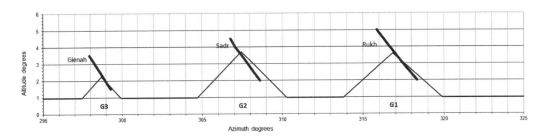

Figure 12.1. View from the convergence point 2940 meters southeast of the peak of the Second Pyramid showing the line of descent of the three Cygnus wing stars circa 2550 BCE.

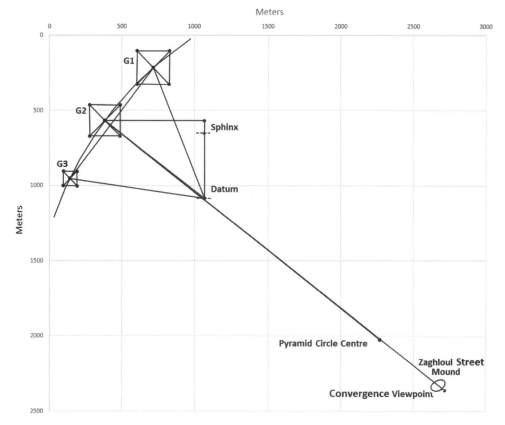

Figure 12.2. Cygnus setting line, from the convergence point to the peak of the Second Pyramid embracing the Zaghloul Street Mound, the center point of the pyramid arc circle, and the datum on Gebel el-Qibli.

All of these azimuth bearings are within 1 degree of variation. This suggests that the convergence point, from which you could have seen the three Cygnus wing stars set into the three pyramid peaks circa 2550–2479 BCE, was a deliberate extension of the Giza pyramid field's gradually emerging grand design.

The stars of Orion were unable to offer a similar visual spectacle. The orientation of the pyramids and astronomical positions of the Orion belt stars as seen from the latitude of Giza during the epoch of circa 2550–2479 BCE never offered a situation in which these three stars synchronized with their respective pyramid peaks. Indeed a distance of more than 10 kilometers would be required before the 3-degree span of the Orion belt stars matched the apparent width of the three pyramid peaks at Giza. Even if the pyramids *had* been visible at this distance, the relative height of their peaks would have been below the extinction level of the Orion belt stars.

STAR-TO-PEAK CORRELATIONS
IN THE VERTICAL PLANE

Although star-to-peak correlations in the vertical plane would never have been observable from ground level, and thus functioned only on a symbolic level, they should not be ignored. So, adhering strictly to the methodology employed by Orofino and Bernardini in their own study,* Hale used the existing spreadsheet data to determine the absolute accuracy of both Orion's belt and the Cygnus wing stars against the peaks of the three main Giza pyramids.

The diagrams resulting from this exercise show that the Cygnus wing stars still matched the pyramid peaks better than those of the Orion belt stars. More significantly, the *order* of the three Cygnus wing stars featured in this overhead synchronization *corresponded exactly with that found in connection with the star-to-peak correlation in the horizontal plane.* This was a highly significant discovery, because it meant that the Cygnus-Giza correlation functioned in *both the horizontal and vertical planes,* in other words, *in a three-dimensional reality.*

DENEB AND THE SECOND PYRAMID

Furthermore, the spreadsheet additionally showed that during the epoch of construction of the pyramid field, circa 2550–2479 BCE, a person standing on Gebel el-Qibli gazing out toward the Second Pyramid would have seen Deneb, Cygnus's brightest star, descend each night into its peak (see fig. 12.3). This must have been a quite magnificent spectacle.

Gebel el-Qibli is located immediately to the west of the recently discovered "Lost City of the Pyramids." This extensive settlement acted as the village and seaport for those employed in construction and maintenance on the pyramid field.[14] It is separated from the pyramid field to the north by a 200-meter-long, 10-meter-high wall of megalithic construction known in Egyptian Arabic as Heit el-Ghurab, the "Wall of the Crow" (see plate 19). That privileged individuals, perhaps attached to this settlement, could have ascended Gebel el-Qibli to watch Deneb set precisely into the peak of the Second Pyramid strengthens the case for the importance of Cygnus to the cosmological beliefs of the pyramid builders.

---

*All calculations were made using the Carte du Ciel sky program. Any spatial offset between stars and peaks has been averaged out across all three pyramids.

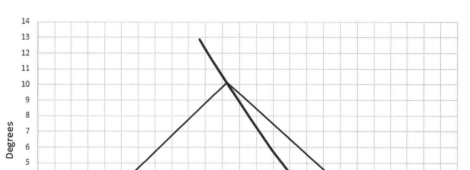

Figure 12.3. The setting path of Deneb into the peak of Giza's Second Pyramid, as viewed from the datum on Gebel el-Qibli circa 2550 BCE.

EXPLORING THE CONVERGENCE POINT

Geographically, the convergence point is located on Zaghloul Street (29°57′36″ N, 31°9′17″ E) just south of the village of Kafr el-Gebel. Although no excavations have taken place in the vicinity, an extensive settlement of mud-brick buildings is known to have extended southeast from the modern village of Nazlet el-Samman, east of the Giza pyramid field, to embrace the area now occupied by the villages of Nazlet el-Sissi, Nazlet el-Batran, and Kafr el-Gebel.[15] This settlement was uncovered in the late 1980s and early 1990s, during the construction of a new sewage system to prevent wastewater from rising close to the Giza pyramid field. Several thousand pieces of pottery were found, most of it dating from the Old Kingdom, as were mud sealings from the reigns of Khufu and Khafre. The remains of the mud-brick buildings, along with the discovery of the pottery, suggest that this extensive settlement formed part of the pyramid city connected with the cult of Khufu.[16]

In addition to these discoveries, levees running parallel to Zaghloul Street between Nazlet el-Samman and Kafr el-Gebel have been detected using data from the Shuttle Radar Topography Mission.[17] Very likely they formed part of an extended dyke or berm that marked the western limits of the Nile flood-plain toward the end of the Fourth Dynasty, circa 2550–2479 BCE.[18]

The existence of these levees, which correspond today to the north-south course of Zaghloul Street, appears to be connected with the discovery in 1993–94 of a colossal wall 650 meters south of Pyramids Road in Nazlet el-Samman. Constructed from huge limestone blocks capped with a level of basalt slabs, three individual sections of the wall have been uncovered so far through excavation. The largest of these is 70 meters in length[19] and lies on the same north-south alignment as the proposed Zaghloul Street levees.[20] The enormous stone wall probably formed part of a vast marina linking the nearby Nile channel with Khufu's pyramid complex via its now-lost valley temple.[21]

ZAGHLOUL STREET MOUND

Satellite data examined by Rodney Hale and the author show a noticeable area of high ground some 200 meters to the north and northwest of the convergence point. Oval-shaped and aligned approximately north-south, it rises above the local landscape to a height of just over 21 meters above sea level.

This isolated area of raised ground, which we shall call the Zaghloul Street Mound, is unique to the area. Thus it is unlikely to be simply the result of a natural deposition of Nile mud and silt across a prolonged period of time. Moreover, it lies extremely close to the line that connects the convergence point with the center of the pyramid arc circle, Gebel el-Qibli, and the peak of the Second Pyramid.

Both the convergence point and the Zaghloul Street Mound would have been located close to the western limits of the Nile River circa 2550–2479 BCE. Plausibly, they formed part of the above-mentioned dyke or berm connected with a place of debarkation used by boats arriving by river, perhaps from the capital city, Memphis. If correct, then the mound could have functioned as a backsight from which to observe the Cygnus wing stars set down into the Giza pyramids.[22]

Clearly any procession approaching the plateau from the southeast could not have followed the exact route of the convergence line. This would have taken it over the top of Gebel el-Qibli, which falls away sharply on its northern side. More likely it would have diverted slightly toward the east and crossed through the Lost City of the Pyramids, entering the pyramid field via the huge cyclopean gateway in the Heit el-Ghurab, the Wall of the Crow. This would have acted as an effective barrier to what might have been perceived as a realm of the dead lying to the north of the wall, the land of the living being the Lost City on its southern side. If correct, then this is further confirmation that the ancient Egyptians of the Old Kingdom saw the placement of the Giza pyramids as important when viewed from the southeast. It lends further weight also to the idea that it was the stars of the northern night sky that featured in any major ground-sky correlations at Giza, with those of Cygnus being the most obvious candidates.

Orofino and Bernardini, in their detailed study of possible star correlations at Giza, used statistical probability to validate the Orion correlation theory and dismiss the Cygnus-Giza correlation. Obviously their findings are at odds with those outlined within these pages. Rodney Hale and I demonstrate quite convincingly that star-to-peak matches involving Cygnus stars in both the horizontal and vertical plane exist at Giza. Almost certainly the stars of Cygnus played an integral role in the pyramid field's grand design from its very inception circa 2550 BCE. The fact that the alignments in question functioned not simply in two dimensions, but in a three-dimensional reality, adds considerably to this argument.

Next we will explore the purpose behind the employment of the Cygnus stars at Giza, for as Robert Bauval rightly pointed out in 2007, it is not simply accuracy that is important in any proposed ground-sky correlation, but *context*.

13

OSIRIS ARISEN

Giza's three main pyramids contain no inscriptions (only workers' graffiti), meaning that there is no surviving contemporary evidence outlining what the kings of the Fourth Dynasty might have believed about the soul's journey to the afterlife. Funerary inscriptions from nearby tombs and mastabas located elsewhere on the plateau at Giza can provide some clues regarding what the ancient Egyptians believed about the hereafter. These were, however, built for priests, officials, courtiers, and lesser members of the royal dynasty, who may not have shared the same death journey as those responsible for the construction of the pyramids. These were, of course, the kings Khufu, Khafre, and Menkaure, who not only venerated the sun god Re, but were also seen as incarnations of the hawk or falcon god Horus.

THE PYRAMID TEXTS

In contrast, pyramids left behind by the immediate successors of Giza's ruling dynasty, the kings of the Fifth and Sixth Dynasties, circa 2479–2193 BCE, contain an entire corpus of inscriptions known today as the Pyramid Texts. (They appear also in the pyramids and tombs of some queens from the Sixth Dynasty onward.) These are collections of magical spells, sayings, and instructions that the deceased's spirit would need to memorize in order to achieve rebirth and enter the afterlife. Their contents reveal that their construction was much influenced by the Re priesthood of Heliopolis, the ancient cult center situated just to the northeast of modern-day Cairo.

The earliest appearance of the Pyramid Texts is in the pyramid of Unas, the last king of the Fifth Dynasty, who ruled circa 2342–2322 BCE. They continue to be used in the Sixth Dynasty and beyond into the Middle Kingdom, when they are finally replaced, first by the Coffin Texts, and eventually by the various so-called Books of the Underworld, or Books of the Dead. However, there is every indication that some parts of the Pyramid Texts existed at a much earlier age, arguably even at the beginning of dynastic history, circa 3120 BCE.

Whatever the origins of the Pyramid Texts, there can be little doubt that they had a profound effect on the design, layout, and construction of pyramids built throughout the Old Kingdom period, including those at Giza. So understanding the cosmological beliefs and ideas contained in the Pyramid Texts can provide us with a clearer picture of what the kings of the Fourth Dynasty believed about the soul's journey, and why exactly the three main pyramids at Giza might have been aligned to key stars of the night sky.

ORIGINS OF OSIRIS

The Pyramid Texts contain some of the oldest references to the god Osiris, whom the deceased king literally became at the moment of death, so much so that in many passages, or "utterances," as they are known, he is actually addressed as Osiris. For a long time it was thought that the earliest mention of Osiris outside the Pyramid Texts was in the tomb of a minor princess named Hemet-re located at Giza.[1] She is thought to have lived during the Fifth Dynasty. However, the name Osiris, used as a funerary epithet, appears in a slightly earlier inscription relating to a prince named Neb-em-akhet in one of his two tombs at Giza (LG12).[2] Since he is considered to have been an elder son of Khafre, the builder of Giza's Second Pyramid, the inscription is probably contemporary with his father's reign.

Various passages in the Pyramid Texts equate the deceased in his guise as Osiris with a god named Sah (*Sȝḥ*), who since the early nineteenth century has been identified with the constellation of Orion.[3] Supporters of the Orion correlation theory cite this perceived relationship to explain why the three main pyramids at Giza reflect the astronomical positions of the Orion belt stars. By laying out the pyramids in this manner, the pharaohs of the Fourth Dynasty were aligning these monuments with the destination of the king's soul, the place of the afterlife, seen in terms of Orion.[4]

The identification of Sah as Orion, and of Orion as Osiris, is crucial to understanding the death journey of the pharoahs during Old Kingdom times. It is therefore important to examine what the Pyramid Texts actually say about Sah, who in one passage is addressed as "father of the gods."[5]

SAH AS ORION

There can be little question that the texts equate the king's spirit with Sah; it is as if the two come together as lost brothers, or as a father embracing his son.[6] Elsewhere in the Pyramid Texts the king is borne by the sky goddess Nut alongside Sah.[7] His spirit is also connected with the birth of Sah.[8] He traverses the sky with Sah,[9] and in one utterance Sah offers the deceased his arm, a symbol of his strength.[10]

Sah certainly possessed a celestial form, since there is reference to a "place of *Sȝḥ.*"[11] This "place" appears to be in the sky, as in one passage the deceased takes a ramp "trodden for thee to the *Dȝ.t* to the place where *Sȝḥ* is."[12] The *Dȝ.t,* usually transliterated as Duat, is the dark, tunnel-like underworld through which the sun was thought to journey each night. On one occasion the deceased is said to go "to the side of his father, to the side of *Sȝḥ,* to heaven."[13] Another utterance actually speaks of the deceased as "he who is in *Sȝḥ,*"[14] an allusion to the deceased as Osiris having entered the "place of *Sȝḥ.*"

The Pyramid Texts link Sah with the goddess Sopdet (*Spdt*), who is seen as his sister.[15] Like Sah, she has a celestial form, usually identified as Sirius (α Canis Majoris), the brightest star in the night sky. One passage describes Sah and Sopdet as the deceased's brother and sister,[16] while in another the king is "seated between them above this earth for ever."[17]

Sah continues to be associated with Sopdet on the calendrical coffin lids found at Asyut in Middle Egypt, which belong to the First Intermediate Period, 2150–2030 BCE.[18] Here Sah is shown as a human figure standing to the left of Sopdet, his head facing away from her and his feet toward her. He holds the *was*-scepter in one hand and an ankh, the symbol of life, in the other. Later, in the Ramesside star clocks of the New Kingdom, circa 1550–1069 BCE, Sah is usually on the right side of Sopdet. He still holds the *was*-scepter and ankh, but now stands on a reed bark (see fig. 13.1) in which he traverses the sky. In these star clocks Sah and Sopdet probably signify two of the 36 decans, or

Figure 13.1. The god Sah on a sky bark surrounded by stars.

10-day weeks, of the Egyptian 360-day calendar. This relationship between Sah and Sopdet expressed in the Ramesside star clocks is thought to be reflected in the astronomical relationship between Orion and Sirius, the former rising shortly before the latter.[19]

Sah's identification as Orion has rarely been challenged. So confident are Egyptologists of this appellation that the god name Sah is automatically changed to Orion in any translation of ancient Egyptian inscriptions, even in translations of the Pyramid Texts.[20] *Yet nowhere do the ancient Egyptians of the Pyramid Age directly identify Sah, or indeed Osiris, with Orion.* Nevertheless, Egyptologists and archaeoastronomers remain convinced that Sah is Orion, or at least a group of stars in the general vicinity of Orion. Even assuming this is correct, we shall see that Sah is not the final destination of the king's spirit. Indeed, the Pyramid Texts provide compelling evidence that the destination of the reborn king was not in the eastern or southern night sky, where we find Sah and Sopdet, but in the north, in the vicinity of the northern celestial pole.

14

STARRY
DESTINY

Although the Pyramid Texts vary slightly regarding how the deceased reaches the afterlife, the basic journey is pretty consistent. Like the dying sun, identified in the Pyramid Texts as the sun god Re, the king's soul or spirit (actually his *ba,* a word meaning something like "soul essence") departed toward the west, where it entered the Duat, the ancient Egyptian equivalent of Hades. This dark chthonic realm, where the deceased underwent a series of trials and tribulations, was filled with waterways. It was imagined also as the interior body of the sky goddess Nut, the mother of both Osiris and Re. At some point during its death journey the king's spirit would receive revivification before entering a place called the Akhet, a term meaning both "horizon" and the "place of becoming *akh*."[1] Here the spirit received new life and henceforth became an *akh,* a concept that will be explained shortly. It should be pointed out that the spirit of the deceased was not, however, seen as the *actual* sun in the underworld; it was simply equated with the sun's journey through the underworld and its eventual rebirth and reemergence each morning on the eastern horizon.

On ascending to heaven following his release from the Akhet, the king would take his place alongside the other stars of heaven. These were known as the Ikhemw-sek, the "Imperishable Stars," which are expressly stated as existing in the northern part of the sky.[2] Egyptologists generally identify the

Imperishable Stars as the circumpolar stars, those that revolve around the northern celestial pole without ever setting.[3] There is, however, a growing shift in the field of archaeoastronomy suggesting that the Imperishable Stars should include not only grazing stars (i.e., those that set only briefly), but *all* stars that rise and set north of the ecliptic.[4]

NORTHERN SOUL

The northerly destination of the king's spirit was recognized by British Egyptologist and philologist Raymond O. Faulkner, who produced a definitive translation of the Pyramid Texts.[5] In his summation of their celestial themes he concluded that they contain two contrasting strata of passages—one "concerned entirely with the circumpolar stars [i.e., the Imperishable Stars] and the northern night sky, *which appears as the abode of the illustrious royal dead whither the King journeys on his departure from the world.*"[6]

The other stratum, Faulkner wrote, concerned Sah and Sopdet—identified by him as Orion and Sirius—along with two stars named the Morning Star (Venus) and the Lone Star (identity unknown). These two strata, he noted, "overlap very little" and "while one deals only with the *ultimate abode of the dead King in the northern sky,* the other . . . appears to be concerned with those celestial bodies which mark the passage of time in the course of the year."[7]

So while the northern night sky was the destination of the soul in the Pyramid Texts, stars such as Sah and Sopdet related more to seasonal cycles and the passage of time, just as they did 1200 years later in the star clocks of the Ramesside period. Here then was confirmation that the ancient Egyptians of the Pyramid Age did not see Orion as the destination of the soul. It was simply an entry point to the eastern sky, providing an occasion for the king's spirit to embrace a close celestial relative (Sah) before its onward journey to the afterlife.

Such a surmise is emphasized, for instance, in the inscription on the north face of the pyramidion that once capped the pyramid of Twelfth Dynasty pharaoh Amenemhet III, who reigned circa 1859–1813 BCE. It proclaims that the "soul of the king is [now] higher than Sah [i.e., Orion]" and that the "soul of the sky is [that of] the king,"[8] making it clear that the king's spirit has ascended past Sah and is now entering the afterlife.

PYRAMID SUBSTRUCTURE

A more up-to-date translation of the Pyramid Texts is the one by American Egyptologist James P. Allen.[9] His work includes a detailed study not only of the texts themselves, but also of their placement and location inside the pyramid tombs. This has revealed what he describes as the "role physical location plays in the choice and meaning of each text in the pyramid."[10] It is reflected, Allen notes, in the spatial placement of texts inscribed on different walls. Again and again, these explicitly convey the perceived west-to-east movement of the deceased king's spirit as it passes through the tomb's substructure on its journey to the afterlife (see fig. 14.1).

The journey begins with the texts inscribed in the vicinity of the sarcophagus, positioned usually at the western end of a stone-lined room known as the sarcophagus chamber. The inscriptions make it clear that the sarcophagus is to be seen as the womb of the sky goddess Nut, where reanimation of the spirit takes place. The sarcophagus chamber thus acts as the Duat, the darkness inside the womb of the goddess, as well as the hinterland through which the deceased travels to achieve resurrection.[11] The flow of the texts continues, like the king's spirit and the sun's nightly journey, in an easterly

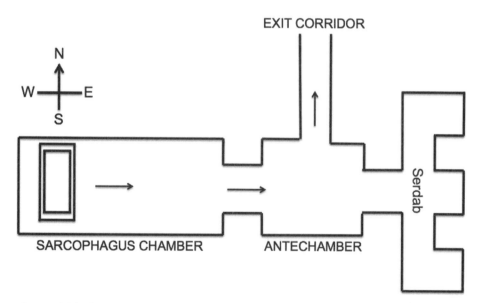

Figure 14.1. Plan of the tomb of the pharaoh Unas of the Fifth Dynasty, showing the directionality of the Pyramid Texts as written on the walls of the sarcophagus chamber (the Duat) and the antechamber (the Akhet).

direction through the sarcophagus chamber via a connecting passageway into an antechamber. This, the inscriptions imply, represents the Akhet, the pre-dawn light seen prior to the sun's appearance, where the deceased's "newly awakened spirit" becomes an akh.[12] In the past the word *akh* has been inter-preted as meaning "glorious spirit," but today it is considered to relate more to the spirit's ability to become "effective" in the afterlife following its reani-mation in the womb of Nut.[13]

On the east side of the antechamber is usually a recessed area containing three vertical niches. This is the *serdab,* a word deriving from the Arabic word for "cellar," since it was once believed that this was where offerings and grave goods were deposited following the interment of the deceased. It is now consid-ered possible that the serdab possessed a cosmological function, representing, according to Allen, "the eastern limit of the Akhet, the point at which the Sun, and the deceased's spirit, left the womb of the Duat to proceed into Nut's birth canal."[14] Since this is the most dangerous time in a birth, spells on the east wall of the serdab protect the spirit against potentially harmful forces and also allow its independent existence. There is also "a Morning Ritual to accompany its eventual appearance at dawn,"[15] confirming the spirit's ascent toward the stars of the eastern sky.

But the texts found on the east wall of the serdab do not mark the end of the soul's perceived journey to the afterlife. Others appear on the northern wall of the antechamber. These enable the spirit of the deceased to exit the antechamber and enter Nut's birth canal. Architecturally, this is represented, according to Allen, by the pyramid's northerly oriented corridor, along with the so-called vestibule and ascending corridor, which leads to the outside of the pyramid. Inscriptions on the north wall around the exit to the antechamber are concerned with the deceased's emergence from the Akhet "in company with the sun" and other gods on his journey into the sky.[16]

ORIGINS OF A NORTHERLY HEAVEN

Allen makes it clear that from the "north wall of the antechamber onward, the direction of the spirit's journey is *from south to north* rather than eastward with the rising sun."[17] The reason behind this 90-degree shift of direction is unclear, although Allen suspects it is most likely "a legacy of pyramid architecture prior to the end of the Fourth Dynasty, when the specific substructure associated with the Pyramid Texts came into use."[18] He adds that the "exact nature of the afterlife by the builders of the first pyramids is not known, but it may have involved the king's eternal existence in the company with *"the 'Imperishable Stars' of the northern night sky."*[19]

So in Allen's opinion the northern destination of the death journey, as outlined in the Pyramid Texts and reflected in the substructure of pyramids built during the Fifth and Sixth Dynasties and beyond, originated with an earlier phase of pyramid construction before the close of the Fourth Dynasty. This is important, because the internal architecture of the Giza pyramids, built toward the end of the Fourth Dynasty, displays the same basic layout as the later pyramids containing the Pyramid Texts. For instance, in the Great Pyramid the sarcophagus is positioned at the western end of a double-sized, granite-lined room known as the King's Chamber (see fig. 14.2).

The double size of the room replaces the individual sarcophagus chamber and antechamber of later designs; most likely a screen partition once divided the two halves.[20] At the eastern end of this antechamber is a small opening at ground level that leads to the top of what is known as the Grand Gallery. This descends toward the north, eventually becoming the Ascending Passage, which finally meets the Descending Passage. This then rises until it exits the pyramid on its northern side. Important here is the fact that Khufu called his pyramid Akhet Khufu. Although usually interpreted as meaning

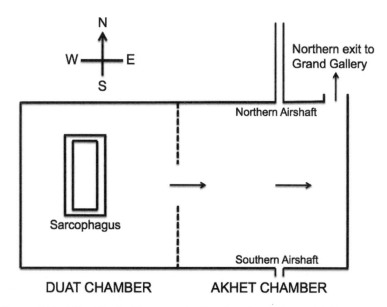

Figure 14.2. The King's Chamber inside the Great Pyramid showing the proposed directionality of the reborn spirit of the king.

the "horizon of Khufu," the name probably implies the place where Khufu's spirit was expected to become an akh through resurrection or new life inside the Great Pyramid.

Incidentally, there is no serdab at the eastern end of the King's Chamber. There is, however, one in the Queen's Chamber, which sits immediately below the King's Chamber and exits on the north side into the area where the Grand Gallery begins and the Ascending Passage ends. Whether or not the Queen's Chamber was the original burial chamber in the pyramid, which was then abandoned in favor of the King's Chamber, or whether it was intended for another person, arguably a son or wife of Khufu, is not known. But the existence of the serdab at the eastern end of the chamber shows its relationship to much later pyramid construction at sites like Abusir and Saqqara elsewhere in the Memphite necropolis.

Even though there are variations in the substructure of the other two main pyramids at Giza, including extra chambers and corridors, their basic design remains the same. Each has a large double room acting as the sarcophagus chamber and antechamber with a sarcophagus at the western end and an ascending corridor exiting the pyramid toward the north. Thus all three main pyramids at Giza reflect the same basic journey of the soul from west to east, and then toward the north, reflecting the directionally oriented Pyramid Texts found in later pyramids. So when the layout of the Giza pyramids was determined sometime circa 2550 BCE, the direction of heaven and the place of the afterlife were very firmly toward the *north*.

THE WOMB OF NUT

We can also say that the stone sarcophagi in all pyramids, including those at Giza, were seen as physical representations of the womb of Nut, who was the mother of Osiris and, in a separate tradition, the mother of Re, the sun god. Indeed, their basic internal architecture acted as the interior body of the sky goddess in its role as the Duat and Akhet. Their exit corridors penetrating through to the outside world thus formed the goddess's birth canal, through which the akh spirit achieved release for its final passage to the afterlife.

Exactly why the destination of the soul during the Fourth Dynasty and beyond was toward the north remains a matter of debate. Allen speculates that this belief could have been linked to the directional flow of the Nile, which is from south to north.[21] In ancient Egyptian tradition, the source of all life emanated from the south, as this was the direction from which the surging waters came that brought new life to the Nile floodplain each year. For this reason the primary direction of orientation in ancient Egypt was toward the south. (It is also why Upper Egypt is located in the south and Lower Egypt in the north.) In contrast, the north was the direction of darkness, death, and the afterlife,[22] the flow of the Nile perhaps suggesting the direction that the spirit must take to reach its final destination among the stars. If this is correct, it explains why Giza's Lost City of the Pyramids was located on the south side of the Wall of the Crow, outside the influence of the main pyramid field. To pass from the realm of the living in the south to the domain of the dead in the north, the inhabitants would have had to pass through the megalithic gateway in the Wall of the Crow, an act that might well have been seen as highly symbolic in nature.

FLY LIKE A BIRD

In hieroglyphic form the akh spirit is signified by the ibis, a bird of creation at Hermopolis in Middle Egypt, the cult center of Thoth, the god of writing and the moon. The Pyramid Texts speak of the spirit of the deceased flying, or possessing wings, like those of a bird. Usually they identify the bird in question as the divine falcon (a symbol of the god Horus, whose cult centers were at Nekhem and Edfu in southern Egypt),[23] the kite (a symbol of the goddesses Isis and Nephthys), or the goose[24] (a symbol of the earth god Geb).

Swallows, on the other hand, are described in the Pyramid Texts as divine spirits identified with the Imperishable Stars that alight on "the great island in the midst of the Marsh of Offerings [a celestial location in the north]."[25] They "give" to the deceased "the tree of life whereof they live, that N. [name of the deceased] may, at the same time, live thereof."[26] Allen believes that this connection with birds, and migrating birds in particular, might have been important to the idea that the soul's journey was originally from south to north:

> In ancient times, these [migratory] birds [entering Egypt from the direction of the Mediterranean] were thought to come from a northern exit of the Duat. For that reason they were seen as *akhs,* spirits of the deceased emerging into the world. The northern exit of the pyramids may reflect a similar concept.[27]

Almost certainly the "tree of life" mentioned in the Pyramid Texts is a metaphor for the northern celestial pole in its role as the cosmic axis or turning point of the heavens. In animistic traditions across the Eurasian continent, particularly in Siberia and central Asia, human souls, or alternately those of shamans, were said to perch on the upper branches of the World Tree as "soul-birds" before, during, or after incarnation.[28] This World Tree was thought to be located either at the center of the world[29] or in the center of the sky,[30] which the myths of central and northern Asia saw as existing in the north.[31] Similar ideas, it would seem, were present also in the Pyramid Texts, hinting at their origin outside of Egypt.

Another revealing passage from the Pyramid Texts is found just a few lines beneath the one mentioning the Tree of Life and reads:

> I will eat of what you eat, I will drink of what you drink, and you will give satiety to me at the pole, at that which is the foremost of its flagstaffs. . . . You shall set me to be a magistrate among the spirits, the Imperishable Stars in the north of the sky.[32]

Archaeoastronomer Juan Belmonte states that if "pole" is the correct rendering for the hieroglyphic text in this instance, then "one of the objectives of the king is to reside at the Pole of the Heavens,"[33] in other words somewhere in the vicinity of the northern celestial pole.

NORTH, NOT SOUTH

From the architectural design and directional orientation of all three main pyramids at Giza, it is clear that these funerary monuments cannot have targeted the belt stars of Orion, or any other star or asterism of the eastern or southern night sky. What is more, there is nothing in the Pyramid Texts that might suggest otherwise. Claims that the southern airshaft in the King's Chamber, which has an ascent angle of 45°14′,[34] targeted one or another of the belt stars of Orion during the Pyramid Age, and thus carried the king's spirit to the stars in question,[35] is an interesting theory. Yet on its own it cannot validate the idea that the destination of the king's spirit was Orion.

What is more, if the southern airshaft enabled the king's spirit to ascend to Orion, there would be no clear purpose for a second airshaft on the northern side of the same chamber. This second shaft climbs at an angle of approximately 32°28′ and comes close to targeting the upper culmination of the star Thuban (α Draconis),[36] the polestar of around 2800 BCE. These airshafts, along with two others in the Queen's Chamber, are unique in pyramid design and do not appear outside of the Great Pyramid; thus their function must remain a matter of speculation at this time.*

The Orion correlation theory is said to be further validated by the proposal that the angle made on the ground by the positioning of the three Giza pyramids matches that of Orion's belt as it crossed the meridian in 10,500 BCE, a date cited as the age of the gods.[37] Although this is a subject outside the scope of this present book,[38] introducing dates many thousands of years before the age of construction of a monument to justify its orientation and placement is ultimately unhelpful. This is not to say that monuments cannot be aligned to astronomical events in the past or the future, only that from a scholarly perspective such statements can only help muddy the situation.

SUMMARY

From the detailed examinations of the Pyramid Texts undertaken by two of their most celebrated translators, Raymond O. Faulkner and James P. Allen, we can see that in the age of the pyramid builders, the soul's death journey was clearly toward a northerly placed heaven. This is reflected in the entrance corridors of almost all key pyramids, which exit on their north side. There is little if anything to show that after the deceased's soul assumes the identity of Osiris, its final destination was the constellation of Orion.

Nonetheless, there can be no doubting the importance of Orion's role as Sah in the stellar destiny of the king's spirit. Sah would appear to have been its initial destination after exiting the Duat. In other words, there appears to have been three stages in the soul's journey to the afterlife. The first was from west to east through the Duat underworld, synonymous with the body of the sky goddess Nut. The second took it from the predawn light on the eastern horizon up toward Orion, while the third and final stage then carried it northward

---

*A similar shaft can be found in the Red Pyramid at Dahshur, although this one rises vertically from the main tomb area. Its function is even less understood than those seen in the Great Pyramid.

to the realm of the *akhu*—celestial beings and celebrated ancestors whose light was that of the Imperishable Stars. Yet as we will see next, to enter heaven the soul of the deceased had first to be reborn from the womb of Nut, the mother of Osiris. It is her stellar identity that reveals the true destination of the soul during the Pyramid Age as well as the exact route necessary to get there.

15

WOMB
OF THE STARS

The Pyramid Texts tell us that in death the king's spirit automatically became Osiris, the god of the underworld. Yet Osiris did not merely preside over the soul of the deceased; he was the expression of death itself, a dead god killed by the treachery of his evil brother Set. So until the point that he was reborn from the womb of his mother, the sky goddess Nut, the soul of the deceased existed in the same limbo state as Osiris, which is why funerary architecture during the Pyramid Age was specifically designed to enable the king's spirit to make the transition from dead god to ascended soul as efficiently as possible.

For this reason, the sarcophagus and sarcophagus chamber inside the pyramid acted as the goddess's womb, where the resurrection process could begin after the seventy-day mourning period, when the body of the deceased was ritually prepared for its transformation into an akh spirit. It is a concept ably expressed in the following passage from the Pyramid Texts, which reads: "As you are given to your mother Nut in her name of 'sarcophagus'; she has drawn you together in her name of 'burial chambers,' as you are made to rise up to her in her name of 'tomb.'"[1]

So with the sarcophagus representing Nut's womb enclosing the body of Osiris, the tomb quite literally became her body in its role as the Duat, with the exit corridor forming her birth canal. (James P. Allen has interpreted the name Nut [*nwt*] as meaning both "watery" and "oval,"[2] an allusion to the shape of the womb.) In doing this, the ancient Egyptians attempted to replicate in physical form the body of the goddess, as she appeared both in the sky and in her otherworldly guise. The Pyramid Texts make it clear also that on achieving rebirth in the afterlife, the king's spirit as Osiris receives the warm embrace of his mother, Nut, who in her celestial form exists in the northern part of the sky. There are various instances of this union between mother and child in the Pyramid Texts,[3] although two good examples will suffice:

> To the king, to this Osiris N. [name of deceased], as he ascends to heaven among the stars, among the imperishable stars, . . . N. goes therewith to his mother Nut; N. climbs upon her, in this her name of "Ladder."[4]

And then here:

> This N. [name of deceased] comes to thee Nut; this N. comes to thee Nut. . . . Thou openest thy place in heaven, among the stars of heaven."[5]

GODDESS OF THE MILKY WAY

Although the ancient Egyptians saw the goddess Nut as an expression of the night sky, there seems every reason to believe that she was also visually equated with the Milky Way as it appears north of the ecliptic. Indeed, the form she takes in the Pyramid Texts and also within the interior architecture of pyramid tombs preempts the role she plays in the art of the New Kingdom period, in which she is depicted arching naked over the earth, her feet on one horizon and her fingers touching the other. Often her brother and lover, the earth god Geb, is shown beneath her, with his penis erect, the pair having just been parted by their father Shu, the god of air, in order to create the division between sky and earth. Very often Nut's body is shown festooned with stars, even though no other stars are displayed around her. Clearly this is meant to imply that her body is itself a stream of stars—a reference to the Milky Way as it arches across the sky. Free of light pollution, the Milky Way becomes a shining arch stretching from horizon to horizon—a visual spectacle few people today ever get a chance to experience.

BORN AGAIN

In the cenotaph of Seti I at Abydos in southern Egypt, and in many tombs from the New Kingdom period, Nut is depicted swallowing the dying sun. This is shown as a red solar orb positioned at various places either inside or next to her body, starting with her neck and ending in her groin area. The message is that the sun is navigating her body in its guise as the Duat. Accompanying texts speak of the solar orb being swallowed by the goddess each night only to be reborn anew from between her thighs the following morning.[6] This same concept seems to be present in the Pyramid Texts in connection with the rebirth of the deceased in his role as Osiris and also as Re. Like the sun, the king's spirit is "swallowed" by Nut on the western horizon. It then passes through her body in its role as the Duat, before being reanimated in her womb and reborn from her birth canal so that it might climb into the sky and receive her warm embrace on entering heaven.

One passage in the Pyramid Texts speaks of the king's spirit as having arrived in heaven, which is seen as "between the two thighs of Nut,"[7] toward which it has been "swimming,"[8] like a fetus swimming in the waters of the amniotic sac prior to birth. Is it possible that the mummy wrappings, coffin, and even the sarcophagus actually represented the amniotic sac? Such ideas are certainly in line with those of James P. Allen, who has described Nut as an *"amniotic sac,* from which the deceased king, like the sun, was born each day."[9]

As we saw in chapter 6, this same concept of a second birth in the afterlife was present among the Bronze Age peoples of Anatolia circa 3500–1200 BCE.[10] They called it "the day of (one's) mother,"[11] the transformation process being achieved through the intercession, not of a biological mother, but of a primeval mother, whose chthonic womb enabled rebirth in the next world. Very often she was portrayed in human form. Yet, as the genetrix of a tribe or society, she might very well have possessed an animistic guise, such as that of a swan, wolf, elk, reindeer, bear, or, as in the case of Nut, a heavenly cow or vulture.

It is even possible that Egypt's original sky mother was conceived of as a primordial leopard, her spots representing the stars. In a theory proposed by German Egyptologist Wolfhart Westendorf,[12] this primordial sky deity, like Nut herself, was thought to swallow the sun at night and give birth to it again the following morning.

CYGNUS AND THE
WOMB OF NUT

Various Egyptologists have acknowledged the uncanny similarity between New Kingdom depictions of Nut arching over the earth and the Milky Way as it stretches from horizon to horizon in the northern night sky.[13] American astronomer Ronald A. Wells went further in proposing that as the Milky Way, Nut's head and outstretched arms were located in the region of the constellations of Taurus and Gemini (and thus Orion), close to the ecliptic, the place where the sun crosses the Milky Way on one side of the sky. On the other side of the sky, her legs were formed by the twin streams created by the Milky Way's Dark Rift, meaning that her feet were located where the sun crosses the starry stream in the vicinity of Scorpius and Sagittarius. Having established the orientation of Nut's body, Wells went on to identify her womb and birth canal with the Dark Rift's northern opening, marked, of course, by the stars of the Cygnus constellation.*[14]

At its moment of release, the sun, having passed through Nut's entire body, would then be perceived to slide down between her "thighs," represented by the twin arms of the Dark Rift, and then "drop" to the "earth." This artificial horizon, or "earth," Wells suggested, coincided with the position that the sun actually crossed the Milky Way in the vicinity of Scorpius and Sagittarius.[15] (see fig. 15.1).

NATIVE AMERICAN
DEATH JOURNEY

Similar ideas about the cosmic geography behind the rebirth of the soul existed among a number of Plains and Woodlands tribes in North America.[16] Here the soul would first make a leap onto the Milky Way, known generally as the

---

*Egyptologist Arielle Kozloff also proposes that Nut is reflected in the humanlike form of the Milky Way. But in her opinion the sky goddess faces the opposite direction, with her feet in the vicinity of Gemini and Taurus, her head in the area of the Cygnus constellation and her outstretched arms created by the twin streams of the Dark Rift. Kozloff sees similarities here with the design of offering spoons that appear during the New Kingdom, which take the form of a "swimming" goddess shown as a nude young woman holding something in her outstretched hands. Usually it is an offering bowl, either for cosmetic use or perhaps for the offering of water to the dead. Occasionally Nut holds a duck, which is the hieroglyph for "son," an allusion perhaps to the king in his role as "son of Re."

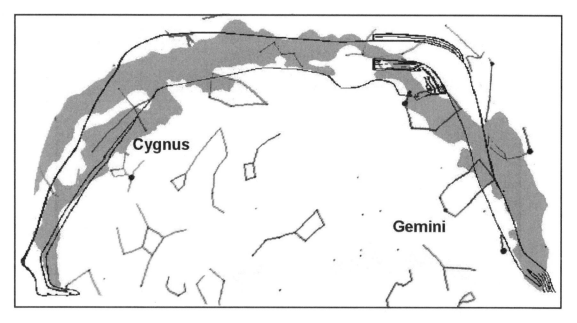

Figure 15.1. The sky goddess Nut as seen in New Kingdom tombs overlaid on the
Milky Way north of the ecliptic (after Ronald A. Wells).

Path of Souls, via an *ogee,* a rip or tear in the sky, located in the constellation of Orion and identified with the Orion nebula (M42).[17] As mentioned in chapter 4, the soul would then continue its journey along the Milky Way until it met a raptor-headed sky figure called Brain Smasher, located where the starry stream split to create the Dark Rift and identified with the Cygnus star Deneb.[18] Thereafter it was allowed to continue its journey to the afterlife, which lay in the direction of a supernatural creature known as the Water Panther or Great Snake, identified with the constellation of Scorpius.[19]

Thus the Native American death journey, which is reflected in stellar alignments toward Cygnus and Orion at a number of different mound complexes dating to the Hopewell period, circa 200 BCE–500 CE,[20] mimics the alignment proposed in connection with the ancient Egyptian world by Ronald A. Wells. It also makes sense of why the soul of the pharaoh had to encounter the Orion constellation in the form of the god Sah prior to embarking on its greater journey toward an afterlife in the vicinity of the circumpolar or nearly circumpolar stars. All of these elements formed part of a much greater cosmic geography that would eventually become fragmented, and even contradictory in its later forms. Yet it is clear that in ancient Egypt, just as it was in

Native American tradition, the key constellations associated with the rebirth of the soul were Orion and Cygnus.

AS ABOVE, SO BELOW

In his theory, which remains controversial,[21] Wells had in mind only the death and resurrection of Re, who belonged to a very ancient cult promoted by the Heliopolitan priesthood. Yet as we have seen, the Pyramid Texts relate how in his role as Osiris, the deceased king is likewise reborn from the womb of his mother, the sky goddess Nut. In other words, Wells's ideas can apply both to the rebirth of Re *and* the resurrection of the king in his role as Osiris, both of whom were seen as the offspring of Nut. If this is correct, then there is every reason to connect the area of the Milky Way occupied by Cygnus with the revivification of Osiris as displayed in the interior architecture of pyramid tombs built from the Fourth Dynasty onward.

If Cygnus and the northern entrance to the Dark Rift did, as Wells believed, signify the location of Nut's womb and birth canal, then aligning the three main pyramids of Giza with the setting of the Cygnus wing stars makes perfect sense. Creating the star-to-peak correlations described in chapter 12 made it possible to synchronize the stellar influence of both Cygnus and the Dark Rift with the interior architecture of the pyramids.

The purpose of this practice would have been to ensure that the king's spirit as Osiris achieved reanimation, gestation, and eventual rebirth within the primeval womb of his mother, Nut. Thus the two "wombs," one structural, the other otherworldly, were harmonized in a manner expressed by the Hermetic axiom of "as above, so below." In this way the king's akh spirit, arguably in the form of a bird, was then able to enter a "heaven" seen in terms of a realm dominated by the presence of a Tree of Life, a cosmic axis synonymous with the northern celestial pole. Here it became one of the heavenly children of Nut—an immortal spirit in the form of an imperishable star that forever shone brightly in the northern night sky.

WORLD SUPPORTS

These cosmological notions regarding the importance of Nut in the ancient Egyptian death journey reflect the religious beliefs and practices contained in the Pyramid Texts. As James P. Allen relates, they are likely to have taken shape sometime toward the end of the Fourth Dynasty, circa 2550–2479 BCE, when the three main pyramids at Giza were under construction. Much later, during the First Intermediate Period, circa 2150–2030 BCE, Nut appears alongside three other celestial forms on a series of calendrical coffin lids found at Asyut in southern Egypt. They are *Mśḫtiw,* the bull's foreleg, identified as the seven principal stars of Ursa Major, the Great Bear; the god Sah as Orion; and the goddess Sopdet in her role as Sirius, the brightest star in the night sky.

These coffin lids tell us very clearly that by the First Intermediate Period Sah and Sopdet, in other words Orion and Sirius, had become the most important celestial objects of the southern night sky, with Mśḫtiw as Ursa Major and Nut as the Milky Way. Indeed Nut here is arguably even to be identified with Cygnus, as her stance, with arms upraised and palms up toward the sky, exactly mimics the extended cross shape of the constellation in its role as the Northern Cross (see fig. 15.2). Together these four asterisms—Orion, Sirius,

Figure 15.2. The sky goddess Nut as seen on coffin lids from Asyut in southern Egypt, which date to the First Intermediate Period, circa 2150–2030 BCE; the example shown being from the tomb of Tefabi. The sky goddess's stance matches that of the stars of Cygnus during the epoch in question.

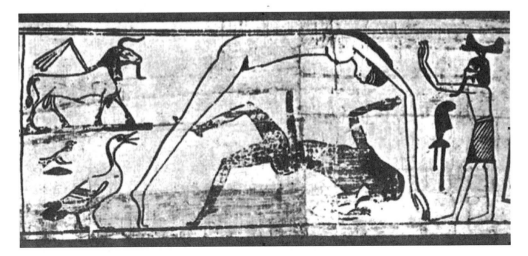

Figure 15.3. The sky goddess Nut with her twin and lover, the earth god Geb. His animistic form, the goose Gengen-wer, the Great Cackler, is seen by Nut's feet.

Ursa Major and Cygnus—would appear to have symbolized the four corners, or four supports, of the heavenly vault, a role played in later times by Nut herself.

BIRTH OF THE *BENNU* BIRD

A further clue that Cygnus might have been associated with the womb and birth canal of Nut, as well as the place of resurrection of Re and Osiris, comes from the Greek historian Diodorus Siculus (90–30 BCE). In his *Library of History* he writes that Osiris was the eldest son of Cronus, that is, the earth god Geb, born of a "fair and noble egg."[22] The egg in question is that of Gengen-wer, the Great Cackler, a form of the earth god Geb as a goose. He is said to have laid the primeval egg from which emerged the soul of Re as the *bennu* bird (see fig. 15.3).[23] Yet in addition to being associated with the sun god, the bennu also signified the soul of Osiris,[24] showing a clear relationship between the two quite separate traditions, both of which were promoted by the Heliopolitan priesthood.

THE GREAT CACKLER

In the various Books of the Dead, which replaced the Pyramid Texts and later Coffin Texts as sources of magic spells to be used by the soul on its journey to the afterlife, the deceased addresses the goddess Nut in her form as the sacred sycamore, promising to protect the "egg of the Great Cackler."[25] This is an interesting statement, for it was said that around "the sycamore of Nut" in the city of Heliopolis were the plants "among which the Great Cackler Seb [i.e., the god Geb] laid the Egg of the sun."[26] According to Heliopolitan tradition, it was here that Nut and Geb produced the egg from which sprang the sun in the form of the sacred bennu bird (see fig. 15.4).[27] Geb, and not Nut, came to be associated with the laying of the egg because the goose was the form the god took to fly through the air; the bird often being shown mounted on his head in ancient Egyptian art.

The chapter of the Book of the Dead where the deceased addresses Nut, saying it will protect the "egg of the Great Cackler," is called the "chapter of giving air." By identifying with the egg, the deceased becomes the "embryo" inside the shell, the air being necessary so that the spirit can breathe and gestate inside the tomb, which has become synonymous with the egg of creation.[28] In this manner the idea of the tomb as the shell of the egg produced by Geb simply replaces the womb and birth chamber of his wife and sister Nut as the place of resurrection of the deceased's spirit.

Although these themes derive from sources outside the Pyramid Texts, they mimic the conception and birth of Re within the cosmic womb of Nut. Furthermore, the goose that accompanies the god with a mace on the round zodiac from Dendera in Middle Egypt has been identified as Deneb.[29] The French Egyptologist Georges Daressy (1864–1938) saw in this goose the

Figure 15.4. The bennu, the bird of creation in Heliopolitan tradition, perched on the primeval hill or mound of creation, synonymous with the *benben* stone.

swan that seduced Leda, who afterward laid the eggs from which emerged the twins Castor and Pollux.[30] This, of course, is a story linked with Cygnus in its role as the celestial swan of Hellenic star lore. An even closer parallel with the story of the Great Cackler is that of Tündér Ilona, the queen of the fairies in Hungarian-Magyar folklore. In legend she takes the form of a swan to lay the egg from which the sun god hatches.[31] Her home in the sky is named Tündérek Fordulója, "the turning of the fairies," identified with the Cygnus star Deneb.[32]

This ethnological exercise tells us that Cygnus, often identified as the celestial swan or goose (and also an ibis), was once universally perceived as the womb of a primordial mother that gave birth to the sun, sometimes in the form of a sun-egg.

THE PHOENIX OF OSIRIS

As to the celestial identity of the bennu bird, seen as the soul both of Osiris *and* the sun god Re, the matter was adequately addressed as far back as 1851 by the English archaeologist, numismatist, and orientalist Reginald Stuart Poole (1832–1895). In his *Horæ Ægyptiacæ or The Chronology of Ancient Egypt* he wrote that the bennu bird, the "Bennu Osir" or "phoenix of Osiris," as he calls it, most likely "corresponded to Cygnus, the 'Bird' (Ορνις) of the Greeks, and perhaps also included Aquila, or corresponded to part of each of those constellations."[33] He made this conclusion after studying the bird's placement on the zodiacal ceiling at the Ramesseum of El-Kurneh, located on the west bank of the Nile at Thebes in southern Egypt.[34]

A PURE SOUL

Others followed Poole in identifying the bennu bird with Cygnus, including English mythologist and poet Gerald Massey (1828–1907). He wrote that "the Egyptian bennu in the tree" corresponded to "Cygnus as the bird, the swan of the Greeks, the eagle of the Romans, and the peacock of the Hindus."[35] Poole, however, went further, recognizing that one name given to the bennu bird, or phoenix, was "rekheet" or "ruk-h" (modern *rekh*), a bird of undefined character with human hands, which signified "a pure soul."[36] This he compared linguistically with the mythical bird of Persian and Arab tradition called the Rukh, Anka, or Simurgh, citing the fact that, like the phoenix, the Anka was connected with a specific time cycle, the former, according to Herodotus, being 500 years and the later 1700 years.[37] Poole noted that the "similarity of 'Rekheet' and 'Ruk-h' to 'Rukh' is very striking."[38] It suggested a northern origin behind all these traditions of a mythical bird associated both with the mysteries of the soul and with recurring cycles of time.

Important here is the fact that the Rukh, or Roc, of Arabic fable has long been identified with Cygnus.[39] Indeed, Rukh (رخ) is the Arabic name for Delta Cygni, the wing star corresponding to the Great Pyramid in the Cygnus-Giza correlation. The word *rukh* might well derive from the name of the Akkakian storm bird Urakhga, although this name has also been proposed in connection with the neighboring constellation of Lyra.[40] As Poole rightly surmised, the word *rukh*—Arabic for a "monstrous bird" or "bird of mighty wing" as big as an albatross[41]—can be written *rekh,* just like the Egyptian bird with human hands, or even *rakham,* meaning "a bird shaped like a vulture."[42] The same word is found also in Hebrew and Aramaic, which, like Arabic, are West Semitic languages. Here *racham* (רָחָם) or *rachamah* means "carrion vulture,"[43] and even "Egyptian vulture,"[44] while the similarly spelled *rechem* (רֶחֶם) means "womb, uterus."[45]

In ancient Egypt the vulture was the symbol of a mother goddess, who bore names such as Nekhbet, Mut, and Nut. In her role as protector of the dead, Nut was often shown on coffin lids as a woman with her open arms displaying the outstretched wings of the vulture. As we saw in connection with Çatalhöyük in Anatolia and Jerf el-Ahmar in Syria, the vulture would appear to have been an important symbol of a primordial mother goddess from the Pre-Pottery Neolithic age onward. More significantly, since fetuses are shown in the bodies of vultures at Çatalhöyük, it would seem that these huge scavenger birds were believed to accompany or carry souls into incarnation just as they would accompany souls into the afterlife following excarnation. As outlined in chapter 4, the point of origin and destination of human souls during the Pre-Pottery Neolithic period was most likely seen as Cygnus, identified in Hellenic, Mesopotamian, and Armenian sky lore with the vulture.

EGYPTIAN PSYCHOPOMP

It is perhaps worth recalling the words of James P. Allen at this point. He sees a connection between birds, migrating birds in particular, and the ancient Egyptian death journey as outlined in the Pyramid Texts:

In ancient times, these [migratory] birds [entering Egypt from the direction of the Mediterranean] were thought to come from a northern exit of the Duat. For that reason they were seen as *akhs,* spirits of the deceased emerging into the world. The northern exit of the pyramids may reflect a similar concept.[46]

Like swans and geese, vultures are migratory. They enter Egypt and North Africa in general from the direction of the Mediterranean, having spent the summer months in Europe. Their sudden appearance in the Nile Valley after a long period of absence could easily have been equated with the bringing forth of new souls, while their departure northward toward the northern celestial pole, with its imagined Tree of Life, was always going to evoke the idea of souls of the deceased returning from whence they came, or at least entering an afterlife seen as situated in the northern part of the sky.

So did an understanding of Cygnus as the source of cosmic life associated with the womb of a celestial bird enter Egypt in prehistoric times, and did it influence the foundation of religious beliefs and practices at cult centers like Heliopolis? Did these ideas, through the intervention of the Heliopolitan priesthood, come to influence the design and layout of not just the three main pyramids at Giza, but *all* pyramids constructed during Egypt's Old Kingdom period? If so, do they all, somehow, reflect an interest in the stars of Cygnus, the constellation, along with Orion, at the core of the ancient Egyptian death journey?

THE ROLE OF USERKAF

It has long been speculated that the lower (valley) temple attached to the sun temple of Userkaf, the first king of the Fifth Dynasty, who reigned circa 2479–2471 BCE, was oriented toward the rising of Deneb.[47] On his accession to the throne, Userkaf set about reviving the beliefs and practices associated with the cult of Re, upheld by his immediate ancestors, the builders of the three main pyramids at Giza. (Userkaf was very possibly a great grandson of Khufu.[48])

It may have been Userkaf's promotion of the cult of Re, and the construction of his magnificent sun temple immediately south of Giza at Abusir, the first of several built by kings of the Fifth Dynasty, that paved the way for the Heliopolitan-inspired Pyramid Texts to be inscribed on the walls of later pyramids. A closer study of Userkaf and his successors might provide further clues about the role Cygnus played in the minds of the ruling dynasty at this time.

Yet even with the advent of the Pyramid Age, the cosmological ideas of the dynastic Egyptians are likely to have been many thousands of years old. How they came to enter the Nile Valley is something that will lead us back to the Pre-Pottery Neolithic worlds of Göbekli Tepe in Anatolia and Helwan in northern Egypt. Yet before we can explore these matters further, we must return to the Giza pyramid field, where during the spring of 2016 an even greater piece of its grand design was about to reveal itself.

PART FOUR

COSMIC CODE

16

GIZA
REVELATION

On Saturday, March 13, 2016, Rodney Hale and I finally submitted our paper on the Giza pyramid field's underlying geometry and its proposed relationship to the stars. It was a process that had begun four months earlier, with the commencement of Hale's new study of the digital positioning of the three main pyramids in both the horizontal and vertical planes. This, of course, was initiated in response to a paper on the same subject by Italian academics Vincenzo Orofino and Paolo Bernardini. They had used statistical probability to validate the Orion correlation theory at the expense of the Cygnus-Giza correlation, something that was found to be completely at odds with our own general findings on the subject.[1]

With the matter put to bed, I did not expect the subject of Giza's grand design to rear its head for a while. Yet something happened later that same day which would expand immeasurably our understanding of the genesis and evolution of Egypt's most famous pyramid field.

INTUITIVE INSIGHT

As I talked that evening to my friend and colleague Richard Ward, author of *Echoes from the Primal Grimoire*,[2] he asked what would happen if an east-west line were to be drawn from the back end of the Sphinx across to the southeast corner of the Second Pyramid. Would this reveal something of significance? His hunch was that it would.

The east-west axis line of the Sphinx does indeed hit a point on the east side of the Second Pyramid, close to its southeast corner. At first this did not seem to be of any significance. Yet I quickly realized that this line exactly truncated the 3-4-5 triangle proposed by Rodney Hale as linking the datum on Gebel el-Qibli with the peak of the Second Pyramid and the north-south datum line that connects the head of the Sphinx with Gebel el-Qibli in the south. Indeed, this new east-west line revealed a brand new, much smaller, 3-4-5 triangle that ran from the datum on Gebel el-Qibli due north to the head of the Sphinx, making the side of 3 units. It then turned westward at 90 degrees—the line suggested by Richard—to reach the eastern edge of the Second Pyramid, close to its southeast corner. This constituted the side of 4 units. The triangle's hypotenuse, or side of 5 units, could then be traced between Gebel el-Qibli and the same point on the east side of the Second Pyramid, close to the southeast corner (see fig. 16.1). This hypotenuse line coincided with the setting of Deneb, as witnessed from the heights of Gebel el-Qibli, as well as the setting of the Cygnus wing star Sadr, as viewed from the convergence point, 2940 meters

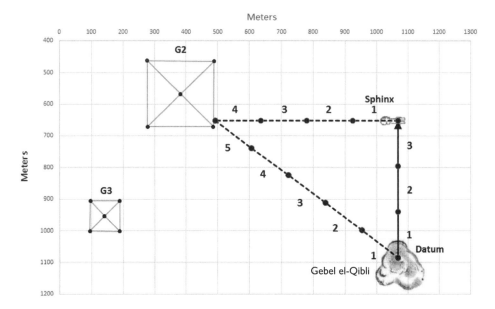

Figure 16.1. The Giza pyramid field showing the base 3-4-5 triangle embracing the datum on Gebel el-Qibli, along with the head of the Sphinx and the eastern side of the Second Pyramid close to the southeast corner.

southeast of the Second Pyramid. It also aligned with the center of the arc circle defined by the curvilinear arrangement of the three main pyramids.

A BASE 3-4-5 TRIANGLE

On its own, the existence of this base 3-4-5 triangle, as we shall call it, was certainly interesting. However, it made very little difference to the underlying geometry at Giza proposed by Rodney Hale and myself in our paper. Indeed we made it clear that an understanding of the basic geometry and triangulation at Giza could easily be extended to reveal further geometry if required. However, I quickly realized that the base 3-4-5 triangle's existence was the key to understanding the placement of other major monuments on the plateau. For instance, if this triangle was flipped northward along its east-west axis, its northeast corner defined the east-west latitude of the Great Pyramid's vertex, and center line, within an error of just 6 meters. What is more, this second, mirrored 3-4-5 triangle, together with the base 3-4-5 triangle, created the outline of a double-sized triangle with a height-to-base ratio of 3:2 (see fig. 16.2).

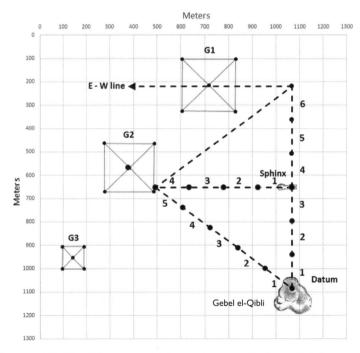

Figure 16.2. The Giza pyramid field, showing the base 3-4-5 triangle flipped northward along its east-west line linking the Sphinx with the eastern edge of the Second Pyramid.

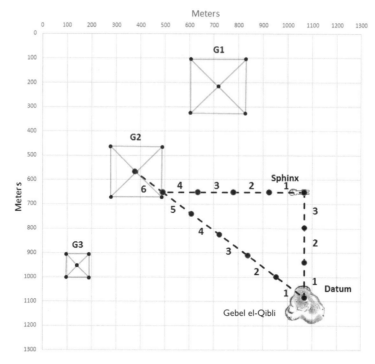

Figure 16.3. A sixth unit applied to the hypotenuse of the Giza pyramid field's base 3-4-5 triangle, creating 6 equal units between Gebel el-Qibli and the peak of the Second Pyramid.

In addition to this, if the base 3-4-5 triangle's hypotenuse, its side of 5 units, was extended northwestward by 1 further unit, making 6 in total, it defined the position of the peak or vertex of the Second Pyramid to within 1 percent of error (see fig. 16.3).

TWO NEW DATUM LINES

Then, using the newly found vertex of the Second Pyramid, create a second north-south datum line halfway between this point and the original datum line projected north from the datum on Gebel el-Qibli through the head of the Sphinx (see fig. 16.4). The northern end of this third line will meet the east-west axis defined by the northern extent of the mirrored 3-4-5 triangle to create the position of the Great Pyramid's own peak or vertex.

Thus the geographical positions of both the Great Pyramid and Second Pyramid, along with that of the Sphinx, can all be determined by the creation of just two back-to-back 3-4-5 triangles. This left the placement of the

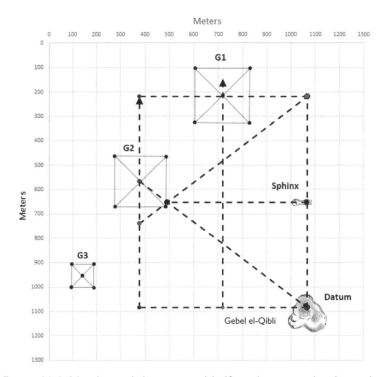

Figure 16.4. North-south line created halfway between the datum line running northward from Gebel el-Qibli and a longitudinal line through the peak of the Second Pyramid. When combined with the east-west line created by the northern extent of the mirrored 3-4-5 triangle, it defines the position of the peak or vertex of the Great Pyramid.

Third Pyramid. How might its location fit into this gradually emerging geometry? Well, as we saw in chapter 11, an equilateral triangle with two of its corners coinciding with the datum on Gebel el-Qibli and the peak of the Great Pyramid defines the peak of the Third Pyramid with its third corner. What is more, this equilateral triangle is bisected within just 1 degree of error by the hypotenuse of the base 3-4-5 triangle. This same line, we should recall, embraces not only Gebel el-Qibli, but also the center of the pyramid arc circle *and* the convergence point. From here, of course, the three Cygnus wing stars could have been seen to set each night into the peaks of the three main pyramids at Giza.

SCHWALLER DE LUBICZ

Justification for projecting a sixth unit out from the hypotenuse of the base 3-4-5 triangle to define the vertex of the Second Pyramid might seem like a random move for determining the extent of Giza's underlying geometry. However, the inspiration for this decision comes from the keen observations and inspired workmanship of French occultist, Egyptologist, and student of sacred sciences René A. Schwaller de Lubicz (1887–1961). In 1937 he visited Luxor in southern Egypt,[3] and while there entered a royal tomb in the Valley of the Kings known as KV6. This had once housed the body of Rameses IX, who reigned circa 1126–1108 BCE.

On one of the tomb's interior walls, Schwaller de Lubicz saw hidden among the usual pictorial scenes from the books of the underworld something of immense significance. It was the image of an ithyphallic, mummiform god with false beard, wig, and arms outstretched above his head. Almost certainly it was a representation of the god Amun in his guise as Min, one of the most ancient deities in Egypt. The mummiform figure was resting on the sloping hypotenuse of what was quite clearly a 3-4-5 triangle suggested by the shape made by the body of a snake, its head immediately behind that of the god. Confirming

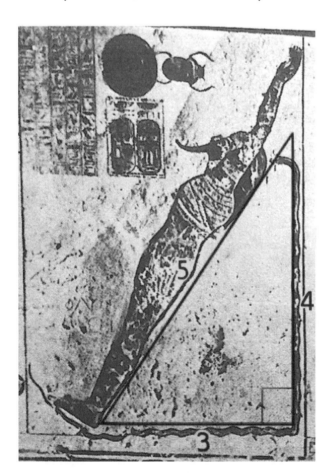

Figure 16.5. Amun-Min on the wall of Rameses IX's tomb in the Valley of the Kings with a 3-4-5 triangle overlaid upon his serpentine support.

the image's profound symmetry was the fact that the angle at which the figure lay on the hypotenuse of the triangle was approximately 37°. This matched one of the two angles of the hypotenuse of a 3-4-5 triangle, which is 36°52′12″. Clearly the artist had created this perfect symmetry to ensure that the viewer knew exactly what was being represented here (see fig. 16.5).

PYTHAGOREAN THEOREM

To Schwaller de Lubicz, the existence of this painted image, created over 3000 years ago and little understood even today, was compelling evidence that the ancient Egyptians employed the use of a right-angled triangle—its sides 3, 4, and 5 units in length—several hundred years before its celebrated "discovery" by Pythagoras of Samos (circa 569–475 BCE), who used its existence to devise what has become known as the Pythagorean theorem. This supposes that the square of the hypotenuse of a right-angled 3-4-5 triangle is equal to the sum of the squares of the other two sides (thus $3^2 + 4^2 = 5^2$).

Schwaller de Lubicz realized something else about this unique painted image in the Valley of the Kings. He determined that the outstretched arms of the god were positioned in such a way as to create a sixth, extra unit on the end of the hypotenuse. Once again, this was unquestionably a deliberate act on the part of the artist—one demonstrating that the units of a 3-4-5 triangle could be detached and used individually when required. Yet to Schwaller de Lubicz the extension of the hypotenuse from 5 to 6 units meant far more than simply accommodating the outstretched arms of the god, for this transition expressed a new value of 6/5 of a whole, or 1.2 if the hypotenuse had ideally been 1 unit of measure in the first place. To him this provided compelling evidence that the ancient Egyptians knew the value both of φ (phi) and of π (pi), for 1.2 (that is, 6/5) times phi (1.618. . .) squared equals 3.1416408 . . . , very approximately the value of pi (its true value is 3.14159265359 . . .).

This profound revelation would persuade Schaller de Lubicz to remain in Egypt for the next twelve years so that he might study the sacred geometry and divine proportion of its temples, statues, and relief art.

ROPE STRETCHERS

Schwaller de Lubicz was, of course, right. The ancient Egyptians did indeed have knowledge of the right-angled 3-4-5 triangle. Land surveyors known as "rope stretchers" used long cords with twelve equal spaces created by twelve equally positioned knots to define triangular plots of land with sides of 3, 4, and 5 units in length (see fig. 16.6). The initial triangle would then be flipped to create a double triangle (exactly as was done at Giza to create the double-sized 3-4-5 triangle with a 3:2 ratio), and then this double triangle would be replicated to create a rectangular area of land.[4] This process was very often carried out to reestablish field boundaries washed away by the annual inundation of the Nile, or to mark out the foundations of buildings.

Clearly, the larger the area being marked, the more difficult it became to use ropes, suggesting that when required, wooden poles would have been substituted. Measuring even larger areas of land like that used to create pyramid complexes, or even entire pyramid fields, would have been a far more difficult task, although arguably this was still achieved on a symbolic level at least. The underlying geometry at Giza, which seems to rely heavily on the use of 3-4-5 triangles, would appear to bear out this view. Moreover, using measurements based on individual units derived from the use of such triangles also seems feasible given the representation of the mummiform god Amun-Min, with its single-unit extension to the 3-4-5 triangle's hypotenuse.

Figure 16.6. Left, illustration by Nick Burton showing Egyptian rope stretchers using a cord of twelve equally spaced knots to create a 3-4-5 triangle with a perfect right angle, and, right, the twelve-knotted rope used to create a north-south-aligned rectangle.

THE MYSTERY OF MIN

The god Amun-Min presided over agriculture and the fecundity of the land, in which capacity he was the patron of land cultivation. Carved reliefs of the god from the New Kingdom depict him as mummiform in appearance with an erect phallus, a symbol of his fertility. His arm is usually shown upraised and he holds a flail, which is an agricultural tool used for threshing. Yet when you look more closely at these reliefs, the god's raised hand does not actually hold the flail; it is as if the tool is floating in midair. Moreover, there appears to be a triangular relationship between the two angled parts of the flail (the stick and the swipple) and the position of Min's arm. When measured, this can be shown to be a near perfect 3-4-5 triangle (see fig. 16.7), an act that seems not only purposeful, but also perhaps representative of the twelve-knot cords used by the rope stretchers to establish 3-4-5 triangles. If this is the case, it strengthens the apparent relationship between the image of Amun-Min in the tomb of Rameses IX and the 3-4-5 triangle first noted by Schwaller de Lubicz in 1937.

Figure 16.7. The god Amun-Min showing a 3-4-5 triangle overlaid on the flail seen floating above his raised hand.

That the right-angled, 3-4-5 triangle, also known as the Pythagorean triangle, was indeed used in large-scale architectural design during the Pyramid Age is not in question. Evidence has been offered for its presence within the Third Dynasty pyramid complex of Djoser at Saqqara,[5] located around 15 kilometers southeast of the Giza pyramid field, while 4:3 proportions have been detected in the height-to-base ratios of several Old Kingdom pyramids, especially those of the Fifth and Sixth Dynasties.[6] Moreover, as we shall see next, the use of the 3-4-5 triangle for positioning the three main pyramids of Giza reveals something else of importance: that originally the Second Pyramid was just as important as its more illustrious neighbor, the Great Pyramid.

17

THE HIDDEN KEY

I n the days that followed the discovery of Giza's underlying geometry using a simple base 3-4-5 triangle I asked Rodney Hale to verify these findings and also establish as precisely as possible the distance from the datum on Gebel el-Qibli to the head of the Sphinx. The resulting figure, when divided by three, would reveal the length of one of the units of the base 3-4-5 triangle. This was needed to confirm the validity of the extension by one extra unit of the triangle's hypotenuse, which defined the position of the peak or vertex of the Second Pyramid. This is what Rodney wrote back:

> Distance from datum [i.e., Gebel el-Qibli] to Sphinx = 432.19 meters
> Dividing by three for our "unit length" = 144.06 meters or 472.64 feet.[1]

When I read these words, something struck me. I was sure that this "unit length" of 144.06 meters or 472.64 feet (5671.68 inches) was similar to the vertex or center line defining the *height* of the Second Pyramid. So I quickly checked and found that this is estimated to be 144.02 meters or 472.5 feet (5670 inches), a figure extremely close to the length of one of the units of the base 3-4-5 triangle at Giza. Indeed, there was just 4 centimeters (around 1.7 inches) difference between the two measures. So finding that the height of the Second Pyramid and the unit of measure used in the base 3-4-5 triangle were essentially the same could not be without meaning.

Then I realized the staggering implications of this discovery. The height of the Second Pyramid formed a seventh unit on the existing hypotenuse of five units with its extra sixth unit already defining the position of the pyramid's peak or vertex. In other words, there were six units in the horizontal plane with a seventh one appended at its northwestern end that rose in the vertical plane to define the height of the Second Pyramid.

PYRAMID GRAND DESIGN

Yet there was more, for a cross section of the Second Pyramid shows that the height, which we know to be one unit of measure of the base 3-4-5 triangle, is two-thirds the width of the pyramid at its base, providing it with a base-to-height ratio of 3:2. In other words its base is one and a half Giza units, giving it an ideal length of 216.03 meters or 708.75 feet.

What all this also tells us is that the 3:2 triangle created by the height-to-base ratio of the Second Pyramid (see fig. 17.1a) is a scaled down model of the double triangle found within Giza's underlying geometry produced by the two 3-4-5 triangles mirrored back to back (see fig. 17.1b). Indeed, not only is the pyramid's cross section exactly one-quarter the size of the pyramid field's double triangle, it also contains the 3-4-5 triangle as well. This is made up of half the length of its base combined with the vertex (or center line) and apothem

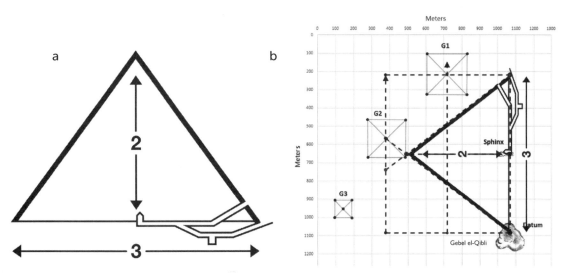

Figure 17.1. Left, the Second Pyramid, showing its 3:2 base-to-height ratio, and, right, the pyramid overlaid on the Giza's pyramid field's 3:2 triangle to show the relationship between the two.

(the point from the middle of the pyramid's base to its apex), creating the triangle's sides of three, four and five parts, respectively.

Everything suggests that the Second Pyramid was designed as a natural projection of Giza's underlying geometry, whereas the placement of the two other main pyramids, although conforming to its triangulation, would seem to have been of secondary importance to the pyramid field's grand design.

SECOND PYRAMID FIRST

By far the best position on the plateau to build a pyramid was the site of the Second Pyramid. This allowed for a causeway to be constructed across to the eastern edge of the plateau, where the preexisting Sphinx knoll was to be found. If, as Serena Love proposes, this rocky promontory had been important during the predynastic age, then surely the builder of the first pyramid on the plateau would have incorporated this natural feature into their funerary complex. Yet this was not the case. The Sphinx features as a part, not of the pyramid complex of Khufu, the assumed originator of the pyramid field, but of that accredited to his son Khafre, the builder of the Second Pyramid. Why, then, did Khafre get the plateau's premier site, which enabled his pyramid complex to incorporate the presence of the Sphinx knoll? An understanding of Giza's newfound underlying geometry helps provide some answers.

Is it possible that the Second Pyramid was built first, or that the plot was originally intended for Khufu's pyramid? Did something happen (some bad omen perhaps) to make the architects and surveyors shift their attentions away from the site of the Second Pyramid to the intended location of the Great Pyramid? The undeniable connection between the design of the Second Pyramid and Giza's underlying geometry argues for the fact that the two were integrally related and of primary concern to the original creators of the pyramid field.

THE SPHINX PUZZLE

There are also other indications that the Second Pyramid and its causeway were built or planned before the construction of the Great Pyramid. For instance, the Sphinx enclosure, the carved sunken area around the monument that permitted its lower body to be sculpted from the bedrock and provided the core masonry for the construction of the Sphinx temple immediately to the east, abuts the Second Pyramid's causeway on its south side. This means that the causeway must have been in place, or at least planned, *before* the creation not just of the Sphinx enclosure, but also of the Sphinx itself. More significant, however, is that to the west of the Sphinx enclosure is a quarry created for the construction of the Great Pyramid, which lies immediately to the north.[2] While the eastern edge of this quarry abuts the ridge left behind following the construction of the Sphinx enclosure, its southern edge abuts the Second Pyramid's causeway, meaning that the quarry must have been created *after* the construction of both the Second Pyramid's causeway and, presumably, the Sphinx enclosure.[3] In other words, the location of the Second Pyramid, its causeway, *and* the Sphinx monument would seem to have existed before the exploitation of the quarry area used to provide core masonry for the Great Pyramid.

Finally, the Second Pyramid's causeway ends at the eastern edge of the plateau. Here we find Khafre's valley temple, which lies immediately southeast of the Sphinx. This was attached to a dock or quay that served the Second Pyramid, allowing vessels from the Nile to easily access the pyramid complex.[4] However, the valley temple and marina attached to the Great Pyramid are much farther east. Since we know that from around 3000 BCE onward the Nile was migrating steadily eastward,[5] it seems likely that the Great Pyramid's marina, valley temple, and extended causeway, all of which are lost today beneath the streets of Nazlet el-Samman, were constructed *after* Khafre's own pyramid complex, the Nile by then being much farther away from the pyramid field.

These are all strong indications that the Second Pyramid was planned, and maybe even constructed, before the Great Pyramid. If correct, it indicates that its site was extremely important to the pyramid field's grand design, although why exactly is unclear. Was it simply the fact that it lay at the northwestern termination of the hypotenuse of the base 3-4-5 triangle, and was positioned so that the Cygnus star Sadr would be seen to set into its capstone as viewed from the convergence point, while at the same time allowing the bright star Deneb to descend into its summit as viewed from the datum on Gebel el-Qibli? Perhaps. Yet was there more to the location of the Second Pyramid than simply this?

MEGALITHIC PLATFORM

In the author's opinion, one of two scenarios is possible. Either the Second Pyramid was meant to have been the tomb of Khufu, the earliest of the three Fourth Dynasty pharaohs responsible for pyramid construction, and/or it was

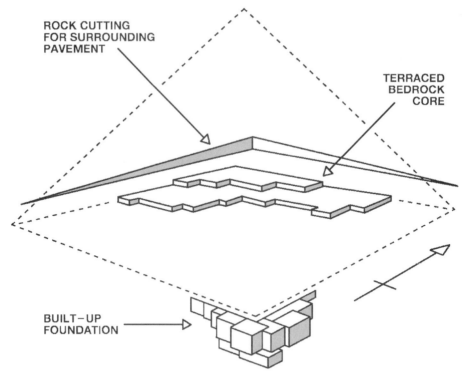

ROCK CUTTING
FOR SURROUNDING
PAVEMENT

TERRACED
BEDROCK
CORE

BUILT–UP
FOUNDATION

Figure 17.2. The Second Pyramid's southeast corner,
showing its underlying megalithic platform.

built on the site of a preexisting monument. In the area of its southeast corner, exactly where the base 3-4-5 triangle and its mirror image to the north
reach the eastern edge of the pyramid, is an enormous stone platform made
up of huge megalithic blocks positioned both vertically and horizontally (see
fig. 17.2). Each one is thought to be as much as 100 tons in weight and up to
3 meters in thickness.[6] Although this structure is believed to have been constructed to create a stable support for the southeast corner of the pyramid (since
the bedrock drops away at this point), it remains possible that this structure is
either older than the pyramid, and/or that it conceals or protects something
hidden beneath it.

UNDERGROUND STRUCTURES

In 1977 geophysical surveys conducted by the Stanford Research Institute in
association with Cairo's Ain Shams University located hollow cavities 50 and
14 meters beneath the huge stone blocks making up the megalithic platform

beneath the southeast corner of the Second Pyramid. These, they concluded, might well be artificial in construction:

> The origin of the echoes at 50 and 14 m range remains unknown. We cannot at present rule out the possibility of a significant subsurface man-made structure under the southeast corner, though the echoes could also be of geologic origin.[7]

The hollows themselves are, as they say, probably linked to natural fissures and even cave tunnels aligned with faults following the northwest-southeast trend of the plateau. Not only do these fissures pass directly beneath the burial chamber (Belzoni's Chamber) located in the bedrock beneath the pyramid,[8] but they are also plainly visible in the carved bedrock area forming its northwest corner. Furthermore, these fissures might well link with the cave system rediscovered in 2008 within the plateau's northern cliff face, which almost certainly goes off in the direction of the Second Pyramid.[9]

The existence of the hollow anomalies beneath the Second Pyramid's southeast corner, close to where the apex of the base 3-4-5 triangle and its mirror counterpart touch the pyramid, seems unlikely to be coincidence. Is it possible that the base 3-4-5 triangle linking the datum on Gebel el-Qibli with the Sphinx knoll and the future eastern edge of the Second Pyramid, close to its southeast corner, was established to lock a preexisting structure into the pyramid field's underlying geometry? What exactly this structure might have represented, or what it meant to the pyramid builders of the Fourth Dynasty, is unclear. Whatever the answer, there can be little doubt that the megalithic platform in the southeast corner of the Second Pyramid conforms to the underlying geometry outlined in these pages.

SACRED MEASURES

With a greater understanding of the importance of the spatial dimensions of Giza's underlying geometry, I now looked more closely at the length of the unit defining the sides of the base 3-4-5 triangle to see whether it might reflect an ancient unit of measure known to have been used by the ancient Egyptians. Looking into this matter, I found that 144.02 meters or 472.5 feet (5670 inches), the height of the Second Pyramid, is ideally 270 long cubits of 21 inches ($21 \times 270 = 5670$). Once again, this was so close to the unit length derived from the pyramid field's base 3-4-5 triangle, which is 144.06 meters or 472.64 feet (5671.68 inches), that I was forced to conclude the two were one and the same. Moreover, I determined that 270 long cubits was the equivalent of 45 Hebrew reeds of 10.5 feet or 126 inches (45 × 10.5 = 472.5 feet or 5670 inches).

So applying these same equivalent measures to the Giza pyramid field's base 3-4-5 triangle meant that its side of 3 units was 135 reeds (810 long cubits or 432.054 meters) in length, its side of 4 units was 180 reeds (1080 long cubits or 576.072 meters) in length, while its hypotenuse was 225 reeds (1350 long cubits or 720.09 meters) in length. Adding the sixth unit to the end increased the hypotenuse's length to 270 reeds (1620 long cubits, 864.11 meters). By strange coincidence, 270 reeds was also the total length of the north-south datum line. This, as we have seen, runs between Gebel el-Qibli and the east-west line defining the vertex of the Great Pyramid, forming also the base of the double triangle, which consists of 6 unit lengths of our measure. Since this triangle has a 3:2 base-to-height ratio, its vertex, running between the Sphinx knoll and the base of the Second Pyramid, was precisely four units or 180 reeds (1080 long cubits or 3456.43 meters) in length. If we use these same units of measure, it means that the Second Pyramid has a base length of 67.5 reeds or 405 long cubits and a height of exactly 45 reeds or 270 long cubits, adequately showing its own 3:2 base-to-height ratio.

REEDS, REMEN, AND CUBITS

Some might question the use of both the long cubit of 21 inches and the Hebrew reed of 10.5 feet or 126 inches in the design of a Fourth Dynasty Egyptian pyramid field. However, there is ample evidence to show that the long cubit of 21 inches formed part of a system of ancient Egyptian measures based on palm- or hand-breadths of 3 inches (7.62 centimeters). For instance, the Egyptian unit of measure known as the *remen* was 5 palms or hand-breadths in length, thus ideally 15 inches or 38.1 centimeters.[10] The small cubit was 6 palms in size, making it 18 inches or 45.72 centimeters in length,[11] while the royal cubit (also known as the great cubit) was the length of 1 standard cubit plus a hand-breadth (in other words seven palms),[12] making it 21 inches or 0.5334 meters in total, the same as the Hebrew long cubit.[13] However, there were different variations of the royal cubit, with a figure of 0.523.7 to 0.523.8 meters (20.59–20.62 inches) usually being cited in the construction of the Great Pyramid.

An examination of the measurements and dimensions of stone blocks and architectural features of the Giza pyramid field, particularly that made by Flinders Petrie in the early 1880s, tends to support the idea that the pyramid builders did indeed use the long cubit of 21 inches,[14] which may well have constituted the true, or at least the ideal, length of the so-called royal cubit.

The fact that 1 unit of measure in Giza's underlying geometry is exactly 45 Hebrew reeds might easily be dismissed as coincidental, and nothing more. Yet as we shall see next, the reed also features prominently in the measurements of the Great Pyramid. Indeed, it is present to such a degree that it becomes difficult to deny that the reed did not have some special meaning to those responsible for the construction of the Giza pyramid field. What is more, there appears to be powerful evidence that both the reed and the long cubit of 21 inches were specifically employed at Giza to encode a cosmic number symmetry that, as this book will demonstrate, can be shown to have existed as much as 21,000 years before the rise of dynastic Egypt.

18

COSMIC SYMMETRY

British engineer John Legon determined that the dimensions of the Great Pyramid were based on the use of an Egyptian cubit equivalent to 20.62 inches or 0.52375 meters. This meant that the intended length of each of its sides, estimated ideally to be 756 feet or 9072 inches (70.234 meters), was 440 cubits, a realization that helped support his own case for a grand design at Giza.[1]

All this might be correct. Yet it is a simple fact that the base length of the Great Pyramid on all four sides is also, ideally, 432 long cubits of 21 inches. Since there are 6 long cubits in a reed of 10.5 feet (126 inches or 3.2 meters), each of the pyramid's four sides are exactly 72 reeds in length, something that, if meaningful, provides an extraordinary insight into the minds of those responsible for this most remarkable monument of the ancient world.[2]

Using these measurements, we can calculate that the intended height of the Great Pyramid was 275 long cubits, which is 481.25 feet or 146.69 meters. To confirm this figure I used the equation $275 \times 2 = 550$ (the corner-to-corner length of the Great Pyramid) times pi (3.141592) to determine the circumference, which turns out to be 1727.88 cubits. This is almost exactly 1728, the sum total in long cubits of all four sides of the pyramid, at a value of 432 cubits per side. Multiply 550 cubits (the diameter of a circle of 1728 cubits) by 43,200, and it comes to 7875 miles or 12,673.58 kilometers, just under 25 miles short of the diameter of the earth from pole to pole, which is 7899.86 miles or 12,713.6 kilometers (the earth's equatorial diameter is 7926 miles or 12,756 kilometers). This can be confirmed by the following calculation: 481.25 × 43,200 = 20,790,000 feet, which is 3937.50 miles, providing a diameter (2 × 3937.50) of 7875 miles.

These calculations not only demonstrate the value of pi in the design of the Great Pyramid, but they also show that it is a scale model of the Northern Hemisphere to a ratio of 1/43,200, something strangely hinted at by the fact that its sides are 432 long cubits in length; 432 being 1/100 of 43,200. Skeptics dismiss such correlations between the size and measurements of manmade monuments and the dimensions of the earth, or indeed of any celestial body, as simple coincidence. Yet, knowingly or otherwise, the pyramid builders employed a specific number system at Giza that reflects a recurring fractionalization of cosmic time cycles about which, in theory, they can have known nothing about.

For instance, if we now consider the sequence of numbers creating the perimeter of the Great Pyramid, we find something else of interest. In reeds, this is 72, 144, 216, 288, which are all 1/5 portions of a circle of 360 degrees. In long cubits, the number sequence runs 432, 864, 1296, 1728, which are all 1/5 portions of a circle of 2160. This is the length in years of a complete precessional age—the time it takes for the equinoctial sun to traverse one zodiacal house (which in astrology occupies 30 degrees of a 360-degree circle). The length of each side of the pyramid in long cubits, 432, is also 1/60 of a precessional cycle of 25,920 years based on the so-called Great Year or Perfect Year of Plato.[3]

We can go further. The Great Pyramid's surface area in reeds is 5184 (72 × 72), which is exactly 1/5 of a Platonic Great Year of 25,920 years.* Once again there is the inference of a 1/5 progression of a cycle. Why not 1/4, or 1/6, or even 1/2? The answer might well lie in the geometrical division of a solar year. The Babylonians and their ancestors, the Akkadians and Sumerians, originally conceived of a year of 360 days corresponding to a circle fractionalized into 360 parts or degrees. But because a tropical year has 365.2422 days and not 360 days, every 72 days, that is, 1/5 of a 360-day year, an extra day was generated, with each of these five extra days creating their own extra 1/20 of a day, making an additional 1/4 (i.e., 5/20) of a day by the end of the year. Today the need to rectify the appearance of this extra 1/4 day is achieved by the introduction of a leap year every four years.

*The pyramid's angle of ascent is 51°84', which, when written in decimals, is 51.845 degrees, close to a figure of 5184, the fingerprint of the Great Pyramid in reeds.

AN OSIRIAN YEAR

Of undoubted relevance to this debate is the ancient Egyptian legend featuring the divine scribe Thoth, god of the moon. As a favor to Nut, he is said to have won 1/72 part of each day of the year from the moon during a game of checkers, making a total of 5 days (i.e., 1/72 × 365 = ~5 days).[4] These became the 5 so-called intercalary days added at the end of the ancient Egyptians' 360-day calendar, which Nut then used to give birth, one each day, to the gods Osiris, Isis, Set, Nephtys, and Horus the Elder.[5] Also perhaps of importance here is that in legend Osiris is killed by his brother Set with the help of Aso, queen of Ethiopia, and 72 coconspirators.[6] They help Set trap Osiris in a coffin, which is then thrown in the Nile, causing the god's death. Very likely both these stories relate to Osiris's original role as an agricultural deity who experiences death and resurrection on a yearly basis, as well as the proposed former existence of an Osirian year of 360 days, split into 5 seasons of 72 days each, with an additional 5 intercalary days.[7]

A very similar five-phase calendar of ancient origin exists among the Yi or Lolo population of southwest China. This also has 5 seasons of 72 days, each one broken down into two corresponding halves of 36 days, with a further 5–6 New Years' days, making up a complete solar calendar of 365.24 days.[8] The Chinese credit the Yi with inventing not only Taoist philosophy and thought, but also writing. Indeed some Chinese scholars have proposed that the Yi writing system is the oldest in the world, having existed at least 9000 years.[9] They conclude also that the Yi writing system spread westward and southward, where it influenced the intellectual foundation of the three great civilizations of the ancient world—those of Mesopotamia, Vedic India, and ancient Egypt.[10] Although such theories might be dismissed as products of Chinese nationalism, there seems to be an important connection between the Yi peoples and the diffusion of profound cosmological notions into the West. It is a matter we take up in chapter 34.

With these thoughts in mind, we return now to the Giza pyramid field, where we find that a very similar sequence of cosmic numbers can be found in connection with both Giza's underlying geometry and the measurements and proportions of the Second Pyramid.

19

HARMONIC CONVERGENCE

According to the Babylonian writer Berosus (fl. 290–278 BCE) in his lost book the *Babyloniaca,* the Babylonian Great Year was 432,000 terrestrial years long. This length was based on the reigns of the ten antediluvian or pre-flood kings.[1] Each one is named, and the length of their extraordinarily long reigns given. Whether or not these kings existed as real people living in some former epoch of humanity, or they are simply mnemonic devices carrying valuable information regarding long-term time cycles, does not matter. What does matter is that here again we see the use of the number 432. This, as we saw in the last chapter, echoes the fact that the length of each of the sides of the Great Pyramid is ideally 432 long cubits, while the monument's height, exterior dimensions, and ground area all express a proportional representation of the Northern Hemisphere based on a scale of 1:43,200. (The positions of the decimal places and the use of additional zeros are irrelevant; only the base number and its multiples are important.)

SEXAGESIMAL SYSTEM

The significance of the number 432 in solar years is that it is ⅟₆₀ of an ideal precessional cycle of 25,920 years and ⅕ of a precessional age of 2160 years.

Moreover, the reigns of the ten antediluvian kings add up to precisely 120 *saroi* (singular *saros*).* These are long-term time cycles reckoned to be 60 × 60 years in length (60 × 60 = 3600 × 120 = 432,000).[2]

The saroi counting process reflects multiples and fractions of the number 60, from which we derive the division of the circle of 360 degrees (6 × 60 degrees) into degrees, minutes, seconds, as well as the use of hours, minutes, and seconds in the reckoning of time. The invention of the sexagesimal system is accredited to the Babylonians, who rose to power from their principal seat of Babylon in lower Mesopotamia (modern-day lower Iraq), circa 1894 BCE. More likely, however, is that it derived from their territorial forerunners, the Sumerians and Akkadians.[3]

This information is important to our understanding of the Giza pyramid field's underlying geometry, because the equilateral triangle that extends from the datum on Gebel el-Qibli to embrace the peaks of the Great Pyramid and Third Pyramid creates an angle between the two peaks of 60 degrees, or ⅙ of

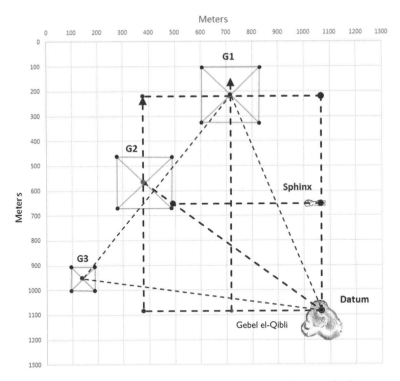

Figure 19.1. Giza's underlying geometry, complete with the equilateral triangle linking the datum on Gebel el-Qibli with the peaks of the Great Pyramid and Third Pyramid.

---

*These saros cycles are not to be confused with the saros eclipse cycle of 18 years, which is featured in chapter 36 of this book.

a circle, something known in the sexagesimal system of the Babylonians as a *sextant*. Apparently a sextant of 60 degrees is relatively easy to create using a simple ruler and compass. Further evidence of the use of the sexagesimal system at Giza is the fact that when viewed from Gebel el-Qibli, the peak of the Second Pyramid lies halfway between the other two pyramids, splitting their 60-degree angle into two equal halves of approximately 30 degrees each (see fig. 19.1).*

The presence of the sexagesimally inspired triangulation in the layout of the three main pyramids at Giza once again offers compelling evidence that the pyramid field adheres to a grand design—one centered squarely on Gebel el-Qibli. It also emphasizes the importance of triangulation in the precision placement of the Giza pyramids and their conformity to the plateau's underlying geometry.

MEANING IN THE GEOMETRY

So are the same sequences of cosmic numbers that are found in connection with the dimensions of the Great Pyramid present also within Giza's underlying geometry? As demonstrated, this ground-based geometry is created by the invisible presence of just two 3-4-5 triangles using a base unit with a length of 5671.5 inches (144.06 meters). This estimated figure is just 1.5 inches out from being exactly 45 reeds or 270 long cubits of 21 inches. Not only does this unit of measure allow us to construct the plateau's base 3-4-5 triangle, but it also makes up the additional sixth unit appended to the northwestern end of the triangle's hypotenuse, its side of 5 units, giving it a combined length of 6⁄5 of its original size. In addition to this, the Giza unit, as we are calling it, forms the exact height of the Second Pyramid, creating a seventh and final extension to the hypotenuse, while 1½ of these units make up the pyramid's base length, creating a base-to-height ratio of 3:2. None of this can have happened by chance alone, meaning that the Second Pyramid is a direct reflection of Giza's underlying geometry based on a unit of 45 reeds or 270 long cubits.

---

*As seen from Gebel el-Qibli, the peak of the Third Pyramid sits at approximately 288 degrees, with the Great Pyramid at 338 degrees. The vertex of the Second Pyramid as viewed from the datum point sits at approximately 306.95 degrees, just over 1 degree out from the halfway point between the other two points.

OCTAGESIMAL SYSTEM

Even beyond this extraordinary revelation is the simple fact that each Giza unit, when added together (e.g., 45, 90, 135, 180, 225, 270), produces ⅛, or 45-degree, increments in the construction of a circle of 360 degrees. So whereas the length of the sides of the Great Pyramid, that is 72 reeds, reflects the progression of a circle of 360 degrees in ⅕ increments, the plateau's underlying geometry creates a progression around a circle in ⅛ increments.

Moving on to 432, the length of the sides of the Great Pyramid in long cubits, and 270, the length of the Giza unit in long cubits, we find that whereas 432 is ⅕ of 2160, a value of 270 is ⅛ of 2160. Consequently, multiples of each figure create a progression around a cycle of 2160 years in steps of ⅕ and ⅛ inclination, respectively, showing a clear 8:5 ratio.

THIRD PYRAMID

Before leaving this matter, it seems pertinent to explore the Third Pyramid, built as a sepulcher for the pharaoh Menkaure sometime around the beginning of the twenty-fifth century BCE. In Giza's underlying geometry, its presence is marked by the southwest corner of the equilateral triangle linking its vertex with the datum on Gebel el-Qibli and the peak of the Great Pyramid. Whereas the base-to-height ratio of the Second Pyramid is 3:2, and that of the Great Pyramid 11:7, the ideal base-to-height ratio of the Third Pyramid is 8:5.[4] This is strangely reminiscent of the fivefold and eightfold progression of the circle found in connection with the Great Pyramid and Second Pyramid. This same 8:5 ratio relationship is expressed in a *reverse* fashion by the lengths of the sides of the Great Pyramid and the Giza unit used in the plateau's underlying geometry, in other words 72 reeds against 45 reeds. In this we see a ratio of 8:5 or, to put it another way, 45 is ⅝ of 72, while 72 is 8⁄5 of 45.

THE SECRET OF PHI

Was there something special about this relationship between the numbers 8 and 5, or, alternately, 5 and 8? I soon discovered the answer—8:5 or 8⁄5 is the closest single-number approximation of ϕ (phi), which has a value of 1.6180339 . . . (henceforth 1.618). Phi is known also as the Divine Proportion, Golden Section, Golden Ratio, or Golden Mean. In contrast, 5:8 as an approximation is the so-called inverse form of the Golden Ratio, a figure calculated at 0.618. However, the two work together in perfect harmony.

Although phi can be used to solve many mathematical problems, one of its primary attributes is that it is the approximate ratio or proportion between each consecutive number making up the Fibonacci sequence—first discovered by Leonardo Bonacci, otherwise known as Fibonacci (circa 1175–1250)—the first 11 numbers of which are 0, 1, 1, 2, 3, 5, 8, 13, 21, 34, 55. So, for instance, if you divide 34 into 55, you get 1.6176 (or approximately ⅗), which is a close approximation to phi. Alternately, if you divide 55 into 34 you get 0.618 (or, approximately ⅝), phi's inverse form. What this means is that, by accident or design, the relationship between the dimensions of the Great Pyramid and both the Second Pyramid and Giza's underlying geometry express the value both of phi (⅗ or 1.618) and its inverse form (⅝ or 0.618).

DIVERGENCE ANGLE

Phi is also found in nature, particularly with respect to the so-called Golden Angle of 137.5 degrees. This occurs naturally in the growth of leaves and florets in some plant species. So as not to be blocked by the shade of an existing leaf, a new leaf ideally appears at around 137.5 degrees away from its predecessor. The next one occurs at 137.5 degrees away from that, and so on and so forth. Similar patterns determined by the so-called divergence angle of 137.5 degrees appear also in spruce cones, pineapples, daisies, and the pattern of seeds in a sunflower head.[5] Phyllotaxis, the study of spirals made by plant growth, can be traced back to the Greek philosopher Theophrastus of Lesbos (371–287 BCE), who alludes to the matter in his work *Enquiry into Plants*.[6] Phyllotaxis is anticipated also by Leonardo da Vinci (1452–1519), who mentions the geometrical patterns made by plants in one of his notebooks.[7] However, the subject of the divergence angle was not properly understood until the first half of the nineteenth century.[8]

In the sexagesimal system, a circle has 360 degrees, and when 137.5 degrees is subtracted from the whole, you are left with 222.5 degrees. Divide 137.5 into 222.5 and you get 1.618, the number of phi. Divide 222.5 into 360 and again you get 1.618, the number of phi. Divide 137.5 into 360 and you get 2.618, phi squared. A 5:8 ratio is the closest single-number approximation to the Golden Angle of 137.5 degrees and its inverse form of 222.5 degrees, which together make a complete circle (see fig. 19.2). So this can also be said to be expressed

GOLDEN ANGLE

222.5°   **137.5°**

Figure 19.2. The division of a circle of 360 degrees into the Golden Angle of 137.5 degrees and its inverse form of 222.5 degrees.

by the relationship between the dimensions of the Great Pyramid and both the Second Pyramid and Giza's underlying geometry.

Now, we have already met with phi in connection with the sixth unit appended to the hypotenuse of the base 3-4-5 triangle in Giza's underlying geometry. When found in the tomb of Rameses IX by Schwaller de Lubicz, it caused him to suspect that the ancient Egyptians knew the value both of phi and pi. As we have seen, 1.2 (that is, ⁶⁄₅) times phi (1.618) squared equals 3.1416408, which is a close approximation of the value of pi. Phi also appears in connection with the measurements of the Great Pyramid. If you divide the pyramid's apothem—the distance from the center of one of its sides to the peak—by half the length of one of its sides, it gives you a figure of 1.618, the mathematical value of phi.*

That phi appears in this way within the design of the Great Pyramid is unlikely to be without meaning. Schwaller de Lubicz would appear to have been correct when he proposed that the ancient Egyptians were not just aware of the value of phi and pi, they saw them as integral to sacred art and architectural design. Thus, through the use of mathematics, geometry, trigonometry, cosmic numbers, and, as we have seen, a profound understanding of astronomy, the ancient Egyptians attempted to lock the Giza pyramids into a harmonic convergence of time, space, and creation in the natural world, which was itself based on the fractionalization of a circle.

---

*The presence of phi in the relationship between the base length of the Great Pyramid and its apothem is best explained using royal cubits (rc) of 20.62 inches (52.375 centimeters) each. If we take the base length of a side as 440 rc, half this would be 220 rc. With the apothem calculated at 356 rc, if 220 rc is divided into 356 rc, we get a figure of 1.61818182, which is a close approximation to the correct value of phi, which is 1.61803399.

From the spiral patterns expressed within nature to the slow precession of the stars of the night sky, everything was once seen to harmonize in a manner that conveyed a perfect relationship with the soul of the universe, something that would only find full expression 2000 years later in the teachings of enlightened spirits such as Pythagoras and Plato. It is their worlds we must now explore to truly comprehend not only the origins, but also the function and purpose of this profound ancient wisdom.

20

MUSIC OF
THE SPHERES

Giza's underlying geometry and its relationship to fractal symmetry, celestial motion, and cyclic precession is extraordinary. It permits us a new insight into the minds of the pyramid builders. The fact also that the cosmic numbers expressed by the Great Pyramid belonged to the same basic canon as that found in the Second Pyramid, as well as other key monuments on the plateau, suggests that nothing here was random. Everything at Giza formed part of a much greater whole, its size, proportion, height, and placement having a definite function and purpose reflected in alignments toward the stars of Cygnus, the celestial bird and womb of the cosmic mother Nut. Here the human soul originated before birth, and returned in death as a shining akh spirit, taking its place among the circumpolar and near circumpolar stars of the northern night sky.

MUSICAL INTERVALS

Yet lingering questions remained, like why did the ancient Egyptians of the Pyramid Age place such a heavy emphasis on 3-4-5 triangles? What might these triangles have meant to them, beyond their obvious role of marking out right-angled tracts of land?

In the book *Beneath the Pyramids* (2009)[1] I speculated that the presence of right-angled triangles on the Giza plateau reflected the ancient Egyptians' deep interest in sound acoustics, intoning, and something that Pythagoras and Plato saw in terms of *musica universalis,* "universal music," or, as it is more popularly known today, the music of the spheres.[2] This was the imagined, inaudible hum or sound created by the perceived mechanical motion of the seven movable "stars" (moon, sun, Mercury, Venus, Mars, Jupiter, and Saturn), as well as that of the so-called fixed stars (those that revolve around the northern celestial pole each night). It was a belief first promoted by the Pythagoreans and later taken up by Plato and his apologists, the Neoplatonists.[3]

Whatever the nature of these inaudible sounds, they had their own science and were thought to be re-created audibly using musical intervals, that is, proportional divisions of a musical scale. Since these intervals remained constant and were thus repeatable, they provided evidence of a mathematical pattern behind the music of the spheres, which could thus be expressed through number, form, and shape. In this manner the spatial harmony expressed by musical intervals could be translated into architecture, art, and, of course, the underlying geometry of sacred and even secular buildings. The importance of this classical science is so important to our understanding of what the pyramid builders were attempting to achieve, and how it relates to both Cygnus and Göbekli Tepe, that it is necessary to provide a brief account of the known origins of the use of musical intervals and the seven-note musical scale devised to define them.

PYTHAGORAS'S REVELATION

Pythagoras is accredited as the first person to recognize the importance of numeric proportions or ratios in music. According to the story, it came about after he passed by a blacksmith's shop and heard the ringing sounds being made by various different types of hammers. What apparently happened next is recorded by Nicomachus of Gerasa (circa 60–120 CE), a Syrian Greek mathematician and Pythagorean, in his treatise titled *The Manual of Harmonics:*

> Elated, therefore, since it was as if his purpose was being divinely accomplished, he [Pythagoras] ran into the smithy and found by various experiments that the difference of sound arose from the weight of the hammers, but not from the force of the blows, nor from the shapes of the hammers, nor from the alteration of the iron being forged. After carefully examining

the weights of the hammers and their impacts, which were identical, he went home.[4]

Thereafter Pythagoras attempted to replicate the effect of the tones made by the hammers. To do this, he suspended four different-sized weights on four identical strings, each of the same material, thickness, and torsion. One weight was set at 6 pounds, a second at 8 pounds, a third at 9 pounds, and a fourth at 12 pounds.[5] The strings were then vibrated in pairs, and when Pythagoras perceived a tone pleasurable to the ear, he decided that he had found a harmonious ratio or proportion. These so-called musical intervals, consonances, or harmonic proportions are as follows:

Weights	Name	Interval	Description
12 lb and 6 lb	Octave	2:1	One full and one half note of an octave
12 lb and 9 lb	Fourth	4:3	4 parts to 3
12 lb and 8 lb	Fifth	3:2	3 parts to 2
9 lb and 8 lb	Tone	9:8	9 parts to 8

The last-mentioned tone, with a ratio of 9:8, was found to be discordant, that is, when played it produced a jarring sound. Yet it becomes essential in calculating the total sum of the intervals, that is, gaps, between the eight notes on a seven-note scale (the eighth note is simply the first note, but with double the frequency or pitch).

Pythagoras re-created the intervals first on a monochord or sonometer, a musical instrument with only one string, so that a movable bridge could be used to produce individual intervals. After that, he replicated the intervals on a lute, which had three strings, as well as on a lyre, which, having seven strings, employs the seven-note musical scale. He also used a set of bronze disks to produce the intervals. All weights were of the same diameter, but each had a varying thickness based on the proportions of the principal musical intervals—the fourth, fifth, and octave, that is 4:3, 3:2, 2:1.

ARCHITECTURAL SPACE AND SOUND

Musical intervals have a clear relationship to both the 3-4-5 triangle and the 3:2 triangle, formed from two 3-4-5 triangles back to back, mirror-fashion, like those in Giza's underlying geometry. This can be shown in the fact that in addition to using four identical strings with weights of varying size to re-create musical intervals, Pythagoras replicated the effect by dividing four strings holding the same-sized weights into different ratios. For the octave, that is, 2:1, he divided one of the strings into two equal parts and played it against a string without any division. For the fifth, that is, 3:2, he took a string and created a division of ⅔ and struck this to produce the interval. For the fourth, that is, 4:3, he took a string and created a division of ¾ and struck this to produce the interval. So each of the divisions of the strings, that is, ½, ⅔, ¾, was an inverse measurement of its interval.

This simple exercise demonstrated to Pythagoras that these proportions have representational lengths when compared against the string used to create the full note. These proportional measurements can be applied to rectilinear forms using triangles with right-angled sides of 2:1, 3:2, and 4:3, each of which, when translated into three-dimensional architecture, will, if designed correctly, produce tonal acoustics that reflect their correct musical intervals.

What this means is that 3-4-5 triangles become essential in re-creating the inferred influence of the 4:3 musical interval, while triangles with a ratio of 3:2 are necessary to create the influence of the perfect fifth. Clearly this is not going to happen if these proportions are in a two-dimensional space, as will have been the case with the underlying geometry of the Giza pyramid field. Here, however, the act would have been more symbolic than practical: the placement of monumental architecture within a set grid plan being seen to harmonize with the cosmic sounds thought to be made by the movement of both the movable and fixed stars.

That such a system of comprehending the inaudible sounds made by the celestial bodies, the so-called music of the spheres, existed at Giza when its pyramid field was created has yet to be proved. However, the presence there of an underlying geometry featuring a 3:2 triangle made from two 4:3 or 3-4-5 triangles placed back-to-back, mirror fashion, hints strongly at a relationship between these ideas and those that first surfaced during the life times of Pythagoras and Plato. Very clearly the 3-4-5 triangles reflect the perfect fourth, with its 4:3 ratio, while the larger 3:2 triangle reflects the influence of the perfect fifth, with its 3:2 ratio. Interestingly, the perfect fifth is the inverse form of the perfect fourth, and vice versa, showing the dual relationship of these intervals.

ORIGINS OF THE MUSICAL SCALE

Pythagoras did not invent the seven-note musical scale or the concept of intervals; he merely rediscovered their importance. Indeed, there is every reason to believe that he expanded his knowledge of these profound subjects after spending time with the astronomer-priests of ancient Egypt. This seems certain from the fact that the ancient Egyptians almost certainly knew of the seven-note musical scale. This can be inferred from the writings of Demetrius of Phaleron (circa 350–280 BCE), an Athenian orator and early librarian at Alexandria. He records that "in Egypt the priests, when singing hymns in praise of the gods, employ the seven vowels, which they utter in due succession; and the sound of these letters is so euphonious that men listen to it in preference to [the] flute and lyre."[6]

Following the demise of dynastic Egypt, this intoning process would seem to have been preserved by the Coptic Christians, who have long been known to use a seven-vowel musical scale in their services.[7] So is it really possible that Pythagoras gained his own knowledge of the seven-note musical scale, and perhaps even his understanding of musical intervals, from the ancient Egyptians? It is time to examine more closely the life of Pythagoras to determine the true nature of the influences responsible for catalyzing the birth of music during the classical age.

21

SECRETS OF THE GODS

Pythagoras is known to have stayed in Egypt for an extended period of time, having arrived during the reign of King Amasis, circa 535 BCE.[1] Once in the country he immediately set about learning "the language of the Egyptians,"[2] and thereafter visited Heliopolis and Memphis,[3] spending time in the company of the temple priests discussing matters such as mathematics and astronomy.

Antonius Diogenes (mid–second century CE), a Greek fiction writer and author of *The Wonders beyond Thule,* writes that from the Egyptians, among others, Pythagoras learned "the exact knowledge of dreams."[4] Diogenes Laertius (fl. third century BCE), a biographer of the Greek philosopher, records that Pythagoras descended "into *aduta* ['crypts'] whilst in Egypt," where he "learned the secrets of the gods."[5] This "descent into underground chambers," presumably under the guidance of Egyptian priests, has led some Pythagorean scholars to propose that Pythagoras underwent "some sort of mystery-initiation."[6] The situation has even been compared with that of a shaman gaining divine insights through contact with the supernatural world:

> In this practice it associates him [Pythagoras] both with other Greek shamans, in particular Epimenides and . . . with Egyptian sorcerers and their crypts.[7]

Interestingly, the original word *aduta* or *adyta,* singular *adyton* (Greek: Ἄδυτον, and Latin, *adytum*), is interpreted here as "crypts." However, it generally translates as "not to be entered,"[8] and refers usually to either "the hidden and secret parts of the temple,"[9] or to its "innermost chambers,"[10] in other words its holy of holies or inner shrine. Yet equally *aduta* can mean "chasms,"[11] as in deep holes or fissures, as well as cave chambers (like those created underground as Mithraea for worship of the god Mithras during the Roman era).[12] This vivid impression of aduta conjures to mind the subterranean chamber of the Great Pyramid, as well as the extensive system of cave chambers entered through Giza's Tomb of the Birds.

The fact that when in northern Egypt Pythagoras visited both Heliopolis and Memphis means that there is no way he can have avoided the Giza pyramids. They are located almost halfway between the two sites, and are clearly visible when traveling along the Nile Valley. It is thus easy to imagine that at least one of the aduta into which Pythagoras descended to learn the "secrets of the gods" was at Giza. Around the time of his visit to Egypt in the sixth century BCE, there was a revival of interest in all things Old Kingdom. The Giza monuments were revered once more. New tombs were constructed, and those of the Fourth Dynasty kings reconsecrated.

PYTHAGORAS IN BABYLON

In 525 BCE Egypt was invaded by the Persians under King Cambyses II. After the decisive battle of Pelusium in the eastern Delta, and the fall of Heliopolis and Memphis, Pythagoras was transported as a prisoner of war to Babylon. Iamblichus of Apamea (242–327 CE), a Syrian Neoplatonist philosopher and author of the *Life of Pythagoras,* tells us that while there Pythagoras "gladly associated with the Magoi [a Persian priestly caste] . . . and was instructed in their sacred rites and learnt about a very mystical worship of the gods. He also reached the acme of perfection in arithmetic and music and the other mathematical sciences taught by the Babylonians."[13]

There is compelling evidence that the Sumerians and Akkadians utilized the seven-note musical scale, called today the heptatonic diatonic system, and made use of musical intervals as early as the third millennium BCE.[14] Thus it seems likely that this was one of the primary sources that provided Pythagoras with his knowledge of "music and the other mathematical sciences," which must have added immeasurably to anything he might have learned when in Egypt.

Pythagoras departed from Babylon in 520 BCE and went first to his home at Samos in Greece. Here he formed a mystery school called the Semicircle before leaving in 518 BCE for Croton (modern Crotone) in southern Italy. Here he founded yet another philosophical and religious school, the inner circle of which was known as the *mathematikoi.* They studied science and mathematics, and saw as their spiritual patrons both Apollo[15] and Orpheus (see below).

THE WORLD SOUL

Certainly there was a close relationship between Pythagoras and Apollo, the former identifying himself with the latter, while the many writings attributed to Orpheus were seen as Pythagoras's principal source of inspiration. Indeed in his *Life of Pythagoras* Iamblichus records that the "writings of Orpheus" contained "the Pythagoric theology according to numbers,"[16] these being the numbers seen as important in the construction of the living universe, something that Plato would come to call the *psychè toû kósmou,* the "Soul of the World," or "World Soul" (Latin, *anima mundi*).[17] This was the creative force behind the animation of the physical universe, including the *musica universalis,* the music of the spheres, the inaudible sounds thought to be made by the celestial bodies.

In his work the *Timaeus,* written circa 355 BCE, Plato offers an arithmetical puzzle to explain the manner in which the World Soul is made known in the mundane world. This is achieved through the presence of numeration in connection with the seven-note musical scale and three specific musical intervals—the perfect fourth (4:3); its inverse form, the perfect fifth (3:2); and a full tone (9:8), which Pythagoras found to be discordant.[18]

As we have seen, two of these musical intervals—the perfect fourth and its inverse form, the perfect fifth—are expressed in the underlying geometry at Giza, and also within the design of the Second Pyramid, suggesting that neither Pythagoras nor Plato was responsible for inventing the concept of the World Soul. It was knowledge that might already have been known to the dynastic Egyptians.

THE SACRED DISCOURSE

So were these musical intervals to be identified with "the Pythagoric theology according to numbers"[19] alluded to by Iamblichus? It is an important question, and one in which the answer might well lie in what Iamblichus tells us is written in the *Sacred Discourse,* a text attributed to Pythagoras, which is no longer extant:

> Orpheus, the son of Calliope, having learnt wisdom from his mother in the mountain Pangæus, said, the eternal essence of number is the most providential principle of the universe, of heaven and earth, and the intermediate nature; and farther still, that it is the root of the permanency of divine natures, of Gods and demons.[20]

After offering these lines from the *Sacred Discourse,* Iamblichus tells us, "From these things, therefore, it is evident that he [Pythagoras] learnt from the Orphic writers that the essence of the Gods is defined by number."[21]

Just who were these "Orphic writers"? Did they come from Egypt, Babylon, Greece, or somewhere else altogether? Syrianus (d. 437 CE), a Greek Neoplatonist philosopher and head of Plato's Academy in Athens, affirms this connection between Orpheus, Pythagoras, and cosmic numbers, writing, "The Pythagoreans received from the theology of Orpheus, the principles of intelligible and intellectual numbers, [and] they assigned them an abundant progression, and extended their dominion as far as to sensibles themselves. Hence that proverb was peculiar to the Pythagoreans, that all things are assimilated to number."[22] (In Platonic terms "sensibles" are those who perceive the world only through the normal senses.)

And there is every reason to conclude that the cosmic numbers outlined in both the writings of Orpheus and in Pythagoras's *Sacred Discourse,* which Iamblichus says contained "the flower of the most mystical place in Orpheus,"[23] related in some manner to the inaudible sounds emitted during the perceived mechanical-like movement of the celestial bodies. These, it was believed, could be replicated audibly through the use of musical intervals. This seems confirmed by Thomas Taylor (1758–1835), the English Neoplatonist, in his translation of *Iamblichus's Life of Pythagoras,* when he writes:

> Pythagoras . . . seems to have said that he heard the celestial harmony, as understanding the harmonic proportions in numbers, of the heavenly bodies, and that which is audible in them. . . . [Moreover, that] to the most ancient and artificially ruling deity, number is the canon, the artificial reason, the intellect also, and the most undeviating balance of the composition and generation of all things.[24]

Simplicius of Cilicia (490–560 CE), one of the last Neoplatonists, also alludes to this matter:

> The Pythagoreans [said] . . . that an harmonic sound was produced from the motion of the celestial bodies, and they scientifically collected this from the analogy of their [musical] intervals; since not only the ratios of the sun and moon, of Venus and Mercury, but also of the other stars, were discovered by them.[25]

So was the "canon" of numbers referred to by Iamblichus simply the ratios and measurements expressed by these musical intervals? Or did it include also the sequences of cosmic numbers found in connection with the measurements of both the Great Pyramid and the Giza pyramid field?

PLATO'S PERFECT YEAR

The exact nature of this canon of cosmic numbers is not made clear in any of the biographies of Pythagoras, or even in the works of Plato. It cannot be coincidence, however, that in Plato's *Timaeus*—the same work that contains Plato's initial account of the lost island continent of Atlantis[26]—the Greek philosopher introduces the concept of the so-called Great Year or Perfect Year almost directly after his mathematical exercise outlining the manner in which musical intervals express the actions of the World Soul within a material existence.[27] This is what he says on the subject:

> None the less, however, can we observe that the perfect number of time fulfils the perfect year at the moment when the relative swiftness of all the eight revolutions accomplish their course together and reach their starting-point, being measured by the circle of the same and uniformly moving. In this way then and for these causes were created all such of the stars as wander through the heavens and turn about therein, in order that this universe may be most like to the perfect and ideal animal by its assimilation to the eternal being.[28]

The mention of "eight revolutions" relates here to the motion of the seven movable stars with the eighth revolution being, presumably, that of all other celestial bodies.[29] If correct, this makes it clear that Plato is referring to the return to their original positions not just of the sun, moon, and planets, but also of the fixed stars as well. This confirms that the World Soul, seen to give both manifestation and motion to the physical universe, was intimately connected with the "perfect number of time" required to compute the length of a Great Year.

THE PERFECT YEAR

The "perfect number" in question is discussed in chapter 37. However, the Perfect Year is thought to have been 25,920 years, the time span of an ideal precessional age, when all the fixed stars return to their original positions in the night sky.[30] Today a complete precessional cycle is thought to be approximately 25,776 years, although the ancient figure is close enough, and, as we shall see, it has important numerical connotations in its own right. If all this is correct, then the number sequences associated with the World Soul's cyclic animation of the physical universe, as perceived through the rotation of the movable and fixed stars and the manifestation of musical intervals, must relate to the canon of numbers expressed in the measurements of the Great Pyramid and in Giza's underlying geometry. We speak here of 45, 72, 216, 270, 432, 1728, 2160, 5184, and so on, all of which are whole-number fractionizations of 25,920.

Thus we can see that every aspect of the Pythagorean doctrine regarding celestial harmonies is reflected in the measurements of the Great Pyramid and the underlying geometry at Giza. The latter's use of 3-4-5 triangles adequately reflects the influence of two specific musical intervals—the perfect fourth (4:3) and its inverse form, the perfect fifth (3:2)—in a manner that tells us that behind the pyramid field's grand design is a very ancient science of number cosmology associated both with sound acoustics and astronomical precession.

Despite everything that Pythagoras either discovered himself or learned from the priests of ancient Egypt and Babylon, it was from the writings of Orpheus, as laid down by the "Orphic writers," that he would find confirmation of the "harmonic sound . . . produced from the motion of the celestial bodies." Plato, a follower of Pythagoras's teachings, showed that these same musical intervals were associated with not only the celestial harmonies, but also with the motion of the fixed stars across the Perfect Year or Great Year, in other words one complete precessional cycle of 25,920 years. Furthermore, Plato attempted to convey his conviction that all these ideas were simply manifestations of the *psychè toû kósmou*, the Soul of the World, the animating force of the universe.

Did this profound mathematical and cosmological knowledge come originally from a single ancient source? Pythagoras tells us it originated with Orpheus. But who exactly was Orpheus, and how did this mythical character of Greek legend become the principal source of knowledge regarding the music of the spheres and the attainment of enlightenment through divine inspiration? As we see next, understanding Orpheus's relationship to his divine father, the god Apollo, and his mother, the Muse Calliope, provides us with a much earlier source for the seven-note musical scale and its relationship to the stars.

22

CELESTIAL SWAN SONG

Orpheus was a celebrated musician and poet of the mythical age, who came to prominence in Greek literature sometime around the beginning of the sixth century BCE.[*1] Apollo, god of music and poetry, is said to have been his father. It was he who gave Orpheus his celebrated golden lyre, which had seven strings corresponding to the seven-note musical scale. Apollo taught Orpheus how to play the lyre, while his mother, Calliope, instructed him on how to create song and verse. Orpheus's sweet song and music enchanted nature itself, taming wild animals and bringing rocks and trees to life (see plate 20). His musical charms were so persuasive that they even caused Hades, the king of the dead, to release Orpheus's wife, Eurydice, from the underworld.

Calliope was the eldest and the foremost of the Muses, the nine daughters of the Titaness Mnemosyne, goddess of memory. The Muses (Greek *Moûsai*) were nymphs who inspired creativity and inspiration in mortal kind. Each one presided over a different aspect of the liberal arts and sciences, including

---

*This is *onomáklyton Orphéa,* "Orpheus famous of name," which features in a fragment of text by Ibycus, a poet of the sixth century BCE. What this indicates is that even by this time Orpheus was a popular character in Greek tradition.

music, poetry, song, and dance. (In fact, the English words *music, museum, amuse,* and so on, all come from *Moûsa* via the Greek *mousiké* and the Latin *musica.*) Calliope herself is said to have inspired epic poetry and rhetoric (the art of effective or persuasive speaking or writing). Her name means "beautiful-voiced," from the Greek καλός (*kalós*), "beauty," and ὄψ (*ops*), "voice," showing her own connection with vocalized music. The epic poet Homer is said to have beseeched Calliope to inspire him while writing the *Iliad* and the *Odyssey,* which is why she is often shown holding laurels in one hand and the two Homeric poems in the other.

Orpheus's doctrine on the transmigration of the soul, shared by Orphites and Pythagoreans alike, was gained apparently during his travels to Egypt.[2] According to legend, Orpheus's soul was transformed upon death into a swan so that he might never again be carried by a woman: a reference to his demise at the hands of the Maenads, the frenzied followers of Bacchus-Dionysus.[3] In order to be near his beloved lyre, which following his death had become the constellation of Lyra,[4] Orpheus's soul was elevated into the heavens, where it became the neighboring constellation of Cygnus, the celestial swan.[5]

HEAVENLY LYRE

Some versions of Orpheus's translation say that the Muses "grac'd his lyre with nine stars,"[6] presumably because they were seen as the source of divinely inspired music, song, and dance. Which stars might have been meant by this statement is not made clear. It could refer to the seven planets, with the eighth and/or ninth stars being a reference to the Milky Way and the starry vault as a whole. In the knowledge, however, that in some parts of Greece there were only three Muses,[7] and not nine, there is every chance that the nine stars included the three bright stars making up the Summer Triangle—Deneb in Cygnus, Vega in Lyra, and Altair in Aquila. This conclusion is strengthened in the knowledge that the lyre, which in classical times looked like a letter *U* strung with strings, was originally triangular in shape. Orphic scholar Johann Gesner first made this observation in 1764 following the discovery of a relief among the ruins of Herculaneum in Italy showing an archaic form of the lyre.[8] This would make it similar in appearance to the harp, the stringed instrument used extensively in western Europe. However, the oldest depictions of triangular harps come not from Europe, but from Egypt, where they appear on the walls of tombs as early as 2500 BCE.[9]

BIRDS OF THE MUSES

Swans were "the birds of the Muses," in which form they sang seven songs as they circled seven times around the island of Delos at the birth of Apollo.[10] Through his own association with the Muses, Apollo's totem also became the swan. It was Zeus, Apollo's father, who gave him his famous lyre, which had been carved from tortoiseshell by the god Hermes. At the same time Zeus presented his son with a heavenly car driven by swans, the reason why in Greek art Apollo is shown either riding on the back of a swan or in a chariot pulled by swans (see plate 21).

Figure 22.1. *The Singing Swan,* a woodcut by Reinier van Persijn (circa 1655), expressing the close relationship between the swan and musical melody.

Thus the swan becomes the clear connection between the Muses, Apollo, and Orpheus. All are in turn associated, like the bird itself, with music, song, and dance—important elements of the shamanic tradition. The powerful connection between swans and music is further brought out in an account by the poet Callimachus (310–240 BCE), who writes about the nine swans that circled Delos when Leto, the daughter of the Titans, gave birth to Apollo:

> Now the swans, Apollo's future companions, most musical of birds, birds of the Muses, leaving behind Maionian Paktolos [a river in southwest Asia Minor], flew in circles seven times around Delos (later the child god strung his lyre with seven strings, to match the seven songs they sang wheeling overhead).[11]

Thus in Callimachus's time swans were considered the "most musical of birds," which was why they were the animistic totems of the Muses, who were seen as the source of divine or poetic inspiration (see fig. 22.1). Yet Callimachus emphasizes a direct connection between the nine swans circling Delos seven times, the seven songs they sang as they made their perambulations, and the decision to give the lyre seven strings.

MUSIC OF THE SEVEN STRINGS

We learn from the Athenian tragedian Euripides (circa 480–406 BCE) in his play *Ion* that Apollo's lyre "is itself attuned to the song of the swan,"[12] suggesting that this was significant in some manner. Moreover, the philosopher Macrobius (fl. 390–430 CE) tells us that "Apollo's lyre of seven strings provides understanding of the motions of all the celestial spheres over which nature has set the Sun as the moderator."[13] Thus the connection of the lyre of Apollo with the songs of the nine swans shows the relationship between the symbol of the swan, the source of the music of the spheres, and through this their audible manifestation using the seven note musical scale. This, of course, was the cosmic philosophy regarding the animation of the universe favored by Pythagoras and Plato, and explained by the latter as the intervention of the *psychè toû kósmou,* the World Soul. So was the swan in fact an expression or vehicle of the World Soul?

PYTHAGORAS,
SOCRATES, AND PLATO

Pythagoras, we are told, had much to say about swans, stating that "their souls were immortal, and how before their death, they rejoice and sing as going to a better life."[14] Various classical writers attested to this death song of the swan, from which we derive the term *swan song*. According to Plato, Socrates (471–399 BCE), who is accredited with the foundation of Western philosophy, likened himself just before his execution to "the swan that sings beautifully before it dies."[15]

Socrates is also said to have experienced a dream in which a cygnet (young swan) appeared out of nowhere. It emerged from his chest and settled on his lap, quickly transforming into a full-fledged swan. It then "flew forth into the open sky uttering a song that charmed all hearers."[16] The next day Socrates met Plato, who would become his star pupil and ultimately his biographer. What Plato would go on to write about Socrates would be enough to immortalize his mentor forever. The probable meaning of this anecdote is that the swan symbolized Plato's eternal soul coming forth from Socrates.

In actuality swans do not emit any unusual sounds at the moment of death. Their connection with death is clearly that of psychopomp, accompanying the soul from one world to the next, while at the same time acting as a symbol of the person's higher self, through which divine inspiration was presumably thought to flow. This connection is reinforced by the knowledge that the swan was a symbol of Cygnus, which was associated not just with Orpheus, whose soul became a swan in death, but also with the harmonies produced by his seven-stringed lyre and the very inspiration of the Muses themselves.

So was this the source of Pythagoras's inspiration regarding "harmonic sound . . . produced from the motion of the celestial bodies," which he said was given to him by the "Orphic writers," that is those who promulgated the divine philosophy of Orpheus? Did they preserve knowledge of the importance of Cygnus as a symbol not only of Orpheus and the World Soul in the form of a swan, but also as the inspiration behind the Music of the Spheres? Did they understand also the clear relationship between the music of the spheres and the construction of monumental architecture using divine harmonies and musical intervals? As we have seen, these profound cosmological notions appear to have been incorporated into the design and measurements of the Great Pyramid and Giza's underlying geometry, both of which seem to reflect a profound interest in the stars of Cygnus. What is more, these same ideas, carried across time by Pythagoras's unknown Orphic writers, are, as we see next, found also in connection with key enclosures at Göbekli Tepe.

23

SONIC TEMPLES

While writing my book *Göbekli Tepe: Genesis of the Gods* (2014), I had noted something curious about the ellipsoid shape of the most accomplished enclosures at Göbekli Tepe. The length-to-breadth ratios of Enclosures B, C, and D, as well as the outline in the bedrock of the now-vanished Enclosure E, all seemed to be more or less identical regardless of their individual dimensions. Using the external measurements of the installations, I worked out that this ratio was approximately 5:4 in proportion; in other words the width of each enclosure was ⅘ the size of its length.[1] This finding led me to propose that the Göbekli builders might have had "a basic understanding of cosmic harmony and proportion."[2]

LION PILLARS BUILDING REVISITED

Fast forward to March 2016, and as I was writing the section in this book on Göbekli Tepe's Lion Pillars Building (see chapter 6) I noticed something potentially significant about its length-to-breadth ratio. Its east-west walls could be divided into four parts, while its north-south walls divided exactly into three parts, which, if correct, would mean that its ground plan was composed of two 3-4-5 triangles placed together to create a rectangle. I asked Rodney Hale to investigate the matter on my behalf. Using an available survey plan of the installation, Hale was easily able to confirm that the Lion

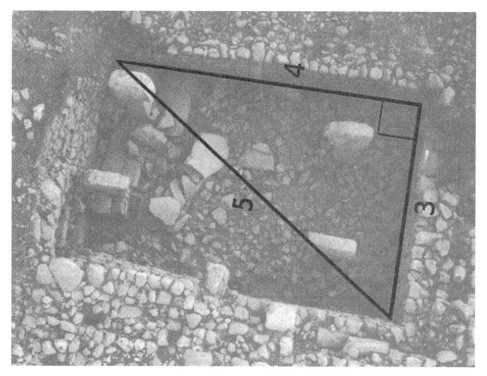

Figure 23.1. Göbekli Tepe's Lion Pillars Building, showing its 4:3 length-to-width ratio.

Pillars Building's ground plan adequately expressed a 4:3 length-to-width ratio (see fig. 23.1).

The implications of this finding were enormous, as it hinted at the builders' deliberate choice to use a specific ratio or proportion, arguably in the knowledge that it had a practical function. Was it to fine-tune the structure's acoustics to produce a sound quality featuring a 4:3 musical interval, in other words a perfect fourth?

Such speculation could not hold weight without further confirmation that the Göbekli Tepe builders were indeed familiar with the concept of enhancing the acoustic properties of architectural features. This proposition made me look again at the larger, and much older, ellipsoid structures at Göbekli Tepe. Even though I had previously determined an approximate 5:4 ratio in the length-to-breadth dimensions of various enclosures, I now looked at their basic shape. My initial observations had been based on the approximate size of their exterior boundary walls. This time I focused on the internal dimensions of their ringwalls, within which the T-shaped pillars had stood. Only these would be able to tell me anything about the enclosures' acoustic properties.

ENCLOSURE D RATIOS

I looked first at Enclosure D, correlating its layout with an ellipse that was 4 parts in length across its long axis and 3 parts across its short axis. (An ellipse is an oval with two symmetrical axes.) The match worked well enough for me to ask Rodney Hale to check my findings. Using an available survey plan, he applied a 4:3 ellipse grid to the structure's interior ringwall. It matched almost perfectly.

Not only did this show that Enclosure D's internal structure bore an internal length-to-breadth ratio of 4:3, but it also meant that its nearly perfect ellipsoid form could contain a diamond consisting of four 4:3 triangles or two 3:2 triangles. This meant that the underlying geometry of Giza was present also within Göbekli Tepe's oldest and most accomplished installation. More incredibly, the center line of the ellipse marking its short axis corresponded very well with the line of sight between the central area of the twin central pillars and the circular aperture of the porthole stone standing in the north-northwestern section of its ringwall. It was almost as if a 4:3-ratio ellipse had been used as the blueprint for the layout of the enclosure.

Hale made another astute observation while examining the ellipse grid's relationship to its internal structure. Seeing that the ellipse's focus points, in other words the centers of its lengthwise curves, were slightly off from matching the positions of the installation's twin central monoliths, he had a sudden moment of insight. The twin focus points of a 4:3 ellipse, he realized, were located at approximately 2.65 units along the length of the enclosure's 4-unit-long axis. This value was so close to two-thirds of a whole that he now decided to divide the ellipse's long axis into 3 equal parts. Looking again at Enclosure D's twin central pillars, he saw that they fell exactly upon the ⅓ and ⅔ divisions of its long axis (see fig. 23.2).[3] This hardly seemed a coincidence, and indicated that there really was some kind of underlying geometry behind the design of the installation, which involved the use of an ellipse with a 4:3 ratio.

ENCLOSURE C REEXAMINED

Hale now applied a 4:3 ellipse grid to Enclosure D's closest neighbor, Enclosure C, to see if this too conformed to the same geometric principles. The inner ringwall, he found, created to reduce the overall size of the structure, was almost a perfect 4:3 ellipse, and when a larger 4:3 ellipse was applied to the

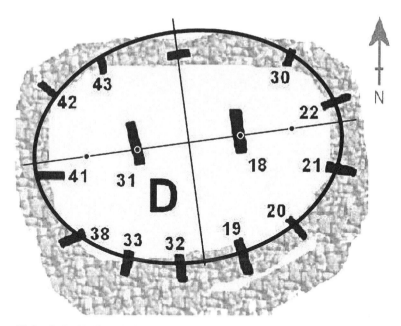

Figure 23.2. Göbekli Tepe's Enclosure D, overlaid with a 4:3-ratio ellipse showing lines of orientation. Note how the one-third divisions of the long axis match the positions of the central pillars, while the main center line corresponds to the angle and position of the aperture in the porthole stone.

outer ringwall, the center line across its short axis matched the original position of the porthole stone and lined up with the positions of the twin central monoliths (see fig. 23.3).

With a pattern emerging, Hale examined further enclosures at Göbekli Tepe to see whether a similar pattern might be found. The outline of Enclosure E easily fitted the 4:3-ratio ellipse grid, its center line of 3 parts accurately reflecting the center line of the two rock-cut pedestals that once supported the structure's twin central pillars.

In contrast, Enclosures A, B, and F do not appear to be good matches to the ellipse grid, at least not according to an examination of the T-pillars remaining today.

ENCLOSURE H REVISITED

The final structure checked was Enclosure H, the most recent installation to be uncovered at the site. Hale found that the positions of the eight T-pillars revealed so far conform to the general shape of the 4:3-ratio ellipse grid, its

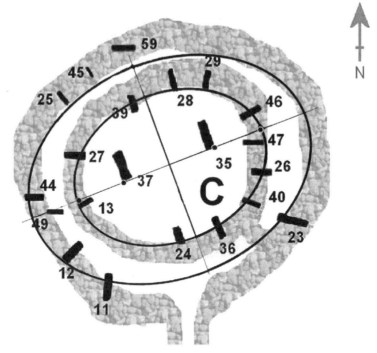

Figure 23.3. Göbekli Tepe's Enclosure C, overlaid with two 4:3-ratio ellipses. One embraces its outer ringwall of T-pillars and the other, its inner ringwall. Note how in both cases the short axis targets the former position of the porthole stone (Pillar 59).

short axis corresponding pretty well to the position of the porthole stone (see fig. 23.4). This now meant that three of the oldest and most sophisticated enclosures found to date at Göbekli Tepe—Enclosures C, D, and H—possess a basic 4:3-ratio elliptical ground plan that incorporates the aperture of their individual porthole stones, and in the case of Enclosures C and D their twin central monoliths as well. Thus, with the Lion Pillars Building's rectilinear ground plan also reflecting a 4:3 ratio, there was every reason to conclude that this apparent interest at Göbekli Tepe in 4:3-ratio triangles, ellipses, and rectangles was purposeful and meaningful.

OPTIMIZING ACOUSTICS

What might the builders at Göbekli Tepe have been attempting to achieve in creating structures with these ratios? One possible answer is offered by present-day engineering for optimizing sound acoustics in theaters. In this handbook on the methodology and mathematics of building construction we read:

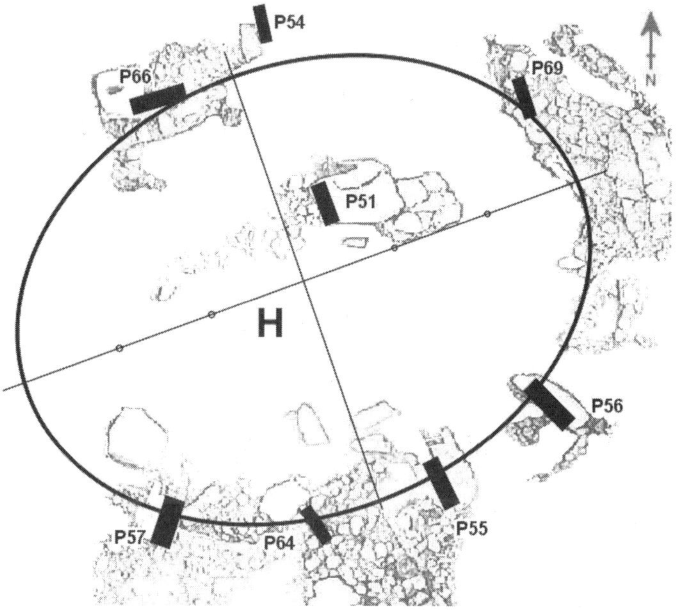

Figure 23.4. Göbekli Tepe's Enclosure H overlaid with a 4:3-ratio ellipse. This comparison is tentative only, as the installation remains half excavated.

From a series of experiments it has been found that a sound which can be heard at a distance of 3.5 meters in front of the speaker is heard at a distance of 2.5 meters on both sides. . . . Hence, remembering this fact the seat of the speaker should be judiciously selected. Consequently, the seats should be arranged such that they are along the circumference of an ellipse with the semimajor and semiminor axes ratio as 4:3.[4]

These might well have been the written instructions given to those constructing Enclosure D. The installation is built to very similar specifications, with the position of the "speaker," arguably an officiating priest or shaman, being between the twin central pillars. This suggests that the enclosure was built to ensure that celebrants entering the structure for rites and ceremonies experienced optimum acoustics.

The "seats" at Göbekli Tepe would have been defined by the positions of the T-pillars and stone benches incorporated into the ringwalls. Their location, close to the circumference of the ellipse, would not only have enabled celebrants seated on the benches to experience the best possible sound quality, but would also have optimized tonal acoustics in the form of a musical interval with a 4:3 ratio, in other words a perfect fourth.

VENUES FOR PERFORMANCES

Suggesting that Göbekli Tepe's stone enclosures were optimized for acoustics is not something new to this field. Archaeologist and archaeoacoustics expert Alexis McBride of the University of Liverpool proposed such a concept as far back as 2014:

> The larger structures at Nevalı Çori and Göbekli Tepe were perhaps more likely used as venues for performances, with participants in the middle speaking or performing an activity, while those around the perimeter watched and listened. . . . This analysis of acoustics highlights how important performance might have been within the larger structures.

With regard to what might have been going on at the center of the largest structures, such as Enclosures C , D and H, McBride speculated that this could demonstrate "the existence of specialist ritual practitioners; or the space may have been more fluid with many different participants taking a turn in the centre of the structure in a community-in-council model; or perhaps these structures were venues for elaborate dramatic performances with many different performers and activities taking place at once."[5]

McBride urges that further research be done into this subject, including on-site acoustic testing, and I could not agree more with her observations. It is easy to see the origins of the ritual buildings and theaters of the classical age deriving from cult buildings like those built at Göbekli Tepe in the Neolithic age. They would appear to have been constructed with the express purpose of carrying sound from a central position to an audience seated or standing around its outer edges. The instructions given to the architects and engineers behind these projects would have been very similar to those offered today for optimizing sound acoustics, and this, as we have seen, includes the utilization of the 4:3 ellipse, which would induce the tonal presence of the 4:3 musical interval, that is, the perfect fourth, as well as its inverse form, the perfect fifth, with its 3:2 or double 4:3 ratio.

THE INFLUENCE OF CYGNUS

Even though Göbekli Tepe's Lion Pillars Building was aligned east toward the rising sun at the time of the equinoxes, three older elliptical installations at the site—Enclosures C, D, and H—were aligned via their porthole stone apertures and twin central monoliths toward the setting of the Cygnus star Deneb during the epoch of their construction. So in the knowledge that in the case of Enclosures C and D at least, the porthole stone's aperture synchronizes with the enclosure's 4:3-ratio-inspired elliptical design, does this suggest that the Göbekli builders saw the influence of Cygnus as important in the production of the correct sound acoustics? Were the sounds generated inside the installations seen as in some way representative of the connection with Cygnus?

The fact that the swan—the form of Cygnus identified in ancient Greek astronomy with, among others, Orpheus, the son of Apollo, god of music and poetry—would appear to have symbolized the celestial influence of the Music of the Spheres and through this the influence of the nine Muses, would tend to indicate that this was indeed the case. If correct, then there is every chance that the close association between Cygnus and the generation of sound acoustics through the use of dimensional space and shape was carried from the Pre-Pottery Neolithic world of Anatolia into Egypt's Nile Valley at a very early date. Did this knowledge linger here through to the dynastic age? Was it later utilized in the design and construction of the three main pyramids at Giza? Here, as we have seen, are alignments toward the setting of the stars of Cygnus, along with the use of musical intervals in the creation of the pyramid field's underlying geometry.

As we shall see next, very similar acoustic optimization appears to have been incorporated into the design of megalithic chambered tombs in southwest England many thousands of years after the abandonment of Göbekli Tepe and the spread of the Neolithic revolution westward from Anatolia into Europe. What is more, we find it linked once again with alignments toward the bright star Deneb.

24

SHAPING SOUND

British archaeological researcher, writer, and musician Steve Marshall has made a detailed study of the acoustic properties of Neolithic long barrows in southwest England.[1] These are stone-built structures, usually rectilinear in shape, that incorporate entrance corridors leading into individual side chambers. Long barrows were constructed during the earliest phases of the Neolithic in Britain, circa 4000–3500 BCE. Marshall's principal site of investigation was the West Kennet long barrow, located in the Avebury ritual landscape around 26 kilometers north-northeast of Stonehenge.

The barrow's orientation is almost precisely east-west. It consists of a long entrance corridor with two side chambers on either side and a hemispherical chamber at its western end. Different tests were conducted inside the various parts of the megalithic structure across an extended period. These determined that the first pair of side chambers, at the monument's eastern end, resonated at approximately 84 Hz, which is around the low note E2, while the more westerly pair of chambers resonated at about 110 Hz, which is the note A2.[2] Together these two notes produced a perfect fourth musical interval, in other words a pitch ratio of 4:3.[3] These findings were significant in themselves. Their importance to our own study, however, is that the creation of this musical interval was emphasized by the 4:3 ratio of the *shape* of the corresponding chambers.

Marshall has pointed out that as early as 1962, British archaeologist Stuart Piggott (1910–1996), who excavated the West Kennet barrow in 1955–1956, observed that "it is clear that some kind of a regular plan was envisaged [in the monument's construction], presumably to definite units of measurement and with a knowledge of ratios."[4] This prompted Marshall to comment: "Piggott may not have been thinking of audible ratios, but it is conceivable that the 4:3 ratio was recognized by the tomb builders and perhaps regarded with significance."[5]

Of even closer relevance to this debate is that archaeoastronomer Professor John North conducted a detailed study of the orientation of the various key components making up the West Kennet long barrow, looking for possible astronomical alignments. In his important work titled *Stonehenge: Neolithic Man and the Cosmos* (1996/2007) he wrote that two of its chambers, Z and Y, the easternmost and westernmost compartments on the barrow's northern side, were each aligned to the setting of the Cygnus star Deneb.[6]

Both chambers feature in the generation of the perfect fourth musical interval discovered by Steve Marshall, showing once again a link between sound acoustics and the influence of the stars of Cygnus, something we have seen already at Göbekli Tepe in Anatolia and also at Giza in Egypt. Even though the alignment of the chambers toward Deneb could not have been seen once the long barrow was covered over with stone and earth, they might well have acted on a symbolic level, allowing the influence of the Cygnus constellation to permeate inside the individual compartments, especially when being used to create the 4:3 musical interval.

Marshall went on to examine the acoustics of several other long barrows in the southwest of England. These too showed a 4:3 ratio in their design.[7] Among the examples studied were Stoney Littleton in Gloucestershire, which revealed that the ratio of its chambers was exactly 4:3 (4.4 meters and 3.3 meters respectively), and also the Luckington barrow in neighboring Wiltshire. Although this was devoid of an entrance corridor, it possessed side chambers showing that "two of their lengths were again proportioned 4:3."[8] This was enough for Marshall to realize the importance of both the 4:3 musical interval and sound acoustics in general in the creation of Neolithic stone chambers during the Neolithic age.

INFRASOUND

Steve Marshall went on to conduct various other sound-related experiments at the West Kennet long barrow and found that its central east-west passage had a low resonance of less than 20 Hz, later refined to 8–9 Hz after further tests and a series of mathematical calculations. These are frequencies below the normal range of human hearing and so are classified as infrasound, which is known to induce strange effects on the human senses, including fear, tension, and anxiety. All of these effects could be produced through sound tests conducted both inside the monument and immediately outside in front of its megalithic façade. Infrasound is also known to induce a sense of presence (the feeling that you are not alone), and also altered states of consciousness, which, when combined, can lead to the belief that entering such structures made it possible to connect with the spirit world.

BLACK CIRCLES AND IMAGINARY PASSAGES

One test conducted with a young, enthusiastic "initiate," a fourteen-year-old boy, inside the West Kennet long barrow's central corridor induced infrasound by means of a miniature bass drum hit loudly with sticks by a skilled drummer positioned immediately outside the monument. What transpired is of extreme interest, for as Marshall records:

> The boy later reported that with eyes open, he could just make out the end stones of the W chamber, which at first appeared to be moving slightly. On one stone of the back wall a small black circle appeared, which grew in size; it took on the appearance of a passage leading to another chamber, which he thought he could see into. He then continued to listen with eyes closed and was convinced that on two occasions someone had joined him [in] the chamber, but he had been entirely alone.[9]

The appearance of the "black circle" that became an imaginary passage leading out of the long barrow reminds us of the soul-hole apertures in the porthole stones at Göbekli Tepe. These were almost certainly physical representations of the same type of opening experienced by the youth. Such passages were most likely thought to act as portals between the world of the living and the realm of spirit.

Clearly the shape and design of the West Kennet long barrow, as well as that of the various other megalithic structures examined by Marshall and his colleagues, show that the Neolithic peoples who reached western Europe circa 5000–4000 BCE, and Britain circa 4000–3500 BCE, were carrying with them an advanced knowledge not only of sound acoustics, but also of how to utilize musical intervals in architectural design. Almost certainly the purpose for establishing tonal resonances that reflected the musical intervals, most obviously the perfect fourth, was to create environments where the mind might more easily enter altered states of consciousness, aided by the use of everything from drumbeats to dancing, singing, chanting, sensory deprivation, fasting, and the use of herbal and fungal hallucinogens.

That the megalithic builders of western Europe possessed an acute knowledge of sound acoustics does not seem in question. What *is* in question, however, is where exactly this knowledge might have come from. Most likely it derived from a much earlier age, and originated among the Upper Paleolithic societies that used cave environments through till the end of the last ice age, circa 9600 BCE. Thereafter it was inherited by the Pre-Pottery Neolithic communities at places like Göbekli Tepe, being spread out from there following the Neolithic revolution. Did this knowledge enter western Europe with the spread of agriculture and animal husbandry, and was it carried eventually to Britain, where it was used in the construction of Neolithic stone chambers, circa 4000–3500 BCE? If so, then where else was it carried? Where else can we find Neolithic architectural structures displaying clear evidence of acoustic enhancement?

HOUSE OF AUROCHS

To answer this question, Rodney Hale examined cult buildings at various sites in the Near East that might have been influenced by the spread of knowledge from places like Göbekli Tepe to see if a pattern might emerge. For instance, at the Pre-Pottery Neolithic site of Jerf el-Ahmar in northern Syria, his eyes fell on an elliptical building uncovered by French archaeologist Danielle Stordeur

Figure 24.1. Jerf el-Ahmar's House of Aurochs, overlaid with a 4:3-ratio ellipse.

and her team during excavations at the site in the 1990s. A bucrania of aurochs were found to have been set into the structure's curvilinear wall, making it clear that this was a communal room, most likely used for ritual as well as secular functions. Hale applied a 4:3-ratio ellipse grid to the ground plan, and it fitted perfectly (see fig. 24.1). Other buildings were more rounded and did not fit the same profile, although the precise manner in which the 4:3 ellipse matched the ground plan of the House of Aurochs, as it is known, appears beyond simple coincidence. Its 4:3-proportioned layout would have permitted it a sound quality expressing a perfect fourth musical interval.

THE WALLS OF JERICHO

Farther south, Hale looked at the Pre-Pottery Neolithic site of Tell es-Sultan, located on the west side of the Jordan Valley. This was the location of the legendary city of Jericho during the Bronze Age, its walls brought down, according to Old Testament tradition, by the sound of trumpets. Tell es-Sultan was occupied from the Natufian period, circa 10,000 BCE, through to the Bronze Age and beyond. Here Hale found a good example of a rectilinear structure of Pre-Pottery Neolithic age that fitted the 4:3 grid plan very well. Once again, this choice of proportion is unlikely to have been random, and no doubt was used to optimize the transpersonal effects of singing, chanting, intoning, and arguably even ecstatic dancing.

Other Pre-Pottery Neolithic sites in the Levant almost certainly possess either elliptical or rectilinear structures with the all-important 4:3-ratio ground plan. Further research is needed into this area of study. Yet we can see a trend emerging, beginning during the Pre-Pottery Neolithic A period with the construction of elliptical enclosures bearing a 4:3 ratio. The same proportions were incorporated into rectilinear structures from the Pre-Pottery Neolithic B period onward, both in Anatolia and as far afield as southwest England during the fourth millennium BCE. Very likely it was a wave of activity that spread outward from Anatolia in all directions, including south through the Levant, until eventually it entered northeast Africa and Egypt's Nile Valley in particular.

ENTRY INTO EGYPT

Other than the presence of buildings displaying a clear 4:3 ratio in their design and construction, there is one thing that all the above sites—Göbekli Tepe,

Jerf el-Ahmar, and Tell es-Sultan—have in common, and this is the Helwan point. Examples have been found at every one of these locations,[10] showing a trend that almost certainly began in southeast Anatolia and spread very rapidly southward through the Levant. As we saw in chapters 9 and 10, this very specific type of projectile point probably appears at Helwan no later than circa 8500–7800 BCE. More significantly, the presence at Helwan of high-quality stone tools and points, some of which were fashioned from exotic materials such as rock crystal, implies that those who carried these high-status items may not have been indigenous to the area. If this is correct, they may have been members of a nomadic elite—shamans, priests, and even traders—who entered Helwan only occasionally, having arrived from the southern Levant via key sites such Tell es-Sultan in the Jordan Valley, Beidha in Jordan, and various post-Harifian sites in the Egyptian Sinai and the Negev region of Israel.[11]

This is certainly plausible. Yet it is also possible that at least some of the visitors to Helwan came from farther afield, having originated at places like Göbekli Tepe and Jerf el-Ahmar. Did they bring with them not only the Helwan point, but also a profound knowledge of the use of sound acoustics in architectural design? Was it these individuals who carried with them a knowledge of the importance of the stars of Cygnus, and their connection with both the music of the spheres and what Plato would come to call the *psychè toû kósmou,* the World Soul? Were these individuals the forerunners to the unnamed Orphic writers who informed Pythagoras "that the essence of the Gods is defined by number"? Was this the knowledge that would one day inspire the layout and design of the Giza pyramid field?

Having been engulfed in recent years by an ever-expanding industrial complex, Helwan might not be ready to impart its secrets from the past anytime soon. Today many, if not all, the major sites where in the late nineteenth and early twentieth centuries thousands of flint tools were picked up by Europeans have now been destroyed, their value to archaeology lost forever. There is, however, another way of trying to understand Helwan's role in the birth of ancient Egypt, and for this we must now return to Giza, where during the spring of 2016 further developments were about to unfold.

PART FIVE

GENESIS POINT

25

THE ROAD TO HELWAN

Adirect relationship between Giza's underlying geometry and geometric proportions based on a profound knowledge of musical intervals now seemed inescapable. Moreover, there was every reason to suppose that this knowledge entered the Nile Valley during the Early Pre-Pottery Neolithic B period, circa 8800–7600 BCE. This in turn had been influenced by the spread of new technologies from Göbekli Tepe.

Shortly after all these ideas had emerged in March 2016, another inspired suggestion from my colleague Richard Ward (in April 2016) led to a fresh insight in understanding not only the extent of Giza's underlying geometry and its astronomical alignments, but also its potential point of origin. We knew already that the hypotenuse line created by the base 3-4-5 triangle, when projected southeastward, coincided with the center of the arc circle created by the placement of the three main pyramids of Giza. Extending this line still farther brought you to the position just over 2.9 kilometers from the Second Pyramid, where the three wing stars of Cygnus—Gienah, Sadr, and Rukh—could have been seen setting, one after the after, into the peaks of the Third Pyramid, Second Pyramid, and Great Pyramid, respectively, circa 2550–2479 BCE. Yet what if the already established triangulation at Giza was to be extended southeastward? Would it conform to a much larger geometry embracing key sites in the vicinity of Memphis, the capital of Upper and Lower Egypt following the unification of the country's two lands at the beginning of dynastic history?

EXTENDING GIZA'S UNDERLYING GEOMETRY

Clearly such an undertaking would require a great deal of trial and error. After I initially tried to extend the base 3-4-5 triangle southeastward without much success, a new idea came to me. Instead of using a 3-4-5 triangle, why not try an equilateral triangle, like the example embracing the datum on Gebel el-Qibli and the peaks of the Great Pyramid and Third Pyramid?

This exercise showed that creating an equilateral triangle with one point on the peak of the Second Pyramid and another on the peak of the so-called Red Pyramid at Dahshur allowed the third point to fall on an elevated location immediately above the northernmost quarries of Gebel Tura. It was from here that the high-quality Tura limestone came from that was used during the Old Kingdom in the construction of the various pyramid fields making up the Memphite necropolis. This realization intrigued me enough to look into the history of the Red Pyramid, which is thought to have been the third and final pyramid constructed by Khufu's father, Snofru, who reigned circa 2575–2551 BCE (the others being the Bent Pyramid, located just to the south of the Red Pyramid, and the "collapsed" pyramid of Meidum, which is around 65 kilometers to the south of Giza).

THE RED PYRAMID

With a height of 104 meters and base length of 220 meters, the Red Pyramid has the second-largest base area of any pyramid after the Great Pyramid. Originally it was covered in gleaming white Tura limestone, but this was stripped away to expose its red sandstone core masonry, hence its name the Red Pyramid. Since it was the first "perfect" pyramid to be built, it can be seen as the prototype for the Great Pyramid in particular. Like the main pyramids at Giza, the Red Pyramid has a north-facing entrance passageway. This descends into the substructure at an angle of approximately 27 degrees and ends in a horizontal passage, beyond which is a burial chamber with an accomplished corbelled roof of enormous granite blocks. It is 12 meters in height and rises in eleven reverse steps. A short horizontal passage at the room's southern end leads to a second chamber.

The Red Pyramid's corbelled roof has characteristics in common with the one seen in the Great Pyramid's Grand Gallery, and there can be no denying the impact of one upon the other. Very clearly the former was constructed in the same general time frame as the latter, suggesting that the underlying geometry at Giza might well have extended to Dahshur's Red Pyramid, which was probably the last pyramid to be built prior to the emergence of the Giza pyramid field.

THE BIG TRIANGLE

Exploring the site of the equilateral triangle's third and final point on the summit of Gebel Tura was made utterly impossible because of the presence of a huge limestone quarry at the exact location. This might well have been the end to the exercise had I not thought about the possible relationship between this "big triangle," as I was now calling it, and the hypotenuse line created by Giza's base 3-4-5 triangle. This, as we have seen, starts with the vertex of the Second Pyramid and extends southeastward to embrace the pyramid's southeast corner area, the datum on Gebel el-Qibli, the center of the pyramid arc circle, and the convergence point, from which the stars of Cygnus would have been seen to set down into the peaks of the three main pyramids at Giza during the epoch of

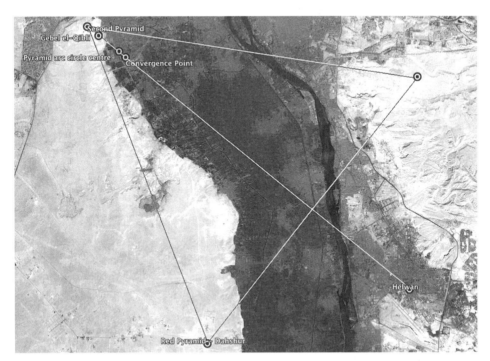

Figure 25.1. The Sadr setting line or convergence line is bisecting the Big Triangle, and embracing the peaks of the Second Pyramid of Giza and Red Pyramid of Dahshur, as well as a high point at the northern edge of Gebel Tura.

their construction, circa 2550–2479 BCE. What I found stunned me, because if the hypotenuse was extended beyond the convergence point, *it bisected the "big" equilateral triangle with an angle of error of just 1 degree* (see fig. 25.1).

OCCUPATIONAL KOMS

In addition to this, along its course the Big Triangle's bisecting line intersects the central mound or *kom* on which the medieval town of Shabramont was built. (A *kom* is the Arabic name for an occupational mound located in the Nile flood plain that was created originally by a buildup of sand and silt, and expanded in height and size by thousands of years of human debris.) Here in the past I have found various examples of cut-and-dressed stone blocks of Aswan granite that almost certainly once belonged to a dynastic building that stood on the site. Even farther southeast, the bisecting line targets another prominent kom covered in palm trees and surrounded by low-lying cultivated land. An examination of high-resolution satellite images has revealed the outline of what appears to be a large rectilinear feature, which remains under investigation.

FURTHER DOWN THE LINE

Satisfied that the Great Triangle embracing the peak of the Second Pyramid at Giza along with the peak of the Red Pyramid at Dahshur and the heights of Gebel Tura had opened up some productive lines of enquiry, I was just about to leave the subject when I realized something of potential significance. If the hypotenuse line, or Sadr setting line, as we shall call it, is extended from the peak of the Second Pyramid southeastward beyond the Nile at a distance of just over 24.5 kilometers, it reaches the center of Helwan. (The distance from the peak of the Second Pyramid to the baths at Helwan is 24.64 kilometers, according to Google Earth.) Indeed, a line drawn from the former site of the sulfur springs close to the Helwan hammam or bathhouse back to the peak of Giza's Second Pyramid created a projected azimuth bearing of 307.4 degrees. This was just 9 minutes of arc askew of the angle defining the line between the convergence point and the peak of the Second Pyramid.

Thinking further about this matter made me realize something else—the bisecting line of the Great Triangle was most probably oriented not southeastward to Helwan, but northwestward to *target* the Giza pyramid field. An astronomer priest standing on high ground at Helwan in circa 2550–2479 BCE would have been able to watch the Cygnus star Sadr set down into the heights of Gebel el-Qibli, clearly visible on the northwestern horizon. Thereafter the peak of the Second Pyramid would have been seen to arise from just behind the same position, since it was located immediately beyond Gebel el-Qibli on the same Sadr setting line. Incidentally, Helwan would have been a perfect place to view not only the construction of the Giza pyramids, but also every other pyramid field in the Memphis necropolis, including those at Dahshur, as can be seen from figure 25.2.

Such a conclusion made better sense of the arc circle created by the geographical positioning of the Giza pyramids. The fact that its center falls on the bisecting line of the Big Triangle, around 2.38 kilometers southeast of the Second Pyramid, makes it seem as if the pyramids are honoring the southeasterly orientation of the line. Are they in fact honoring Helwan out of some kind of reverence to its role as the genesis point of Egyptian civilization, or, alternately, was Helwan seen as a place of the ancestors, its influence being conveyed via the Sadr setting line to each of the three Giza pyramids?

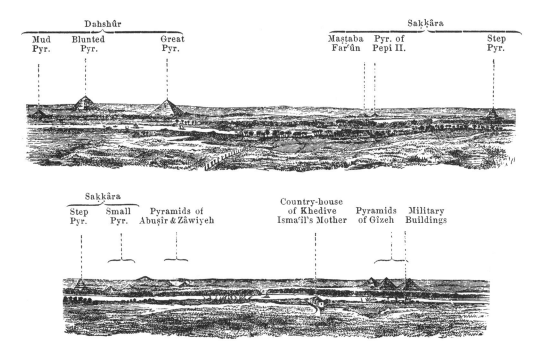

Sketch of the Pyramids as seen from Ḥelwân.

Figure 25.2. Illustration from the Baedeker travel guide to Lower Egypt published in 1885, showing the view from Helwan toward the various pyramid fields, including Dahshur and Giza.

Just how important *was* Helwan to the dynastic Egyptians? Answering this question led me to a staggering conclusion: Helwan's rightful claim to being the genesis point of Egyptian civilization was very clearly *stolen* by its greatest rival, Heliopolis, the city of the sun god Re, located around 30 kilometers to the north. It is a diabolical story that must finally be told.

26

DIVISION OF THE
TWO LANDS

Even before the ancient Egyptians began constructing a series of pyramid fields on the border between the Libyan Desert and the western edge of the Nile floodplain, the inhabitants of the nearby city of Memphis had built a vast necropolis just across the river at Helwan. It was located in the rich alluvial deposits brought down by rainwater washing through the normally dry Wadi Hôf immediately to the east. The site of the cemetery is today marked by the small hamlet of Ezbit el-Walda, situated just to the northwest of Helwan's former spa resort. Indeed, between the late predynastic age and the end of the Third Dynasty, circa 3150–2575 BCE, as much as 10,000 tombs were constructed within an area of just 100 hectares.[1]

Yet how exactly the ancient Egyptians perceived the importance of Helwan and its ancient springs has until now been difficult to ascertain, as has its ancient name. From all the evidence available this would appear to have been Ainu,[2] Ayan,[3] and perhaps even Ain-an.*[4] All derive from the

---

*Ayan is identified often with the limestone quarries of Gebel Tura, north of Helwan. However, Gebel Tura's ancient name is more correctly Ta-roau, "place of Roau," (Brugsch 1879, I, 74) or just Roau. This is a location either synonymous with or mentioned in association with Ayan, or 'Ainu (Lichtheim 1980, 56), where 'Ainu is said to be "of the eastern Memphite nome" and is "called by name" Roau. The ancient Greeks knew Gebel Tura as Troia, from Ta-raou (Brugsch 1879, I, 74).

Semitic root *ain, ayan,* or *ainu,* meaning, variously, "spring," "fountain," "flowing water," and "eye."*5

THE TWO LANDS

Despite what little is known about Helwan during dynastic times, there is compelling evidence that it played an important role following the unification of Upper and Lower Egypt circa 3120 BCE. This information comes from the so-called Memphite Theology, a cosmogonic text containing the genealogy and history of the gods of Egypt as presented by the Memphite priesthood of the god Ptah. It is inscribed on the so-called Shabaka Stone, carved at the command of the pharaoh Shabaka, who ruled circa 712–698 BCE. The text itself was apparently copied from an Old Kingdom original so as to preserve its contents for future generations.

According to the Shabaka Stone, which can be seen today in the British Museum, Geb, described as "lord of the gods," gathered the Nine Gods (the so-called Ennead), and in their presence judged between the warring gods Set and Horus. Geb gave Set Upper Egypt, "up to the place where he was born," while Horus was allotted Lower Egypt, "up to the place where his father [Osiris] was drowned, which is [the] 'Division of the Two Lands.'" Thus with Horus standing over his region and Set his, they made peace "over the Two Lands at Ayan [i.e., Helwan]. That was the division of the Two Lands."6 Having done this, Geb changed his mind, and decided to give Horus the whole of the Two Lands, making him the legendary first king of Upper and Lower Egypt, a title later adopted by all pharaohs, after which the text continues:

> He is Horus who arose as King of Upper and Lower Egypt, who united the Two Lands in the Nome of the Wall [i.e., Memphis], the place in which the Two Lands were united. Reed and papyrus were placed on the double door of the House of Ptah [the temple of Ptah at Memphis]. That means Horus

(cont.) On the relationship between Roau and 'Ainu, Miriam Lichtheim points out that the English philologist Alan Gardiner wrote that 'Ainu "was either an early synonym of Ro-au or else a rather more extended term for Ro-au and its neighborhood." (Lichtheim 1973, 57 n. 6.)
*Hebrew אהין (AhYN): Well, spring, fountain, eye in the ground. In Akkadian it is *enu* or *inu,* in Phoenician *enu* or *inu,* and in Aramaic it is *ena* or *'ayna.'* In Persian and Arabic *'ain* is "fountain, source, conduit . . . [of] flowing water," with *'ainu l'haiwan (hayat)* being the "Fountain of life or immortality." See also Urdu (derived from Persian) *ayaan,* a "spring with multiple streams and sides, basically a 'dynamic' spring."

and Seth, pacified and united. They fraternized so as to cease quarrelling in whatever place they might be; being united in the House of Ptah, the "Balance of the Two Lands" in which Upper and Lower Egypt had been weighed.[7]

From this text it is clear that Ayan signified the point of demarcation between Upper and Lower Egypt. Confirmation that Ayan was Helwan comes from the fact that it is said to have been located at the same latitude as the House of Ptah in Memphis, with both representing the "Balance of the Two Lands," exactly the situation of Helwan and Memphis, which sit opposite each other on either side of the Nile.

SYMBOL OF THE TWO LANDS

The reference in the Memphite Theology to "reed and papyrus" is an allusion to the two plants that symbolized, respectively, Upper and Lower Egypt. These are shown in scenes that depict the "Balance of the Two Lands." In these Horus and Set pull on a rope that ends on one side with a reed and on the other with a papyrus. The rope is looped around a columnar device known as the *sema-tawy,* the symbol of the actual Balance of the Two Lands. Looking like a downward-pointing spade, it is in fact a pair of lungs attached to the trachea, incorporating the larynx at its upper end (see fig. 26.1). This strange device is difficult to comprehend, although very likely it signified the rhythmic breath of life brought to Egypt through the unification and stability of the Two Lands. Either the lungs and trachea are purely conceptual, or they belonged to the god Osiris, who, as the Memphite Theology indicates, was drowned at Ayan, presumably in the Nile, which flowed around the city of Memphis during the Old Kingdom period. (The river later drifted away to the east, leaving the city high and dry.)

The Memphite Theology indicates that Helwan, as Ayan, was recognized as an extremely ancient site even before the unification of the Two Lands. Moreover, it states that it was here that the god Geb, in the presence of the Ennead, brought together Set and Horus not only to bring peace to the country but also to decide how best Egypt should be divided between the two gods.

Yet Ayan appears in the Memphite Theology quite beyond its association with the point of unification of the Two Lands, for it is here, apparently, that "his [i.e., Horus's] father was drowned." This is a reference to the earlier

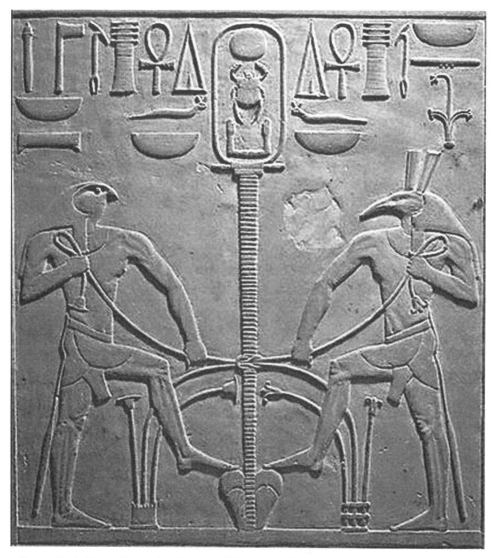

Figure 26.1. Scene from the throne of the pharaoh Sesostris I (1956–1911/10 BCE), showing the gods Horus and Set tugging on ropes that terminate in the reed (left) and papyrus (right). These symbolize, respectively, Upper and Lower Egypt. The ropes support the symbolic device known as the *sema-tawy*, the "Uniter of the Two Lands."

rivalry between the brothers Osiris and Set, the latter eventually tricking the former into a bespoke coffin, an obvious symbol of death and resurrection, and then throwing this into the water, where the god drowns. Osiris's wife, Isis, then retrieves the body of her husband. She later uses magic to reanimate the corpse so that she might copulate with it. It is this act that brings forth the child god Horus, who on reaching adulthood seeks revenge for the death of his father. (This Horus is not to be confused with Horus the Elder, or Horus the Behdetite, the patron of Edfu in southern Egypt: see chapter 30).

So Helwan was also where Set had thrown the coffin containing his brother Osiris into the nearby Nile. Assuming that this murderous act did not take place at some random place, it was obviously either the location of Set's earthly abode or a site important to Osiris himself. Since Set was a very ancient god, a trickster figure vilified as an evil god during the New Kingdom, circa 1550–1070 BCE, there seems every chance that Helwan was a cult center to the god prior to the unification of the Two Lands.

It is important here to remember that the Memphite Theology, although clearly filtered through the priesthood of Ptah at Memphis, cites the presumably much older and obviously important cosmogony of the Ennead, the Nine Gods of Heliopolis, a celebrated city located around 30 kilometers north-northeast of Memphis. In other words, the text provides the story line behind the pantheon of gods celebrated in the various temples at Heliopolis, which in the ancient Egyptian language was known as Iwnw, Iunu, Annu, Anu, or simply An (the biblical On).

As we saw in chapter 13, Heliopolis was the home of the highly influential Re priesthood, the creators of the Pyramid Texts, in which the pharaoh at death takes on the role of Osiris. Thus there was every reason to cast Set in the role of the trickster and villain in the story of Osiris' death, since Set was obviously the memory of something that had preceded the rise in popularity of the Heliopolitan priesthood.

DEATH OF OSIRIS

The Memphite Theology contains its own form of the death of Osiris, which is itself important in revealing the even greater significance of the location where the god was drowned:

> This is the land . . . the burial of Osiris in the House of Sokar. [Arrived] Isis and Nephtys [Set's sister-wife] without delay, for Osiris had drowned in his water [the Nile]. Isis [and Nephtys] looked out [beheld Osiris and attended to him]. Horus speaks to Isis and Nephtys: "Hurry, grasp him [from the water] . . ." Isis and Nephtys speak to Osiris: "We come, we take you. [They heeded in time] and brought him to [land. He entered the hidden

portals. . . . Thus Osiris came into] the earth at the royal fortress, to the north of [the land to which he had come.][8]

Having retrieved the body, Isis and Nephtys remove it to the "House of Sokar," also known as the Shetayet, the "Tomb of God," where Osiris enters between the "hidden portals," which were clearly located somewhere in the vicinity of Memphis, the "royal fortress" mentioned in the text. Where exactly the tomb of Osiris might have been located I address adequately elsewhere.[9] Suffice to say that there is compelling evidence to suggest that the secret chamber in which Osiris's body, or essence, was thought to be located existed somewhere in the vicinity of Upper Rostau, modern Nazlet el-Batran, very close to the Sadr setting line between Helwan and the three main pyramids of Giza.

Thus, if you remove the veneer overlaid upon this cosmogony of the gods of Heliopolis, there remains an underlying importance to Ayan, where Geb had Set and Horus make peace, Osiris was drowned, and the balance of the Two Lands was to be found. In the knowledge that histories are always written by the victors, this seems to imply that Helwan, in its role as Ayan, had a far greater role in the emergence of the Heliopolitan cosmogony and Memphite Theology than has previously been recognized.

At this juncture it is important to recall once again that the myth of Osiris grew in popularity through the concerted efforts of the Heliopolitan priesthood, whose influence on ancient Egypt's ruling dynasties began in earnest during the second half of the Fourth Dynasty, just about the time of construction of the Giza pyramid field. It is then that Osiris's name begins to appear in funerary inscriptions, the oldest being found at Giza itself (see chapter 13). The Heliopolitan priesthood's heavy promotion of the Osiris cult included the codification of the spells and sayings that would eventually form the Pyramid Texts. They appear for the first time at the end of the Fifth Dynasty, during the reign of King Unas, circa 2342–2322 BCE. Yet as we have seen, the cosmological notions promulgated by the Heliopolitan priesthood would have come to bear on the design of funerary architecture much earlier, arguably during the age of Khufu, Khafre, and Menkaure, the builders of the three main pyramids at Giza.

So the fact that the Memphite Theology is based on Heliopolitan traditions tells us that it was likely to be at Heliopolis that the role of Ayan or Helwan in the story of the murder of Osiris was preserved. Yet the fact that Ayan's true history is sidelined, ignored even, is very revealing indeed. It indicates that Helwan was once so important that its memory could not entirely be expunged from the cosmogonic records of the gods of Heliopolis. More than this, it suggests that the Heliopolitan priesthood might well have stolen aspects of Helwan's history in order to convey their own myths and legends of the gods. As far-fetched as this scenario might seem, I would certainly not be the first author to make this assertion.

27

WHO STOLE IWNW?

German archaeologist and former Catholic priest Hermann Junker (1877–1962) is best known for his excavation of the Chalcolithic age site of Merimde Beni-Salame in the western Nile Delta, which thrived circa 5500–4500 BCE. Yet somehow he also recognized the greater importance of Helwan. According to Egyptian archaeologist Zaki Y. Saad (1901–1982), who excavated Helwan's vast cemetery complex between 1942 and 1954,[1] Junker "contended that in the prehistoric period, before the kingdoms of Upper and Lower Egypt were united, there existed a city called Iwnw, or Heliopolis, near the site of present-day Helwan. Junker's theory seems to have been borne out by the excavations at Helwan."[2] Saad goes on to say:

> This lost city was the capital of the region for many years, but it began to lose importance during the First Dynasty with the establishment of the new capital [just across the river] at Memphis. . . . When Iwnw, or Heliopolis, was abandoned, another city bearing the same name was constructed to the north, where El-Matariya stands today. . . . Many Egyptologists believe that in time the location of the original Iwnw will be discovered."[3]

This hypothesis is remarkable. It begins to make sense of everything we know so far about the origins of Helwan in the Epipaleolithic age, as well as its continued importance in the Pre-Pottery Neolithic B period, circa 8800–7600 BCE, and even beyond that into the later Chalcolithic period, circa 5500–4500 BCE. It was at this time that new settlements arose at El Omari, which lies to the north of Helwan in the vicinity of Ma'sarah and Wadi Hôf.[4] The El Omari culture was roughly contemporary to that of the Merimde Beni-Salame settlement. Indeed it was probably this fact that began to convince Junker that Helwan might well have had a much greater role in the genesis of Egyptian civilization than had previously been acknowledged.

Even later in time, circa 3900–3200 BCE, the settlement at Maadi, located on the east bank of the Nile, around 15 kilometers north of Helwan, flourished. As we saw in chapter 11, burials belonging to the Maadi culture have been found in the vicinity of the Sphinx monument at Giza, suggesting that the site was already a place of special veneration by this time. Contemporary to the emergence of the Maadi settlement was a cemetery belonging to the same culture uncovered in the area of Heliopolis, which marks the site's earliest known beginnings as a cult center. As Saad states, it soon grew to become a major city named Iwnw, or Iunu, meaning "Place of Pillars." Heliopolis is the Greek name of the city and means "city of the sun," a reference to it as the site of the cult of the sun god Re.

Yet both Junker and Saad apparently believed that the city of Iwnw in the El-Matariya district of Cairo merely replaced another of the same name that had previously flourished at Helwan. Saad even argued that the name Helwan was a corruption of Iwnw, the toponym having been adopted by the first Coptic Christians to occupy the area. In his opinion, the village of Helwan might have been a suburb of the old capital Iwnw and bore the name Her-Iwnw, meaning "City above Iwnw." The Arab Egyptians later changed Her-Iwnw to Helwan,[5] using the Arabic *helw,* or *halw,* meaning "sweet, pleasant (to the eye, mind, or taste)."[6]

Yet if Iwnw, the "old capital" of northern Egypt during the First Dynasty (and to date it must be pointed out that no such city has been uncovered beneath the urban sprawl that is the modern metropolis of Helwan), then did its successor, Heliopolis, steal more than its predecessor's name?

TREE OF THE VIRGIN MARY

Just as at Helwan, the second Iwnw, located at El-Matariya northeast of Cairo, was also focused around a major spring. Known in Arabic as Ain Shams, meaning the "spring or fountain of the sun," it remains even today as a place of devotion and pilgrimage. Currently the spring is dedicated to the Virgin Mary. Indeed it is believed that the root behind the name El-Matariya is the Latin *mater*, "mother." Next to the spring is an ancient sycamore tree known as the Tree of the Virgin Mary, and although this was only planted in 1672, it is believed to have replaced an original tree under which Mary, Joseph, and the Holy Child are said to have taken rest during the flight into Egypt. This was almost certainly the Christianization of a tree that had stood close to the same site in dynastic times. It was from within a sacred sycamore that Nut was said to have nourished the spirits of the dead (a role she shared with the goddess Hathor, who bore many of Nut's traits).[7] Although this sycamore was unquestionably thought to be the one at Heliopolis, there is no indication that this was Nut's principal cult center.

The various Books of the Dead have the deceased address Nut in her form as the sacred sycamore promising to protect the "egg of the Great Cackler."[8] As we saw in chapter 15, it was among the plants growing beneath this "sycamore of Nut," said to have been located in Heliopolis, that "the Great Cackler Seb [i.e., the god Geb] laid the Egg of the sun,"[9] in other words the sun god Re. This seems to be a variation of the story that tells of Nut and Geb, in his form as the Great Cackler, producing the egg from which the sun emerges as the sacred bennu bird.[10]

The bennu bird, as we have seen, was of utmost importance to the Heliopolitan cosmological story. This is because it was in this form that the spirit of the creator god Atum landed on the primeval mound at the moment the sun rose at dawn on the first day, bringing forth light to the world and initiating the passage of time. From this mound, which rose from the watery void known as the Nun, the mundane world came into being. Atum himself became the progenitor of the Ennead, the nine gods of Heliopolis. These were Shu and Tefnut, who gave birth to Geb and Nut. They in turn produced the two sets of twins Osiris and Isis and Set and Nephthys. With Atum himself, they composed the Ennead.

NOURISHMENT OF THE SOUL

So given that Heliopolis might well have stolen Helwan's identity as the original Iwnw, did it also steal its creation myths and claim them as its own? Is it possible that the stories that tell of Nut nourishing the dead with water in her guise as the sacred sycamore derive originally not from Heliopolis, but from the area around the saline, sulfur, and chalybeate springs in Helwan and nearby Ma'sarah? British Egyptologist David Jeffreys informs us that the decision to situate a major cemetery so close to Helwan's natural springs very likely related to ancient Egyptian mortuary beliefs concerning the soul's nourishment in preparation for its journey to the afterlife,[11] the responsibility, of course, of the goddess Nut.

So if Nut's original cult center really was Helwan, then what about her brother and consort Geb, the Great Cackler, whom the Memphite Theology refers to as "lord of the gods"? Was his cult center also originally Helwan? Remember, it was Geb who was said to have brought together Set and Osiris so that they might make peace at Ayan, the location marking the division of the Two Lands, which can be identified with Helwan.

Geb's animistic form was that of the goose, a primary symbol of cosmic creation in ancient Egypt, identified with the Cygnus star Deneb.[12] As we have seen, his sister and wife, the sky goddess Nut, was the personification of the Milky Way, her womb and birth canal marked by the stars of Cygnus; she might even have been personified as Cygnus itself on coffin lids from Asyut in southern Egypt dating the First Intermediate Period (see chapter 15). So both Nut and Geb would seem to have been associated with the very same area of the northern night sky. Indeed, there is every reason to suspect that the Egyptian afterlife, entered after resurrection in the womb of Nut, was itself seen as the abode of Geb. This is demonstrated in various utterances from the Pyramid Texts, such as:

> The blessed dead lament for thee (after) the imperishable stars bore thee (away). Enter the abode of thy father, to the abode of Geb.[13]

Did these cosmological beliefs, which surface for the first time in the Heliopolitan-inspired Pyramid Texts, derive originally not from Heliopolis, but from Helwan's "lost city" of Iwnw? Had Cygnus and the Milky Way been important to the city's inhabitants during the prehistoric age?

PLACE OF THE PILLAR

There is a clue in the fact that the name Iwnw, although usually rendered into English as "Place of Pillars," or "City of the Pillars," should more correctly read "Place of the Pillar." It is a theory borne out by the hieroglyphs used to spell

Figure 27.1. The name of the ancient cult center of Iwnw, An, Anu, or Annu, the Greek Heliopolis. We see on the left the towerlike hieroglyph representing the word *an*, meaning "pillar" or "obelisk." We see also the hieroglyph denoting "place," which is the cross inside the circle on the lower right, and the round pot representing the syllable *nu*, used also in the name of the sky goddess Nut.

Iwnw, which usually either consist of the pillar sign alongside the hieroglyph for place (a circle containing an X) and the hieroglyph for *nu* (the water pot, a symbol also of Nut), or alternately the pillar sign on its own (see fig. 27.1). In its singular form, the pillar sign probably alludes not to standing obelisks, as is generally believed, but to the mythical *benben* stone, on which the bennu bird was said to have alighted at dawn on the first day. It was an act celebrated at Heliopolis in the Mansion of the Bennu (or Mansion of the Phoenix), considered the location of the original primeval mound of creation. This belief is expressed in Utterance 600 of the Heliopolitan-inspired Pyramid Texts:

> O Atum-Khepri [a form of Atum as the midnight sun], when thou didst mount as a hill, and didst shine as *bnw* [i.e., the bennu bird] of the *ben* (or, *benben*) in the temple of the "phoenix" [i.e., bennu bird] in Heliopolis.[14]

Is it possible that this first act of creation did not occur at El-Matariya, the modern Heliopolis, but at the true site of Iwnw, the "City of the Pillar," farther south at Helwan? Was this the original site of the primeval mound, the "hill" or benben stone on which the bennu bird alighted at dawn on the first day?

BIR EL-HADÍD, THE IRON WELL

Unable to provide any satisfactory answers to these questions, I began turning my attention back toward Helwan's Epipaleolithic and later Pre-Pottery

Neolithic settlements to more fully investigate this subject for the earlier chapters of this book. One site I became particularly interested in was Bir El-Hadíd, "the iron (Arabic *hadíd*) well (*bir*)."[15] This was a chalybeate spring located close to the entrance of Wadi Karáfish, near the village of Ma'sarah, around 9 kilometers north-northwest of Helwan. Here a large number of stone tools and projectile points were found during the nineteenth century.[16] Wondering why this site had become so important to the prehistoric peoples of the area, I started looking for clues in old accounts from European travelers. I already knew that from Ma'sarah north to the entrance of Wadi Tura, which divides the Mokattam Hills in the north from the Gebel Tura range in the south, were a number of deeply cut cave tunnels. They were not natural, but had been created from the Pyramid Age onward by dynastic Egyptian quarrymen cutting their way into the bedrock to remove blocks of Tura limestone for use in religious and secular buildings throughout Egypt.

With the completion of a particular assignment, the quarrymen would leave inscriptions either on the surrounding cliffs, on stone stelae, or inside the cave tunnels. Many of these were still clearly visible when the first European travelers reached the area during the nineteenth century. One such person was pioneering Egyptologist Sir John Gardner Wilkinson (1797–1875), and a chance discovery he was to make in one of these quarries could well go some way to confirm Helwan's true role in the Heliopolitan creation story.

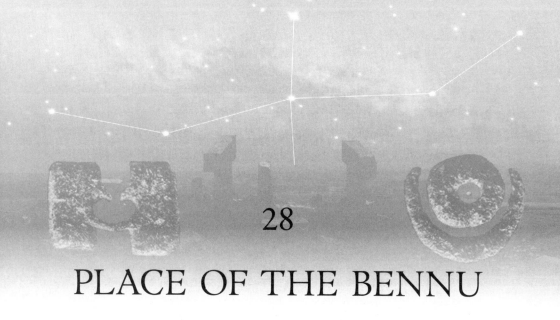

28

PLACE OF THE BENNU

Sir John Gardner Wilkinson began his celebrated travels to Egypt in October 1821. They continued through until 1833, when he returned to England for health reasons. Thereafter he would write extensively on life in both ancient and modern Egypt, producing various lengthy tomes including *The Topography of Thebes and General View of Egypt,* published in 1835,[1] and *Manners and Customs of the Ancient Egyptians,* a three-volume set published in 1837.[2] Even today these fascinating books stand as perfect introductions to Egyptian culture, history, and religion, made all the more accessible through the graphic illustrations of English artist Joseph Bonomi (1796–1878). Wilkinson's books were so popular and influential that in 1839 they would earn him a knighthood, assuring his place in history as Britain's first great Egyptologist.

The big difference between Wilkinson and many of the other early pioneers in Egyptology is that he could read hieroglyphs and understand the ancient Egyptian language. This had only become possible during the first few years of his travels in Egypt because of the incredible efforts of the Frenchman Jean-François Champollion (1790–1832) and the Englishman Thomas Young (1773–1829). Working on either side of the English Channel, both men had managed to make translations of the hieroglyphic language of the ancient Egyptians. This was made possible following the discovery in 1799 of the famous Rosetta Stone, with its trilingual inscription in Greek, Egyptian hieroglyphics, and demotic, a cruder form of the Egyptian written language used by ordinary people.³ Thus Wilkinson was among the first scholars to actually be able to read hieroglyphic texts, a crucial fact, since it is likely that many carved or handwritten inscriptions discovered at this time would later be lost or destroyed through vandalism or natural erosion. This makes some of Wilkinson's observations during his travels between Cairo and Beni Suef in Middle Egypt very important indeed, for while in the area of Tura and Ma'sarah, immediately to the north of Helwan, he spent time recording the inscriptions to be found in various of the limestone quarries. These are reproduced in volume 2 of *Modern Egypt and Thebes,* published in 1843.⁴

WILKINSON'S VISIT TO THE TURA QUARRIES

In one quarry, which he describes as "towards the south," a reference apparently to the southern end of Ma'sarah, he discovered a "larger tablet," most likely a carved stela, on which was shown a king by the name of "Amyrtæus."⁵ Today we know this king under the name of Amun-rut. He ruled during the Twentieth-Eighth Dynasty, circa 460 BCE, and is remembered for having expelled the Persians from Egypt.⁶

Wilkinson writes that the king was shown presenting offerings to a triad of deities, whom he names as "[the god] Thoth, the goddess Nehimeou, and Horus (Nofre-Hor, the 'lord of the land of Bahet')."⁷ Thoth is the divine scribe as well as the god of the moon. His cult center was Hermopolis, in what is today Middle Egypt. The goddess "Nehimeou," whom Wilkinson says elsewhere sported a vulture headdress with a box shrine from which water plants sprouted, bore the titles "Mistress of the Eight Regions of the Land, Dominatrix of Tentyris [i.e., Dendera in southern Egypt]," and "daughter of Ra."⁸ She can be identified with Nehem(t)-'auit, a consort of Thoth.⁹ Horus appears to be in his guise as Horus the Behdetite, the patron of Edfu in southern Egypt.

Below the king, according to Wilkinson, stood "a small figure, in the act of cutting the stone with a chisel and mallet. Besides the hieroglyphic ovals of the kings, are several names and inscriptions in enchorial [i.e., demotic script]; and here and there are various numbers, and quarry-marks, frequently with lines indicating the size of each stone."¹⁰ Yet it is what Wilkinson says next that instantly drew my attention, for he tells us that "the name of the place appears to be Benno."¹¹ This is Wilkinson's rendering of the word *bnw,* that is, *benu* or *bennu,* the name of the Heliopolitan bird of creation and the phoenix of classical tradition.

This is an incredibly important statement, which, if correct, reveals the true name of the area "towards the south" of the dynastic quarries at Ma'sarah, which takes us within just 3 kilometers of Helwan's late predynastic and early dynastic cemeteries at Ezbit el-Walda and 8–9 kilometers from the center of Helwan. Remember also that the northernmost spring at Helwan, where large quantities of stone tools and projectile points were found, was Bir El-Hadíd, situated close to Ma'sarah itself.

BIRD OF CREATION

Evidence that Wilkinson's use of the word *benno* does indeed refer to the Egyptian word *bennu,* the name given to the Heliopolitan bird of creation, comes from his work *A Second Series of the Manners and Customs of the Ancient Egyptians,* published in two volumes in 1841. Here he talks about the tamarisk tree, chosen by the ancient Egyptians he says to "overshadow the sepulcher of Osiris."[12] An accompanying illustration (volume 2, no. 465) shows the heronlike bennu bird sitting in the tree's upper branches (see fig. 28.1).

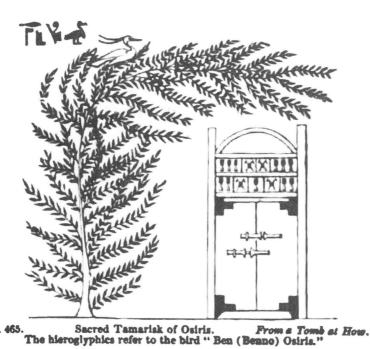

No. 465. Sacred Tamarisk of Osiris. *From a Tomb at How.*
The hieroglyphics refer to the bird " Ben (Benno) Osiris."

Figure 28.1. Illustration no. 465 from *A Second Series of the Manners and Customs of the Ancient Egyptians* (volume 2) by Sir John Gardner Wilkinson showing the "Benno" bird perched in the sacred tamarisk tree overshadowing the sepulcher of Osiris.

An accompanying caption reads: "Sacred Tamarisk of Osiris. The hieroglyph-ics refer to the bird 'Ben (Benno) Osiris.'"[13] The text itself states: "In the lat-ter [illustration] the bird Benno is seated in its branches, accompanied by the name of Osiris, of whom it was an emblem."[14] Elsewhere in the same volume, an entry on the "tufted Benno" reaffirms that it is "one of the emblems of Osiris, who was sometimes figured with the head of this bird."[15]

Wilkinson does not use the word *benno* in any other context in any of his published works. Thus there can be little question that the hieroglyphic and demotic inscription he recorded in the quarry "towards the south" of Ma'sarah records that the name of the locality was Bennu, assuredly a reference to the Heliopolitan bird of creation, which alights on the benben stone at dawn on the first day.

Since Heliopolis was itself identified with this same place of first creation, did it really steal this mythological tradition from Helwan's own, presumably much earlier, role as the place of first creation? More importantly, why has just one inscription been found suggesting that the Helwan area was once called Bennu? Surely there should be more attestations of this ancient Egyptian top-onym in the many inscriptions found throughout the area.

THE CLUE TO HERMOPOLIS

One clue is in the fact that the late-dynastic inscription Wilkinson found at Ma'sarah is very clearly *not* of Heliopolitan origin. Its triad of deities in the form of Thoth, his consort Nehem(t)-'auit (identified with Hathor of Dendera), and Horus (presumably the Behdetite of Edfu) belie the fact that those responsible for its creation venerated the gods of Hermopolis in middle Egypt and Edfu in southern Egypt. The Hermopolitan priesthood borrowed aspects of the Heliopolitan cosmogony in its own creation myth, whereby the ibis, Thoth's totemic form, replaces the heron as bird of creation. At Hermopolis it is the ibis that lays the egg from which Re emerges to bring forth the physical world, and not the bennu bird. Clearly this version of the creation story was a hybrid of two different myths from two separate cult centers in Egypt, which had been forged together as one at some point.

Thus the highly influential priesthood of Heliopolis would not have pro-moted the fact that Helwan might once have been the original place of cre-ation, wanting to claim this role for their own cult center whenever possible. However, at Hermopolis the attitude toward Helwan's claims might well have been different, meaning that its priests had no problem in admitting that the Helwan district should be identified as Bennu, a clear reference to the Heliopolitan bird of creation.

The fact that the Memphite Theology tells us that Ayan, that is Helwan, is where Osiris was murdered, and Set and Horus came together to make peace at the balance of the Two Lands, only strengthens the case for Helwan being the original place of first creation in Heliopolitan tradition. Very likely this age-old tradition was stolen by Heliopolis at the same time that it set itself up as the new Iwnw, the new "Place of the Pillar," sometime during the early dynastic period, circa 3120–2650 BCE. Further confirmation of these conclusions comes from a second inscription found near the stone quarries at Ma'sarah. It reveals yet another ancient name for the area around Helwan, which, as we see next, dovetails perfectly with the realization that here was the original place of creation in Heliopolitan tradition.

29

THE MOUNTAIN
OF ANU

A further indication of the manner in which Heliopolis adopted the former great sanctity of Helwan and its surrounding area comes from a second inscription found in the limestone quarries in the vicinity of Tura and Ma'sarah. This example was published by the French Egyptologist Georges Daressy in 1911, and comes from the reign of the Twenty-Sixth Dynasty king Necho II, who ruled circa 610–595 BCE.[1] Written on a carved standing slab, or stela, it sets out the geographical boundaries of the Tura quarries, named as "Ro-au," in order to restrict access to the area. The text proclaims that no one is permitted to enter the mountain "east of the stone pillar" because the king (meaning his work gangs) is extracting limestone for construction purposes.

AN OF HIS ANCESTORS

The mountain in question is named on the stela, quite enigmatically, as "An of his ancestors," a title that instantly drew my attention. An or Anu was also the name of Heliopolis, although clearly the stone inscription left in the Tura-Ma'sarah area by Necho II did not refer to Heliopolis. Was the mountain of "An of his ancestors" viewed by the king as the place of his own ancestors, or those of the dynastic Egyptians in general? Remember, the inscription refers to

232

the mountain specifically, and not to Ro-au, the name given to the Tura area as a whole.

The hieroglyph used to represent the name An, an eye enclosed in an oval, has above it the hieroglyph meaning "sky" or "heaven," and below it the mouth symbol, used usually to denote the letter *R* (see fig. 29.1). I was unsure why the mouth symbol should appear, although the presence of the sky symbol suggested that the correct rendering of the text should be "the heavenly [or sky] mountain [named] An of the king's ancestors." This mountain must have had a special status among the Egyptians of the period, which might well have reflected the procurement of the area's fine-quality Tura limestone at this time.

So where exactly was this mountain? What was its present-day identity, and what was known about it both in terms of its mythology and archaeology? The only clue offered by the text is that the mountain existed to the east of the stone stela. Since it would have been located somewhere in the vicinity of Ma'sarah, or even slightly farther north, this would place the mountain in the hills making up the Gebel Tura range to the northeast of Helwan. The geography of the district suggests that the "heavenly mountain An" is most likely to be identified with a location the ancient writers referred to as "Mons Troicus," the "Mountain of the Trojans," after an anecdote recorded by the Greek geographer Strabo (63 BCE–24 CE) to the effect that Tura derived its name from Troia, that is, Troy, since it was once inhabited by a colony of Trojans.[2]

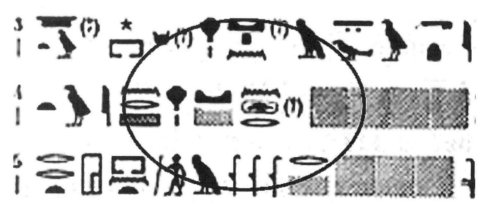

Figure 29.1. Inscription found in the vicinity of Ma'sarah, north of Helwan, from the reign of Necho II. In the center we see the saddleback hieroglyph denoting "mountain" (above the lacuna shown as a blurred area), To its right is the sign for "heaven," or "sky" (the bar with downturned ends), beneath which is an ellipse with an eye inside representing the toponym "An" or "Anu," and underneath this is the "mouth" sign denoting the letter R.

A detailed map of the Helwan district executed in 1895–1896 by Georg August Schweinfurth (1836–1925), a famous Baltic German botanist, traveler, and ethnologist, to accompany the book *Helwan and the Egyptian Desert* written by W. Page May and published in 1901,[3] shows *"Mons troicus"* as being located close to the summit of Gebel Hôf (coordinates 29°54′0″ N 31°21′0″ E). This is a prominent mountain plateau that rises to a height of 286 meters (68 meters above sea level) and overlooks Wadi Hôf, a deep curling ravine that ends abruptly in a vertical cliff face at its eastern end (see fig. 7.1 on page 70). Both Gebel Hôf and Wadi Hôf lie due east of Ma'sarah, making it likely that the former is the mountain named in the inscription as "An of his ancestors." Both locations were also sites of the Chalcolithic El Omari culture, which thrived in the area circa 5500–4500 BCE. This superseded Helwan's much earlier Epipaleolithic and later Pre-Pottery Neolithic settlements. Furthermore, the main Helwan cemetery at Ezbit el-Walda lies within the paleofan, the outpouring of alluvial deposits, that emerges from Wadi Hôf.

WHITE WALLS

Although not the highest mountain in the Gebel Tura range, Gebel Hôf is by far the most imposing, being visible not just from the area of the Helwan cemetery, but also from across the Nile at Memphis.[4] Indeed its commanding presence on the eastern horizon might even have influenced the choice of location of the early dynastic elite cemetery at North Saqqara, positioned on high ground above the Nile floodplain northwest of the city. David Jeffreys suggests that, as seen from North Saqqara, the sight of the white cliffs of Gebel Tura, with Gebel Hôf towering above them, might well have led to Memphis being called the "White Walls."[5]

So if Gebel Hôf *is* the "heavenly An," the mountain of the ancestors, what more can be determined about this important location? An or Anu (transliterated from the original texts as *'n* and *'nw*) turns out to be a variation of the name used to denote the entire area immediately to the north of Helwan. Indeed, the high-quality Tura limestone of the local quarries also bore the name *an*, suggesting that the stone itself might have borne some special quality associated directly with the area. So what exactly was the root of the name An or Anu, used seemingly in connection with Gebel Hôf in its role as a holy mountain?

SEMITIC EYE

Egyptologist James P. Allen, in his *Middle Egyptian: An Introduction to the Language and Culture of Hieroglyphs* (2014), states that the eye hieroglyph denoting the place-name '*nw* (which he identifies with Tura) derives from the Semitic root '*in,* meaning "eye."[6] This, of course, is correct, Semitic '*in,* usually written as *ain,* '*ayin,* or *ayan,* does indeed mean "eye." Yet as we saw in chapter 26, it can also mean "spring," "fountain," or "flowing water," a reference unquestionably to the springs of Helwan and Ma'sarah. We have seen also how in the Memphite Theology the name of the location where Set and Horus make peace is Ayan, which is simply another form of the name An or Anu, derived from the Semitic '*in.* However, An or Anu cannot have been the name given to the Tura quarries, as is proposed by Allen, because they have their own name, which is Ro-au (*r-3w*). Indeed, this name is attested as early as the age of Khufu. A papyrus text dating to his reign and found in 2013 at what is being referred to as the seaport or harbor of Khufu, located at Wadi al-Jarf on the Egyptian Red Sea coast, records how limestone was procured from the northern and southern quarries of Tura, named as *r-3w rsj* and *r-3w mhtj,* for transportation to the "Horizon of Khufu," the Egyptian name for the Great Pyramid.[7]

Thus it becomes clear that An, Anu, or Ayan is simply the ancient name, not of Tura and its quarries, but of the Helwan district. This would have extended from Ma'sarah, Gebel Hôf, and Wadi Hôf in the north all the way down to the site of the old village and hammam (bathhouse) in the south, in other words the area once occupied by the thermal and mineral springs so important to Helwan's prehistoric age. But why should Necho II have singled out a local mountain, calling it "An of his ancestors"? Did this title have something to do with the area's long history of occupation, which went back to the Epipaleolithic age, circa 18,000–9600 BCE?

ABODE OF THE BLESSED

One possible clue to this mystery is Heliopolis's own use of the names An or Anu.[8] This seems to have been based on the belief that its city was the terrestrial form of a heavenly location of the same name. The topic was discussed by English Egyptologist Sir E. A. Wallis Budge (1857–1934), who in 1913 wrote: "The abode of the blessed in heaven was called Anu, and it was asserted that the souls of the just were there united to their spiritual or glorified bodies, and that they lived there face to face with the deity for all eternity."[9]

Budge added that "the heavenly Anu was the capital of the mythological world, and was, to the spirits of men, what the earthly Anu [that is, Heliopolis] was to their bodies, *i.e.,* the abode of the gods and the centre and source of all divine instruction."[10] From this we can determine that Anu was the name given to the celestial destination of the souls of the deceased on entering the afterlife, which, as we have seen, was reached via the Imperishable Stars—the circumpolar and nearly circumpolar stars of the northern sky. Yet because this same name was used also for Heliopolis, some natural confusion and overlap would result from any reference to the two locations—one celestial and the other terrestrial. This was perhaps intentional on the part of the Heliopolitan priesthood, who might easily have made a point of blurring the boundaries between the two different Anus to promote the belief that their own cult center was a mundane reflection of the heavenly abode of the gods.

This situation is clearly brought out in the Heliopolitan-inspired Pyramid Texts. They emphasize that the king's true place of origin is Anu, where the Ennead, the gods of Heliopolis, were themselves born, and where the bennu bird alighted on the benben stone at the beginning of time.[11] Such propaganda not only established Heliopolis as the terrestrial abode of the gods, but also as the place of first creation in the physical world; everything thereafter emerging from Heliopolis. Yet as we have seen, this association between Heliopolis and the ancient creation myth would appear to have been a fallacy, based on the city's adoption of Helwan's own mythic traditions. This involved the importance of Helwan and the surrounding area as Bennu, the place of the bird of creation, and its original name of *'in* or *'nw,* that is, An or Anu, deriving from the Semitic root for "eye," "fountain," or "spring." As a reference to the area's thermal and mineral springs, these were most likely seen as sources of life and creation in the physical world and as places of nourishment for the dead as they departed for the heavenly Anu.

THE SKY FALCON

If the Helwan district was the original site of the terrestrial An or Anu, where exactly was its heavenly counterpart? Could it be connected in some way with why one of the local peaks, most obviously Gebel Hôf, was known as the heavenly An or Anu, the place of the ancestors? An answer can be gleaned from

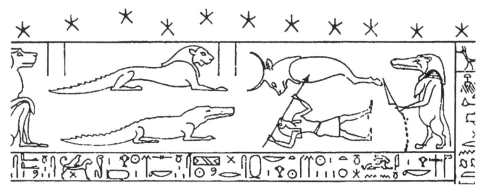

Figure 29.2. The falcon-headed god An or Anu, with raised spear,
sparring with Mšhtiw, the ox leg, or bovine.

ancient Egyptian astronomy. One of the principal sky figures of the Egyptian heavens shown on the walls of tombs from the Middle Kingdom onward was An or Anu. He is depicted as an anthropomorphic sky falcon with outstretched arms that hold, horizontally between them, either a polelike or spearlike object, or in some cases a long, taut rope. Always in opposition to the sky falcon is Mšhtiw, the ox leg, identified with Ursa Major (see fig. 29.2). The two figures are sometimes linked via the rope, or the falcon's spear points toward the ox leg, which can also take the form of a bull's head and torso, or even a complete bovine. The relationship between Mšhtiw, the ox thigh, and the sky falcon goes back at least to the Eleventh Dynasty, circa 2124–1981 BCE, since they are found together on the coffin of an individual named Heny, which dates to this period. This implies that even by this age the two constellations featured in the funerary beliefs of the ancient Egyptians, arguably in connection with the soul's journey to the afterlife.

SPARRING PARTNERS

The first scholar to attempt to identify the sky falcon was English Egyptologist Gerald Avery Wainwright (1879–1964). He was a leading authority on the sky religion of ancient Egypt, and in an article published in 1932 wrote that the opposition between An or Anu and Mšhtiw was indicative of the astronomical relationship between Ursa Major, as the ox leg, and the constellation of Cygnus as the falcon. In particular he singled out the stars Deneb, Gienah, Sadr, and Delta Cygni,[12] which together form an asterism known as the Triangles.[13] Ursa Major and Cygnus do indeed revolve around each other in the night sky, never getting any closer or farther away, a relationship that might suggest they are

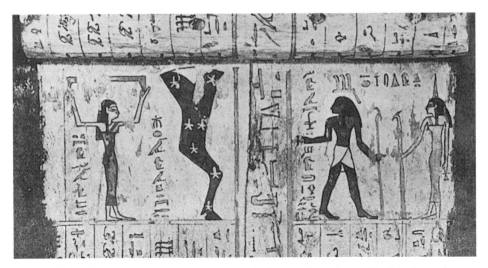

Figure 29.3. The four sky figures consistently featured in the coffin lids from Asyut dating to the First Intermediate Period. This example comes from the tomb of Tefabi. From left to right we see the sky goddess Nut (Cygnus) and the ox leg Mšhtiw (Ursa Major), representing the northern night sky, and Sah (Orion) and Sopdet (Sirius), representing the southern sky.

forever sparring in opposition, like two boxers moving around a boxing ring.

Remember also that on the astronomically themed coffin lids from Asyut dating to the First Intermediate Period, circa 2150–2030 BCE, just four sky figures are represented. We see two from the southern sky—Sah (Orion) and Sopdet (Sirius)—and two from the northern night sky—the ox leg, Mšhtiw (Ursa Major), and the sky goddess Nut (see fig. 29.3). As we have seen, she can be identified both with the Milky Way and, more importantly, with Cygnus. Indeed the coffin lids might well indicate that at this time Nut was specifically identified with Cygnus: the stance she adopts, with her arms outstretched, almost exactly replicates the positioning of its stars during this epoch (see fig. 15.2 on page 137). If this is the case, then sometime later, arguably during the Middle Kingdom, Nut's role as Mšhtiw's celestial partner was replaced by the sky falcon An or Anu, suggesting that the two figures represent the same two sets of stars—those of Ursa Major and Cygnus.

FINDING NORTH

Modern archaeoastronomers argue that the distance between Cygnus and Ursa Major is too great for the former to be identified as the sky falcon An or Anu, forcing them to look for its presence either within the patterns made by one of the lesser constellations in the vicinity of Ursa Major, or among the minor stars of Ursa Major that do not feature in the Mšhtiw asterism.[14] This exercise seems completely unnecessary, because Cygnus and Ursa Major are just two and a half palm-widths distance from each other in the night sky. Furthermore, the pole, rope, or spear connecting the two sky figures might well reflect the true relationship between the two asterisms.

As seen from the latitude of Giza during the Pyramid Age, Cygnus would have culminated on the meridian exactly as the seven main stars of Ursa Major, that is, Mšhtiw, crossed beneath the northern celestial pole on their lower transit. To be more precise, as the Cygnus star Sadr crossed the meridian two of Ursa Major's brightest stars—Megrez (δ Ursae Majoris) and Phecda (also known as Phad, γ Ursae Majoris)—would have been about to cross the meridian within about 3 arc minutes of each other. So if the identification of these two sky figures is correct, the rope, pole, or spear linking them together signifies the meridian line.

Following Wainwright's lead, I proposed in my book *The Cygnus Mystery* (2006a) that the sky falcon could indeed be identified with the stars of Cygnus.[15] This suggestion met with fierce opposition from those who believe that Cygnus played no major role in ancient Egypt.[16] However, many noted authorities on ancient Egyptian astronomy have accepted Wainwright's original identification.[17] Indeed, Egyptologists today either identity the sky falcon as Cygnus,[18] or propose that it is an asterism nearby, such as Aquila.[19]

In my opinion there seems no reason not to conclude that the most likely identification of the sky falcon An or Anu is Cygnus. What is more, the sky falcon was thought to be located in the vicinity of the circumpolar or nearly circumpolar stars of the northern night sky, exactly where, according to Budge, the celestial abode of An or Anu was said to exist. This is unlikely to be a coincidence, especially as in ancient Egyptian funerary tradition the soul of the deceased, the ba, took the form of a human-headed falcon. Once released from the physical body, the ba was thought to be able to journey between the tomb and the celestial abode with relative ease, and was often depicted as a bird hovering over the mummy of the deceased. This is expressed quite beautifully in Utterance 245 of the Pyramid Texts:

This N [name of deceased] comes to thee Nut; this N. comes to thee Nut. He has thrown his father [i.e., Osiris] to the ground; he has left Horus behind him. His two wings are grown as (those of) a falcon; (his) two feathers as (those of) a *gmḥsw*-falcon. His ba has brought him (here); his magic power has equipped him. Thou openest thy place in heaven, among the stars of heaven.[20]

This shows that on release from the underworld, the soul of the deceased was expected to fly into the embrace of its "mother" Nut, where as an akh spirit it would reside for all eternity. Indeed, chapters from the Pyramid Texts such as the one quoted above emphasize the manner in which the soul of the deceased ascended to the sky in the form of a falcon (even though the symbol for an akh spirit was in fact the ibis hieroglyph).

THE FOUNTAIN OF LIFE

If Cygnus really was identified in ancient Egyptian tradition with the celestial realm of An or Anu, could this connection by linked in some manner with the heavenly mountain of An, seemingly identified with Gebel Hôf? In theory, the answer is no, because the ancient name of the Helwan/Ma'sarah area was derived from its springs, although the connection might be deeper than this, with the celestial and terrestrial forms of An or Anu meaning more than simply "spring," "fountain," or "eye." More likely it was a metaphor for the fountain or source of life, reflected on earth within water sources like the springs at Helwan and Ma'sarah, and in the sky within the celestial waters of the Milky Way. (The Pyramid Texts and Coffin Texts refer to a celestial location called the Great Winding Waterway, which is likely to be a name of the Milky Way.)[21] In this way a dual relationship existed between the various different forms of An or Anu, which were seen simply as reflections of each other. Thus the mountain of An bore its heavenly attribution not only because of its proximity to Helwan and Ma'sarah, as an original place of the ancestors, but also because its heights were seen as reaching toward its heavenly counterpart.

FALCON OR HERON?

Yet was there a link between the falcon in its role as the soul bird of the ancient Egyptians and the bennu as bird of creation? Paintings and reliefs show the bennu as a species of heron. It is definitely not a falcon. The falcon and bennu are, however, identified with the spirits of both Osiris and Re, the release of the soul from the physical body being likened to the rebirth of the sun each morning.

So in this way the falcon as the ba and the bennu as the spirit of both Osiris and Re are really one and the same. Only the species of bird changes, and arguably even these avian forms were but substitutes for a more primeval soul bird that has now been lost to us, perhaps the goose of Geb or the vulture of Nut.

WADI OF THE VULTURE

I find it intriguing that the innermost part of Wadi Hôf, which bends toward the north as it navigates the base of Gebel Hôf, bears the name Wadi Rakham, which means "wadi of the vulture."[22] It is several hundred meters in length, is bordered on either side by immense walls of limestone, and ends abruptly at the foot of a steep cliff face (see fig. 29.4). Evidence of the Chalcolithic El Omari culure has been found at the entrance to Wadi Hôf, while various "circles of rude stones, marking the tombs of desert tribes in the early centuries of the Christian era" were to be seen here at the turn of the twentieth century.[23] However, in the light of Fernand Debono's investigations of the area in 1936 and 1941, these stone circles, which were found to conceal human burials, are

Figure 29.4. Nineteenth-century photo of the quite dramatic setting of Wadi Hôf, north of Helwan. In this vicinity thrived the Chalcolithic El Omari culture, circa 5500–4500 BCE.

likely to have been many thousands of years older than the Christian era.[24]

In this instance, *vulture* refers more specifically to the Egyptian vulture (*Neophron percnopterus*). How old this place-name might be is unknown. It could be hundreds or even thousands of years old. That the West Semitic word *rakham* derives from the same root as Rukh, or roc, a monstrous bird identified not only with the stars of Cygnus, but also with the "ruk-h" (modern *rekh*), a form of the bennu bird, is intriguing, to say the least.

Whatever the true identity of the bennu bird, we have seen how at the moment of first creation it was thought to alight on the benben stone, heralding the first appearance of the sun on the first day. Ma'sarah and Helwan's tentative identity as a place called Bennu, as well as its role as Iwnw and An/Anu, supports the conclusion that this is where this act was originally thought to have taken place, and not Heliopolis, as the Heliopolitan priesthood would later promote in their own creation myth.

As we shall see next, the benben stone, as the perch of the primordial bird of creation, might well reflect the memory of an actual pillar that once stood in Egypt's earliest cult building. Moreover, there are powerful reasons to suppose that this archaic structure, the role model and blueprint for all later temples built in Egypt, existed at Helwan. Evidence for this view can be found in the inscriptions that are seen to this day at the Temple of Edfu in southern Egypt.

30

HOMELAND OF THE PRIMEVAL ONES

Part I—The Coming of the Shebtiw

At Edfu in southern Egypt is a record of the construction of what might be one of the earliest cult structures ever built in the country. It can be found on the walls of its Ptolemaic-period temple, built circa 237–57 CE, to replace a much older building that had stood on the spot since Old Kingdom times. The account takes the form of so-called foundation texts, which speak of the emergence of the primordial world and the erection of the first sacred enclosure—the memory of which would define the shape, size, and function of all inner sanctuaries built in much larger temple complexes in ancient Egypt.

The Edfu building texts, as they are popularly known, are more or less unique. Not only are they extremely detailed and almost complete (something that is, sadly, not the case at other Egyptian temple sites), but they are also thought to preserve the oldest remaining account of how the ancient Egyptians believed the world came into being and why their temples had to conform to a preexisting pattern set down during the age of the gods (*sep tpy*).

THE WORK OF EVE REYMOND

By far the most important contribution to our understanding of the Edfu records is a book by Polish-born Egyptologist Eve Reymond, née Jelinkova PhD (1923–1986), of Manchester University in England. Titled *The Mythical Origin of the Egyptian Temple* (1969), it takes the form of a comprehensive précis of the texts located on both interior and exterior walls at various locations within the temple complex. What is so important about Reymond's contribution is her incredible understanding of how the dynastic Egyptians perceived the foundation of their cultus places, as she calls them. Moreover, she eloquently outlines how the achievements of the confusing array of mythical beings cited in the Edfu texts as responsible for the emergence of the physical world can be categorized and placed in their correct order of appearance. Without her lifelong interest in this subject, there is every chance that the greater importance of these texts would have gone unnoticed, and we might never have known that there exist very real accounts of the establishment of primitive cult structures in Egypt. As we shall see, these almost certainly had their foundation during the Early Pre-Pottery Neolithic B period, circa 8800–7600 BCE, and most likely replaced a much earlier cult site that existed during the Epipaleolithic age, circa 18,000–9600 BCE.

THE ARRIVAL OF THE SHEBTIW

The Edfu building texts begin with the arrival at a place called the Island of Trampling (*iw titi*), also known as the Homeland of the Primeval Ones, of two divine beings called Wa and 'Aa. They are described as Shebtiw (*sbtyw*), a term denoting a certain group of mythical beings, eight (or even ten) in number, involved with the early stages of establishing the first sacred enclosure in Egypt. Wa and 'Aa are never described, their sex never given, and yet they are clearly, like many of the other principal characters in the story, anthropomorphic in appearance and corporeal in nature. Indeed it is even stated that after they completed their mission on the Island of Trampling, they continued their journey to Heracleopolis in Middle Egypt, where their bodies were laid to rest, a cult in their honor surviving there through to dynastic times.[1] Where they came from is unclear. Reymond suggested that they simply emerged from the Nun, the primeval waters that surrounded the mythical island in every direction.

Figure 30.1. Three examples of djed-pillar amulets in the British Museum.

The Shebtiw appear following a period of darkness and a great destruction, which has devastated an earlier phase of building on the island.[2] This has caused it to be lost beneath the primeval waters, leaving only an enigmatic field of reeds as evidence of its former existence.[3] The destruction has also caused the death of the island's previous inhabitants, who are described in the texts as *ddw,* a word meaning something like "ghosts."[4] They had occupied and maintained a primitive cultus place located at the edge of a pool of reeds.[5] Its main focus had been something called the *ḏd,*[6] a word usually transliterated as *djed.* This suggests it was the prototype of the later djed pillars associated with the cults of Ptah and Osiris (see fig. 30.1), which represented not only the backbone of these gods, but also the cosmic axis or pole holding up the sky. This primeval pillar had acted as a perch for a divine being said to have been a *drty,* a type of bird usually identified either as a kite or, as Reymond prefers, a falcon.[7] To her, this indicated that this drty was in fact "a physical personality conceived as a bird."[8]

LORD OF THE WING

The drty falcon is named only as *Pn,* "This One,"[9] and he would appear to have been the "Sanctified Ruler"[10] of the cultus place, which had emerged originally as the seat of a nameless creator in the form of an earth god. Arguably, as Reymond admits, the nameless creator has some relationship to the later Sanctified Ruler, who bears the title Lord of the Wing (*ndm ndb*).[11] In other words, the *Pn*-god was simply the divine essence or soul of the earth god transformed into the guise of a bird atop the ḏd pillar.[12]

The Shebtiw are there on the Island of Trampling to prepare the way for the coming of another divine being, called the Falcon.[13] He is represented by a hieroglyph showing a falcon, which can also be used to denote the word *ntr,* or *neter,* meaning "divinized being" or "god."[14] The Falcon is referred to also as *ndb,* interpreted by Reymond as the "Winged One,"[15] showing his association with the former Sanctified Ruler of the island. Clearly the Falcon, like his predecessor, is a divine being in the form of a bird. Even though he is not to be confused with the falcon god Horus the Behdetite, who was the patron of Edfu, there is little question that the original being known as the Falcon went on to influence the much later cult of Horus the Elder.[16]

ANCESTORS OF THE FIRST OCCASION

Prior to the arrival of the Falcon, the *ka* (spirit double) of the former Sanctified Ruler, the *Pn*-god or drty falcon, turns up to assist the Shebtiw in their duties.[17] This ka had remained among the Field of Reeds, which marked the former position of the ḏd pillar destroyed during the period of darkness. This was also the site where the former inhabitants of the island had drowned at the time of the great destruction. They are referred to as the original divine dwellers of the Field of Reeds as well as the "Company of gods, the Ancestors [*tpyw*] of the First Occasion [*sep tpy*]."[18] They are also collectively known as the drty falcons, showing that the entire company, and not just the *Pn*-god, have avian attributes.[19]

THE FLYING BA

Confusingly (and there is much confusion in the Edfu building texts, which take the form of late redactions of sections from several different works attributed to the primeval age), the soul (ba) of the former Sanctified Ruler of the island, the *Pn*-god, returns from its place in the sky under the name of the "Flying Ba."[20] This takes up residence within the primitive cult structure built by the Shebtiw under the guidance and instructions of the *Pn*-god's ka, or spirit double,[21] which Reymond suspected was also that of the original creator of the island.[22] This primitive enclosure is built either on or very close to the site of the former ḏd pillar destroyed at the time of the great destruction.[23]

The new shrine is built to contain the *djeba* (*ḏja*), an ancient Egyptian word usually meaning "finger." It alludes to the djeba's polelike form, similar to that of the ḏd pillar, which it replaces as perch for the soon-to-arrive character known as the Falcon.[24] Reymond believed that both the ḏd pillar and the djeba perch were considered real pillars. She saw them as fashioned from reeds bound together and erected in the center of the cult structures in question, one existing before the great destruction and the other afterward.[25] Indeed she suspected that the entire structure erected by the Shebtiw functioned as a real enclosure, and that it too had been constructed from reeds woven together to create very basic walls.[26]

MADE IN STONE

Despite Reymond's assumptions about both the ḏd and djeba pillars, a good case might be made to suggest that they were in fact made of stone. Reymond, it should be remembered, was basing her opinions on the understanding that prior to the early dynastic age, the ancient Egyptians did not use stone masonry in building construction. It was also believed that during this early period cult structures employing the use of stone were rare in the Near East, and virtually nonexistent in Egypt. We now know that this is incorrect, not least because of the discovery of a 7000-year-old stone calendar circle at Nabta Playa in the Nubian Desert, located some 100 kilometers west of Abu Simbel in southern Egypt.

The Nabta Playa calendar circle features outlying stelae and more complex structures that, when viewed from the stone circle (built circa 4600–3600 BCE), marked the rising of key stars in the night sky.[27] Stone circles and cromlechs also featured as part of the El Omari culture, which thrived in the area of Gebel Hôf and Wadi Hôf, north of Helwan, circa 5500–4500 BCE.[28] There is also every reason to believe that even older cult structures, built by Post-Harifian and later Pre-Pottery Neolithic peoples, might once have existed in northern Egypt. Although generally made of materials such as wood, reed, and a basic form of wattle and daub, both domestic and early cult buildings built during the Natufian and later Pre-Pottery Neolithic periods would often feature foundations composed of fair-sized stone boulders, as well as walls made from piles of flat stones held together by clay mortar.[29]

More significantly, and as we saw in chapter 8, Israeli archaeologist Uzi Avner proposes that some of these early communal structures possessed masseboth, standing pillars of a cultic nature like those seen at the Epipaleolithic sites of Abu Salem and Ros Zin in the central Negev, both of which are likely to be as much as 12,000 years old. Did something similar exist within the earliest cult structures described in the Edfu building texts? It is a matter we return to in due course.

MAGIC SPELLS

Returning now to the Edfu records, we find the ka of the former Sanctified Ruler instructing the Shebtiw Wa and 'Aa, not only on the construction of a cult structure to surround the djeba perch, but also on how to use magic spells to make the waters recede from the edges of the sacred domain.[30] Carrying out these spells exposes a structure known as the Underworld of the Soul (*dw3t n B3*), which has remained hidden since the time of the great destruction.[31] In here are certain "relics" (*iht*) associated with the first period of creation on the island,[32] as well as the physical remains of the *Pn*-god, This One, along with those of the other divine inhabitants, who were drowned when the island was lost beneath the primeval waters.[33]

ARRIVAL OF THE FALCON

When all is ready, the new ruler of the Island of Trampling appears. This is the Falcon, known as the Winged One (*ndb*). Where he comes from is not stated, although Reymond suspected that he had left behind his "ancestral territory" to journey to the island.[34] "Ancestral territory" implies a land far away, but where exactly this might have been remains open to speculation.

On his arrival, the Falcon is uplifted by the djeba, where he takes his place under the new title of Lord of the Perch (*nb dj3*).[35] This act provides the sacred domain with a new name: Wetjeset-Neter (*wts-ntr*),[36] which means something like "that which uplifts the god."[37] The texts tell us also that the Falcon is the rightful successor of the original Sanctified Ruler, the *Pn*-god, who was Lord of the Wing.[38] Once the Falcon has been installed on his perch, the Flying Ba, the soul of the former occupier of the ḏd pillar, appears and reveals to the Falcon and the Shebtiw, Wa and 'Aa, everything that has transpired on the island prior to their arrival.[39]

THE ENEMY SNAKE

What is stated next is crucial to our understanding of events on the island before the great destruction, for after the establishment of the sacred enclosure with its ḏd pillar, there had come into the primeval world an "enemy snake" (rȝ),[40] known as the Great Leaping One (nhp-wr).[41]

This "enemy" attacked the island and its divine inhabitants, causing absolute catastrophe and leaving devastation in its wake. Exactly what went on is cryptically alluded to in the account given. One statement records how the Great Leaping One oppresses the head of a divine inhabitant named Heter-her, who is defenseless against its actions. His feet are pierced, and the ground of the sacred domain is split apart, prompting Reymond to remark, "This is a clear picture of a disaster."[42] She adds that "a storm, perhaps, came over the island during which an attack was made by an enemy pictured as a snake. The aggression was so violent that it destroyed the sacred land."[43] Not only did it devastate the island, reducing its original cult structure—enigmatically named the Mansion of Isden—to debris, but it also drowned the divine inhabitants[44] and left the world in complete darkness.[45] It was in this state that Wa and 'Aa found it upon their arrival at the beginning of the second phase of construction on the island.[46]

ECHOES OF OSIRIS

Reymond saw echoes in this story of the entombment and drowning of Osiris at the hands of Set. Just like Osiris, the original inhabitants of the Island of Trampling, as a consequence of the actions of the enemy snake, were entombed and drowned inside a structure, in this case the so-called Underworld of the Soul (dwȝt n bȝ).[47] Symbolic tombs of Osiris, such as the Osireion of Seti I at Abydos in southern Egypt and the so-called Tomb of Osiris or Osiris Shaft located beneath Khafre's causeway at Giza,[48] have raised islandlike areas surrounded by channels of water, perhaps symbolizing the island of creation surrounded and even submerged by the primeval waters of Nun. Are these structures abstract representations of the Island of Trampling, which eventually became associated with the drowning of Osiris inside the bespoke coffin? We should recall that according to the Memphite Theology as recorded on the Shabaka Stone, the drowning of Osiris took place at Ayan, in other words Helwan.

YOUNGER DRYAS EVENT

The nature of the island's destruction is open to speculation. However, in previous works I have speculated that the Edfu records preserve the abstract memory of an actual cataclysm that befell Egypt during the prehistoric age.[49] In the absence of any other candidates, the most likely cause was the Younger Dryas impact event, which science is now recognizing as having devastated large areas of the Northern Hemisphere sometime around 10,800 BCE.[50] The enemy snake is suggestive of a comet (comets are very often interpreted abstractly as snakes and serpents);[51] the period of darkness would then be the nuclear winter caused by the ash and debris thrust into the upper atmosphere, which would block out the sun for an extended period of time. The drowning of the first sacred domain and the submergence of the island could be a memory of the intense floods of the Younger Dryas. Should these assumptions prove correct, then the first phase of construction in Egypt's Isle of Trampling occurred *prior* to this period of turmoil, in other words toward the end of the late Epipaleolithic age, perhaps circa 13,500–10,500 BCE.

BIRDS IN HUMAN FORM

From these deductions we can determine that the island's original cultus place with its ḏd pillar was constructed during the Epipaleolithic age. Reymond believed that this enclosure was erected for a nameless creator in the form of a drty falcon and his companions, who, like their leader, were anthropomorphic beings in the form of birds. So were these individuals actually shamans who adopted the mantle of a bird to perform their ceremonies and rituals? If so, they must have existed during the Epipaleolithic age, their community eventually being decimated by a cataclysm that we can identify with the Younger Dryas event. This brought turmoil to the world for a period of several hundred years and almost certainly triggered a 1200-year cold spell that ended very suddenly, circa 9600 BCE.[52]

On the other hand, the Shebtiw Wa and 'Aa, along with the Falcon and Crew of the Falcon, do not arrive on the "island" until after the great destruction, so post circa 9600 BCE. The fact that the Falcon is himself described as the Winged One and Lord of the Perch tells us that he too is to be seen as a priest or shaman in the guise of a bird, one perhaps related to or descended from the former group of drty falcons who occupied the Homeland of the Primeval Ones during the first phase of construction. In other words, the Falcon is simply returning to the place of his ancestors. This is what Reymond had to say on the matter:

> If we recall the name of the divine being for whom it [the cult structure] was created, the Winged One, we may venture to suggest that there is preserved either an extract or an abbreviated version of what might well have been a single myth about the origin of the place of worship of a sacred bird. The bird might have been later identified with the Sacred Falcon, and thus the story of his cultus-place was adopted and adapted for the explanation of the beginnings of the cult of the Falcon.[53]

The Falcon's arrival on the island was thus a revivification of the original sacred domain, which had now become, as Reymond notes, a place of veneration of the ancestors (*tpyw*),[54] who were its original inhabitants.[55] We should also keep in mind that the ancient Egyptians regarded this primeval structure as the role model for all subsequent forms of the inner sanctuary or "holy of holies" at the heart of temple complexes.[56] This is made clear by the fact that the manner of creation of these built structures is specifically recorded—their size, appearance, and function,[57] which we shall examine shortly. But, having dealt with the first and second phases of construction on the Island of Trampling, or Wetjeset-Neter as it had now become, we must move forward in time to examine what happened next in the Homeland of the Primeval Ones.

31

HOMELAND OF THE PRIMEVAL ONES

Part II—Memphite Origins

After the arrival of the Falcon and his companions on the Island of Trampling, the Shebtiw Wa and 'Aa begin the process of creating other sacred domains on the margins of Wetjeset-Neter. This constitutes the third phase of construction in the Homeland of the Primeval Ones. It involves the creation of primeval mounds or hills on newly emerged portions of land known as *pāy*-lands.[1] Each one is brought into existence through the use of "learned spells" (*dʒjsw*).[2]

Clearly this original island of creation was only considered an island at the beginning, the emergence of the pāy-lands leaving it high and dry within a gradually emerging landmass. The manner in which these pāy-lands were added to the existing island landmass might be likened to continually affixing previously unknown pieces of a jigsaw puzzle to the edges of an existing picture, each new piece appearing as if out of nowhere to take its place on the board. Each of these new pāy-lands would itself become a cultus place, with its own cult structure containing a replica of the primeval ḏd pillar or djeba perch.

In this manner Wetjeset-Neter's original cult structure became the role model for the inner sanctuaries or shrines at the heart of every temple complex built in both Upper and Lower Egypt. These cult buildings symbolized the place of first creation in the physical world, an honor that would afterward be claimed by several locations, including Heliopolis in Lower Egypt, Hermopolis in Middle Egypt, Thebes in Upper Egypt and even Edfu itself, which became known as Djeba,[3] the same name as the sacred pillar that had once stood in the sacred enclosure of Wetjeset-Neter. Very clearly this djeba perch or pillar onto which the Falcon had been uplifted was the model also for the benben stone of Heliopolis on which the bennu bird perched at the commencement of the primeval age.

RETURN OF THE ENEMY SNAKE

According to the Edfu records, on the completion of the pāy-lands, the enemy snake known as the Great Leaping One returns to threaten the Homeland of the Primeval Ones. The Shebtiw once again recite spells, and this results in the appearance of a protector god (*ntr-hn*),[4] who is replaced in later texts by another divine being known as the God of the Temple.[5] His role is to protect the island against further attack from the enemy snake. This involves the building of a more substantial enclosure (*sbht*) around the sanctuary housing the djeba pillar, as well as the cutting of a channel around its perimeter, making it an island in its own right.[6] This channel was said to contain sanctified water that helped protect the sbht enclosure from the influence of the enemy snake. The making of the first actual temple in Egypt's history was now firmly under way.

The God of the Temple is in turn replaced by, or becomes, a new deity called Tanen.[7] He conducts a ceremony in which the Falcon is presented with a mace, as well as other power objects, including two stakes personified as living entities named Sekhem-her and Segemeh, along with a fragment of the original *dd* pillar.[8] All this is to strengthen the protection of the sacred domain against further attacks from the enemy snake, which appears to work.

The enemy snake's second attack on the Homeland of the Primeval Ones, which occurs on the edges of the island landmass, is countered by the appearance of a plethora of new mythical beings. They are formed into four groups, known collectively as the Soldiers of Tanen. The snake is overthrown, and the new gods of Wetjeset-Neter are victorious.[9] What exactly was going on here is difficult now to unravel, although the fact that the Falcon is said to have engaged in a battle with a snake both in the sky and in the primeval waters[10] suggests that this story derives from the memory of a cosmic event that once again threatened Egypt's earliest settlements. The battles that are said to have taken place on the margins of the island perhaps reflect the physical conflicts that must have resulted from the arrival into the region of displaced peoples from other parts of the ancient world. Very likely they would have come up against the island's inhabitants. They are said to have amassed an army to defeat these invaders, whose actions are put down to the presence of the enemy snake.

MEMPHITE ORIGINS

Usually Tanen is seen as one of the names of Memphis's creator god Ptah, his temple being the largest and most important in the capital city. However, at this stage in the Edfu records this might not have been the case.[11] Only later on in the texts does Tanen assume the name Ptah, who thereafter becomes identified with the original creator of the Homeland of the Primeval Ones.[12] This is our first indication that the origins of the Edfu building texts are to be sought, not in southern Egypt, where Edfu is located, or in Hermopolis, the cult center of the god Thoth,[13] which possessed its own interrelated creation account, but in northern Egypt, in the area around Memphis.

Indeed Egyptologist Eve Reymond found overwhelming evidence from many different areas of the Edfu records to suggest that their construction took place in the vicinity of Memphis under the influence of the Memphite priesthood.[14] Moreover, she concluded that the texts alluded to an actual sacred domain that was once thought to have existed somewhere to "the north of Memphis."[15] In her words, "The Memphite connexion of the creative deities, all point to the Memphite region as the source of the original form of the myth. Consequently, it may be expected that in the formulation of this myth there are reflected traditions attached to the early sacred places of that region."[16] One section of the Edfu texts even states that these sacred accounts of the primeval world derived from "the Ancestors," and had come originally from *a book which descended from the sky to the north of Memphis.*"[17] In conclusion Reymond proposed that "the basis of the Egyptian temple was formulated at Memphis, just as Heliopolis and its temples were the basis of the ordinary daily ritual of the temple."[18] This is a highly significant realization, to which we shall have cause to return shortly.

SEAT OF THE FIRST OCCASION

It is about this stage in the development of Wetjeset-Neter that a willow tree suddenly replaces the role and function of the djeba perch.[19] The Falcon is now uplifted onto this tree, making it into some kind of divine seat or throne standing at the center of the sacred enclosure.[20] For example, it is stated that the Falcon "arrived and settled down on the willow," leading Reymond to suspect that it was seen as the new seat of the First Occasion (sep tpy), the title given to the first period of construction on the Island of Trampling.[21] The Edfu texts tell us that this sacred willow stood at the foot of a structure referred to as the *bw-hnm*.[22] Understanding what this name represents will become crucial in determining the true location of the Homeland of the Primeval Ones.

The prefix *bw* implies a foundation ground or place, while *hnm* is a problematic word suggesting either "still water," such as a pool, cistern, or well,[23] and/or a construction of some kind.[24] Eve Reymond felt it was perhaps a water source within Wetjeset-Neter, arguably the "place from which the subterranean water welled out, whereupon the creative powers might eventually have been brought out of Nun [i.e., the primeval waters], in the first instance Tanen."[25] He, as we have seen, was the proto-form of the Memphite creator god Ptah. This tells us that the bw-hnm, if it existed as a physical place, was thought to have been located somewhere in the vicinity of Memphis.

PRIMEVAL WELL

The bw-hnm also bore the title *bw-w3*, "the place of Wa,"[26] one of the two Shebtiw involved in the creation at Wetjeset-Neter. To Reymond, this implied that it was here, in this "primeval well" or "primeval spring," that the Shebtiw had removed the iht-relics before reciting the magical spells that had brought the pāy-lands into existence.[27] If this was the case, then the bw-hnm was considered the point of connection between the first phase of creation on the Island of Trampling and everything that came after. What is more, it constituted a structure located somewhere in the Memphite area and identified with what appears to have been a primeval spring, well, cistern, or pool of some kind. From here the "subterranean water" was thought to have "welled up" in order to initiate creation in the outside world.

In Eve Reymond's words, "It would follow that this *bw-hnm* was regarded as being the place of origin and the realm of the creative powers acting in the second period of the creation of the Earth. . . . The picture of a willow standing near a well gives a clear idea of a primitive sacred place as it might once have existed in Egypt."[28]

PLACE OF THE FIRST OCCASION

Is this site, the bw-hnm, a reference perhaps to the springs around Helwan and Ma'sarah, which, as we have seen, have been the focus of human activity since the Epipaleolithic age, circa 18,000–9,600 BCE? Was this area the original Homeland of the Primeval Ones, the site of Wetjeset-Neter, where the Falcon was lifted onto his perch? Is this where the primeval cult structure containing the dd pillar and later djeba perch was to be found—in the vicinity of Helwan, toward which the arc circle created by the geographical positioning of the Giza pyramids is directed, the same line that forms the hypotenuse of the pyramid field's base 3-4-5 triangle and targeted the setting of the Cygnus star Sadr during the Pyramid Age, circa 2550–2479 BCE?

Reymond linked the story of the entombment and drowning of Osiris with the death of the primeval inhabitants of the Island of Trampling, even further reinforcing a connection of this tradition with the area. As we have seen, the Memphite Theology records that Osiris met his fate at the hands of his evil brother Set at Ayan, the ancient name for Helwan.

THE SACRED WILLOW

A further clue that Helwan was the Homeland of the Primeval Ones comes from the fact that in the Edfu texts the sacred willow replaced the dd pillar and djeba perch as the resting place of the Falcon. In Heliopolitan tradition, the willow was the seat not of a divine falcon, but of the bennu, connecting the willow directly with Heliopolis in its role as the place of first creation. The tree was thus a metaphor for the benben stone, the original perch on which Re as the bennu alighted on the first day. It is also on the sacred willow that the soul of Osiris, again in the form of the bennu bird, perched following his resurrection. So important was the sacred willow to Heliopolitan tradition that it was said to have actually stood in Heliopolis's Mansion of the Bennu Bird.[29]

Heliopolis's sacred willow tree was eventually replaced by the ancient sycamore that stood in the vicinity of the Ain Shams spring in El-Matariya. It was beneath this sycamore tree that the sky goddess Nut and her brother and lover, the earth god Geb, in his guise as the Great Cackler, are said to have produced the egg of creation from which Re emerged in the form of the bennu bird.[30] Were these two separate traditions both garbled forms of an original creation myth associated with another site altogether?

Unquestionably the Heliopolitan priesthood saw their city as the true site of the primeval mound and benben stone. During the dynastic age the Mansion of the Bennu Bird occupied this all-important mythical location. Yet as we have seen, Heliopolis's claim to be the place of first creation was very likely false: the city's sacred identity as Iwnw or Anu being stolen, or at least adopted, from an original cultus place bearing the same name, or names. This primeval location was almost certainly situated in the vicinity of the thermal and mineral springs of Helwan and Ma'sarah, with the heavenly mountain of An or Anu, the place of the ancestors according to the inscription left in the area by the pharaoh Necho II, being nearby Gebel Hôf.

"NORTH OF MEMPHIS"

Perhaps now is the time to attempt to understand exactly what the Edfu records represent in historical and archaeological terms. In the first place, Eve Reymond freely admitted that, to date, absolutely no archaeological evidence has ever emerged to confirm the existence of prehistoric cult structures of the type described in the texts. This said, she clearly believed that the very vivid description of the sacred enclosure and shrine surrounding the djeba perch related to an actual built structure that had existed somewhere to the "north of Memphis."[31] She said to the "north of Memphis" because it was here that the book containing the knowledge of the Homeland of the Primeval Ones, which was afterward used to construct the Edfu records, had "*descended from the sky.*"[32]

To the northwest of Memphis, Eve Reymond's eyes fell upon the early dynastic cemetery at Saqqara. This is located on high ground facing toward Gebel Hôf and the Nile flood basin. Was it near here, she speculated, that the mythical book containing the original account of the Homeland of the Primeval Ones was thought to have descended from the sky?[33] Was it here too that she would find a clue to the true place of construction mentioned in the Edfu records? Under the assumption that the answer was going to be "yes," she began examining the type of tombs making up the necropolis at Saqqara. Here she focused her attentions on Tomb 3505, which she deemed of "special interest" to this debate.[34] Indeed she saw in its construction, which incorporated both a tomb and small temple, "the same combination of temple and place of funerary cults . . . that . . . was one of the essential features in the constitution of the original temple of the Falcon."[35]

Yet Reymond also emphasized that in no way did the tombs of the Saqqara cemetery resemble Wetjeset-Neter's mythical cult structure. She claimed only that there were "undeniable points of contact between the actual constructions of the Archaic Cemetery and the theoretical reconstructions that can be made on the basis of the Edfu records. It may be that at Sakkara and Edfu we have, in the one in brick and the other in hieroglyphic, aspects of what was essentially the same Memphite tradition."[36] For her there was "not the slightest justification for postulating any constructional material but reed in so far as the first temple, that of the Falcon, is concerned."[37] However, as we have seen, Reymond was either being overly cautious in imagining the cult structure as being constructed primarily of reed, or she was simply not aware of the widespread use of stone masonry in both the Levant and northern Egypt during the prehistoric age.

A LONG-ESTABLISHED TRADITION

I was surprised to see that in her search to find the point of origin of the Edfu records, Reymond did not focus her attentions on the late-predynastic and early dynastic cemetery at Ezbit el-Walda, just to the northwest of Helwan. It is located on the opposite side of the Nile from Saqqara at approximately the same latitude. Just prior to her writing *The Mythical Origin of the Egyptian Temple*, which was published in 1969, over 10,000 tombs had been recorded during excavations carried out there by Zaki Y. Saad. Many of these houses of the dead contained superstructures that were made of cut-and-dressed stone blocks of enormous size (see fig. 31.1). They were also highly sophisticated, perhaps even more so than the elite tombs at Saqqara. Indeed it was the highly advanced nature of the tombs at Helwan that prompted Egyptologist Michael Rice to comment:

> It is frequently asserted that the earliest use of stone [in ancient Egypt] was in the late Second Dynasty but quite apart from the revetment of Hierakonpolis [in the south of the country], the First Dynasty tombs at Helwan (as well as some of the larger, contemporary tombs at Saqqara) demonstrate that this is not so. Some of the blocks used for the wall and floor of the burial chambers are huge, suggesting that they are already the products of *a long-established and assured tradition.*[38]

Figure 31.1 Above and left, two perspectives of a late First Dynasty mastaba tomb, circa 2900 BCE, uncovered in 1945–1946 by Zaki Y. Saad in the cemetery of Ezbit el-Walda, northwest of Helwan. Note the solid stone infrastructure made of Tura limestone.

This "long-established and assured tradition" had begun in the vicinity of Helwan and Ma'sarah at the time of the El Omari culture, circa 5500–4500 BCE, where it had most likely lingered in some form since the earliest days of the Pre-Pottery Neolithic B period. As we have seen, it was at this time that a highly advanced stone-tool-making society had thrived in the area—one with links all the way back to the culture responsible for cult centers like Göbekli Tepe in far off Anatolia. Yet it is what Rice goes on to say that is of the greatest importance here:

> A study of the architecture of the Helwan tombs has concluded that the use of stone in their construction indicates a high level of building skills available in this region of northern Upper Egypt in the First and Second Dynasties. The ability to manipulate stone, it is suggested, *may have contributed to the remarkable achievements of the builders of the monuments at Giza.*[39]

We can begin now to understand why the monuments of Giza are of such sophistication for their age, and where exactly the knowledge and technological skills that went toward their creation actually came from—Helwan. Yet these advances did not stem simply from the late predynastic and early dynastic periods. They came from a long tradition of human activity in the area of Helwan and Ma'sarah stretching back to the Pre-Pottery Neolithic, and beyond even into the Epipaleolithic age.[40]

THE WISDOM OF IMHOTEP

Reymond herself acknowledged the connection between the Edfu records and the establishment of the pyramid complexes in the Memphite district during the Old Kingdom. She saw this fact as encoded in the tale regarding the ancient book containing the original account of the emergence of the Homeland of the Primeval Ones. According to the Edfu account, the knowledge and wisdom in this book was acquired by the great architect Imhotep,[41] the designer of the Step Pyramid at Saqqara on behalf of the pharaoh Djoser, who ruled circa 2630–2611 BCE.

According to the Edfu texts, the "Chief Lector priest Imhotep the Great, son of Ptah," used this information to create "the Book for the Planning of the Temple,"[42] which was in turn "used as the starting-point in drawing the plans of the historical temples."⁴³ Significantly, the Edfu records, Reymond suggests, point "definitely to Lower Egypt [i.e., the area around Memphis] as the place of the prototype constructions which were imitated at a later date in Upper Egypt."⁴⁴

These same plans for the construction of the ideal Egyptian temple unquestionably influenced the design and layout of the pyramid fields in the Memphite district built by Imhotep's immediate successors. Each would have contained at least some of the ideas that were thought to have come from a creator in the form of a bird. We can now reveal with some certainty that this sacred place, seen to be the foundation point of Egyptian civilization, was located somewhere in the vicinity of Helwan and Ma'sarah, to the east and northeast of Memphis.

More poignantly, the knowledge preserved in the Edfu records regarding the size, appearance, and function of the original cult structure of Wetjeset-Neter can be found, as we see next, in the underlying geometry at Giza. What is more, there is every chance that this ancient wisdom came all the way from Göbekli Tepe in southeast Anatolia.

32

HOMELAND OF THE PRIMEVAL ONES

Part III—A Certain Ratio

The potential flow of innovation from the Pre-Pottery Neolithic world of Göbekli Tepe to the Pyramid Age of ancient Egypt probably did not stop at the use of stone masonry and architectural design. Almost certainly it also included abstract memories of the original prime movers behind the birth of Egypt, and the knowledge they introduced via key settlement sites like Helwan as early as 8500–7800 BCE. This can be recognized in the Edfu building texts, which seem to emphasize the manner in which the Shebtiw constructed the original cult structure at Wetjeset-Neter.

LIVING ENTITIES

We are told that this primitive shrine or sanctuary, built to enclose the djeba perch, was 30 cubits in length and 20 cubits in width.[1] It remained this way until it was finally incorporated into the much larger Temple of the Falcon,[2] where it formed its adyton or holy of holies.[3] The sanctuary's function remained the same: to house the essence or spirit of a creator, seen as a drty falcon. Indeed, both the primeval enclosure of Wetjeset-Neter and the subsequent shrines modeled on it were, Egyptologist Eve Reymond suspected, seen in terms of a "living entity," their shape, size, and design making it possible to manifest and contain the deity's primal essence.[4] The pillar or post standing at their center would have served as the symbolic perch upon which the deity had been uplifted.

Most likely the oldest built structures described in the Edfu texts were elliptical in shape like so many of the cult buildings uncovered at Natufian and later Pre-Pottery Neolithic A sites in the Levant. Yet as we saw in connection with Göbekli Tepe during the Pre-Pottery Neolithic B period, some (although not all) communal structures began changing from curvilinear to rectilinear designs, perhaps in order to maximize space in an urban environment. The great trade center of Beidha, immediately north of Petra in Jordan, comes to mind. Here almost all of the excavated buildings are rectilinear and grouped together to create a self-contained urban environment, complete with shops, walkways, dwellings, and communal rooms.

GRAPHIC RECONSTRUCTION

London graphic artist Russell M. Hossain was asked to reconstruct what Wetjeset-Neter's proposed cult building might have looked like, based on known examples of cult buildings and communal rooms from the Natufian and later Pre-Pottery Neolithic tradition in the southern Levant, including the Negev highlands and Egyptian Sinai. After due consideration, it was thought likely that large stone boulders would have featured in its foundations, with piles of flat stones forming its boundary wall. Its floor would probably have been mud plaster and at least partially subsurface, perhaps with a stone slab displaying carved cupules. There might also have been a partial roof, made of wooden struts and reeds, and at its center we shall place a stone pillar or massebah of the sort implied by the Edfu building texts and seen in Post-Harifian communal rooms in the Negev highlands (see plate 22).

Russell Hossain's reconstruction of Wetjeset-Neter's primeval sanctuary beautifully encapsulates what Egypt's first cult building might have looked like around 8500–7800 BCE. To imagine that a stone structure of this appearance once stood in the vicinity of Helwan, and was perhaps the role model for the first adyton or holy of holies in Egypt, is an exciting prospect. To consider also that its builders could have been in contact with nomadic groups coming from as far away as Göbekli Tepe and other sites in southeast Anatolia and the Levant enables us to better comprehend how the technical achievements of these Neolithic peoples might have evolved across a period of several millennia until finally they were utilized in the creation of the Giza pyramid field. Yet if this was the case, then what else can we determine passed between the Neolithic world of southeast Anatolia and the Old Kingdom builders of the three main pyramids at Giza? Was it an understanding of sound acoustics like that found at Göbekli Tepe? Did these ideas really reach the Pyramid builders via Pre-Pottery Neolithic sites like Jerf el-Ahmar in northern Syria, Beidha in Jordan, and Helwan in northern Egypt? The first clue comes from the measurements of the original cult structure at Wetjeset-Neter.

PERFECT RATIOS

An architectural structure with the dimensions of 30×20 cubits, whether curvilinear or rectilinear in shape, might at first seem random. Yet its 3:2 ratio should be familiar to us from the geometry underlying the three main pyramids at Giza. As we have seen (see chapter 16), a 3:2 triangle, composed of two back-to-back 3-4-5 triangles, stretches between the latitudes of Gebel el-Qibli and the peak of the Great Pyramid and the eastern side of the Second Pyramid, close to its southeast corner. A further 3:2 triangle, one quarter of the size of that displayed in Giza's underlying geometry, is found also in the height-to-base ratio of the Second Pyramid.

Triangles with 3:2 ratios are simply two 4:3 ratio or 3-4-5 triangles joined together, back-to-back, while the musical interval known as the perfect fifth, which has a 3:2 ratio, is simply the inverse form of a perfect fourth, with a ratio of 4:3. As we saw in chapters 23 and 24, a 4:3 ratio defines the elliptical shape of various key installations at Göbekli Tepe, as well as the House of Aurochs at Jerf el-Ahmar in Syria. It is found also in connection with at least one Pre-Pottery Neolithic structure at Tell es-Sultan (Jericho) in the West Bank, and was incorporated into the acoustic design of various Neolithic stone chambers in southwest England.

Thus there exists a directly proportional relationship between the geometry underlying the layout of the Giza pyramid field and the length-to-width ratio of the original enclosure of Wetjeset-Neter as outlined in the Edfu building texts. Thereafter the shape, size, and function of this primeval sanctuary were incorporated into the much larger Temple of the Falcon. This in turn, according to the Edfu records, went on to become the model for the adyton or holy of holies of all temples built in Egypt.[5] As a consequence, every Egyptian temple, in theory, contained an inner sanctuary based on the dimensions and proportions of a primitive cult structure that perhaps existed in the Helwan area several thousand years earlier. Were these inner shrines specifically designed to maximize their sound acoustics using an understanding of musical intervals? Remember, it was inside an aduta, that is, adyton, that Diogenes Laertius tells us Pythagoras learned the "secrets of the gods" (see chapter 21). Is it possible that this apparent initiatory experience provided Pythagoras with a knowledge of musical intervals based on the sound acoustics of the adyton in question?

THE SOLAR TEMPLE

Eventually, a variation in the original design of the Temple of the Falcon resulted in the development of what Reymond calls the solar temple, dedicated to the sun god Re. Yet even here the Edfu texts tell us that its inner sanctuary was 30 × 20 cubits in size, just like the primitive enclosure of Wetjeset-Neter. Interestingly, during its second phase of construction, the size of the inner enclosure of the solar temple was expanded to 90 × 20 cubits.[6] This is the equivalent of three 3:2-ratio rectangles, each of 30 × 20 cubits in size. Once again, this hardly seems a coincidence, suggesting that structures bearing 3:2 ratios, or expansions thereof, were considered extremely important in providing the environments necessary to contain the living spirit of the creator god. Enhancing the building's sound acoustics will have helped instill the appropriate state of mind with which to recognize the presence of this divinity.

Even further confirming the apparent potency of the 3:2 ratio in temple construction in ancient Egypt are the overall measurements given for the solar temple. According to the Edfu account, these had to be 300 × 200 cubits in size,[7] which once again preserves the 3:2 proportions of Wetjeset-Neter's original cult structure.

DIRECTED NORTH

Another powerful link between the Edfu building texts and both Göbekli Tepe's and Giza's grand design was the location of Wetjeset-Neter's primeval enclosure within the much larger Temple of the Falcon. It was positioned at the temple's northern end with its northern wall corresponding with the temple complex's own exterior wall. This is what Reymond had to say on the subject:

> The text indicates that the sanctuary was erected at the north rear wall of the enclosure and in its middle. . . . Originally the Temple in the Wetjeset-Neter was probably a mere courtyard having at its north wall very little more than a simple, light structure of reeds erected round the Perch to screen and protect it with its lord and to mark the most sacred part within it. The "booth" might have been the starting-point of the construction of the interior in the primitive temples, and it was from it that the "Holy of Holies" of the later temples eventually developed.[8]

So there is a direct relationship here between the orientation of the "booth" or "sanctuary" containing the djeba perch in the Temple of the Falcon and the layout and orientation of the stone installations at Göbekli Tepe. These, as we will recall, were built with twin central pillars, which, in the cases of Enclosures C, D, and H, were oriented toward the circular apertures of porthole stones located in the north-northwestern section of the ringwall. As we saw in chapter 2, these upright stones would appear to have been specifically positioned to target the setting of the star Deneb during the epoch of their construction. Likewise, the three main pyramids at Giza were built to reflect, in both the horizontal and vertical planes, the setting of the Cygnus stars Gienah, Sadr, and Rukh, while the peak of the Second Pyramid also marked the setting of Deneb as viewed from the summit of Gebel el-Qibli (see chapter 12).

That the original cult structure of Wetjeset-Neter, in its role as the inner shrine of the Temple of the Falcon, was located up against the latter's northern exterior wall tells us that the north was the primary direction of interest to these first Egyptians, just as it was for the builders of Göbekli Tepe. Further emphasizing the sanctuary's position within the temple is that construction occurred outward from this direction and, more importantly, southward. This was most likely to preserve the cult structure's northerly orientation within the gradually expanding building complex.

PLACE OF THE WINGED ONE

That Wetjeset-Neter's cult structure was considered a living entity, containing the essence or spirit of a creator in the form of a bird, tends to suggest that its orientation toward the north reflected an interest in a celestial bird thought to either exist in or be connected with this direction. This is borne out by the fact that in the Edfu records it is the Flying Ba of the Sanctified Ruler in the form of a drty falcon called the *Pn*-god, or Winged One, that returns from the sky to inhabit the sacred enclosure following its revivification by the Shebtiw Wa and 'Aa. This sanctuary, we should recall, was built to contain the divine perch on which the Falcon himself would be uplifted upon his arrival in the Homeland of the Primeval Ones. The clear impression here is that he is an embodiment of the former creator in its guise as a drty falcon. We should recall also that the djeba perch replaced the ḍd pillar, which had previously stood at the center of the very basic shrine erected during the first period of creation on the Island of Trampling. This suggests that the structure's connection with the north might well have reached back to this distant epoch, which we can identity with the final stages of the Epipaleolithic age prior to the Younger Dryas event, thus circa 13,500–10,500 BCE.

Is it possible that the ḍd pillar, as well as the later djeba perch and even the sacred willow tree, all of which acted as perches for a divine falcon in the Edfu texts, were in fact physical representations of a sky pole symbolizing the point of connection between the earth and the sky world? Is this why the inner sanctuary of the Temple of the Falcon had to be located at its northern end, because the perch was a symbol of the northern celestial pole in its role as the cosmic axis, its summit occupied by a creator in the form of a bird? If so, then this cosmic bird might well have occupied the position of the northern celestial pole either during the earliest epoch of construction of the first cult structure on the Island of Trampling, circa 13,500–10,500 BCE, or perhaps even earlier. As we see next, this archaic image of a bird on a pole seen in association with the northern celestial pole is found elsewhere in the ancient world. To examine the matter further, we must transfer our attentions, temporarily at least, to the Upper Paleolithic cave art of southern France.

PART SIX

STARRY WISDOM

33

BIRD ON A POLE

etween 15,750 and 12,750 BCE the stars occupying the position of the
northern celestial pole were those of Cygnus, and even in this age the constellation was almost certainly seen in terms of a celestial bird. By virtue of its
astronomical position, its stars would have been believed to guard and even
control the turning of the heavens as a deity in its own right. In the earliest
days of Egypt this bird would become a creator in the form of a drty falcon,
celebrated in what might have been the first primeval enclosure ever built in
the country. To get a further idea of this very ancient belief in a controlling
force of the heavens in the form of a bird, we must examine a painted relief to
be found on the northern wall of an almost inaccessible pit known as the Well
Shaft, or the Shaft of the Dead Man, in the famous caves at Lascaux in the
Dordogne region of southern France.

Here among the ice-age art created by accomplished Solutrean artists circa
16,500–15,000 BCE,[1] we see a bird perched on a pole, above which is a male
human figure with the head of a bird. He leans at an unnatural angle as if falling backward and, curiously, has an erect penis, just like the headless figure on
Göbekli Tepe's Vulture Stone (Pillar 43, see chapter 4). This is almost certainly
a sign that he is a shaman in a deathlike trance, for men can have erections in
the early stages of an altered state induced by hallucinogens, just as they can
close to the point of death.

To the figure's right is a large bovine, a bison most probably, with a spear in its back and blood and/or guts spilling from its underside. Professor Michael Rappenglück of the University of Munich has identified this painted fresco, found in the Shaft of the Dead Man, situated in the most northerly part of the cave complex, as a representation of the area of sky occupied by the stars making up the Summer Triangle (see figs. 33.1 and 33.2).[2]

Figure 33.1. The bird man, bison, and bird on a pole seen in the Well Shaft of France's Lascaux cave.

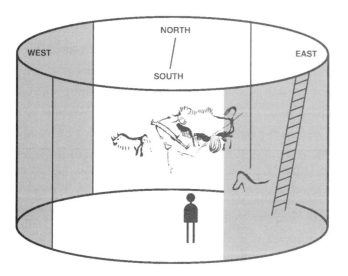

Figure 33.2. Plan of the Lascaux cave's Well Shaft (after Rappenglück), showing the positioning of its cave art. The bird on the pole, bison, and bird man are located almost precisely due north.

GUARDIAN OF THE POLE

Almost certainly the bird in Lascaux's Well Shaft scene is Cygnus in its role as guardian of the northern celestial pole. The sky pole is the bird's perch, just like the ḏd pillar and djeba perch of the Edfu records. Very likely they preserve the memory of a physical representation of a sky pole or cosmic axis, the drty falcon of the Edfu texts playing the same role as the bird in the Lascaux scene.

Just like the headless figure on Göbekli Tepe's Pillar 43, the Lascaux bird man almost certainly signifies the soul of a shaman who, having achieved an altered state of consciousness, has ascended the sky pole to gain access to the Upper World. Indeed, the shaman's ritual paraphernalia mimics the bird itself, much as the Falcon of the Edfu records mimics the Sanctified Ruler in the form of a drty falcon. It is important to remember what Eve Reymond had to say about the divine being known as the Winged One venerated at Wetjeset-Neter:

> We may venture to suggest that there is preserved either an extract or an abbreviated version of what might well have been a single myth about the origin of the place of worship of a sacred bird. The bird might have been later identified with the Sacred Falcon, and thus the story of his cultus-place was adopted and adapted for the explanation of the beginnings of the cult of the Falcon.[3]

The fact that Lascaux's shaft scene is to be found on the circular pit's north wall emphasizes the connection with the primitive enclosure of Wetjeset-Neter, which would afterward become the northerly placed sanctuary of the Temple of the Falcon. Very clearly the Lascaux panel was thought to have been an imaginary window onto the celestial realms in the northern part of the heavens, quite literally an ice-age planetarium correctly orientated toward its chosen celestial targets. Had the primitive enclosure of Wetjeset-Neter represented something similar? Was it where Cygnus had been venerated in the form of a drty falcon? Was this sky falcon eventually portrayed on the astronomical ceilings from Egypt's Middle Kingdom onward under the name of An or Anu, a name given also to the celestial realm of the dead in ancient Egyptian funerary texts? As we have seen, An or Anu was the Helwan district's original place-name and it was here, most likely, that the primeval enclosure of Wetjeset-Neter once stood, having replaced an earlier, more basic structure that had existed when the stars of Cygnus occupied the vicinity of the northern celestial pole, circa 15,750–12,750 BCE.

SIBERIAN SKY POLES

One might question the use of a single example of ice age cave art in southern France to explain the mythical account of a primeval sanctuary that perhaps once existed in northern Egypt. But sky poles with birds at their summits feature heavily in other parts of the ancient world, and these too can be shown to derive from sky-related mythology dating back to the Paleolithic age. For instance, shamans of the Reindeer Tungus tribes of Siberia and Manchuria in northeast Asia erect long wooden poles atop which they affix carved images of swans in flight (see fig. 33.3). These are placed in outdoor environments next to altars where rituals are conducted in which a shaman enters a trance state and "climbs" the pole to induce what are known as "soul flights." These are conducted so that the shaman might enter the sky world.[4] Acting as a visual aid in this process, the swan on the pole is seen both as the soul of the shaman and as guardian of the Upper World.

Figure 33.3. Swan pole erected by shamans belonging to the Reindeer Tungus tribes of northwest Manchuria and Siberia.

AMERICAN BIRD OF CREATION

Although the swan of the Reindeer Tungus shamans is not linked directly with Cygnus, the symbolism mimics that of the bird on the pole in the Lascaux cave, which dates to an age when the identity of the celestial bird would not have been in question. Swans and geese are universal symbols of Cygnus not only in Europe and Asia, but also in North America. For instance, among the Cherokee a bird of creation known as Guwisguwi or Cooweescoowee is identified with Cygnus.[5] According to Cherokee elders, Guwisguwi laid the egg that brought forth the universe; it also governed a world age of humankind.[6] Illustrations show the bird sitting atop a T-shaped cross (see fig. 33.4). Its stem represents the cosmic axis as the turning point of the heavens, while the horizontal bar signifies the sky world over which the bird rules. Guwisguwi was said to have been a "mythical white water bird of tremendous size,"[7] or in another account "a large white bird of uncommon occurrence, perhaps the egret or the swan."[8]

Guwisguwi and similar celestial birds in Native American sky lore, such as the raptor named Brain Smasher, who judges human souls as they reach the Milky Way's Dark Rift and is identified with Deneb,[9] suggest that such traditions arrived in North America from Eurasia prior to the submergence of the Beringia land bridge around 8500 BCE. But there are much clearer indications that the swan atop the Siberian shamanic pole derives from an age when the northern celestial pole coincided with Cygnus.

Figure 33.4. Guwisguwi or Cooweescoowee, the Cherokee bird of creation.

TENGRI THE CREATOR

In the modern religious revival movement of Tengrism or Burkhanism (from the word *burkhan,* the celestial deities of the Altai), which has assimilated preexistent shamanic traditions prevalent among the Turkic-speaking ethnic groups of southern Siberia, the goose is identified with Tengri, the sky god. (The swan is the symbol of his wife, the earth goddess Umai Ana.)[10] Followers of Tengrism, which thrives today in countries such as the Altai Republic, the Republic of Khakassia, and the neighboring Republic of Tuva, preserve a creation myth in which Tengri, in his form as a white goose, glides unerringly over an endless expanse of water, symbolizing time itself. Beneath the water awaits the goddess Ak Ana, "White Mother." She calls out to Tengri, saying, "Create."[11]

To aid him in his task, Tengri first brings forth the god Er Kishi. He is not as pure or as white as Tengri, but together they create the mundane world. Thereafter Er Kishi turns evil, misleading and drawing the human race into dark ways. This causes Tengri to withdraw from the earth and assume the name Tengri Ülgen. From this remote position he now helps humanity, sending guidance to shamans, both male and female, through a series of power animals.[12]

This creation story parallels the Hindu account of how Saraswati, the goddess of poetry, music, and divine inspiration, encourages her husband, the creator god Brahma, to bring forth the physical universe through the call of the swan-goose, Hamsa. In Egypt also the earth god Geb, in his guise as the goose Gengen-wer, the Great Cackler, emits a honk that brings forth the cosmic egg from which emerges the sun god Re at dawn on the first day. Both the goose Gengen-wer and the swan-goose, Hamsa, can be shown to be personifications of the Cygnus constellation.[13]

COSMOLOGY OF THE ALTAI MOUNTAINS

The heavenly abode of Tengri Ülgen is entered through Altyn-Kazik (the "polar star"),[14] reached via a sky pole or cosmic axis called Kangyi.[15] This is held in place by a golden nail or stake that Tengri drove into the universe at the beginning of time, creating order in the cosmos and keeping both the heavens and earth in place.[16] In some variations of this myth, the world axis is a "heavenly tree," a form used by *kams* or shamans to reach the sky world.[17]

Kangyi is said to connect the earth with the sun and, finally, with

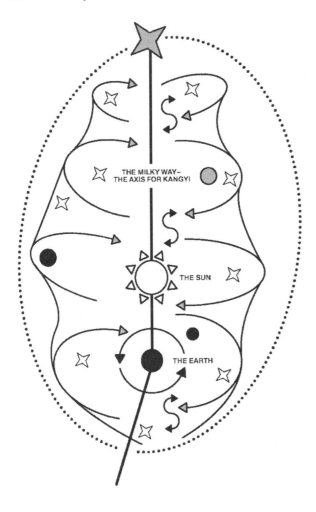

THE MILKY WAY–
THE AXIS FOR KANGYI

THE SUN

THE EARTH

Figure 33.5. The cosmic schema of the Altaic Tengrists, showing the egglike universe through which the sky pole Kangyi passes, symbolizing the Milky Way. Altyn-Kazik, the polestar, seen at the top of the cosmic axis, marks the northern celestial pole.

Altyn-Kazik, the polestar.[18] It also enables the stars to keep their positions while turning about the sky. The whole universe, with Kangyi running through its center as polar axis, is surrounded entirely by a kind of cosmic egg that has the appearance of a placenta or an amniotic sack (see fig. 33.5). Kangyi itself is seen to be an active spirit in its own right, a living entity whose light is felt through the intercession of the burkhans.[19]

Kangyi enables the shamans to travel from the earth via the sun toward Altyn-Kazik, the polestar, shown in pictorial representations as a large four- or eight-pointed star, although in life they are unable to reach it. More importantly, Kangyi is in actuality the Milky Way.[20] It is this that the shamans use to reach the different levels of existence between here and the realm of Tengri Ülgen. Yet clearly no mechanism attached to the Milky Way turns the stars at night, while the polestar cannot be reached simply by ascending the Milky Way.

COSMIC CONUNDRUM

If, as I suspect, the Altaic form of Tengrism is of extreme antiquity, there can be only one answer to this cosmic conundrum: these disparate notions derive from an age when the polestar did indeed embrace the Milky Way. But this last happened when the northern celestial pole passed through the constellation of Cygnus, circa 15,750–12,750 BCE. It was across this 3000-year period that three of its stars—Deneb, Sadr, and Rukh—came close enough to the northern celestial pole to be classed as polestars. Thereafter the northern celestial pole moved into the constellation of Lyra, where sometime around 12,750 BCE it began to align with the bright star Vega, which then became polestar for a period of around 2000 years.

COSMIC TREE

When the northern celestial pole was in Cygnus, the Milky Way would have been seen to pivot around this area of the sky, like some unimaginable propeller on the nose of an invisible cosmic airplane. Moreover, once every night the Milky Way would have been seen standing upright due north, while at the same time passing directly overhead to trail away into the southern sky. This incredible sight would have had an immense impact on the mind-set of our ancestors, creating abstract ideas about a celestial bird (Cygnus) perched on a pole (the Milky Way and cosmic axis of the heavens). Alternately, it might well have been interpreted as a bird that sits within the branches of a cosmic tree, a Tree of Life, with its trunk and roots in the extreme north.

In Norse tradition, for instance, the mythical ash tree Yggdrasil was personified in the night sky as the Milky Way.[21] In this heavenly tree's upper branches sat an unnamed eagle that "has knowledge of many things, and between its eyes sits a hawk called Vedrfolnir."[22] While the eagle has been identified with Cygnus,[23] the hawk was perhaps made up of other stars in the same vicinity. Quite possibly the myths surrounding Yggdrasil, as well as other cosmic trees that were said to exist in the center or northern part of the sky, are echoes of a time when the Milky Way was last seen standing in the extreme north some 14,750 years ago.

Such beliefs would seem to have inspired the creation of the bird on a pole and the bird man seen inside the Shaft of the Dead Man at Lascaux. Thus there seems every likelihood that the wooden swans in flight placed on the top of sky poles used by the Reindeer Tungus shamans to aid soul flight are also abstract echoes of an age when Cygnus played host to the northern celestial pole. These beliefs, it would seem, never died out, and survived in abstract form through to the modern day in many parts of the world.

COSMIC CREATION

From Finland across to the Urals, and beyond into Siberia and the American continent, swans, geese, and other types of wildfowl feature in folk stories regarding the creation of the universe. In other parts of the ancient world, the swan or goose is replaced by raptors, such as eagles and falcons, or vultures, like those that feature so prominently in the carved art of the Neolithic world of Anatolia and the Near East.

Yet questions remain: Where did these ideas originate, and how old are they? Did they really come from Göbekli Tepe, or might they have had their genesis much farther afield? It is the true roots of this starry wisdom that we must now seek in the final chapters of this book.

34

SIBERIAN ROOTS

I t would be difficult to deny that some of the strongest influences on the belief in a cosmic bird that brought forth the physical universe were the shamanic traditions of the Altai region of southern Siberia. The Altaic stories regarding the creator god Tengri or Ülgen Tengri, and the divine path named Kangyi, which coincided with both the cosmic axis and the Milky Way, might, as we have seen, date back to the epoch when the stars of Cygnus acted as polestars, circa 15,750–12,750 BCE. Was it really in southern Siberia during this distant epoch that the bird of creation had its inception?

ALTAIC AGES

Altaic elders employ a counting system based on the number 72. This is seen as the average life span of a person as well as the length of an Altaic "century."[1] They adhere also to cyclic periods that progress in multiples of 72 years and reflect "periods of development in the natural world."[2] This, we shall recall, is also the amount in years it takes for the stars to shift 1 degree against the local horizon, the basis of the precessional cycle.

In Altaic tradition, each successive period of 72 years reveals numbers already familiar to us from the dimensions of the Great Pyramid—72, 144, 216, 288, 360 and, finally, 432.[3] The completion of a sixth cycle (6 × 72), amounting to 432 years and known as *elen chak,* is seen as the turning point of a tribe or nation. Should it fall into decline after this time, it will not survive another cycle of 72 years, but if it thrives and remains in harmony with other tribes and the outside world, it will go on to complete a bonus 72-year cycle, making 504 years in all (72 × 7).[4] After this time, a tribe or nation will go into decline.

We have no way of knowing exactly how old this idea of a 432-year cyclic age among the Altaic peoples might be, although the likelihood is it is extremely old. Indeed, one source of this information says it "goes back right to the very beginnings of civilization."[5] The number 72 (12 × 6), and multiples thereof, reflects the use of the pentagesimal system, whereby a circle of 360 degrees is divided into five equal parts, creating steps in multiples of 72 degrees (i.e., 72, 144, 216, 288, 360), with 432 being a sixth step (72 × 6) and 504 being a seventh step (72 × 7). Did this pentagesimal division of a circle of 360 degrees into 72 degrees, and multiples thereof, come originally from an advanced ancient human society that once thrived in southern Siberia? Was it from here that it traveled at some early date via Göbekli Tepe to Egypt? Is this how it came to be employed in the design of the Great Pyramid?

ORIGINS OF THE YI

In chapter 18 we saw how the Yi people of southwest China possessed a five-phase calendar based on a year divided into five seasons of 72 days, making 360 in total, with 5 to 6 new year's days, creating a tropical year of 365.2422 years. This calendar matches very well the seemingly lost knowledge of an ancient Egyptian calendar of 360 days consisting of five seasons of 72 days and 5 intercalary days.[6] Just as in the case of the Altaic cycle of 432 years, both the Yi calendar of China and the fivefold year of ancient Egypt employ the pentagesimal progression of a circle of 360 degrees in ⅕ increments, each one 72 degrees in length. Is it possible that all three forms of time reckoning—those found among the Altai, the Yi, and the Egyptians—all stem from the same source? If so, then what exactly was that source, and where might evidence of its existence be found?

The Yi people are said to have introduced to Taoism not only the five-phase calendar, but also the eight trigrams of the *I Ching* divination system, along with the concept of yin and yang. This is the philosophy whereby everything has a light and dark balance, and can be divided in two, something that is alleged to have contributed to the invention of binary mathematics.[7] Furthermore, modern Chinese scholars, as we have seen, credit the Yi population with creating the oldest writing system in the world.[8] According to them, it is at least 9000 years old and was carried west and southwest, where it helped inspire the intellectual development of three great civilizations—those of Mesopotamia, Vedic India, and ancient Egypt.[9]

As bold as these assertions might seem, they should not be put down completely to Chinese nationalism. The ancient civilizations of Egypt, Mesopotamia, and Vedic India would all appear to have used cosmic number sequences based on the pentagesimal fractionalization and multiplication of a circle of 360 degrees. So is it possible that the Yi people really do hold the key to understanding the origins of cosmic creation and the generation of precessional numbers? Who exactly are the Yi, otherwise known as the Lolo, and what are their proposed origins? One clue comes from their greatest totem, the white tiger. They are said to have worshipped the tigress[10] and to have introduced the animal as a symbol into Taoism.[11]

In the opinion of the Yi, heaven, earth, and the 10,000 creatures of the natural world all have their origin in the tiger,[12] which in Chinese astronomy is a symbol of the western portion of the heavens. Moreover, the earth is said to have been "set in motion" by the tiger.[13] This suggests the animal was seen originally as a *kosmokrator,* one who controls cosmic time through the turning of the heavens. (The head of the tiger in Yi tradition is the "head of heaven."[14])

THE GREAT TIGRESS

The Yi believe that after death the soul of a person becomes a tiger.[15] This implies a connection between the tiger as a psychopomp and the animal's role as controller of cosmic time and guardian of the realm of the dead. There is an indication also that the tigress venerated by the Yi is in fact the totemic form of Hsi Wang Mu (Xi Wangmu), the Great Mother (or more correctly Great Shamaness) of the West.[16] She weaves the cosmic forces generated by the axis of heaven, showing that she too is a form of kosmokrator. Hsi Wang Mu is said to have guarded the Peach Tree of Immortality, located near the Lake of Gems and Jade Palace on Kunlun Mountain,[17] its three peaks acting as a stairway to the sky world.[18] Here were to be found the Eight Immortals and a race of genii presided over by Hsi Wang Mu herself.[19]

The Peach Tree of Immortality bore fruit once every 3000 years, but it took another 3000 years for them to ripen, a point coinciding with the birthday of Hsi Wang Mu. It was only at such times that she presented the peaches to those mortals worthy of immortality.[20] Hsi Wang Mu is said to have been nourished

Figure 34.1. The ancient Chinese goddess Hsi Wang Mu, Great Mother of the West, shown on the sacred mountain Kunlun. She is seen surrounded by her shamanic animals, including the three phoenixes of the north.

by three phoenixes, which "are found to the north of the Kunlun mountains"[21] (see fig. 34.1). It seems possible that these phoenixes were personifications of the bird constellations of the Summer Triangle—Cygnus, Lyra, and Aquila—even though the goddess herself is more directly linked with Ursa Major.[22]

CENTRAL ASIAN BACKGROUND?

I mention all this because although today the principal territories of the Yi people are in the Chinese provinces of Yunnan, Sichuan, and Guizhou, in the southwest of the country (they are also found in Thailand and Vietnam), there are some indications that their earliest ancestors came from central Asia. European travelers prior to the Chinese revolution noted the predominance among the Yi of tall, high-nosed, long-headed (dolichocephalic), broad-shouldered individuals.[23] This led to speculation that the ancestors of the Yi were to be sought in central Asia.[24] Although mainstream science today frowns upon the use of physical anthropology to prove ancient ethnicity, the language of the Yi, a form of Tibeto-Burman, supports the idea of ancestral migrations from the Tibetan plateau to the northwest of the population's current territories in southwest China.[25]

If at least some of the most distant ancestors of the Yi *did* come originally from central Asia, then they must have thrived somewhere within easy reach of the Altai Mountains of southern Siberia and Mongolia. Yet where, exactly? The Yi's long-held tradition regarding the importance of the tiger totem might well be a clue in this respect, since the most likely candidate for the site of Hsi Wang Mu's Jade Palace and Lake of Gems, and thus the triple-peaked Kunlun Mountain, is Bogda Feng, also known as Bogda Peak. This is the highest mountain of the Bogda Shan range, which forms part of the eastern Tian Shan mountain range, located in China's Xinjiang Uygur Autonomous Region. It has three peaks and its enchanting Yaochi (Jade Lake)—today called Tianchi (Heaven's Lake)—is said to have been the original abode of Hsi Wang Mu.[26] Indeed the temple of Hsi Wang Mu, built on the western slopes of Bogda Peak in the thirteenth century CE, is today one of Taoism's most ancient holy shrines.

ÜRÜMCHI MUMMIES

Was the genesis point of the Yi people somewhere in the vicinity of Bogda Peak, an early site seemingly for the veneration of the Great Mother of the West? Bogda Peak is 110 kilometers east of Ürümchi, a very ancient city

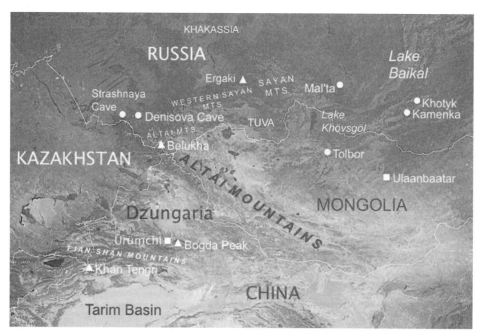

Figure 34.2. Map of the Altai, Tarim Basin, and Baikal regions of central and eastern Asia showing Upper Paleolithic sites and other locations mentioned in this book.

on the western edge of the Gobi Desert, with the vast Tarim Basin and Taklamakan Desert to its south (see fig. 34.2). Over the past 40 years, around the eastern fringes of the Tarim Basin, Chinese archaeologists have uncovered many hundreds of well-preserved mummies that date from the Bronze Age, circa 2000 BCE, through to the first century BCE.

Almost all the older Tarim mummies have dolichocephalic skulls, extended jaws, high-bridged noses, and red hair, usually kept long and sometimes woven into plaits, even for the men.[27] These descriptions match the physical characteristics historically reported in connection with some of the Yi, who, incidentally, also traditionally wear their hair long. Moreover, some of the Tarim mummies, like the Yi, are extremely tall, with males as much as 2 meters in height[28] and females not far behind at 1.8 meters.[29] Some of the bodies were found dressed in extremely high-quality clothes made of intricate woven fabrics.[30] They included beautiful red twill tunics, tartan-style trousers or leggings, and, for the women, tall black felt witches' hats, conical in shape with wide brims.[31]

GENETIC STUDY

An examination of 302 skulls belonging to Tarim mummies found that the closest matches to the region's Bronze Age population were the anatomical remains of both the Afanasevo culture, which thrived in the Altai region of southern Siberia circa 3300–2000 BCE, and the later Andronovo culture, which existed farther west between the Ural Mountains and the Caspian Sea, circa 2200–1500 BCE.[32] Since there is strong evidence that the Tarim Basin people were among the first in the world to ride horses,[33] they are likely to have taken advantage of what would eventually become the so-called Silk Road linking China with western Asia.[34] Nonetheless, their principal homeland during the Bronze Age, and arguably earlier, most probably extended from the Altai Mountains in the north to the Tarim Basin in the south. Beyond here to the south is the Altyn Shan (Altun Tagh) mountain range, which marks the beginning of the Tibetan plateau, across which the ancestors of the Yi perhaps migrated to reach southwest China. Is it possible that these people carried with them the "worship of the tigress"[35] as well as other profound ideas that went on to influence the foundations of Taoism?

Were the ancestors of the Yi connected to the Bronze Age population of the Tarim Basin, and through them the Afanasevo culture of the Altai region of southern Siberia? Were all of these groups related to a much earlier high culture that thrived in either the Altai region and/or the Tarim Basin prior to the age of Göbekli Tepe? Were the ancestors of the Yi people responsible also for the creation of a solar calendar of 360 days divided into five equal parts of 72 days, as well as the 432-year calendar cycle derived from multiples of 72-year periods seen in terms of Altaic "centuries?" As we have seen, this has been preserved among the indigenous people of the Altai through to modern times.

Did the descendants of this advanced population migrate at an early date westward via the Ural Mountains into Europe, Anatolia, and Mesopotamia, as well as southwestward into the Indus Valley of India and Pakistan? Intriguingly, it has long been suspected that both the Sumerian and Akkadian languages, which were certainly present in Mesopotamia circa 3300–3000 BCE, are related to the Uralic and Altaic languages.[36]

PRESSURE-FLAKING ORIGINS

That the Altai region, or the Tarim Basin farther south, might have been the true point of origin of a cosmology featuring the creation of cyclic time by a celestial bird, perhaps identified with the Cygnus constellation, is supported by our knowledge of the spread of the pressure-flaking technique. As we saw in chapter 9, immediately prior to its appearance at sites like Göbekli Tepe, circa 8800–8000 BCE, pressure flaking thrived only in certain areas north of the Black Sea. These included western Russia and Ukraine in eastern Europe.[37] All these territories were occupied by Post-Swiderian cultures that derived much of their stone-toolmaking traditions from the Swiderians themselves, who inhabited large areas of central and eastern Europe both before and during the Younger Dryas event, circa 10,800–9600 BCE. They are thought to have inherited knowledge of the pressure-flaking technique from Epipaleolithic and Mesolithic societies inhabiting the southern Ural Mountains and the steppes of what is today Kazakhstan and Uzbekistan, circa 15,000–11,000 BCE.[38] Not only are these populations known to have mastered the art of pressure flaking, but they are also thought to have been the forerunners of the Swiderian tradition.[39]

Even farther back in time, circa 20,000–15,000 BCE, the Solutreans of western Europe used pressure flaking, while as early as 20,000–30,000 years ago the technique was being employed by Upper Paleolithic societies in central Mongolia (see chapter 40). Is it possible that the Epipaleolithic societies of the southern Urals and the steppes derived their knowledge of pressure flaking from even earlier human societies in central Mongolia? Immediately to the south of the Altai Mountains is Dzungaria, a vast triangular plateau, located in China's Xinjiang province. The transmission of knowledge from the Altai region via the so-called Dzungarian Gate, which forms the border between central Asia and China, westward through Kazakhstan to the southern Urals and the Caspian Sea, would easily have been possible.

SHIGIR IDOL

It is in the central and southern Urals that intriguing evidence of high culture has emerged dating to the end of the Paleolithic age, circa 10,500–9600 BCE. This includes some of the only decorated caves outside of western Europe, as well as the Shigir Idol. This is a wooden totem pole, 2.8 meters tall, that terminates with an abstract human head and has strange designs, including zigzags and secondary heads, along its length. It was found in 1894 in a peat bog at Shigir on the eastern slopes of the middle Urals (see fig. 34.3). Radiocarbon dating shows

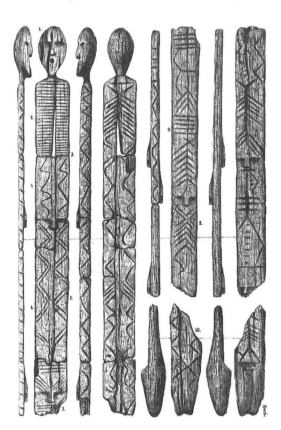

Figure 34.3. The 11,000-year-old Shigir idol discovered in 1894 in a peat bog near Shigir in the middle Ural Mountains (after V. Y. Tolmachev).

it is at least 11,000 years old, classifying it as the product of the Mesolithic age. Its level of sophistication matches that of the various stone-carved totem poles found at Göbekli Tepe and Nevalı Çori, suggesting a possible link between the two contemporary cultures, despite the great distances involved.

Did the cosmological beliefs and sacred geometry encoded into the design of the Great Pyramid, and also within Giza's underlying geometry, come originally from the Altai region of southern Siberia? As we shall see next, there is compelling evidence that this remote region of Asia, the traditional site of the lost kingdom of Shambhala, was almost certainly the genesis point of human civilization.

35

THE
LAND OF DAWN

awn behind the Dawn (1992), by British historian and mythologist Geoffrey Ashe (1923–), is an important book indeed. It details the author's investigation into the recurring appearance of the number 7 in ancient cosmologies and mythologies around the world.[1] Of paramount importance to Ashe's examination of septenary symbolism, as he sees it, is its association with the seven stars of Ursa Major.[2] Indeed he argues that the primary reason for the repeated occurrence of the number 7 is the seven stars' role as the perceived mechanism for the turning of the heavens.[3]

Although Ursa Major is never close enough to the northern celestial pole to allow its stars to become polestars, the fact that they are mostly circumpolar has caused them to be seen as a kind of celestial crank handle controlling the movement of the starry canopy around its cosmic axis. This would have been particularly likely when no bright star marked the northern celestial pole, a situation that prevails for much of the 26,000-year precessional cycle. Through this abstract relationship between the number 7 and the motion of the stars, Ashe proposes, septenary symbolism became associated with an imagined cosmic mountain or Tree of Life located either in the center of the geomythical world or somewhere in the extreme north.[4]

LAKE BAIKAL

Ashe traces the origins behind the veneration of the seven stars of Ursa Major to the shamanic traditions of central Asia and southern North Asia, in particular those that thrive even today among the Turkic and Mongolian tribes of southern Siberia.[5] From here these cosmological notions were carried, he writes, by migrating populations to various parts of the ancient world, including Europe, Mesopotamia, India, Tibet, China, and even as far as Island Southeast Asia. This occurred sometime prior to the rise of civilization, circa 3000 BCE.[6] Ashe additionally proposes that the importance of Ursa Major and its sevenfold symbolism entered the North American continent prior to the drowning of the Beringia land bridge, circa 8500 BCE.[7]

As evidence of the possible veneration of the seven stars of Ursa Major at an even earlier date, Ashe cites the discovery of a sophisticated Upper Paleolithic culture that thrived at a site named Mal'ta on the Belaya River, a branch of the Angara River, west of Lake Baikal.[8] Located in southern-central Siberia, and north and east of the Altai Mountains, Baikal is the world's deepest and most enigmatic inland sea.

THE MAL'TA PLATE

Ashe cites the discovery of a 24,000-year-old mammoth-ivory plate as confirmation of the culture's interest in septenary symbolism.[9] It is trapezoidal in shape, 14.1 centimeters in length, 8.5 centimeters in width, and slightly curved in appearance.[10] On one side is a whole series of punctuates, that is punch or peck marks, creating a central spiral of seven circuits, with three other twin spirals on either side of it, making seven spirals in total.[11] At the center of the large central spiral is a bored hole that penetrates through to the other side of the plate. On its reverse side are engravings of three wriggling snakes, two with large heads that look conspicuously like those of cobras (a species not native to Siberia). They are positioned side by side, their heads all facing the same way.[12] Very likely the centrally placed aperture represents the hole that, according to various shamanic traditions, connects the Upper World via the Middle World with the World Below.

Ashe's findings convinced me still further of an Altaic root behind our ancestors' interest in Cygnus, which, we know, provided three polestars circa 15,750–12,750 BCE. The Mal'ta-Buret' culture, as it is known, thrived around 24,000 years ago, and continued to exist in some form until around

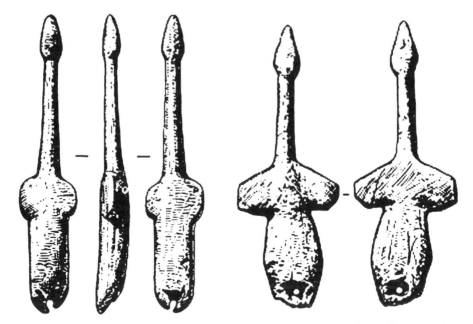

Figure 35.1. Two examples of the mammoth-ivory swan pendants found at the Mal'ta site west of Lake Baikal. They are likely to be as much as 20,000 years old.

17,000 years ago. In fact, in my book *The Cygnus Mystery* (2006) I cite the discovery at Mal'ta of a number of mammoth-ivory swan pendants. They have oval bodies, stubby wings, and long, straight necks resembling Cygnus in its role as the celestial swan (see fig. 35.1 and chapter 36).[13] Ashe does not mention Cygnus in his book. But he does demonstrate the existence of a polarcentric cosmology as early as the Upper Paleolithic, confirming that the prehistoric populations of the Northern Hemisphere saw the circumpolar stars as important in understanding the mechanics of the universe.

THE ALTAIC ORIGINS OF APOLLO

The closest Ashe comes to complementing my theories regarding the importance of Cygnus in the ancient mind-set stems from the fact that in his opinion the Greek cults of both Apollo and his twin sister Artemis originally derive from the Altai region, and were carried into the Hellenic world by Indo-European-speaking peoples during the Neolithic age. Like Apollo, Artemis was linked with a semimythical location named Hyperborea, said to have existed beyond the source of the north wind.[14] Indeed, Leto, the mother of both Artemis and Apollo, was apparently born in Hyperborea, while Apollo himself is said to have departed for Hyperborea each fall on a chariot pulled by swans. Here he would spend three months before flying back to Greece. Ashe proposes that Apollo was originally a form of Tengri or Tengri Ülgen, the Altaic sky god, whose vehicle, as we have seen, was the white goose (the swan being the totem of his wife, the earth goddess Umai Ana). Ashe links Apollo's journey to Hyperborea with the Milky Way because of its association with birds, and particularly with the fact that in northern Europe, in Lithuania for instance, the Milky Way is traditionally known as the Road of the Birds.[15] Artemis, on the other hand, was perhaps the memory of an Altaic shamaness or ancestress, whose cult evolved gradually into that of a mother goddess.[16]

PRIESTS OF APOLLO

Hyperborea was anciently said to be the true home of the cult of Apollo. Here its priesthood thrived. One such priest was Abaris the Hyperborean, a legendary healer, teacher, and sage endowed with the gift of prophecy. He traveled to Greece, having departed his native land during a plague. Here he taught the wisest individuals of the age, including, it is said, Pythagoras. Abaris bears all the hallmarks of a shaman. He is even said to have possessed Apollo's golden arrow, on which he could fly through the air. Arguably this resembled the ritual sticks or pointers carried by Siberian shamans. Of course these are used not for actual flight but to aid shamanic flight during ecstatic states. Abaris was said to have been a priest not only of Apollo, but also of Scythia, the ancient name for the Russian steppe stretching between the Pontic region north of the Black Sea right across to the Dzungarian Gate at the start of the Altai Mountains.

NORTH BEYOND THE NORTH WIND

The oldest known source of information on Hyperborea is a seventh-century BCE poet and miracle worker named Aristeas of Proconnesus. His account (preserved only in fragments) makes it clear that this semimythical land was located not in Europe, as was later believed, but in central Asia. According to him the Issedones, a nomadic people of the steppes, told him that beyond the mountains, which were the source of the North Wind that blew in from the north bringing cold winter air, was the land of Hyperborea (see fig. 35.2 on page 292). Here in a cave—the actual source of the wind—lived Boreas, the purple-winged god of the North World.[17]

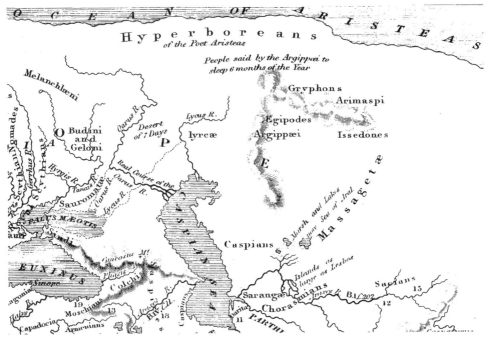

Figure 35.2. Section of a nineteenth-century map based on *The History of Herodotus* (Cramer, 1828, "The World According to Herodotus."). It shows the land of the Hyperboreans in the extreme north of Eurasia. Note at upper right the mountain chain bearing the name *Issedones,* the steppe people who described the Hyperboreans to Aristeas.

Ashe, following the lead of earlier commentators on Aristeas, identified the mountains he mentions as the Altai range.[18] These lie immediately north of Dzungaria, on the north side of which, in the foothills of the Altai chain, is Boreas's legendary home. It is an enormous cavern known locally as the Cave of the Winds.[19] Dzungaria, as previously stated, is located in China's northwestern province of Xinjiang. Northeast of the Altai Mountains are western Mongolia, the Altai Republic, and the Republic of Tuva, homeland of the Turkic population known as the Tuvans, and beyond that Lake Baikal (see fig. 34.2 on page 283 for a map showing the sites in these regions featured in the book).

THE SONS OF BOREAS

Thus as Hyperborea the Altai-Baikal region can be seen as the point of origin of the cults of Apollo and Artemis, the former, as we have seen, god of music and poetry. His lyre of seven strings, which made manifest the inaudible sounds generated by the turning of the stars, the so-called music of the spheres, was given to his son Orpheus, whose soul, upon his death, was transformed into a swan and elevated into the heavens as the constellation of Cygnus. Using this lyre, its seven strings expressing the seven-note musical scale, Orpheus was able to charm the creatures of the natural world. Did these traditions originate among the earliest shamans of the Altai-Baikal region? Connected to this possibility is the fact that Boreas, the legendary leader of the Hyperboreans, was said to have had three sons, born to Chione, the daughter of Arcturus, whom Boreas had abducted. Like Orpheus, the three sons of Boreas are said to have used music to charm the creatures of the natural world. According to Hecataeus of Abdera, a writer and traveler of the late fourth century BCE, in his now-lost work *On the Hyperboreans:*

> This god [i.e., Apollo] has as priests the sons of Boreas and Chione, three in number, brothers by birth, *and six cubits in height.* So when at the customary time they perform the established ritual of the aforesaid god there swoop down from what are called the Rhipaean mountains Swans in clouds, past numbering, and after they have circled round the temple, as though they were purifying it by their flight, they descend into the precinct of the temple, an area of immense size and of surpassing beauty. Now whenever the singers sing their hymns to the god and the harpers accompany the chorus with their harmonious music, thereupon the Swans also with one accord join in the chant and never once do they sing a discordant note or out of tune, but as though they had been given the key by the conductor they chant in unison with the natives who are skilled in the sacred melodies. Then when the hymn is finished the aforesaid winged choristers, so they call them, after their customary service in honor of the god and after singing and celebrating his praises all through the day, depart.[20] [*Rhipaean* derives from the Greek *rhipá,* "blast," a reference to the mountains' perceived role as the source of the North Wind.[21]]

Everything about this remarkable account suggests the actions of powerful shamans. That the sons of Boreas are said also to have had a height of six cubits, approximately 2¾ meters, need not detain us here. What is of most interest is the way the sons of Boreas had control over the flocks of swans drawn to the precinct of the sacred temple in order to "join in the chant."

Like the Reindeer Tungus tribes of northern Siberia, various Turkic tribes venerate the swan and use swan totems.[22] Certain clans, such as the Tuvan sub-group known as the Kuular, whose territory is Tuva's Dzun-Khemchik region,[23] actually see themselves as descendants of a swan ancestor. Similar ideas are held among many other tribes and clans of southern Siberia, including the Soyod of northwest Mongolia[24] and the Mongolians themselves.[25] Such beliefs add weight to the idea that Hecataeus's account of the giant sons of Boreas is the abstract memory of swan shamans of extremely tall stature, priests of a proto-form of Apollo who thrived in the Altai-Baikal region during some former epoch.

All this offers further evidence that the true source of Cygnus's importance to the builders of Göbekli Tepe and of the Giza pyramids originated in the Altai-Baikal region toward the end of the last ice age. Geoffrey Ashe's contribution to this same subject, written many years before I would venture down this same avenue, is stunning in its own right. Yet I could not leave the matter there, for after reading Ashe's book, my mind kept returning to the mammoth-ivory plate found at the Mal'ta site.

Years earlier I had read about a Russian scientist who had found extraordinary correlations between the number and arrangement of the Mal'ta plate's well-defined punctuates and long-term calendar cycles. Ashe's inference that this 24,000-year-old object was crucial to dating the true age of humanity's interest in septenary symbolism and its associations with the stars of Ursa Major prompted me to look again at the findings of this Russian scientist. My discoveries dramatically alter our knowledge about the origins of the sequences of cosmic numbers found in connection with both the Great Pyramid and Giza's underlying geometry. It is a subject of extreme importance to our understanding of these matters, and one that we address next.

36

COUNTING TIME

T he mammoth-ivory plate found at the Mal'ta site, situated on a branch of the Angara River, immediately west of Lake Baikal, is arguably one of the most important discoveries from the Paleolithic age. Its configuration of deeply cut punctuates or rounded peck marks tells us a great deal about its carver and the age in which he or she lived. Excavations at the Mal'ta site in 1928–1931, under the leadership of Russian scientist Mikhail M. Gerasimov (1907–1970), found a number of houses with walls made almost entirely from reindeer bones. One even bore foundations of massive stone slabs set on end. Also discovered were up to thirty ivory figurines of women, many of which bear a realism so striking that one can imagine their models in thick fur garments with hoods of the sort worn even today by the indigenous peoples of North Asia.[1]

BIRD CULT

As previously mentioned, a large number of carved images of birds, mostly swans, all made of mammoth ivory, were found at Mal'ta (see fig. 35.1. on page 290),[2] as well as at another site of the same culture farther along the Angara River at a place called Buret'.[3] Some were clearly pendants, as they had drilled holes through their width, enabling them to be worn around the neck. These were the only animal totems discovered at the site (other than the fragment of a mammoth carving, a small figurine of a squirrel, and the snakes seen etched on the plate itself), suggesting that birds, and the swan in particular, had some special significance to this community.

This assumption is confirmed by the fact that the skeletal remains of birds were found in great numbers at Mal'ta, more so than should have been the case by chance alone.[4] Unfortunately, their species were rarely identified. What we do know is that among the bones were those of the "goose and seagull."[5] In one dwelling the skull of a "large bird," along with some of its cervical vertebrae, was found in a shallow pit, having been deliberately deposited in this manner.[6] More importantly, four or five swan pendants found inside dwellings at Mal'ta had been purposely aligned north-south,[7] something that led Russian paleoarchaeologist Antoiny P. Derevianko to surmise that this deliberate act of directionality was perhaps linked to the north-south migration of birds and the fact that in death the soul was very often seen as a bird. Indeed, he interpreted the ritualistic placement of these miniature bird totems as a "significant first appearance of animism" in Siberia.[8]

PSYCHOPOMP

A link between the swan pendants and the transmigration of the soul was further suggested by the fact that one example was found deliberately placed in the grave of a young boy who lived 24,000 years ago.[9] This hints that the swan was seen as a psychopomp, aiding the soul in its journey to the Upper World. Tuvan shamanism sees the swan as a communicator between worlds, "since it can fly to the upper world and dive under the water."[10]

Very likely the Mal'ta community associated the Upper World with the northerly placed "birdland" or "bird heaven" featured in the swan-maiden tradition,[11] which, as we shall see in chapter 39, almost certainly had its origin in Siberia as far back as Paleolithic times.

MNEMOMIC CALENDRICAL DEVICE

The mammoth-ivory plate found during excavation at the Mal'ta site in 1929 also seems to have been connected with celestial themes, according to Russian scientist Vitaliy Larichev (1932–2014). Before his death, Larichev was for many years professor of archaeology at the Institute of Archaeology and Ethnography at the Novosibirsk State University in Siberia, leading excavations at a number of Upper Paleolithic sites across the region. Larichev concluded that this fascinating Paleolithic relic was a mnemomic calendrical device containing specific information about both short-term and long-term solar, lunar, and eclipse cycles. Since the plate is thought to be around 24,000 years old, this might seem a quite extraordinary claim. Certainly I thought so when I first read about the Mal'ta plate some years ago. But Ashe's proposal that septenary symbolism found across Eurasia and in the Americas originated among the Upper Paleolithic population of the Altai-Baikal region led me to reconsider Larichev's findings.[12] If they are correct, they have incredible implications for our understanding of the emergence of civilization in the ancient world.

SPIRAL COUNT

The upper side of the Mal'ta plate (see fig. 36.1) bears a series of seven spirals. In the center is a large spiral made up of seven circuits, around which are six smaller spirals linked together to form three S-shaped double spirals. The central spiral is composed of 243 peck marks; actually 242 + 1, as one is slightly adrift of the others.[13] The total number of peck marks making up the

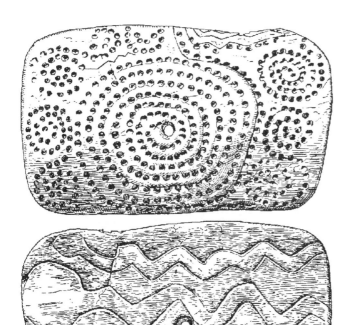

Figure 36.1. The two faces of the 24,000-year-old mammoth-ivory plate discovered in 1929 at the Mal'ta site on the Belaya River, west of Lake Baikal.

three twin spirals to the left of the large spiral is 122, with the same number making up those to its right. The fact that the spirals on both sides add up to 122 should alert us to the fact that something meaningful is implied by the number and arrangement of these peck marks. As Larichev points out, 122 + 243 is 365, the number of days in a solar year.[14] At the base of the plate are 11 peck marks slightly detached from the surrounding twin spirals (although still forming part of them). Subtract 11 from 365 and you get 354, the number of days in a 12-month lunar year, with each month either 29 or 30 days in duration.

Using number counts in this manner to determine the amount of days in a solar or lunar year was common in the ancient world. For instance, at the site of Teotihuacan in Mexico, a standard unit of measure has been found throughout the pyramid complex built around 200 BCE. This is 0.83 meters in length. The sides of the Pyramid of the Sun are precisely 260 of these units—this being the length in days of the Mesoamerican ritual calendar based on the positions of the sun. The nearby Temple of the Moon, on the other hand, has a base length of precisely 105 units. Add 260 and 105 and you get 365, the number of days in a year.

Thus there is every reason to assume that the Mal'ta plate might be a teaching device carrying specific information regarding calendrical cycles. So what more can be determined about its configurations of peck marks?

Larichev came to believe that the plate's individual spirals represented multiples of the synodic lunar month of 29.531 days, which is the time between one new moon to the next.[15] Regarding the 242 + 1 peck marks in the large spiral of seven circuits, he saw this as related to the so-called draconian month, the mean time it takes the moon to return to the same point on the ecliptic as the start of its cycle. This place of crossing on the ecliptic is known as a node, and there are two of these, one in the northern part of the sky and another in the southerly part of the sky, each one being exactly 180 degrees apart. The moon crosses each node once during a draconian month, which lasts 27.2122 days, and it is only at this time that an eclipse, either of the sun or the moon, can occur. Larichev realized that 242 draconian months (that is, 6585.3524 days, or 18 years, 11 days, 8 hours, 27 minutes) is the equivalent of a saros, the name applied in ancient times to one complete eclipse cycle of the sun and the moon (of which, more below). Was the length of a saros in draconian lunar months being implied by the 242 + 1 peck marks on the Mal'ta plate? Larichev certainly thought so.

CANICULAR YEAR

More controversially, Larichev highlighted the fact that the total number of punctuates on the Mal'ta plate, that is, 487, reflected a period of 487 years, exactly one third of a so-called canicular cycle made up of 1461 solar years of 365 days, or 1460 tropical years of 365.2422 days. Since the length of a tropical year is 365.2422 days, and not 365 days, every four years an extra intercalary day has to be added, hence the concept of a leap year. If the extra day is not added, the two cycles go out of sync and do not resynchronize until the completion of 1461 years of 365 days.

The ancient Egyptians were aware of the canicular cycle of 1461 years, using it in association with a civil calendar of 365 days, made up of 12 months of 30 days along with 5 extra days added to the end of the year. On the first year of a cycle its first month, named Thoth, would begin with the rising of the star Sirius immediately before the appearance of the sun (its so-called heliacal rising), a much-anticipated event that would take place shortly after the summer solstice. Yet because no leap year was used, the ancient Egyptians' civil calendar would run retrograde, causing it to wander very slowly out of sync with the tropical year, the two only coinciding once more after a period of 1461 years. This constituted one complete Sothic cycle, named after Sothis, the ancient Greek name for the star Sirius.* It was the anticipation of the synchronization of the two cycles among the ancient Egyptians that probably led to the belief that the phoenix returned to Heliopolis from Arabia after 1461 years. Here it would die and be reborn again, flying back to Arabia for the next cycle of 1461 years.[16] Yet other time periods were also associated with the return of the phoenix, most obviously 500 years,[17] extremely close to 487 years, or one third of a canicular cycle. Is it possible that the Mal'ta community had knowledge of the canicular cycle, breaking it down into three parts of 487 years each? As wild as it might seem, this was the conclusion reached by Vitaliy Larichev.[18]

ECLIPSE CYCLES

What we have seen so far in connection with the Mal'ta plate has simply been a prelude to Larichev's other discoveries. He realized that 486, the Mal'ta plate's

---

*Other stars can be used for this same purpose. The canicular cycle is not exclusive to Sirius, although this is the most obvious star to use, because it is the brightest in the night sky.

lower total, is 9 × 54, with 54 being the number of years in a triple saros,[19] a matter that will need some introduction. As previously mentioned, solar and lunar eclipses are cyclic and can be predicted in the knowledge that every 242 draconian months of 27.2122 days (6585.3524 days, or 18 years, 11 days, 8 hours, 27 minutes) or 223 synodic months of 29.531 days (6585.3238 days, or 18 years, 11 days, 7 hours, 46 minutes), the sun, moon, and earth return to relatively the same position as they were in at the beginning of the cycle. (The actual length of a saros is 6585.3 days or 18 years, 11 days, 8 hours.) What this means is that a solar eclipse, whether partial or total, which occurred at the commencement of a saros cycle, will occur again at the end of the cycle. This was knowledge known to the Chaldeans, the astronomer priests of Harran and nearby Şanlıurfa in southeast Anatolia, who are referred to in medieval Arabic sources as the Sabians or Harranians (see chapter 2).

Yet because of the timing differences between the draconian and synodic months, and the tropical year of 365.2422 days, when a solar eclipse does take place after one complete saros cycle, it occurs around 8 hours later and 120 degrees to the west of the same eclipse one cycle earlier. Yet by some strange quirk of fate, the eclipse cycle resynchronizes every 54 years (in actuality it is 54 years and 34 days), that is after exactly 3 saros cycles of just over 18 years a piece. So every 54 years a solar eclipse will occur at approximately the same time and place as it did at the beginning of a triple saros cycle. The Chaldeans also knew this fact and used it to both predict eclipses and mark the passage of time.[20]

Nine triple saros cycles, or triple saroi, amount to approximately 486 years, 306 days. This reflects not only the 486 + 1 peck marks on the Mal'ta plate, but also one-third of a canicular cycle of 1460/1 years. Another indication that the carver of the plate was aware of the triple saros cycle comes from the fact that 243, the total number of peck marks in its large spiral, is exactly 4.5 × 54, in other words 4½ triple saros cycles.[21]

It should be noted here that 27 triple saros cycles, each of 54 years and 34 days, is just over 1460.51 tropical years, conveniently close to the length of a canicular cycle of 1461 solar years or 1460 tropical years. Whether or not such long-term calendrical systems were ever implemented is unclear. Yet their apparent presence in the sequences of punctuates on the mammoth-ivory plate implies that some knowledge, not only of the canicular cycle, but also of its synchronization with the triple saros eclipse cycle, was available to the Mal'ta community of southern Siberia around 24,000 years ago.

It seems likely also that the Chaldeans might themselves have been aware of the relationship between the canicular cycle of 1460 tropical years and the triple saros cycle of 54 years, if only in a highly abstract manner. The Roman politician and lawyer Marcus Tullius Cicero (106–43 BCE) wrote that "Babylonians" (that is, the Chaldean astronomers, see below), as well as "those astrologers who, from the top of Mount Caucasus, observe the celestial signs and with the aid of mathematics follow the courses of the stars," possess "records" of the observation of the stars covering a period of 470,000 years.[22]

The original source of this statement is perhaps the Greek historian Diodorus Siculus (90–30 BCE), who observed that according to the statement of the Chaldeans, who have the "greatest grasp of astrology," they have "spent on the study of the bodies of the universe," a period of time amounting to no less than 473,000 years,[23] Cicero having rounded down this figure to 470,000 years. Yet Diodorus might himself have rounded down the true number of years, for according to the Rev. William Hales, an Irish scholar and professor of Oriental languages at the University of Dublin, writing in the year 1830, "The correct number is somewhat more, 473,040 years. . . . This correct cycle of 473,040 years was evidently formed by the multiplication of two factors; the square of the Chaldean *Saros*, 18 × 18 = 324, and the Nabonassarean or Sothiacal period of 1460 years."[24] (The Nabonassarean period was a Chaldean or Babylonian form of the canicular cycle.)

Whatever the true nature of this impossibly long time period of stellar observations by the Chaldeans, the figure in question, 473,040 years, is remarkable, for it is not only 324 × 1460, as Hales points out, but also 54 × 8760, showing its synchronization with both the canicular cycle and the 54-year triple saros cycle. We shall encounter this extraordinary figure again very shortly.

All this was quite incredible. Yet, under the assumption that the carver of the Mal'ta plate was also aware of both the canicular cycle and the triple saros cycle, and recorded this information as sequences of punctuates on the object's upper surface, something else might now be said about its total number of peck marks. They can be divided into certain key numbers seen in the past as having a cosmic or sacred significance across the ancient world.

37

REVOLUTION 432

Something really significant can be said about the total number of peck marks on the upper surface of the mammoth ivory plate found at the Upper Paleolithic site of Mal'ta in southern Siberia and carved by a highly talented artist some 24,000 years ago. In addition to displaying knowledge of both the canicular cycle of 1460/1 years and the 54-year triple saros eclipse cycle, they form multiples of certain key numbers that have long been seen as having a cosmic or sacred significance.

One such number is 432, which, as we saw in chapter 18, is the length of the sides of the Great Pyramid in long cubits. It can be found on the Mal'ta plate in the following manner: if you subtract 432 from 486, the lower total of punctuates on its upper surface (the other being 487), it leaves you with 54, the number of years in a triple saros cycle. This connection between 432 and 54 hardly seems a coincidence, especially since 432 is itself 8 × 54, the ideal length of 8 triple saros cycles. Of unquestionable relevance here is that 432, as we saw in chapter 34, is also the length in years of a cyclic age among the Altaians, derived from multiples of 72-year periods seen in terms of Altaic "centuries" (6 × 72 = 432).

How exactly the indigenous peoples of the Altai came to use cycles of 72 years, with 6 cycles lasting 432 years, is unclear.[1] All we are told is that it "goes back right to the very beginnings of civilization."[2] Altaic elders propose that 72 years is important because it is the length of an average life span,[3] and that "wise men used the number 72 in other counting systems relevant to clans, families and the nation as a whole."[4] They state also that the 72-year life cycle, which can further be broken down into periods of 12 years (6 × 12 = 72), is regulated by Ene-Dzhaiachi, the Mother Creator; the fate and destiny she brings being perceived by seers or clairvoyants known as *jarlykchi*.[5]

Even though the average life span of a person might be 72 years today, it is unlikely to have been the case in the past, suggesting that the use of 72-year periods to define a cyclic age must have come from something else. Perhaps it derives from the fact that cyclic precession causes the stars to shift their positions against the local horizon approximately 1 degree in every 72 years. Some might argue that there is no real evidence that our most distant ancestors divided the circle into 360 degrees. But there is another way to achieve a figure of 72 years for a precessional "century." One degree of arc is very close to 2 widths of the sun. Thus it might be said that the background of stars shifts 2 sun's widths, or approximately 1 degree of a circle of 360 degrees, every 72 years.

It is possible that the Altaians' use of a calendrical system based on 6 periods of 72 years, making a complete age of 432 years, with a bonus cycle of 72 years making 504 in total, is not only extremely ancient, but was also once synchronized with the 54-year triple saros eclipse cycle. Remember, 432 is either 6 × 72 years or 8 × 54 years, meaning that, numerically speaking, the two cycles sync together perfectly. If correct, this could explain why the Altaic peoples adopted 432 as the length of a cyclic age, and why (as we shall see shortly) this number became known to ancient cultures and religions across the Eurasian continent. So from the evidence of the Mal'ta plate there is every chance that the importance of the number 432 derives from its use in ancient calendar systems present among the shamanistic traditions of the Altai-Baikal region as much as 24,000 years ago.

CALENDAR SYNCHRONIZATIONS

Nowhere else in the world at this early stage in human development is there any evidence for the use of this same synchronization of cycles, using a combination of precessional "centuries" of 72 years and triple saros eclipse cycles of 54 years. So the fact that one of the most advanced cultures of the Upper Paleolithic age thrived for many thousands of years at the south Siberian site of Mal'ta, close to Lake Baikal, tells us we must seriously consider the possibility

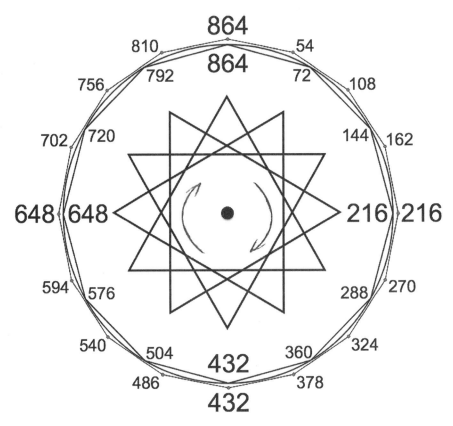

Figure 37.1. Calendar round displaying the proposed grand calendrical system of the Altai-Baikal region, which is perhaps 24,000 years old. It shows 16 triple saros cycles of 54 years and 12 precessional "centuries" of 72 years. Synchronizations between the two cycles occur after 216 years, 432 years, 648 years, and 864 years. Note the presence of 270 years (5 x 54), which is the length of the Giza unit of measure in long cubits, and 486 (9 x 54 or 432 + 54), the lower total of punctuates on the Mal'ta plate.

that this was the birthplace of this remarkable calendrical system outlined in figure 37.1. Here we see that the 72- and 54-year cycles synchronize for the first time after 216 years (3 × 72 or 4 × 54 = 216).

Pythagoras believed that 216 was the number of years between each reincarnation of the soul,[6] while some scholars suggest that Plato's so-called "perfect number," alluded to in his works the *Timaeus*[7] and the *Republic*,[8] was 216.[9] Although this was arguably because 216 is 6 × 6 × 6, that is, 6 cubed ($6^3 = 216$), as well as the sum of the cubes of the Pythagorean 3-4-5 triangle ($3^3 + 4^3 + 5^3 = 6^3$), there seems to be more to its significance than simply this.

The context in which Plato's perfect number appears in the *Timaeus* makes it clear that it relates to a cycle or period of time. So if 216 *is* Plato's perfect number, its purpose is almost certainly calendrical in nature.

PERIOD OF CONSOLIDATION

Significantly, in the Altaic calendrical system only 2 of the 72-year cycles bear names. This is the "turning point" of 432 years, known as elen chak,[10] and 216 years, which is seen as the "period of consolidation" and bears the name *tuutalanar*.[11] This suggests that only the cycles of 216 years and 432 years were taken to be pivotal in the Altaic counting system.[12]

In all possibility 216 years was considered one half cycle in the proposed Altai-Baikal calendar system, with 432, the next point of synchronization between the 72-year precessional period and the 54-year eclipse cycle, being seen as one complete age. If correct, then this not only conforms with the Altai-Baikal calendar, but also implies its incredible antiquity; indeed, there is every reason to conclude that it is an extension of the calendrical system displayed on the Mal'ta plate, which we know to be at least 24,000 years old.

Further synchronizations between the 72-year and 54-year cycles occur after 648 years (1.5 × 432), 864 years (2 × 432), 1080 years (2.5 × 432), 1296 years (3 × 432), and thereafter in multiples of half or full 432-year cycles right up to 2160 years (5 × 432) and 2592 years (6 × 432). This last value, when multiplied by 10, creates a figure of 25,920 years (60 × 432), the Perfect Year or Great Year of Plato, in other words, one complete precessional cycle.

Even though the existence of this prehistoric calendrical system seems evident, whether or not it was ever utilized for practical purposes is quite another matter. Because the triple saros cycle is actually 54 years and 34 days in length, and not an ideal 54 years, it would very quickly have gone out of sync with the 72-year cycle. Moreover, precession itself is now known to occur at a rate of 1 degree every 71.6 years, and not a round 72 years. Most likely the Altai-Baikal calendrical system existed as a conceptual vision of long-term time cycles used by shamans and timekeepers to express the ability to calculate and thus measure time, and in so doing, constrain, control, and define it within a finite reality. This supposition becomes even more apparent when we examine ancient Indian cosmological time, which seems to be based *entirely* on multiples of 432 years.

PURANIC COSMIC TIME

In Puranic tradition the Year of Brahma, the creator god, made up of a Day and Night of Brahma, is 8,640,000,000 terrestrial years (a clear multiple of 864 and 432), of which one single Day or Night of Brahma is 4,320,000,000 terrestrial years (again an obvious multiple of 432). One Day or Night of Brahma is made up of 1000 Mahayugas, each of 4,320,000 years (another multiple of 432). One Mahayuga contains four *yugas* (or cycles): the Satya-yuga of 1,728,000 years; the Treta-yuga of 1,296,000 years, the Dvapara-yuga of 864,000 years, and the Kali-yuga of 432,000 years.[13]

So important is the number 432 to the yuga system that it has even been suggested that it might constitute the length in terrestrial years of a "little" Kali-yuga.[14] If so, then it would be comparable to the Altai-Baikal calendar, which is also based on a recurring cycle of 432 years. What is more, all four yuga values cited above are multiples of idealistic synchronizations between the precessional period of 72 years and the triple saros cycle of 54 years, namely, 1728, 1296, 864, and 432, with these being, respectively, 4 × 432, 3 × 432, 2 × 432, and 1 × 432.

Thus each yuga displays a gradually descending value based on the ratios 4:3 (1,728,000 to 1,296,000), 3:2 (1,296,000 to 864,000), and 2:1 (864,000 to 432,000). These in turn reflect the divisions found in the principal musical intervals: the perfect fourth (4:3), perfect fifth (3:2), and the octave (2:1). What this suggests is that 432 was singled out because it reflected the descending ratios of the musical intervals, in other words 4:3, **3**:2, and **2**:1. This geometrically perfect reduction in the length of each yuga, from four parts to three parts to two parts and then finally one, must have had it own purpose and significance, since it conjures to mind the idea of something slowly descending from a higher state of being down to a denser form of existence, or, indeed, vice versa. It is almost as if these fractional reductions allude to the manifestation of the physical universe, an act, as we know, that Brahma achieves through the call made by the swan-goose, Hamsa, symbolized in Vedic astronomy by the stars of Cygnus. Perhaps sounds or tones played a role in this creation process, with musical intervals, particularly the perfect fourth (4:3) and its inverse form, the perfect fifth (3:2), being the key to understanding how such notions were envisaged, utilizing the fractal symmetry so beautifully encapsulated within the number 432.

Similar numeric themes are to be found also in the myths and legends of

ancient Mesopotamia* and northern Europe,† as well as in the religious traditions of Hinduism,‡ Buddhism,§ and Taoism,¶ showing that this grand system,
conveying the idea of the cyclic passage of time, must have a universal basis
and singular point of origin. Completing the picture are the two half cycles of
Plato's Perfect Year, which are 12,960 years each (30 × 432);[15] the Babylonian
Great Year, which is 432,000 years (1000 × 432),[16] and the Chinese cosmic year
known as the *yuan* (meaning "round"), which is 129,600 years (300 × 432).

Every example cited here, and many more besides, use the same canon of
numbers. These are generated either by the triple saros cycle or precessional
periods of 72 years, or by their points of synchronization (i.e., 216 years,
432 years, 864 years, and so on, see fig. 37.2). Even the incredible, and no
doubt symbolic, length of time the Chaldean astronomers and astrologers were
said by Cicero and Diodorus to have recorded the observation of the stars can
be seen as a mathematical constant of not only the canicular and triple saros
cycles, as previously noted, but also of the Altai-Baikal calendrical system. For
instance, 473,040 is 6570 × 72, 2190 × 216, 1095 × 432, 219 × 2160, and,
most significant of all, 365 × 1296, with 1296 being 1/100 of a Chinese cosmic
year of 129,600 years, and 1/1000 of a Treta-yuga of 1,296,000 years; the 365
denoting a solar year of 365 days.

What all this shows is that a time period of 473,040 years cited in connection with the observation of the stars by the Chaldeans, and also, according to

---

*Here we can read about the 108 essences given by Enki to Inanna, the 216,000 workers used by
King Gudea to build the temple of Ningirsu, and the 108 dates offered to the gods of Uruk.

†From each of the 540 gates of Valhalla, 800 warriors slain in battle will one day ride out, making 432,000 warriors in all. Then we have the 648 (1.5 × 432) great beams in Thor's palace.

‡In Hinduism we have, for instance, the 10,800 stanzas of the Rig Veda, each of 40 syllables
making 432,000 syllables in total; the 10,800 bricks in the Indian fire altar (Agnacayana); the
skull of the demon Lightning Tongue broken into 108 pieces by the monkey god Hanuman,
and the 108 kinds of illusions granted by Brahma and received by Indrajit, the son of the demon
Ravana.

§In Chinese and Tibetan Buddhism we find various examples of the use of cosmic numbers,
such as the rosary made of 108 beads, the 108 blessings of Buddha, the 108 ways to build a
chorten (shrine), the 108 lakes and cemeteries encountered during the *chöd* ritual, the 108 sacred
books of the Kangyur canon, the 108 perambulations of Mount Kailash necessary to achieve
nirvana, the 108 bongs made on a large gong in Japanese Buddhist shrines, and the 54 teachers
visited by a pilgrim named Sudhana.

¶In Taoism we find mention of the 72 auspicious sites of the *xiān* (immortals), the 72 levels of
the Mo Pai Nei Kung system, the 108 movements of tai chi chuan, and the 108 Stars of Destiny
(made up of 36 Heavenly Spirits and 72 Earthly Fiends).

Cicero, by "those astrologers who, from the top of Mount Caucasus [in eastern Asia Minor or Armenia Major], observe the celestial signs and with the aid of mathematics follow the courses of the stars," is by no means a random number. It would appear to have been created by either the Chaldeans or some predecessor as an idealistic cosmic number expressing exact multiples of all the important long-term time cycles mentioned here—a synodic year of 365 days, triple saros of 54 years, precessional "century" of 72 years, grand calendrical period of 432 years, canicular cycle of 1460 tropical years, and, finally, a precessional age of 2160 years. Incredibly, and as we shall see next, many of these same numeric concepts are expressed perfectly in spatial form within Hindu-Buddhist sacred architecture that additionally provides tantalizing confirmation regarding the geographical origins of this extraordinary blueprint to time itself.

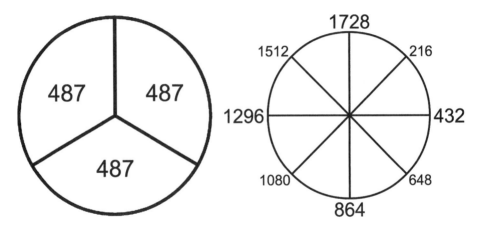

Figure 37.2. Two calendar rounds expressing the numeric system of the mammoth-ivory plate (see fig. 36.1 on page 297). Left: the breakdown of a circle into three 487-year periods of a canicular cycle of synodic 1461 years. Right: the 216-year half-cycle and 432-year full-cycle periods of the grand calendrical cycle.

38

TIME TURNED
TO STONE

At the temple of Borobudur in Java, built during the ninth century CE, there are 72 statues of Buddha on each of the 4 sides of its central tower structure, making 432 Buddhas in all. On the temple's 3 upper tiers are 72 additional Buddhas inside pierced stupas, bringing the total number up to 504.[1] None of this can be by chance alone, suggesting that here, perhaps, we should look for tangible evidence of the origins of this profound sacred understanding of cosmic numbers, derived from synchronizations between the triple saros eclipse cycle of 54 years and a precessional "century" of 72 years.

The Borobudur temple represents the cosmic mountain Sumeru, the Buddhist name for Mount Meru, and in Vedic literature this is located in the extreme north of India, either in the Tian Shan Mountains of China or in the Altai Mountains of southern Siberia and Mongolia.[2] Is this where we will find the origins of these cosmological number sequences? As we have seen, 432 is the length of one complete cyclic period in Altaic calendrical tradition, and yet, just like at Borobudur, with its extra 72 Buddhas, the Altaic cycle allows for a bonus period of 72 years, bringing the total number to 504. Thus at Borobudur we see the concept of cosmic time not only encapsulated in stone, but also envisaged as revolving or turning about a pivot point seen in terms of an *axis mundi,* or axis of the earth.

A connection between the triple saros eclipse cycle and the turning of cosmic time around an axis mundi is hinted at also by the fact that Greek astronomers referred to the triple saros cycle as an *exeligmos,* from the Greek ἐξελιγμός, meaning a "turning or turn of the wheel," something encapsulated in the Buddhist architecture of Borobudur as a physical representation of Sumeru.

MOUNT MERU

Mount Meru, or Sumeru, was a concept based on the idea that the cosmic axis, the turning point of the heavens, revolved about a pivot-like mechanism fixed to the earth. This was most usually imagined as a mountain or tree, which could be substituted when required with a simple pole or post in order that a shaman might climb it to access the sky world. A number of mountain locations have been identified with Mount Meru (for a map of these sites see fig. 34.2 on page 283). For instance, the Russian painter and traveler Nicholas Roerich (1874–1947) identified the Altai chain's highest peak, Belukha, with Sumeru,[3] the Buddhist form of Mount Meru, while Geoffrey Ashe linked Belukha directly with Meru.[4] Interestingly, Belukha is the mountain's Russian name; in Turkic tradition it is Uch-Sumer, meaning "three peaks," or Umai-Uch-Sumer, the "womb of the three peaks," a reference to its role as the earth mother Umai Ana, whose primary totem is the swan. She, of course, is the consort of the sky god Tengri, whose own totem is the white goose.

Geoffrey Ashe has highlighted the importance also of another holy mountain called Khan Tengri,[5] which becomes another candidate for Mount Meru. It is a prominent peak in the Tian Shan range of central Asia, and has been the center of worship for the god Tengri since time immemorial. To this list of potential world mountains we might add Bogda Peak in the Bogda Shan range, an eastern extension of the Tian Shan Mountains. This, as we saw in chapter 34, forms the most likely candidate for the Chinese cosmic mountain named Kunlun, which was the home of the goddess Hsi Wang Mu, the Great Mother of the West.

THE CENTER OF ASIA

Although all these peaks might well be seen as sacred, and may define one part of the "Altaic seedbed," as Ashe calls it,[6] they are all simply physical representations of a conceptual cosmic mountain. It is perhaps wrong to single out any one mountain as marking the absolute center of the earth, around which the heavens are seen to revolve. Nevertheless, a monument to the south of Ürümchi, the city of the sands on the edge of the Tarim Basin, supposedly marks the center of the Asian landmass.[7] Other similar monuments exist in the region. One located several hundred kilometers farther north in Kyzyl, the capital of the Tuva Republic, is known as the Center of Asia monument. It consists of a tall polelike obelisk on a globe with a "solar deer" at its apex. Clearly it is meant to represent the axis of the earth. So did an original axis mundi of extreme antiquity exist somewhere in this region? Was this location the true source behind the stories of the Hindu Meru and the Buddhist Sumeru? Could it be found today? It is a matter we return to in the book's final chapter.

Tuva is situated between the Altai Mountains and Lake Baikal, and in Tuvan shamanic tradition the cosmic mountain is called Sümber-ula,[8] a name that might well have links to the Buddhist concept of Mount Sumeru. Followers of Tengrism or Burkhanism view the entire Altai region as the "twelve faceted Kin-Altai,"[9] as well as the "navel of the earth."[10] It is said to be located at the base of a cosmic tree, its branches stretching out over the Altai and Asia as a whole. The Altai is seen also as linked to an umbilical cord connecting the center of the world with the cosmic axis.[11] This is achieved through Kangyi, the "axis," which coincides with the path of the Milky Way and enters the Upper World via the "North Star,"[12] in other words the polestar, something that last occurred when the northern celestial pole crossed through the constellations of Cepheus, circa 20,000–15,750 BCE, and afterward Cygnus, circa 15,750–12,750 BCE. It is perhaps for this reason that Mount Belukha in its role as a cosmic mountain and birthplace of the world is seen as a personification of the swan mother Umai Ana, for there is every chance that her association with the axis mundi, the axis of the world, goes back to an age when the stars of Cygnus, as the celestial swan, commanded the position of the northern celestial pole.

CHURNING THE OCEAN OF MILK

Very likely Cygnus, and possibly even a combination of stars belonging to both Cygnus and Cepheus, formed the first avian guardian of the cosmic axis and keeper of cosmic time. In Egypt this role was played by the bennu bird, which returned to Heliopolis from Arabia either every 1461 years or else every

500 years. In ancient Mesopotamia it was the Zu bird, while in Hindu Vedic tradition it was the monstrous eagle known as Garuda. This was said to have taken into its care the *amrita* (or *amrit*), the ambrosia or nectar of the gods seen as the elixir of immortality, created when 54 asuras (demons or antigods) and 54 devas (gods) churned the Milky Ocean by pulling back and forth the body of the great snake Vasuki, who had coiled around the postlike Mandhara, a spur of Mount Meru, for this purpose.

The concept of Samudra Manthan, the Churning of the Milky Ocean,[13] is expressed with suitable numeric symbolism at the Bayon, the great temple located at the heart of the late twelfth- and early-thirteenth-century Khymer period religious center of Angkor Thom in Cambodia. This magnificent building complex was originally dedicated to the Hindu god Vishnu, but was later transformed into a Buddhist temple. Like Borobudur in Java, Angkor Thom functions as a physical representation of Mount Meru, being located on a square island surrounded by a large moat. Entrance to the complex was across four bridges located at the cardinal directions. Each bridge displays carved statues of 54 asuras on one side and 54 devas on the other. They are shown holding the stretched-out body of the great snake Vasuki, which they appear to be pulling back and forth in some unimaginable game of tug of war.

Very likely the pulling of the great serpent one way, then the other, was meant to signify the creation of one triple saros cycle of 54 years by the asuras, followed by another cycle created by the devas, thus implying 54 years of darkness followed by 54 years of light, making one complete cycle of 108 years. Standard belief regarding what the Churning of the Milky Ocean represents in celestial terms suggests that the struggle between the asuras and the devas signifies the movement of the sun and moon as they swing back and forth between the solstices each year.[14] Yet this perceived swing between solar and lunar extremes most likely relates, not to the movement of the celestial bodies across the course of a year, but to their movements during what is known as the lunar standstill cycle. This takes 18.61 years to complete, during which time the moon rises more northerly or more southerly of the sun at the time of solstices, while for the other nine years the moon rises within the limits of the sun's most northerly and southerly risings at this time. Since the lunar standstill cycle is similar in length to the 18-year saros eclipse cycle, this interpretation of the Churning of the Milky Ocean supports the view that the account of the 54 asuras and 54 devas pulling the great snake back and forth really does relate to alternating cycles of darkness and light, each one marked by the start of a triple saros eclipse cycle of 54 years in length. What is more, one double cycle of 108 years multipled by four is, of course, 432 years, the time span of a "mini" Kali-yuga.

The importance of the number 432 at the Bayon in Angkor Thom is emphasized by successively adding up the number of asuras and devas on each bridge, that is, 108, 216, 324 and, finally, 432—this last figure constituting 4 periods of equal light and darkness (108 years × 4 = 432 years). The only complication in this perfect synchronization between cosmic time and sacred architecture is the fact that a fifth entrance bridge, the Victory Gate, was created with an additional 54 asuras and 54 devas, bringing the total number of statues up to 540.

RAHU AND KETU

That the story of the Churning of the Milky Ocean alludes to the importance of eclipse cycles is brought out by the fact that after the amrita is produced, it is stolen and consumed by an asura named Svarbhānu, who has the body of a serpent. The god Vishnu pursues Svarbhānu, cutting off his head. However, since Svarbhānu is now immortal, his disembodied head continues to exist, now under the name Rahu (Rahula in Buddhist accounts), while his serpentine body takes the name Ketu. Rahu and Ketu then become the two lunar nodes, which are always 180 degrees apart from each other, one in the northern sky and the other in the southern sky. As we have seen, these points of intersection between the solar and lunar orbits, referred to, respectively, as the ascending node (Rahu) and descending node (Ketu), define where solar and lunar eclipses can occur—Rahu's severed head being seen as the actual cause of eclipses.

Very clearly there exists a relationship between the mythology behind the establishment of the lunar nodes and the 54-year triple saros eclipse cycle, the reason why the numbers 54 and 108 recur repeatedly within the sacred architecture not only at Angkor Thom, but also at nearby Angkor Wat. This is another Khymer-period Hindu-Buddhist temple complex built in the twelfth century and also representing Mount Meru. Here the art and architecture once again feature the number 54 and its double form, 108. For instance, the complex, which like the Bayon at Angkor Thom is in a square plan and surrounded by a square moat, is accessed from the west by a single extended bridge. It is in two parts, with an elongated nāgá snake forming the railings on either side of each section. All four nāgás are supported by 54 balustrade supports, making 108 in each section and 216 in total. An equal number of columns once supported the balustrades themselves. Adding still further to the numerological significance of Angkor Wat's western bridge is the fact that in length each section measures 54 phyeam, a unit of measure made up of four cubits of 0.43545 meters in length.[15] Thus in local cubits the two sections of the bridge are 432 cubits in length, which has been interpreted as a fractional representation of a Kali-yuga of 432,000 years.[16]

Every measurement and number sequence at both Angkor Wat and Angkor Thom are deliberately reflective of cyclic time turning about an axis mundi seen in terms of Mount Meru. This once again raises the question of whether somewhere in the Altai-Baikal region, which Geoffrey Ashe saw in terms of the genesis point of human civilization, there existed a common place of origin for the interconnectness between cosmic number sequences and celestial cycles involving the sun, moon, and stars. If so, then could it be identified today? Could we go on to find the true source of the Altai-Baikal calendar system?

THE SOURCE OF IMMORTALITY

One possible clue is the nature of the amrita, the ambrosia or nectar of the gods, featured in the Samudra Manthan, the Churning of the Milky Ocean. There is every reason to believe that amrita, the source of immortality for the gods and the asuras, was created through the intervention of moonlight. In ancient India moonlight was able to imbue water taken from certain pools, waterfalls, and river sources with a special quality. This then created the amrita, which was able to bestow longevity on the drinker.[17] So water exposed to moonlight in a prescribed manner was thought to be the key to immortality, a realization that adequately confirms the connection between the story of the Churning of the Milky Ocean on Mount Meru and the monitoring of eclipse cycles based on long-term observations of the moon such as the 54-year triple saros eclipse cycle.

Did these profound cosmological notions originate among the Upper Paleolithic peoples of the Altai-Baikal region? Were they carried westward to Göbekli Tepe in southeast Anatolia? Were they afterward taken up by the earliest inhabitants of nearby Harran, which preserved a knowledge of the triple saros eclipse cycle through till classical times? Lastly, did the Chaldeans, the inhabitants of Harran and nearby Şanlıurfa, inherit knowledge of archaic number sequences, like the 473,040 years said by Cicero and Diodorus Siculus to have been the length of time they had been recording the movement of the stars? This number, in similar with those making up the Puranic yuga cycles, derives most probably from multiples of solar and lunar time cycles, including the canicular cycle of 1460/1 years and the Altai-Baikal calendrical system of 216 and 432 years, which most likely had their origins at places like Mal'ta in south-central Siberia at least 24,000 years ago, and arguably much earlier still.

What is more, there is every reason to conclude that many of these cosmological ideas, based on cyclic time, would afterward find their way via the Pre-Pottery Neolithic world of Göbekli Tepe into the Nile Valley of Egypt. Here they would go on to influence the design, layout, and ultimately the function both of the Great Pyramid and of Giza's underlying geometry.

39

THE
CYGNUS KEY

The Great Pyramid is—like the temple of Borobudur in Java, and those of Angkor Thom and Angkor Wat in Cambodia—an axis mundi uniting the earth with the cosmos. It is, if you like, an ancient Egyptian form of Mount Meru. This is something determined by its association with the cyclic number 432, the length of each of its sides in long cubits. When these are added together, one by one, they generate a cyclic progression reflecting the synchronization between the 72-year precessional period and the 54-year triple saros cycle, in other words 432, 864, 1296, and 1728.

All of these numbers are also precise fractional representations of the amount in terrestrial years of the four cosmic time periods or yugas of Indian Puranic tradition (1,728,000, 1,296,000, 864,000, 432,000), which, as we saw in chapter 37, display a descending ratio of 4:3:2:1. This in turn might be linked to the importance of musical intervals in the ancient mind-set, particularly the perfect fourth, with its 4:3 ratio, and the perfect fifth, with its 3:2 ratio. The fact that the Great Pyramid is a scale model of the Northern Hemisphere to a ratio of $\frac{1}{43,200}$ is also likely to be important in the monument's role as a cosmic mountain. That the length of its sides in reeds is 72 only further emphasizes the connection between the monument's dimensions and celestial time cycles, in this case a precessional "century" of 72 years.

TWELVE AND NINE

Over and above all this is the proportional relationship between the 72-year precessional period and the 54-year triple saros cycle, for it reflects a fractional division or ratio of 4:3 (e.g., 8 × 54 = 432 and 6 × 72 = 432), which is hinted at also in the 3-4-5 triangles used to define Giza's underlying geometry. This 4:3 ratio is found in the most obvious fractionalization of 72 and 54, which is 12 and 9, something that features in the numeric symbolism seen in connection with the Great Pyramid. For instance, the length of its sides in reeds and long cubits, 72 and 432, respectively, are both divisible by nine and twelve (72 = 6 × 12 or 8 × 9, with 432 = 36 × 12 or 49 × 9). Nine is also the root number behind Giza's underlying geometry and the dimensions of the Second Pyramid, which, as noted in chapter 17, are defined by a unit of measure equivalent to 45 reeds (5 × 9) or 270 long cubits (30 × 9), the latter additionally being the length in years of 5 triple saros cycles (5 × 54 = 270).

In southern Siberia, 9 is the most important number in the Tuvan shamanistic religion,[1] while 9 and multiples thereof feature heavily in the Taoist-inspired design and layout of Beijing's Temple of Heaven, a matter discussed shortly.[2] In Britain 9 is a key number attached to many Neolithic and Bronze Age stone circles, which often bear names like the Nine Ladies or the Nine Maidens, even though they invariably possess considerably more than nine standing stones. Such archaic number symbolism is meant to convey the idea of women dancing or turning in circles, actions performed perhaps to ensure the perpetuation of cosmic time; failing to do so no doubt leading to its cessation and with it the end of the world.

This concept is brought out in the tales from Norse myth of the Nine Maidens of the Mill. These are "giant maids" who turn the "world-mill," in other words the perceived cosmic axis or turning point of the heavens.[3] It is said that the "great mill" was larger than the whole world, "for out of it the mould of the earth was ground."[4] From this "world-mill" came the blueprint for the mundane world, which was thereafter made manifest by the gods.

THE NINTH HEAVEN

There is a connection here also with the nine Muses of Greek tradition, the nine swans that flew seven times around the island of Delos at Apollo's birth, and far-flung stories of otherworldly swan maidens, who are occasionally said to have been nine in number.[5] Shamans of the Yakut-speaking Dolgan tribe of Russia's Krasnoyarsk Krai (Russian *krai*: "territory"), which lies to the north of the Altai region, are known to have erected nine posts in ascending heights.[6] On top of these they would place wooden swans or geese to give the impression of birds ascending through the nine heavens. During ceremonies the shaman would summon a "goose." After mounting it, he would ride off to the ninth heaven.[7]

The ninth heaven's association with the goose makes it synonymous with the "birdland" or "bird heaven," the celestial home of the swan maidens.[8] When a direction for this is indicated, it is said to be the north.[9] There are hundreds and thousands of swan-maiden stories recorded in every part of the Northern Hemisphere, from North America right across to Europe and the Far East. In these legends, swan maidens come from the sky world to alight on terrestrial bodies of water, such as pools or lakes. Once here, they transform themselves into human form by removing their swan garment or "feather-robe."[10] While they are bathing, a man chances upon them and, seeing their swan cloaks at the water's edge, steals the one belonging to the youngest and/or prettiest member of the group. In doing so, he prevents her departure when the other maidens resume their swan form. Thus the poor girl is forced to remain in the mortal world, where she becomes the wife of her abductor. She bears him children, but forever yearns to return to the sky world. Eventually she either tricks her husband into giving back her swan cloak or finds it through some cunning means. The swan maiden then takes flight (often through a smoke hole in the top of a yurt or tent, symbolizing a spirit hole between this world and the Upper World) and returns from whence she came.

Ethnologists have long realized the extreme antiquity of the swan-maiden tradition, ascribing its genesis to the Paleolithic age.[11] Central Asia, northern Asia, and of course Siberia, where many of the accounts stemmed from, are all good candidates for its point of origin.[12] These stories also reflect a link to the migration of swans and geese to and from Arctic breeding grounds in the north.[13] The Buryats are one of several clans and tribes of southern Siberia that honor an ancestress in the form of a swan.[14] They claim descent from one of nine (or sometimes three) swan maidens who are said to have alighted on the waters of Lake Baikal.[15] In one version of the Buryat myth, the swan maiden, about to depart for the sky world, tells those she is leaving behind that "every spring, when the swans fly north, and every autumn when they return, you must perform special ceremonies in my honour."[16]

Most important of all are the direct links between the swan-maiden tradition and shamanism. The maidens are somehow an amalgam of migrating swans and female shamans, who attain astral flight through the wearing of a feather robe, swans often (although not exclusively) being the totems of shamanesses. In southern Siberia eagles and ravens are usually the totems of male shamans. Among the Buryats the eagle was the father and the swan the mother of the people.[17] This connection with shamanism is highlighted in one swan-maiden story told by the Chorin Buryat of Russia's Irkutsk Oblast, which lies immediately to the west of Lake Baikal, close to the Upper Paleolithic site of Mal'ta, where the discovery of 24,000-year-old swan pendants has been linked with north-south bird migration, the soul as the spirit of a bird, and the birth of animism in Siberia. Here a swan maiden tricks her husband into returning her feather robe. Upon her departure, she tells her "daughters and sons" to "become shamans."[18] This account strongly associates Buryat swan ancestry both with shamanism and with the swan-maiden tradition. Among the Dolgan shamans of Krasnoyarsk Krai, the birdland or bird heaven would appear to have been one and the same as the ninth heaven. So where exactly was it to be found?

THE NINE STARS OF CYGNUS

In Taoist tradition the significance of the number 9 is attributed to *nine* stars, identified today with the seven stars of Ursa Major and two other invisible "attendant" stars nearby.[19] The Tuvans also associate the number 9 with "nine stars," which they see in terms of the seven stars of Ursa Major along with the sun and moon.[20] All this might well be so. But the awkwardness in this identification of the nine stars is self evident. *Seven* is the number of Ursa Major, the Great Bear, as Geoffrey Ashe makes clear. Not the number 9. These explanations of the nine stars are simply bold attempts at trying to explain why the number 9 is so intimately connected with cyclic time and the turning of the heavens, which, as we have seen, is marked out by not only the variable motion of the moon and long-term eclipse cycles, but also by the Great Bear's circumnavigation of the northern celestial pole. So might an alternative solution to this problem of the nine stars be found?

Classical Chinese astronomy identifies the constellation of Cygnus as Tianjin (or Tien c'hin), the Celestial Ford, which is composed of a rectangle of nine stars.[21] In this role Cygnus was the "Heavenly Harbor of the Heavenly River,"[22] in other words the bridge that crossed the Milky Way. So is it possible that the connection between the number 9 and the turning of the heavens around the cosmic axis was compounded by the fact that "nine stars" marked out the Cygnus constellation? If correct, then this would have been especially important when its stars commanded the position of the northern celestial pole, circa 15,750–12,750 BCE, for at this time they would have been seen to revolve around the cosmic axis in a circular motion each night. The connection with the number 9 would have linked Cygnus with the variable motion of the moon and the eclipse cycles in particular, since these were themselves associated with this same number on so many different levels.

The connection between Cygnus and the moon is strengthened in the knowledge that the swan in many parts of Europe was seen to be under the influence of the moon. At a very early date the swan became associated with the night and moonlight,[23] while in Estonia, for instance, the name for the moon, *kukene* ("little moon"), was close to the Greek for swan, both the bird and the constellation, which was Κύκνος ("kuknos"). This is likewise similar to the Finnish and Estonian word *kuu,* which also means "moon."[24]

So it seems possible that the use of nine stars to define China's Tianjin constellation, identified with the Cygnus constellation in the west, came about because of the number's ancient association with the marking of time using both the cyclic variability of the moon and the triple saros eclipse cycle. If correct then this explains why the number 9 is connected with not only the moon and cyclic time, but also with a "ninth" heaven located in the northern night sky that was seen as the ancestral home of the swan maiden. In this way the number 9 also became the key number associated with the wheel-like motion of the cosmic axis, reflected in the story of the nine "giant maids" who turn the "world-mill" in Norse myth, and references to stone circles in Britain being called names like the Nine Ladies or Nine Maidens.

BEIJING'S TEMPLE OF HEAVEN

Chinese mysticism regards the number 9 and multiples thereof as extremely auspicious. As previously mentioned, they feature in the profound cosmological and numeric symbolism encoded within Beijing's Temple of Heaven, built during China's Ming Dynasty (fifteenth–sixteenth centuries CE).[25]

The complex's central feature is the Round Altar (Yuan Qiu) where the Chinese emperor would communicate directly with the embodiment of Sky as part of a unique nine-part ritual conducted each year at the time of the winter solstice. The altar is made up of three platforms, each of which has specific measurements in *zhang,* a unit of measure employed during the Ming Dynasty. A zhang was around 10.5 feet (3.2 meters) in length,[26] the same as the reed found in connection with both the dimensions of the Great Pyramid and Giza's underlying geometry. The Round Altar's first platform is 9 zhang in diameter, the middle one 15 zhang, and the outermost platform 21 zhang. Together this makes 45 zhang (5 × 9), the equivalent of 45 reeds, the unit of measure employed at Giza.[27]

The number of panels on the balustrades surrounding the Round Altar's three platforms also forms multiples of nine. The first platform has 36 panels (4 × 9), the second 72 (8 × 9), and the third 108 (12 × 9), providing a total of 216 panels (9 × 24). The most sacred spot in the entire structure is the stone where the emperor would stand at the center of the upper platform. Around it are nine paving stones. Each ring of paving stones beyond that continues the ninefold theme, with 18 (2 × 9) in the next ring, 27 (3 × 9) in the third, and 81 (9 × 9) in the outermost ring. The second platform's inner ring has 90 (10 × 9) paving stones and its outer ring 162 (18 × 9). The third platform's inner ring has 171 paving stones (19 × 9), while its outer ring has a total of 243 (27 × 9, or 3 × 81), emphasizing the importance of this number, which, as we have seen, appears on the mammoth-ivory plate found at Mal'ta.

ALL SEVENS AND NINES

Although Beijing's Temple of Heaven is only 500 years old, its profound use of ninefold numeric symbolism almost certainly derives from the significance given to the number 9 in Taoism. As we have seen, according to Chinese tradition many of its cosmological notions derived originally from the beliefs and practices of the Yi people of southwest China.[28] This almost certainly included the importance of the number 9, which features prominently alongside the number 7 in Yi folk customs. Nine is seen as male and relating to "white" Yi clans, while seven is seen as female and associated with "black" Yi clans.[29]

As we saw in chapter 34, the ancestors of at least some of the Yi people might well have come originally from beyond the Tibetan plateau, their true homeland being either somewhere close to the Tarim Basin of central Asia or, more likely, farther north in the Altai Mountains of southern Siberia and Mongolia. This last surmise is supported by the fact that Tuvan shamanism, like Yi folk tradition, uses the numbers 9 and 7 together and also gives them male and female genders, respectively.[30] The numbers 9 and 7 also combine in a nine-part grid used by Tuvan shamans to convey the importance of the complex number 41 (which is 9 + 7 + 9 + 7 + 9). It features in a form of divination known as *khuvaanak,* which uses 41 black and white stones[31] that are meant to be collected from 41 different streams.[32] (Interestingly, there are normally 41 solar eclipses in a triple Saros cycle of 54 years and 29 lunar eclipses, making 70 in total.)

These black and white pebbles are laid out in specific sequences, including sets of three and seven.[33] In some instances they are arranged to form the shape of the seven stars of Ursa Major as a turning mechanism of the heavens.[34] Very likely these stones are used not simply for divination, but also to demonstrate the interconnectedness between sevenfold and ninefold symbolism, particularly their relationship to the seven stars and nine stars as regulators of cosmic time. Similar ideas would appear to have been carried at an early date from the Altai-Baikal region via the Tarim Basin and Tibetan plateau into southwest China. Here they would find expression in both the folk magic of the Yi people and, through their influence, the philosophy, beliefs, and sacred architecture of Taoism.

If all this is correct, the nine stars associated with the polarcentric traditions of both northern and eastern Asia related originally not to the *seven* stars of Ursa Major, but to *nine* key stars in the vicinity of Cygnus—the two constellations, the Great Bear and celestial Swan, working together in harmony during the Upper Paleolithic age. It also suggests that the *nine* swans representing the birds of the Muses that flew *seven* times around the island of Delos at Apollo's birth, as well as the nine stars with which the Muses graced the lyre of Orpheus upon its placement in heaven, are to be found in the vicinity of the Summer Triangle, as was proposed in chapter 22. Cygnus then was almost certainly the birdland or bird heaven of the swan-maiden tradition, connecting its influence with both swan ancestry and swan shamanism. All went together in the past, and might never have been separate entities in their own right.

THE CYCLE OF LIFE

The spread of both swan shamanism and the idea of swan ancestry during the Upper Paleolithic would seem to have gone hand in hand with a belief that the human soul was originally thought to emerge into earthly incarnation from a starry realm presided over by a swan or goose. Each spring, flocks of these migratory birds would be seen to fly toward a northerly placed bird heaven and return each fall in a manner replicating the cycle of life itself. Yet because this cosmic source or axis of the heavens was seen also to regulate time, human souls were thought to conform, and even reflect, this same cyclic process—each one entering this world for a prescribed period before leaving incarnation and returning from whence it had come. Since the soul or spirit was seen as eternal, it could wait on the branches of an imagined Tree of Life, synonymous with both the Milky Way and the cosmic axis, before returning to earth and achieving rebirth, starting the whole process all over again. This, of course, was the foundation of a belief in reincarnation, which probably had its inception among the earliest communities of southern Siberia, where shamans promoted this form of spirituality for the first time.

Similar ideas in cosmology, shamanism, and spirituality would most likely have reached the Pre-Pottery Neolithic world of southeast Anatolia via various carrier cultures of the Russian steppe and the Caucasus, where the shamanic bird of choice somehow switched from the swan or goose to the vulture. Most likely this change in species had something to do with climate and terrain as well as with the preexisting beliefs of the cultures inhabiting these regions. Whatever the answer, it now meant that Cygnus, as the entrance to the sky world, instead of being the celestial home of the swan or goose, or even the eagle, now became the domain of the vulture, as well as of a feline identified with the panther-leopard and later with the mythical griffin. In turn, these same ideas were carried via the Levant into the Nile Valley of Egypt, where the bird of creation was seen as a vulture (a totem of Nut), goose (the Gengen-wer of Geb), heron (the bennu bird or phoenix), and falcon (the falcon-headed god An or Anu, and also the drty falcon).

Greek tradition came to associate the swan with heavenly harmonies, the music of the spheres of Pythagoras and Plato, which found expression through the seven strings of Apollo's lyre, given to his son Orpheus. His soul was transformed into a swan, and he became the constellation Cygnus so that he might be near his precious lyre, which had become the neighboring constellation of Lyra.

Such ideas flourished within the cult of Apollo, god of music and poetry, where Orpheus also played an important role. As Geoffrey Ashe concludes in *Dawn behind the Dawn*, Apollo's true origins are to be sought in Hyperborea,[35] a mythical land existing somewhere in the vicinity of the Altai Mountains. The first priests of Apollo, including Abaris the Hyperborean, who supposedly mentored Pythagoras, and the sons of Boreas, can thus be seen as distant echoes of a powerful shamanic elite that thrived in the Altai-Baikal seedbed during some former age. Here, most probably, was the true point of origin, not only of the grand calendrical system outlined in these pages, but also of some of the most ancient and profound ideas in cosmology and spirituality to come out of the Eurasian landmass during the Upper Paleolithic age, circa 43,000–9600 BCE.

Yet can we solely accredit our own human ancestors with the creation of this complex system of ideas? Who exactly were the first priests of Apollo in Hyperborea? The greatest clue comes from the account of Hecataeus of Abdera, who in the fourth century BCE wrote about the bizarre ritual conducted by the three sons of Boreas in the precinct of an enormous Hyperborean temple. As we saw in chapter 35, their actions, which seem shamanic in nature, attracted countless swans, which joined the chant for the duration of the proceedings before taking flight and returning from whence they had come. Where Hecataeus obtained this story, and how old it might have been when first recorded, will probably never be known. His allusion, however, to the fact that the sons of Boreas were a full 6 cubits (2¾ meters) in height might prove to be helpful in their identification. Recent archaeological discoveries in the Altai-Baikal region have revealed important clues regarding a lost chapter in human history—one that might well have led to the genesis of civilization. I speak here of the lost legacy of the Denisovans.

40

THE DENISOVAN LEGACY

In the Altaic region, something began.

GEOFFREY ASHE, 1992[1]

In the Bashelaksky range of the Altai Mountains, within the Denisova Cave, located on the north side of the Anui River (51°23′51.29″ N 84°40′34.34″ E) just inside Russia, archaeologists have uncovered tantalizing evidence of an extinct human type (see fig. 34.2 on page 283 for a map of all Denisovan-linked sites in southern Siberia mentioned in the book). It comes from meager evidence—a fingertip (distal phalanx) of a young girl and a large molar, which both date to circa 40,000–50,000 years before the present,[2] along with two other teeth that are tens of thousands of years older than the other fossils.[3] Over the past decade or so, these human remains have provided vital DNA evidence of the uniqueness of this population in the human evolutionary tree, as well as of its character and distribution in the Asiatic world.

Known today as Denisovans, or, tentatively, *Homo sapiens altaiensis,* after the place of their discovery, these "archaic" humans are thought to have thrived in southern Siberia from perhaps 300,000 years ago down to around 40,000 years ago.[4] Moreover, up to 3–5 percent Denisovan DNA has now been found among human populations in central Asia, southern Asia, northern Asia, eastern Asia, Melanesia, including Papua New Guinea, Fiji and the

Solomon Islands, and Australia.[5] It is present also among the Yi or Lolo peoples of China, Vietnam, and Thailand, the Han Chinese, and the indigenous Sherpa populations of the Tibetan plateau.*[6] Denisovan DNA is even present among certain Native American tribes,[7] opening up all sorts of possibilities concerning the migration of Asiatic populations into the Americas during the Upper Paleolithic age, circa 43,000–9600 BCE.

BIG TEETH

All the indications are that before their extinction sometime after the arrival of the first anatomically modern humans in southern Siberia during the Initial Upper Paleolithic, 45,000–40,000 years ago,[8] some Denisovans were of exceptional size. For instance, the two Denisovan molars found in the Densiova cave are so large that one of them, known as Denisova 8, was initially dismissed as that of a cave bear.[9] The second molar, a wisdom tooth from the upper jaw of a different individual and known as Denisova 4, is described as a "giant tooth."[10]

Paleoanthropologist Bence Viola, PhD, of the University of Toronto and Max Planck Institute for Evolutionary Anthropology in Leipzig, Germany—where DNA testing under the leadership of Svante Pääbo, a Swedish biologist specializing in evolutionary genetics, has revealed the unique nature of the Denisovan fossils—has had much to say about the enormous size of this giant tooth. In a National Geographic TV documentary first screened in 2012, he admitted, "This pretty big tooth belonged to a rather big individual. We don't know how big. There is not a close relationship [to modern humans], but at least big teeth frequently belong to big guys. If this belonged to a woman, I don't want to see the man! [He] might have been pretty big!"[11]

The fossilized fingertip (Denisova 3)—which DNA analysis revealed belonged to a young girl with dark skin, brown hair, and brown eyes[12]—adds weight to the conclusion that some Denisovans were of exceptional size. Before the fingertip's unfortunate destruction during the DNA extraction process, it was said to have been unusually "broad and robust,"[13] suggesting that the individual, originally dubbed "X-woman," was strongly built. Lastly, a fourth fossil (Denisova 2), a tiny worn milk tooth of a young girl of 12 or 13 that was found

---

*Melanesians in Papua New Guinea have the highest levels of Denisovan DNA known today (5 percent), while some mainland Asians, such as the Yi or Lolo, along with Taiwanese aborigines, also possess noticeable levels of Denisovan ancestry (2 percent).

in 2002 and came from a layer in the cave dated to 228,000 to 127,000 years ago, is described as "very large, falling outside of the range of variation seen in modern humans."[14] Thus all four Denisovan fossils recorded so far are much larger than those of anatomically modern humans, a trend that will most likely continue with future discoveries.

HOMO HEIDELBERGENSIS

In addition to this, there are indications that the Denisovans are related to a type of hominin, or human type, known as *Homo heidelbergensis* ("Heidelberg Man"), who might also have been of great size. They thrived in various parts of the African and Eurasian continents from about 800,000 years ago down to around 350,000 years ago. It has even been proposed that Denisovans were an early form of anatomically modern human (*Homo sapiens*) that evolved from a population of *Homo heidelbergensis* in Southwest Asia prior to their suspected arrival in southern Siberia some 300,000 years ago.[15]

DNA analysis of skeletal remains of *Homo heidelbergensis,* found at the Lower Paleolithic cave site of Sima de los Huesos in the Atapuerca Mountains of northern Spain and dated to 430,000 years ago, has shown that this archaic population were more closely related to Denisovans than they were to Neanderthals, *Homo heidelbergensis's* most likely European descendants.[16] Both Denisovans and Neanderthals are today thought to have diverged from *Homo heidelbergensis* or at least a common ancestor around 750,000 years ago.[17] This is about 400,000 years earlier than the suspected first emergence of Denisovans sometime around 350,000 years before the present. Having said this, the results of a DNA study announced in 2017 propose that Denisovans and Neanderthals parted company soon after their split from the common ancestor,[18] meaning that Denisovans existed on their own for far longer than had previously been thought. This does seem to make sense of their unique physiology, which although bearing some similarities to Neanderthals, diverges in other ways, most obviously the incredibly large size of their teeth.

The Neanderthals would go on to occupy Europe, as well as west, central, and northwestern Asia. The Denisovans, on the other hand, moved eastward, occupying southern Siberia and, arguably, territories in northeastern, eastern, and southeastern Asia, where modern human populations containing Denisovan DNA exist today. The borderland between the two human type must have run from the Yenisei River basin and Sayan Mountains in the north down through the Altai-Baikal region to the Bay of Bengal in the south; this being not only the potential point of contact between Denisovans and Neanderthals, but also between Denisovans and anatomically modern humans who entered Siberia from the west.

Although when found in Europe, the skeletons of *Homo heidelbergensis* are no more than 1.73 meters (5 feet, 7 inches) in height, there is powerful evidence that some members of this population were of exceptional size. Fossil bones belonging to *Homo heidelbergensis* found in South Africa suggest that individuals were routinely over 7 feet (2.13 meters) tall.[19] So if the Denisovans really are related to *Homo heidelbergensis,* and may even have been their more direct descendants, then there is every chance that at least some members of their population were of exceptional size and height. Seeing how the examples of Denisovan teeth discovered in the Denisova Cave have chewing areas almost twice the size of modern human teeth makes this possibility very real indeed.[20]

ADVANCED TECHNOLOGY

More significantly, the occupational layer in the Denisova Cave that has revealed the finger bone and molar dated to circa 70,000–40,000 before the present, Layer 11 (the other molar—Denisova 8—was found just below in Layer 12), has also produced evidence of highly advanced human behavior. This includes a beautifully polished arm bracelet now thought to be around 60,000–70,000 years old.[21] Made of bottle-green chloritolite or chlorite, it shows evidence of having been sawed, polished, and, finally, drilled to create a hole through its width so that a second object, perhaps a stone ring or disk, could be hung from a cord. More incredibly, the hole displays characteristic signs of having been created at high speed, suggesting that the drill used for this purpose was of an extremely advanced nature (see plates 23 and 24).[22] Similar precision-made jewelry would not be seen again until the Pre-Pottery Neolithic world of Anatolia over 50,000 years later.

Archaeologists working at the Denisova Cave have additionally found drilled beads made of ostrich eggshell. These are around a centimeter or less in diameter, with centrally drilled holes.[23] They also came across the oldest known needle anywhere in the world. It is 7-centimeter-long, finely polished, with an eyehole at one end for thread.[24] Most likely the needle, fashioned from the bone of a so-far-unidentified large bird, was used to make tailored clothing.

More incredibly, equine DNA discovered in the same layer as the Denisovan remains has raised the possibility that a species of Pleistocene horse known as the ovodov was being domesticated, herded, and even ridden as much as 40,000–70,000 years ago.[25]

What is so important about these discoveries is that Russian archaeologists are now willing to accept that the chloritolite bracelet, bone needle, and ostrich-eggshell beads were the product not of anatomically modern humans, *but of Denisovans*.[26] In other words, before their disappearance around 40,000 years ago the Denisovans perhaps rode horses, wore tailored clothing, and manufactured highly sophisticated jewelry. Indeed, the extraordinary bracelet found in the Denisova Cave was probably worn by a very important Denisovan female, maybe even a shamaness of some kind. If all this is correct, then these extraordinary realizations change everything we know about the origins of civilization, for it seems that its founders were not our own ancestors, but Denisovans, who would appear to have developed a sophisticated society as much as 60,000–70,000 years ago.

ACCELERATED HUMAN BEHAVIOR

Of undoubted relevance here is that a recent study of the first appearance of modern human behavior in southern Siberia shows that it emerged for the first time at sites in the Trans-Baikal, southeast of Lake Baikal, some 44,500 years ago. It then went on to dominate the archaeological record across the region around 40,000–35,000 years before the present.[27] More incredibly, the authors behind this study admit that in the absence of modern human remains from the sites in question—two of which, Khotyk and Kamenka-A, are mentioned below—there is every chance that these "manifestations of modern behavior"—including organized occupations, dwellings with stone foundations, standardized tool kits, symbolic activities, and the specialized hunting of dangerous prey—could have been triggered by the presence of "archaic" groups such as Denisovans and Neanderthals.[28]

INNOVATIONS AND INVENTIONS

In the knowledge that Denisovans interbred with anatomically modern humans, not simply during the Initial Upper Paleolithic period, circa 45,000–40,000 years ago, when our ancestors first reached the

Altai-Baikal region, but arguably much later still,* what kind of impact did the Denisovans really have on the emergence of early human society? Could they, or their hybrid descendants, have developed an advanced knowledge of celestial time cycles that evolved into complex numeric systems of the sort clearly displayed on the 24,000-year-old Mal'ta plate? Were these time cycles based on the observation of eclipse cycles, the sun's canicular cycle, and the slow precession of the stars across their cycle of approximately 26,000 years?

EARLIEST EVER USE OF PRESSURE FLAKING

Both the Denisovans and their hybrid descendants will have moved among the earliest human settlements of southern Siberia, circa 45,000–20,000 years ago, and this will have included those situated on the forest steppe of central Mongolia, immediately to the south of Lake Baikal. Here, at a site named Tolbor-15 located in the Ikh Tulberiin Gol (the Tolbor River) basin, a branch of the Selenga Gol (Selenga River), archaeologists have uncovered evidence of one of the earliest sustained manifestations of pressure flaking.[29] It comes from an occupational layer dating to the Middle Upper Paleolithic, circa 30,000–20,000 BP (before the present).[30]

The importance of this discovery from the Tolbor-15 site cannot be understated, for, as prehistoric stone tool specialist Mikkal Sørensen makes clear, "pressure blade production" emerges "during the Upper Paleolithic around 20,000 B.C. in the [central] Mongolian area" and is then carried from Siberia via the Urals westward as "transmitted knowledge."[31] On its arrival in eastern and central Europe, pressure flaking, he tells us, was adopted by Swiderian-linked cultures such as the Kunda and Butovo sometime during the tenth or ninth millennium BCE.[32]

As I argue elsewhere, either the Swiderians or their Post-Swiderian descendents might well have been responsible for introducing not only pressure-flaking technique to the Pre-Pottery Neolithic world of Anatolia, but also the concept of monumental archiecture at places like Göbekli Tepe.[33] If correct, then this shows their possible impact on the genesis of modern human civilization including that of prehistoric Egypt through contact with important sites

---

*Rasmus Neilsen, professor of computational biology at UC Berkeley, California, in the TV program "Yeti: Myth, Man or Beast?" (first broadcast May 29, 2016, on British Channel 4) admitted that interbreeding between Denisovans and modern humans could have occurred as late as 15,000–7000 years before the present.

like Helwan in the north of the country. That an understanding of this highly specialized type of stone-tool technology, passed on only through instruction from teacher to pupil, might have originated some 30,000 years ago at sites like Tolbor-15 in the forest-steppe of central Mongolia, south of Lake Baikal, is quite extraordinary. Was it inspired originally by the presence across the region either of Denisovans and/or their hybrid descendants?

MICROBLADE TECHNOLOGY

Not unconnected with these discoveries is the fact that the earliest manifestation of what is known as microblade technology is now thought to have emerged out of nowhere within early human settlements in the Altai region around 35,000–30,000 years BP. This evidence has come from the discovery of a number of examples of microblades from various sites excavated during the past fifty years by Russian archaeologists.[34] What is even more significant, however, is that microblades have been found in Layer 11 of the Denisova Cave, which, as we know, dates to circa 70,000–40,000 years BP. This is the same layer that the chloritolite bracelet, bone needle, ostrich-eggshell beads, and fossil remains of the Denisovans have been found.[35]

Microblades are long, thin flakes (nearly always of flint, but occasionally of obsidian or other types of stone) that have been detached from a prepared core, generally (although not always) through the application of the pressure flaking technique. This is done using a specialist tool made from bone, antler, or wood. Microblades generally have either a triangular or trapezoidal cross section, and should by definition have a length that is two and a half times longer than their width. After their initial manufacture, they can be retouched to produce an assortment of different tools including burins, scrapers, and projectile points.

The fact that microblade technology appears for the first time not just in the same geographical area as the Denisovans, but actually in the same occupational layer of the Denisova Cave where their fossil remains have been found, makes it likely that they were its initial innovators. From the earliest human settlements in the Altai region this technology then disperses into other areas of Siberia, before being carried eastward into China and Japan, and westward across the Urals into Europe. Here it manifests for the first time at sites like Kostenki on the west bank of the Don River in Ukraine, sometime around 30,000 years ago.[36] Kostenki was the home of an advanced population known as the Eastern Gravettians, who were the forerunners both of the Solutreans and the Swiderians.

DRILLED OSTRICH-EGGSHELL BEADS

Another possible connection between the Denisovans and both pressure flaking and microblade technology can be gleaned from the fact that the Tolbor site to the south of Lake Baikal has yielded evidence of symbolic or nonfunctional art that has links with the Denisova Cave. At both sites a unique type of "subsquare" bead has been found,[37] as have the finely worked beads made of ostrich eggshell mentioned earlier in this chapter.[38] Indeed, the tiny drilled ostrich-eggshell beads found in the Denisova Cave pose a problem. Not only is the technology more or less unique for 40,000–50,000 years ago, but there are no ostriches in southern Siberia.

It has been proposed that either the eggshells or the finished beads, perhaps both, were imported to the area of the Denisova Cave from the Trans-Baikal, where ostriches *are* thought to have existed.[39] If this is correct, then to reach the Altai region of southern Russia the eggshells and/or the beads will have passed through Upper Paleolithic sites in central Mongolia, immediately below Lake Baikal, which is around 650 kilometers in length from north to south. Could there really have been contact between the Denisovans and the earliest anatomically modern humans to settle in central Mongolia and the Trans-Baikal? If the answer is yes, then it would explain another important connection between the two, and this is the manufacture and use of musical instruments.

BONE FLUTES AND WHISTLES

Liudmila Lbova, a doctor of historical sciences at the Institute of Archaeology and Ethnography at Novosibirsk State University, has made a special study of the flutes and whistles found at Upper Paleolithic sites in both southern Siberia and the Trans-Baikal.[40] She found that they were almost all fashioned from the long bones of birds.[41] One particular fragment of a flute from an Upper Paleolithic site at Khotyk in the Uda River basin, southeast of Lake Baikal, appears to be made from the long bone of a swan.[42] It comes from an occupational layer that has produced radiocarbon dates in the range of 32,700 BP ± 1400 years down to 26,220 BP ± 550 years,[43] which, with the necessary recalibration, suggests that the flute is probably around 30,000–35,000 years old. A similar flute found at the Kamenka-A site, also on the Uda River, is made from the long bone of a goose.[44] According to Lbova and her colleagues, the flute found at Khotyk "can confidently be considered the oldest musical instrument in the territory of Siberia"[45] (although see below for a direct contraction of this fact).

If all this is correct, it is a very exciting prospect, as it implies that some of the earliest melodies played on a musical instrument in the Altai-Baikal region were connected directly with birds, waterfowl in particular. As we know from Greek tradition, the swan was seen as the most musical of birds. It was the totem also of the Muses, of Apollo, god of music and poetry, and also of the divine poet, Orpheus. More poignantly, we are reminded once again of the strange ceremony conducted by the three giant sons of Boreas in the precinct of the Hyperborean temple, which attracted flocks of swans that joined the choral chant and sound of the harps. We are reminded also of the unique swan carvings found at the Mal'ta settlement west of Lake Baikal. Was this region truly the point of origin of the veneration of the swan as a shamanic creature symbolizing divine inspiration attained through musical sounds? Had the swan been an important totemic creature to the Denisovans, and did they themselves use musical instruments?

Amazingly, the answer to these questions could well be yes, for the archaeological layer (Layer 11) at the Denisova Cave that has yielded firm evidence for the presence here of Denisovans as much as 40,000–70,000 years ago, including the discovery of the chloritolite bracelet, bird-bone needle, ostrich-eggshell beads, and microblades, has also produced a bone object identified as a musical instrument.[46] Although identified as a whistle,[47] it could easily have formed part of a much larger flute. Indeed, Lbova describes this object and others of a similar appearance in the following quite remarkable manner:

> The notches and the cuttings, distinguishable technologically, have a clear geometrical rhythm of intervals and form various compositions of graphic lines. . . . A sense of rhythm, counting, and abstraction, demonstrated through graphic marks, point to the generated area of elementary aesthetic perception of reality.[48]

Very clearly we see here an understanding of both sound enhancement and aesthetic quality. Frustratingly, what type of bone the instrument found in the Denisova Cave was made from has not been made clear. Whatever the answer, the object's sheer existence is tantalizing evidence that the Denisovans used whistles and perhaps flutes as much as 40,000–70,000 years ago.

It was in the millennia that followed the appearance of these innovations that the Mal'ta site had its beginnings. Here, on a branch of the Angara River, sometime around 24,000 years ago, an unknown artist carved the mammoth-ivory plate, its upper surface covered with pecked spiral forms. As we saw in chapter 36, their number and arrangement may preserve calendrical information regarding precession, eclipse cycles, and canicular periods of 487 years. In the opinion of the author, this advanced knowledge did indeed come from surviving Denisovans or Denisovan-human hybrids who still occupied the high plateaus and forest-steppe of the Altai-Baikal region immediately prior to this time. I believe they were responsible for creating the complex sequences of cosmic numbers, such as 54, 72, 108, 216, 432, and so on, based on long-term time cycles, that would go on to influence cosmological notions in Mesopotamia, Egypt, northern Europe (Scandinavia in particular), southern Asia (India and Tibet), and eastern Asia (especially China, Camobodia, and Indonesia).

Yet if the Denisovans really were responsible for catalyzing advanced human behavior in the Altai-Baikal seedbed, why has next to no Denisovan DNA been detected in the populations of Europe and western Asia? This is a good question that needs some attention. The fact is that aside from the presence of Denisovans in the Denisova Cave, it would seem that the same territory, and perhaps even the same cave, was at times shared with Neanderthals (*Homo neanderthalensis*).

NEANDERTHAL MIGRATIONS

A Neanderthal population is thought to have reached the Altai Mountains either from Southwest Asia or the Crimea region, north of the Black Sea in what is today Ukraine, sometime around 55,000 years ago,[49] and arguably earlier still.[50] Yet by around 40,000 years ago they had disappeared, seemingly having been assimilated by the Denisovans.[51] A toe bone found in the Denisova Cave's Layer 11 in 2011 is now known to have belonged to a Neanderthal girl who lived around 50,000 years ago. DNA tests showed that the individual's direct ancestors had very likely mated not just with Denisovans,[52] but also, much earlier back, with some of the first anatomically modern humans to leave Africa around 120,000–125,000 years ago.[53] Although these early humans did not reach any further than Southwest Asia, their DNA was carried eastward by members of the Neanderthal population that entered southern Siberia at a much later date.[54]

Almost no fossil remains of early modern humans have been found in southern Siberia. The only exception are those of Ust'-Ishim "Man," discovered in 2008 at a site of this name on the banks of the Irtysh River in Russia's Omsk Oblast, northwest of the Altai Mountains. DNA evidence tells us that the immediate ancestors of this male individual, who lived sometime around 45,770–44,000 years BP, interbred with Neanderthals.[55]

THE REAL MIDDLE EARTH

This evidence shows that at this time at least three different forms of hominin all inhabited the same territory in a manner not unlike that of the Middle Earth of J. R. R. Tolkien novels. Some would have been of great stature (Denisovans), others of normal size (modern humans), while still others might well have been much shorter in height (Neanderthals). Such encounters would have been occasionally friendly, but at other times they unquestionably involved violence and abduction, resulting in new types of human hybrid, some of whom went on to become our own ancestors.

So it might not have been the Denisovans, or even their hybrid descendants, who carried new ideas in cosmology, eclipse cycles, complex number sequences, and timekeeping, along with the rudiments of civilization, westward into western Asia, northeastern Africa, and Europe. Although the knowledge might have *originated* among the Denisovans, and arguably even among Denisovan-Neanderthal hybrids, it could have been transmitted to other parts of the ancient world by modern humans, that is, *Homo sapiens,* or else by hybrids of a different kind—Neanderthal–*Homo sapiens* or even Neanderthal-Denisovan–*Homo sapiens.* All must have coexisted in the distant past, meaning that all of them might well have contributed to the rise of human civilization. Yet from the DNA evidence available so far, there seems little question that before the arrival in northern and central Asia of anatomically modern humans, the Denisovans were the most advanced human type living anywhere on the planet.

SHAMANISTIC POPULATION

So was it really possible that the first "priests of Apollo," remembered in myth as the three sons of Boreas, each of whom was a full "six cubits" (2¾ meters) in height, are an abstract memory of Denisovans living in the Altai-Baikal region sometime before the end of the last ice age? That the most notable totem of both the Mal'ta community and the sons of Boreas was the swan, a primary symbol of the Hyperborean cult of Apollo, as well as that of the Cygnus constellation, tells us that the Denisovans might well have been responsible for the introduction of cygnocentric (swan-centered) cosmological themes regarding the existence of a cosmic bird that controlled the passage of time from its position at the northern celestial pole.

What is more, the Denisovans might well have been the first human species to employ the use of musical instruments, arguably flutes and whistles made of bird bones. In doing so, they perhaps forged a link between swan ancestry, divine melodies, and the music of the spheres, the imagined sounds produced by the slow movement of the celestial bodies. If so, then did the Denisovans also explore the concept of sound acoustics and musical intervals?

SWAN ANCESTRY OF THE SOYOD

Intriguingly, one account of swan ancestry in southern Siberia is actually connected with a musical instrument. The Mongolian tribe called the Soyod, better known today as the Dukha or Tsaatan, are said to derive their ancestry from the offspring of a swan from Lake Khövsgöl. This is a huge freshwater sea 136 kilometers in length, linked to Lake Baikal in the northeast via waterways connected with the Selenga River basin. One day, it is said, a handsome man appeared as if by magic from a piece of green jadeite that burst forth from a rock on the shore of the lake.[56] He began playing his *khuur* (a bowed stringed instrument), and the beautiful sounds it produced were heard by a swan floating on the water. Having fallen in love with the musician's enchanting melodies, the swan transformed into a maiden to be with him. They married and had a baby daughter. When the child was three, the swan, yearning for her homeland, became a bird once more and flew out through the smoke hole in the top of the *toono* (yurt or tent). The daughter of the swan maiden went on to become the ancestor of the Soyod peoples and the man, having lost the original head of his khuur, recarved its end into the shape of a swan. For this reason, even today the instrument bears a head and neck in the likeness of a swan.[57]

Here somewhere is the relationship between otherworldly melodies and a perceived descent from an original ancestor whose animistic form was the swan. Moreover, the fact that the "handsome man" is said to have emerged from a piece of green jadeite is curious, and brings to mind the Denisovans' use of bottle-green chloritolite to fashion jewelry. It hints that there was once some special relationship between the beautiful green minerals found in this region and the manifestation of divine melodies associated with swan ancestry and the symbol of the swan.

THE SWAN MAIDEN AND THE FLUTE

In another variation of the swan-maiden myth, this one from Romania, the transformation of a swan into a swan maiden is directly linked with the sounds of a flute.[58] After she was treacherously killed by a rival, the voice of the swan maiden reveals her plight every time a flute is played that has been cut from a tree growing on the site of her death. So the fact that some of the oldest flutes in the world, not only from Siberia, but also from Europe, are made of swan bone,*[59] confirms the relationship between musical harmonies, swan shamanism, and swan ancestry. Could this connection have begun under the influence of the Denisovans in the Altai-Baikal seedbed some 40,000–70,000 years ago?

SOUNDS OF THE SWAN

The khuur stringed instrument that had its end recarved into the shape of a swan in the Soyon ancestry myth is very similar to a traditional stringed instrument used by Turkic musicians and storytellers throughout the Altai-Baikal region. It is called the *khomys* in Khakassia, the *igil* in neighboring Tuva, and the *topshur* in the Altai Republic. It has a long straight neck and a head shaped like a swan, because the swan, as we have seen, is believed to travel between the upper and lower worlds.[60] The instrument has either two or three strings. Their pitch is of no particular consequence. What matters is that the strings are tuned to create overtones based on two specific musical intervals—the perfect fourth and its inverse form, the perfect fifth.[61] These, apparently, are important to use, because they are seen to have otherworldly associations.[62] Similar overtones (*kai* or *khai*, as they are called) feature in multiple-voiced vocal harmonies created by Khakas, Tuvan, and Altaic throat singers, occasionally for epic storytelling and shamanic invocation.[63]

---

*Two swan-bone flutes from the Geissenklöesterle-Hohle cave in Swabia, Germany, are among the oldest instruments in the world, being circa 42,000–43,000 years old.

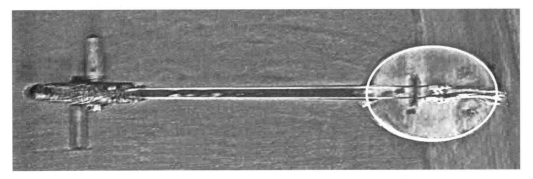

Figure 40.1. The Turkic stringed instrument called the khomys, which has the neck and head of a swan and is traditionally tuned to create overtones based on the perfect fourth (4:3) musical interval and its inverse form, the perfect fifth (3:2). Note its body's elliptical shape, which has a 4:3 ratio.

What is more, the general appearance of the khomys might be likened in shape to the carved swans with stubby wings and long straight necks found at the Upper Paleolithic sites of Mal'ta and Buret', west of Lake Baikal. Most significant of all is the khomys's ellipsoid body. It often has a 4:3 length-to-width ratio (see fig. 40.1), almost certainly to enhance its acoustic properties.

ORIGINS OF THE KHOMYS

One particular folk story from Khakassia tells of how knowledge of the khomys and its unique shape came to be known in this world.[64] Two giants building a bridge across a river came to hear the sound of a mountain girl singing and playing a musical instrument they did not recognize. When they tried to find the source of these beautiful sounds, the girl disappeared as thunder was heard and lightning struck the ground, leaving behind an indentation in the shape of a musical instrument. As a consequence, "They [the giants] made the *khomys* from that imprint, and began to sing to its sound."[65]

The otherwordly girl was most likely a mountain spirit of the type that often features in Khakassian folk stories. Yet the fact that the shape of the musical instrument was made known to "giants," who thereafter create the first khomys and "sing to its sound" hints that knowledge of how properly to make this instrument came originally from the Denisovans, who, as we have seen, might well have been of great stature themselves.

That the khomys's body additionally echoes the shape of the main enclosures at Göbekli Tepe is extraordinary, and goes some way to confirm that their layouts really were designed to enhance acoustics. The fact that even today the khomys and its variants are tuned to produce overtones using musical intervals provides further evidence that this profound understanding of music's other-worldly status was known among the earliest human populations of southern Siberia, and arguably came originally from the Denisovans.

THE DENISOVANS' AUTISTIC MIND-SET

Yet if all this is correct, then the question becomes how and why did the Denisovans come to possess such an extraordinary vision not just of musical harmonies, but also of celestial time cycles and the manner in which they could be multiplied to create incredibly long number sequences like those contained in the Puranic yuga system or indeed the 473,040 years the Chaldean astronomers were said to have recorded the motion of the stars? The answer might well lie in the Denisovan genome, sequenced by the Max Planck Institute for Evolutionary Anthropology in Leipzig, Germany, from the fingertip of "X-woman" found in the Denisova Cave in 2008. This has revealed some major divergences from the modern human genome, eight of which relate to brain function and brain connectivity.

According to Svante Pääbo, the leader of the team of geneticists involved in isolating and sequencing the DNA taken from the finger bone, "Some of them [the divergences] have to do with genes that, for example, can cause autism when these genes are mutated."[66] This does not therefore mean that Denisovans were autistic in the modern sense. However, it remains possible that these genes enabled their brains to operate in a manner *similar* to that of an autistic mind. In other words the Denisovans could well have had a mind-set comparable to that of the "idiot savant." This is a highly gifted individual whose brain is able to instantly perform tasks of memory and calculation, and in so doing take in and remember unbelievably complex information, including extremely long mathematical computations.

If this type of brain can be applied to the Denisovans, and certainly the genome sequencing makes this explanation seem likely indeed, then it would explain how they came to calculate multiple permutations of celestial time cycles and then use this information to formulate complex number sequences. It would also explain their need to do so. For them it was simply a consequence of their savantlike mind-set. It is even possible that the computation of extraordinarily complex numerical systems, derived from tracking the cyclic movement of the celestial bodies, became like a shared mathematical language, which could be expressed in physical form through the creation of symbolic art. A perfect example of this would be the 24,000-year old Mal'ta plate, which is not simply a mnemonic teaching device, but also a series of mathematical number sequences presented as visual art. Very likely, this mathematical language came to be associated with the perceived mechanical nature of the universe, expressed in terms of the slow precession of the stars, the variable motion of the moon, the recurring 54-year eclipse cycle, and the synchronization of the sun's own cycles to create the 1460/1-year canicular period.

THE NINEVEH CONSTANT

Not unconnected to this realization is English writer, philosopher and novelist Colin Wilson's belief that savant syndrome could explain the so-called Nineveh constant. This is a 15-digit number found on a cuneiform clay tablet containing mathematical data discovered among the ruins of the library of the Assyrian king Ashurbanipal (ruled circa 668–630 BCE) at Nineveh in north Iraq during the 1840s. The number in question is 195,955,200,000,000, which has been the subject of much speculation since it was first published in a book in 1952.[67] For instance, it is 70 multiplied by 60 seven times, while its divisors include all the main cosmic numbers found in connection with long-term time cycles including 54, 72, 108, 216, 432, 864, 1296, and 1728.

In 1979 French NASA consultant Maurice Chatelain worked out that the number, which he named the Nineveh constant, was a value in seconds amounting to a figure of just over six million years.[68] Chatelain realized, however, that the exact value in tropical years was out by a twelve-millionth of a day per year. After due thought he found that the figure could be corrected if the fact that the tropical year is getting shorter by a sixth-millionth of a second per year was taken into account. Yet this meant that the original value in seconds reflected the length of a year 64,800 years ago,[69] suggesting that this was the true age of the Nineveh constant. Unable to explain how knowledge of this extraordinary number might have been produced at this time, Chatelain concluded it had to have been given to our distant ancestors by alien visitors.

Colin Wilson (1931–2013), however, had a different take on the matter. He was fascinated by the Nineveh constant and in the epilogue of the revised edition of his book *From Atlantis to the Sphinx* published in 2007, he cited examples of savant syndrome, showing how autistic individuals can instantly work out long periods of time in seconds and retain this information afterward.[70]

He proposed that our ancestors of 64,800 years ago might also have had similar savant qualities, explaining how numbers like the Nineveh constant came into existence.[71] Wilson speculated on who might have been behind its creation, concluding that the most likely answer was the Neanderthals, who are known to have been far smarter than is commonly accepted by mainstream academia.[72]

Back in 2007 nothing was known about the Denisovans, whose existence was not realized until the sequencing of their genome three years later in 2010. Yet knowledge that the Denisovans might well have had a savantlike mind-set, and certainly manufactured exquisite jewellery 60,000–70,000 years ago, makes them the most likely candidates to have created complex numbers like the Nineveh constant. Moreover, the fact that the Altai-Baikal calendrical system existed at least 24,000 years ago in the same region where Denisovans might well have catalyzed advanced human behavior 45,000–30,000 years before the present makes it clear that they, and not the Neanderthals, fit the bill of Colin Wilson's ice age savants who, he suggested, were perhaps the true founders of human civilization.

EXTERNALIZING SOUND

Thus the Denisovans' savantlike mind-set might well have allowed them to associate different sounds with specific shapes, colors, and proportions, a medical condition known as synesthesia. Modern research has shown that synesthesia is common among sufferers of autism.[73] If Denisovans also experienced synesthesia then this might have been one way they came to understand (like Pythagoras tens of thousands of years later) the concept of musical intervals, and their externalization into physical form. We don't know yet how far they might have gone with this creative process, but we can certainly trace its legacy.

Not only might this knowledge have enabled the creation of some of the earliest musical instruments, but these concepts were destined to survive through until the rise of the Pre-Pottery Neolithic world of Anatolia circa 9600 BCE. At Göbekli Tepe, for instance, they would inspire the 4:3-ratio ellipsoid shape of the site's earliest and most sophisticated stone enclosures (Enclosures C, D, and H), and in so doing maximize their sound acoustics. From here, this now extremely ancient wisdom disseminated into other parts of the ancient world, including Helwan in Egypt. This important early settlement, the original Heliopolis, would act as a clearing house of new ideas across a period of several thousand years until finally the surviving knowledge of the Denisovans would be used to encode the importance of the perfect fourth and perfect fifth, expressed in terms of the divine ratios 4:3 and 3:2, into the Giza pyramid field's underlying geometry.

With Khakassian folklore preserving a tradition that knowledge of how to create the precise shape of the khomys was first made known to two "giants," who thereafter began to "sing to its sound," this helps confirm that those who first taught the importance of the khomys' 4:3 ellipsoid shape and its association with the symbol of the swan were the Denisovans. It was they who passed this knowledge on to the earliest modern human societies in the Altai-Baikal region around 45,000–40,000 years before the present. During this approximately 5000-year window, the northern celestial pole in its role as the turning point of the heavens passed through just two constellations— Cepheus, circa 45,000–42,000 BCE, and Cygnus, circa 42,000–39,000 BCE. (These figures, generated by the Stellarium sky program, should be seen as approximate only.)

CYGNOCENTRIC IDEAS

Together or individually these asterisms quite likely provided the earliest human communities with their first celestial timekeepers and guardians of the cosmic axis, beyond which was the entrance to the sky world or Upper World of shamanic tradition. If this is correct, then we have the true answer why the celestial swan was seen as a source of cosmic creation, and why the swan ancestry myth became a metaphor for the foundation of human societies. The first swan maiden was not simply a primeval swan mother or swan shamaness responsible for the birth of clans and tribes, she was also a moment in time when some of the earliest human settlements in southern Siberia adopted cygnocentric beliefs and practices (the Mal'ta site being a latter example of this phenomenon). These beliefs and practices, I suspect, related to a perceived swan ancestry and the importance of the Cygnus constellation as a source of divine inspiration induced, at least in part, through the use of shamanic experiences and musical instruments. These would have included whistles and flutes made from the leg bones of birds, most obviously those of the swan and the goose. Instruments of this type might have been played in the darkened interiors of caves to induce altered states of consciousness, which in turn would have led to perceived contact with the spirit world.

THE PECULIAR PEOPLE

Yet the Denisovans' autistic gene might also now explain other areas of human development at the beginning of the Upper Paleolithic age such as the emergence of shamanism. Toward the end of the Denisovans' existence in Siberia, those of their society who still remained will have been singled out by modern human societies as odd or peculiar due to their strange physiology and strange savantlike abilities. As time went by this situation it likely to have increased, forcing remaining Denisovans to withdraw to more remote localities, most obviously cave environments in the mountains and taiga (the cold Siberian forest terrain). Yet their special abilities will still have been seen as important in establishing contact with the unseen world, meaning that trafficking between Denisovans and modern humans continued, a situation that will have led not only to interbreeding but also to some of the earliest manifestations of shamanism.

The first shamans of Siberia might well have been Denisovans, or at least Denisovan-human hybrids, in other words modern humans who had inherited certain Denisovans genes including those relating to physiology and autism. In this way they retained the peculiar appearance of their ancestors alongside some of their savantlike qualities, which were now seen as an essential part of shamanizing. Individuals of this type will most likely have lived in isolation away from large communities, either on their own or in the company of other Denisovan-human hybrids. Those belonging to these groups will most likely have had a quite different appearance from the earliest anatomically human societies, singling them out as almost otherworldly in nature. (They were probably taller, their heads large and perhaps elongated, their jaws would have been of greater size, while their strange eyes, deep eye sockets, and thick brow ridges would have made them look just a little scary.) As we will see in the final chapter this will have led to these individuals being remembered as legendary figures possessing supernatural attributes.

Oddly related to this scenario is a curious legend attached to the Denisova Cave (named after a local hermit who inhabited the site in the eighteenth century called Dionisij, or Denis), which the Altaians call Aju-Tasch, that is "Bear Rock." It refers to an "evil sorcerer" who became very angry at the local people and so made it rain for many years. Those affected went to a good sorcerer for help. He expelled the evil magician and tangled all the rain into a ball, which was then turned to stone and concealed beneath the ground of the cave.[74] Is there some abstract memory here of Denisovan shamanism (the evil sorcerer) being superseded by the "good" magic of later human societies, with the perpetual rain being an allusion to a cataclcysm that affected the region during some former age? Does the stone ball relate to the archaeology of the Denisovans now being uncovered inside the Denisova Cave? These are tempting thoughts indeed.

A relationship between shamanism and autism has long been suspected. One of the leading figures in this field is cognitive and social evolution expert Michael Winkelman, MPH, PhD, of the Department of Anthropology, Arizona State University, who asks:

> What if shamans resembled autistic savants some of the time? What if the very activity of shamanizing rendered these people in some respects functionally autistic, so that at the time they made the drawings [i.e., cave art] they were temporarily in a non-conceptualizing state of mind? Given new ideas about the origins of savant skills, I think there is reason to take this possibility seriously.[75]

In the knowledge that Denisovans are known to have possessed an autistic gene that perhaps allowed them to function in a similar manner to savants, then I strongly suspect that, in part at least, they were indeed responsible for the emergence of shamanism in Siberia. This in itself would have led to the development and dissemination of one of the earliest cosmological systems anywhere in the world.

In the opinion of the author, this integration of Denisovan knowledge among the earliest human societies to reach the Altai-Baikal region began around 45,000 years ago (even though encounters with Denisovans are liable to have taken place as early as 50,000–65,000 years ago when some of the first anatomically modern humans passed through central and southern Asia en route to Australia). It would, however, have taken many thousands of years of contact with the Denisovans and their hybrid descendents for this integration process to take full effect. Thereafter these ideas were spread throughout the Eurasian continent, entering also the Americas. They were then given a reboot when Cygnus once again controlled the northern celestial pole, circa 15,750–12,750 BCE.

Denisovan-inspired cosmology might have been set to take over the planet. But then something happened to change all that—the global cataclysm remembered today as the Younger Dryas cosmic impact event, which occurred circa 10,800 BCE with aftereffects lasting for hundreds of years afterward. Not only would this devastate the world, and decimate human populations, but it would also delay the birth of our own civilization by many thousands of years. Eventually, however, the first flowering of civilization did begin to take place at places like Göbekli Tepe in Anatolia and Helwan in Egypt, as well as many other parts of the Eurasian continent. Yet the unfortunate consequence of this delayed start to civilization was that we forgot where this profound cosmological knowledge had come from, and who had given it to us. The part played by the Denisovans was totally blanked out, while only vague ideas remained concerning the origins of civilization in the Altai-Baikal seedbed. Geoffrey Ashe came to realize the importance of the Altai-Baikal region during the writing of *Dawn behind the Dawn,* a book I see as an incredibly important contribution to this subject.

Yet, as we shall see in the final chapter, not only are these shamanically based ideas in cosmology and spirituality reemerging into popular consciousness at this time, they are also gaining a major boost from the imminent fulfilment of a potent ancient prophecy. What is more, it is a prophecy attached to a specific location—a gigantic gateway of the gods—that might well turn out to be the original nerve center of the Denisovans as well as the true location of Mount Meru.

41

GATEWAY
OF THE GODS

Very likely the myths and legends of the indigenous populations of northern and central Asia have preserved a memory of the Denisovans. Across the millennia these powerful individuals, whose physique might well have resembled that of a large wrestler (see the description of the Denisovans in the book's preface, "Last of the Denisovans"), would have been regarded as celebrated warriors, terrible demons, and, most important of all, legendary ancestors of great stature.

It cannot be coincidence that Alyp-Manash (or Manas), the great warrior hero of Altaic and Kyrgyz folk tradition, who possessed supernatural invulnerability and rode a warhorse capable of effecting magical transformations, is said to have been a giant (Turkic *alp* or *alyp*).[1] Is Alyp-Manash's survival in the Altaic folk memory derived from the former presence in the region of the Denisovans and their hybrid descendants?

Ay-čürök, the wife of Alyp-Manash's son Semetey, is described as "a seer and swan-maiden."[2] She "dons her swan-habit" to assume swan form and flies over the earth in search of her future husband.[3] Could Ay-čürök be the collective memory of a powerful swan shamaness, or group of shamanesses, whose deeds contributed to the emergence of swan ancestry among the earliest peoples of southern Siberia?

THE GIANT SARTAKPAI

Among the Tuvans of the Tuva Republic their "creator-founder" is said to be the "giant" Sartakpai.[4] He appears also in the storytelling epics of the neighboring Republic of Khakassia and also in the Altai itself under the name Sartakpai, or simply Sartak.[5] Altaic history is divided into four world ages called *yurgyuld'i*.[6] During the earliest of these it is recorded that there were several ice ages. Various types of beings inhabited the region during this time. There were the "human-like *almisi*, [the] *oborotni* and sphere-headed (*bolchokbashi*) pygmies/ dwarfs," the latter apparently feeding on "the meat of small children."[7] After the pygmies died out, the region became the domain of "giants," whose former presence is preserved in the folk stories surrounding Sartakpai and his kin.[8] Eventually the giants were replaced by, first, the "new people," and then by the *turguti*, seen as ancestors of the current Turkic population.[9]

This information is of extreme value to our study. Turkic peoples take their ancestry and legendary history very seriously, preserving it across count- less generations in storytelling epics. If they say the region was once occupied by a race of pygmies who were then replaced by "giants," the chances are this is indeed what happened. (Were the pygmies an early hominin perhaps, not unlike *Homo floresiensis*, the so-called "hobbit," who inhabited the island of Flores in Indonesia as recently as 13,000 years ago?)

There are many accounts surrounding Sartakpai and his kin, although these are mainly related to the supernatural sculpting of geographical features such as mountains, lakes, and rivers.[10] One story, curiously, has Sartakpai build- ing a bridge, and becoming frustrated when things don't go right. Venting his frustrations on his son, Adoochee, and his wife, Oimok, he hurls a huge boul- der at them, forcing them to transform into grey geese to escape his fury. The offending projectile thereafter becomes a notable rock feature, while Adoochee and Oimok are so scared they remain thereafter as geese.[11] Does this story hint that the goose, like the swan in the story of the three sons of Boreas, was a totem of the giants?

Sartakpai's bridge-making exploits remind us of the two giants in the Khakassian tale (see chapter 40) who while building a bridge find the imprint of the shape of the khomys instrument after hearing a female mountain spirit singing a sound they had never heard before. Thereafter they create the first khomys and "sing to its sound." Was this a story originally about Sartakpai and his kin?

STRASHNAYA CAVE

In Khakas tradition, Sartakpai spends his youth in the area of the Middle Yenisei River near Abakan, the capital city of Khakassia, as well as a little farther south in the nearby Sayan Mountains.[12] According to legend he then relocates to the Altai and makes his home on the Inya (or Ini) River, close to where it joins the Charysh River.[13] What is interesting here is that located on the Inya River is the Strashnaya Cave, a well-documented habitation site of the prehistoric age. Archaeologists have found evidence of Paleolithic occupation of the cave circa 50,000–35,000 years BP, including a large number of diagnostic stone tools. Some of these match very well those recovered from the Denisovan layer (Layer 11) of the better-known Denisova Cave around 125 kilometers to the east.

Recent finds from the Strashnaya (Russian: "scary," "terrifying") Cave have included fragments of a human skull and rib expected to be no less than 50,000 years old, as well as a small piece of finger bone approximately 35,000 years old.[14] DNA testing of these fossil remains will hopefully determine whether they belong to Denisovans, Neanderthals, modern humans, or a hybrid mixture of all of them. Since the Inya River is only 110 kilometers in length, to find that it contains a cave site possibly associated with Denisovan habitation, as well as a legend concerning a giant that once lived in the same area, seems unlikely to be coincidence.

If the Denisovans really were of exceptional size and height, then there is every reason to assume that Sartakpai and his kin are indeed reflections of the former presence in the Altai-Sayan Mountains of the Denisovans. The "new people" alluded to in the world ages of Altaic myth would then be the first modern humans to enter the same region no later than 45,000 years ago. That the Tuvans additionally express direct ancestry from the giant Sartakpan might well preserve the memory of hybridization between the Denisovans and modern humans, as well as the debt owed to the former for catalyzing the growth and spread of modern human behavior in this region.

Across the millennia, Sartakpai's memory merged with that of other great warrior heroes such as Kezer-Chinggis, better known as Gesar Khan.[15] He is a part god, part culture hero of Buryat, Tuvan, Mongolian, and Tibetan tradition. It is said that when the time is right Gesar Khan will awaken from his eternal slumber and, like an Asiatic King Arthur, rise up to defeat the demonic forces laying waste to the world.[16]

THE
SLEEPING WARRIOR

In the shamanic religion of Burkhanism the return of this great culture hero is associated with the reawakening of what is known as the Sleeping Warrior.[17] Indeed among the Tuvan, Khakas, and Altaian populations this idea has taken on eschatological proportions, being connected with the recent resurgence of interest in language, customs, and traditional ways of life, along with the promotion of their age-old swan ancestry.[18] This not only includes localized forms of shamanism but also song, dance, and the recitation of historical epics. Furthermore, the Tuvan and Khakas peoples point out the very place the Sleeping Warrior will reawaken. It is located in the western Sayan Mountains, immediately to the north of the Altai range.[19]

Sleeping Sayan, as he or she is known (Sayan in Khakas tradition is female), is seen as a mighty giant and great warrior who became Master of the Taiga (the subarctic forests of Siberia). When the shadow of death loomed, the gods deemed that Sayan should be transformed into stone so that he or she might continue to guard the region and be reawakened only when a suitable replacement had arisen to take his or her place.

The sleeping giant's unique profile is formed by a cluster of mountain peaks within the Ergaki National Park in Russia's Krasnoyarsk Krai,[20] a region that borders Khakassia to the west and Tuva to the south. Ergaki is the pearl of the Sayan Mountains. According to legend it was here that the gods of the past (modernly described as Atlanteans and Lemurians) would assemble for their meetings.[21] Indeed, only gods and shamans were allowed to visit Ergaki. Normal people were forbidden from entering the mountains and instead had to worship them from afar.[22]

Ergaki is seen also as the center of the world, its tallest peak called Zvezdnyi ("Star"), or Paletz ("Finger"), being a "finger" or "nail" reaching all the way to heaven.[23] Indeed, Ergaki as a place-name probably derives from the Tuvan *ergek*, meaning "finger." Curiously, Ergaki does actually sit close to the geographical center of the Eurasian landmass, giving some credibility to its mythological role as a functioning axis mundi. Other, more outlandish claims suggest Ergaki is a "star gate,"[24] and perhaps even a portal to other dimensions.[25]

TWIN PEAKS

At the heart of Ergaki is a secluded granite plateau enclosed by a series of ridges and peaks, the four most prominent of which are Zvezdnyi ("Star"), Ptitsa ("Bird"), and the Bratia ("Brothers"), situated at coordinates 52°50'23.67" N 93°23'57.35" E. These last two peaks stand close to the northwest edge of the mountain plateau, and are like gigantic twin horns forming some unimaginable gateway of the gods. They are said to be brothers turned to stone by the mountain spirits to protect something precious.[26] These spirits give their name to a highly mysterious, north-south-orientated expanse of water situated immediately to the east of the "younger," easternmost brother. It is known today as Ozero Gornykh Dukhov, "Lake of Mountain Spirits."

The highly polished convex surface stretching between the twin peaks of the Brothers is said to be the siblings holding hands.[27] This enormous natural gateway, its twin horns rising to approximately 260 meters (the elder brother) and 150 meters (the younger brother) above the lake, is today known as the Parabola, because of its resemblance to this geometric form. From the south and southeast visitors to the elevated plateau can watch the Milky Way's Dark Rift and the stars of Cygnus setting between the Parabola (see plate 25).

PREHISTORIC LUNAR OBSERVATORY

In addition to this, I have determined that the full moon can be seen to set between the Parabola's crescentlike horns as the lunar orb reaches its most northerly point during its 18.61-year standstill cycle.* As we saw in chapter 38, this cycle very gradually shifts the moon's rising and setting positions, allowing it to rise and set farther north than the sun's own most northerly rising and setting positions for a full nine years, following which the moon rises and sets within the range of the sun's own most northerly and southerly risings for another nine years. The twin horns of the Parabola are positioned in just such a way as to allow the viewer to witness the moon to set between them exactly as it reaches its northerly most position on the horizon, something that occurs only once every 18.61 years.

---

*Based on the gap between the Parabola being approximately 316–318 degrees azimuth as viewed from the south side of the Lake of Mountain Spirits, and the most northerly setting of the full moon being 317–318 degrees azimuth, according to the Stellarium sky program.

Such a unique alignment tells us that in the past Ergaki's elevated plateau might very well have functioned as a gigantic lunar observatory, where the passage of time could have been recorded through long-term observations of the moon's lunar standstill cycle.[28] Yet if this was the case, who were Ergaki's first astronomers? In the knowledge that in legend the site was the domain only of gods and shamans, were those first astronomers Denisovans? As we shall see, there is much evidence that this was indeed the case.

STRANGE GLYPHS

When I first saw the mighty twin peaks constituting the Brothers of Ergaki, my thoughts went immediately to the twin monoliths at the centers of the main enclosures at Göbekli Tepe. I thought about those in Enclosure D, the largest, oldest, and most impressive of the installations uncovered so far. Around the neck of the easternmost of the two huge T-pillars (Pillar 18), both of which are around 5.5 meters in height, are two carved glyphs. They are like personal insignia or emblems of office, one placed above the other. The upper example is at first glance like a letter H, being two upright parallel pillars linked by a centrally placed crossbar. However, a closer examination of the glyph shows that the center of the crossbar is hollow and open at the top, revealing that the vertical pillars are in fact two anthropomorphic figures with birdlike faces holding hands (see fig. 41.1). Arguably this symbolic

Figure 41.1. The two glyphs, one above the other, on the neck of Göbekli Tepe's Pillar 18 standing at the center of Enclosure D.

device represents the monoliths themselves, which are also anthropomorphic in nature and perhaps to be seen as brothers. (They both wear fox-pelt loincloths as if to cover male genitalia.)

Is it remotely possible that here at Göbekli Tepe was some distant echo of an unforgettable location 7000 kilometers away in the Sayan Mountains of southern Siberia? Did the ancestors of Göbekli Tepe know Ergaki? The second glyph on the neck of Pillar 18 is just as enigmatic. It shows a stylized crescent, its horns turned upward, within which is a raised circle with a hole at its center. It has the distinct likeness of an eye, the crescent representing the lower eyelid. Did this eye-and-crescent glyph seen below the *H* symbol on Göbekli Tepe's Pillar 18 signify Ergaki's Parabola—the "eye" being the full moon setting between its crescentlike horns? Myths and legends across both the Eurasian and American continents portray the sun and moon as the eyes of a sky deity. The fact that Ergaki's natural amphitheater is oriented north and northwest, similar to the main enclosures at Göbekli Tepe *and* the Pyramids of Giza, should not be overlooked here. Nor should the fact that stone tools belonging to a Paleolithic culture have been found on the shores of Lake Oyskoe or Ozero Oyskoye.[29] This lies within the boundaries of the Ergaki National Park and is one of the largest high-altitude lakes in the region. The discovery here of prehistoric stone tools confirms that Ergaki was utilized by a local population in Upper Paleolithic times, and arguably even earlier still. But who exactly was present here? Was it really the Denisovans and their hybrid descendents?

A LOST CIVILIZATION?

In Tuvan, Khakas, and Altaic folklore, the legendary giant Sartakpai is accredited with creating not only natural features like mountains, lakes, and rivers, but also (as we saw earlier) with the construction of bridges,[30] irrigation channels, and even the first dams.[31] Such claims take on a special significance in the knowledge that various examples of "ancient hydrological structures" have been found in the Ergaki National Park, including "dams and bypass channels."[32] Archaeologists have been unable to determine who made these mysterious features,[33] implying that they are of extreme antiquity.[34] Elsewhere in Ergaki "traces of discharges and bypass canals" testify, we are told, to the "high level of the civilization" existing in the Sayan Mountains many thousands of years ago.[35] So who was responsible for these apparently artifical features of megalithic construction?

THE WHITE-EYED PEOPLE

Folk stories from neighboring Khakassia speak of a race of alyp, "giants," known as 'Akh Kharakh, meaning the "white-eyed people,"[36] a name gained since their eyes appeared entirely white because they had no irises, just black pupils.[37] Of possible relevance is the fact that extremely pale irises, which make them look white, is a common trait of albinism. Although albinism is a genetic disorder, it can recur across successive generations among certain isolated populations. Indeed, when the Challenger expedition reached the Melanesian island of Fiji in 1874 it was reported that many of the children bore albino traits including irises that were a "pale grey colour,"[38] making them look almost white. I there-fore find it of interest that DNA research indicates that Fijian islanders, and Melanesians in general, retain a high level of Denisovan DNA.[39] If so, then it becomes possible that the Khakassian giants known as the 'Akh Kharakh were a memory of not only the Denisovans and their hybrid descendents, but also, in some instances, of Denisovan albinos, hence their name the "white-eyed people."

Tradition asserts that the 'Akh Kharakh inhabited the Middle Yenisei and Abakan River basins,[40] close to the foothills of the western Sayan Mountains, and thus Ergaki itself. They are said to have employed large stone slabs to con-struct "houses," "temples," and "castles."[41] However, when their greatest sha-man, Palabankam, recognized the signs suggesting that their time had come to an end, the white-eyed people are said to have disappeared inside their kur-gans[42] and buried themselves alive. Apparently it is for this reason that their large bones are even today found at such sites.[43] As in the stories of Sartakpai and his kin, the 'Akh Kharakh are accredited with having built the first irriga-tion channels.[44]

The stone and earthen monuments of the Altai-Sayan region, gener-ally referred to under the collective term *kurgan* (Turkic "fortress"), are not thought to date any earlier than the time of the Iron Age Pazyryk culture, circa 500–300 BCE. Yet legends attached to such sites concerning the former pres-ence in the Yenisei and Abakan River basins of the 'Akh Kharakh might easily reflect the memory of a much earlier period, since the kurgans were probably built at locations that had been important for many thousands of years. Yet are there any megalithic constructions in the region that *can* be directly attrib-uted to the 'Akh Kharakh, or indeed the Denisovans themselves? The answer at this time is no, although the great strength and savantlike qualities of the

Denisovans could have led to them moving about large blocks just as the legends concerning the 'Akh Kharakh suggest. This in turn resulted perhaps in the creation not only of crude megalithic constructions, perhaps like makeshift dolmens, but also the first dams, waterways, bridges, and canals.

In many ways the Denisovans, as the 'Akh Kharakh, are likely to be the real source behind the stories of a "lost civilization" that seeded our own toward the end of the last ice age. If so, then it is distinctly possible that a memory of Ergaki lingered in the minds of those who carried the ancient wisdom and technical capabilities of the Denisovans to other parts of the ancient world.

THE TRUE MOUNT MERU

Finally, we must ask whether Ergaki in its role as an axis mundi was the original source of stories regarding the Mount Meru of Hindu tradition, located not only at the center of the world, but also to the north of India. The Tuvan form of Meru, the Buddhist Sumeru, is Sümber-ula. On its summit is the mysterious Süt-khöl, the Milk Lake, the waters of which are said to glimmer white when touched by light.[45] Likewise, at night Ergaki's Lake of Mountain Spirits is seen to emit an inexplicable luminescence.[46] So magical are its waters that visitors take them away to rejuvenate contaminated springs and wells.[47] Is it possible that Sümber-ula is in fact Ergaki, its Milk Lake the Lake of Mountain Spirits? Were its waters deemed special because of their prolonged exposure to either moonlight or starlight?

There is a connection here perhaps with the story of the manufacture of the amrita, the ambrosia or nectar of the gods. This was once believed to be created through the exposure of certain types of water sources, such as pools, waterfalls, and river heads, to moonlight. If so, could the story of the 54 asuras and 54 devas churning the Milky Ocean to generate the amrita be a memory of long-term lunar observations at Ergaki in the distant past? Are the devas (the gods), and more particularly their antithesis, the asuras (anti-gods), some form of abstract memory of the Denisovans and their connection with Ergaki and southern Siberia in general? When we look at the ugly faces of the asuras in the Hindu art at places like Angkor Thom in Cambodia are we looking at the way our ancestors came to recall the presence of the Denisovans at sites like Ergaki?

The fact that Ergaki's Lake of Mountain Spirits is thought by some to be artificial, having been created by a gigantic dam of huge stone boulders located at its northern end,[48] makes this an exciting prospect indeed. Ergaki could have easily functioned as a nerve center of the Denisovans and their hybrid descendants, who utilized its elevated plateau with its breathtaking, twin-horned gateway as a gigantic lunar observatory. Very possibly it was seen as a primordial axis mundi, linking earth with the sky world via the northern celestial pole; Ergaki's northerly orientation very clearly highlighting the Denisovan's deep interest in the stars and constellations of the northern night sky.

Most important of all though was the Milky Way, especially when it stood upright in the extreme north forming the silvery trunk of the World Tree, the Tree of Life itself. Here, in the fork between its branches, was a great bird (Cygnus) marked out by nine stars that, together with a nearby group of seven stars (Ursa Major), controlled the turning of the heavens. The bird also provided guardianship to those souls entering incarnation or, at the end of their life, returning from whence they'd come. This was a starry world that came to be called the Ninth Heaven, which for many early human societies, and perhaps even for the Denisovans themselves, was to be found somewhere in the heart of Cygnus, the celestial swan.

SAYAN'S RETURN

That for the Tuvan and Khakas peoples of the Altai-Sayan region Ergaki is where the legendary Sleeping Warrior will reawaken is a powerful thought to keep. On one of its ridges a huge rocking stone, anything up to 100–200 metric tons in weight and made of granite-syenite, rests precariously on the edge of a 1000-meter precipice. It is held in place by just a few centimeters of contact with the sloping bedrock beneath it.

Called the Hanging Rock (Visiachiy Kamen), the boulder in question, shaped like the capstone of a gigantic megalithic dolmen, is said to be Sayan's beating heart, torn from his or her chest by the ancient gods.[49] When eventually it falls into the lake below, it will awaken the slumbering giant, who will once again become flesh and blood. In 2016 *The Siberian Times* reported that the Hanging Rock has recently developed a noticeable crack,[50] suggesting that the prophecy may soon be realized.

Such powerful ideas are unlikely to be without meaning. The mostly Turkic and Mongolian populations of southern Siberia see themselves as guardians of the spiritual heart of the Asian world. They ever await the return of the old ways, suppressed until the 1980s by Soviet rule. Stories and beliefs of this kind, as eschatological as they might seem, are crucial, for they relate not just to the origins of shamanism and tribal ancestry, but also to their continued survival through to future generations of humanity. The ancient religions still held true by the indigenous peoples of southern Siberia could easily have been inspired by the former presence in the region of what might well turn out to be the true founders of human civilization—the Denisovans and their hybrid descendants. With the recent discovery of the lost Denisovan legacy, it appears that the Sleeping Warrior's reawakening has now finally begun.[51]

NOTES

CHAPTER 1. AN ARTIST'S WORK

1. Personal communication with Lee Clare, PhD in 2015. See also Dietrich 2017a.
2. Dietrich 2017a.
3. Schmidt 2012, 141–42.
4. Schmidt 2012, 99.
5. Thapar 2004, 95.
6. Koster 1983; Avetisian 1999/2000.
7. Schwierz 2011.
8. Lukan 1979, 55.
9. Frazer 1939, 160.
10. Personal communication between the author and various retired nurses between 2014 and the publication of this book.
11. Siikala 1978, 145, 176, 194.
12. Siikala 1978, 286.

CHAPTER 2. MYSTERY OF THE NORTH

1. For a full account of this trip, see Collins 2004 and Collins 2006.
2. Dodge 1967, 69.
3. Dodge 1967, 69.
4. Dodge 1967, 60.
5. Dodge 1967, 63.
6. Dodge 1967, 64–65, 70.
7. Dodge 1967, 70.
8. Dodge 1967, 74–75.
9. Dodge 1967, 62.
10. Green 1992, 192–95.

11. Green 1992, 211.
12. Dodge 1967, 70.
13. Dodge 1967, 84.
14. Yardimci 2008, 362–64.
15. See Lloyd and Brice 1951, 77–111. They report on surface finds at Harran, including distinctive ceramic ware belonging to the Halaf culture.
16. Collins 2014, 80–82. Based on Schmidt and Dietrich 2010.
17. Schmidt and Dietrich 2010.
18. Dietrich 2017a.
19. Dietrich 2016b.
20. Dietrich 2016b.
21. Dietrich 2016b.
22. Collins 2014, 85.
23. Lorenzis and Orofino 2015.
24. Lorenzis and Orofino 2015, 42.
25. Schoch 2014, 54–55.
26. Magli 2013.
27. Collins 2014, 77–80; Collins and Hale 2013.
28. Dietrich, Notroff, and Schmidt 2014, 6, fig. 2.
29. Becker et al. 2014, 5. See Dietrich et al. 2016, 64–65, fig. 11.
30. Dietrich et al. 2016, 59, 62, fig. 12.

CHAPTER 3. CELESTIAL SIGNS

1. See, for instance, Collins 2015a and Collins 2015b.
2. For Hugh Newman's Megalithomania video "First Pictorial Representation of Göbekli Tepe Found—New Discovery," see https://www.youtube.com/watch?v=NfU-nFXlZMU (accessed October 22, 2017).
3. Allen 1899, s.v. "Cygnus, the Swan," 192–98.
4. Hale 2015.
5. Dietrich 2017b.
6. Collins 2014, 83.
7. Çelik 2000a; Çelik 2011.
8. See Collins 2014a.

CHAPTER 4. THE ENIGMA OF PILLAR 43

1. Belmonte 2010.
2. Allen 1899, s.v. "Aquila, the Eagle," 55–61.

3. Brown 1899, 1:34–36, 234; Brown 1900, 2:17, 148.

4. Brown 1899, 1:34–36, 234; Brown 1900, 2:17, 148; for Aquila, Brown 1899, 1:44–46; for Cygnus, Brown 1899, 1:35–37; for Lyra, Brown 1899, 1:34–36.

5. Thomas 1837, s.v. "Harpies," 159. See Shaw 1790, s.v. "Alpine vulture," npn.

6. Allen 1899, s.v. "Aquila, the Eagle," 55–61; Allen 1899, s.v. "Cygnus, the Swan," 192–98, and Allen 1899, s.v. "Lyra, the Lyre or Harp," 280–88.

7. Najarian, 2016.

8. Vahradyan and Vahradyan 2013. See also Mkrtcyan 2014.

9. Vahradyan and Vahradyan 2013.

10. Herouni 2004.

11. Herouni 2004.

12. Najarian 2016.

13. Tedlock 1996, 356; and also Jenkins 1998.

14. Lankford 2007b, 182–4.

15. Lankford 2007b, 208.

16. Horowitz 1998, 35.

17. Najarian 2016.

18. White 2007, 159–60.

19. Klaus Schmidt, television interview by Graham Phillips, "Death Cult Temple and Bog Bodies of Ireland," *Ancient X-Files,* National Geographic Channel, 2012.

20. Uyanik 1974, 12.

21. Barentine 2015, 131.

22. Pettitt 2013, 212–13.

23. Personal inspection of the shrine in question in 2013.

24. Mellaart 1967, 104.

25. Mellaart 1967, 167.

26. Mellaart 1967, 167.

27. See, for example, Collins 1996, 132–6, 138, 248–51; Collins 2006, 18–19, 26, 36, 40; Collins 2014, 98–101.

28. Gourichon 2002, 140–41, table 1.

29. Gourichon 2002, 144–45.

30. Solecki and Solecki 2004, 120.

31. Solecki 1977.

32. Solecki 1977.

33. Gourichon 2002, 149 and fig. 10.

34. Gourichon 2002, 149 and fig. 10.

35. Mellaart 1974, 92, 126.

36. Schüz and König 1983.

37. Gourichon 2002, 149.

38. Collins 1996, 132–39; Collins 2006, 18–19; Collins 2014, 96–104.

39. Dodge 1967, 60, 69–70.

40. Dodge 1967, 73.

41. Dietrich et al. 2016, 62.

42. Dietrich et al. 2016, 62.

43. Dietrich et al. 2016, 58.

44. Dietrich et al. 2016, 58.

45. "Signs of World's First Pictograph Found in Göbeklitepe," *Hurriyet Daily News,* July 15, 2015; www.hurriyetdailynews.com/signs-of-worlds-first-pictograph-found -in-Göbeklitepe-.aspx?PageID=238andNID=85438andNewsCatID=375 (accessed November 28, 2017).

CHAPTER 5. SCORPIONIC GATEWAY

1. Santillana and von Dechend 1969, 243–44.

2. See Lankford 2007a, 128–31; Lankford 2007b, 178. Also Little 2014 for a general review of this subject.

CHAPTER 6. CULT OF THE LEOPARD

1. Peters and Schmidt 2004, 184.

2. Dietrich et al. 2016, 64–65.

3. Black, George, and Postgate 2000, s.v. "Ukaduhha, Kadduhha," 419.

4. Rogers 1998, 12; Black, George, and Postgate 2000, s.v. "Ukaduhha, Kadduhha," 419.

5. Najarian, 2016.

6. NationMaster.com Encyclopedia, s.v. "Common Griffon Vulture," www.statemaster .com/encyclopedia/Common-Griffon-Vulture (accessed October 22, 2017).

7. White 2007, 159–60.

8. Green 1992, 195.

9. Mellaart 1967, 180–83; Hodder 2006, 86–87, 91–92, 94, 207–08, 259–61.

10. Mellaart 1967, 180.

11. Hodder 2006, 260–61.

12. Hodder 2006, 260.

13. Peters and Schmidt 2004, 183.

14. Hodder 2006, 261, pl. 24.

15. Hodder 2006, 261.

16. Hodder 2006, 123.

17. Mellaart 1967, 24.

18. Blasweiler 2014, 7.
19. Blasweiler 2014, 10.
20. Blasweiler 2014, 7.
21. Blasweiler 2014, 8.
22. Blasweiler 2014, 8.
23. Mustacich 2012.
24. Mustacich 2012.
25. Heun et al. 1997.
26. Deitrich et al. 2012; Dietrich 2016a.
27. Pseudo-Oppian, 3:78–83, as cited in English translation by Weitzmann 2014, 130. This anonymous author wrote under the name of Oppian, a second-century Greco-Roman poet from Cilicia in southern Anatolia.
28. Graf and Johnston 2013, 21, 35, 109–10, 112–14.
29. Graf and Johnston 2013, 129.
30. Graf and Johnston 2013, 100–2, 104, 108–9; Torjussen 2014, 41.
31. Torjussen 2014, 41.

CHAPTER 7.
THE LOST OASIS

1. Egyptian chronology, where possible, after von Beckerath 1997, and "List of Rulers of Ancient Egypt and Nubia," 2000. See www.metmuseum.org/toah/hd/phar/hd_phar.htm (accessed October 22, 2017).
2. For confirmation of the line of sight observation between Helwan and the Giza pyramid field, see "Helwan Observatory," UNESCO, http://whc.unesco.org/en/tentativelists/5574 (accessed October 22, 2017).
3. Debono and Mortensen 1990, 8.
4. For Wilhelm Reil's life and his associations with Helwan, see Pflugradt-AbdelAziz 1994, 259–79, and Reil 1888.
5. May, Schweinfurth, and Sayce 1901, 65. See also "Helwan les Baines: Thermal Spa," Oasis magazine articles, www.livinginegypt.org/portal/Publications/OasisMagazine/Articles/tabid/199/ID/4487/Helwan-les-Baines-Thermal-Spa.aspx#.V0hVGte9PMA (accessed October 27, 2008).
6. May, Schweinfurth, and Sayce 1901, 1–3.
7. For a full account of Wilhelm Reil's time at Helwan, see Plflugradt-AbdelAziz 1994.
8. For the etymology of Helwan's place-name, see Peterson 1893, 19. For the meaning of the root "Helwa," see Johnson 1852, s.v. "halw," 490.
9. Peterson 1893, 19.

10. Burton 1879, 305.

11. Vyse 1840, 4; Burton 1879, 306.

12. Jeffreys 2005, s.v. "Helwan," 367–68. See also Reil 1888, 11.

13. May, Schweinfurth, and Sayce 1901, 5.

14. Khaled 2012.

15. "Helwan les Baines: Thermal Spa." Oasis magazine article, CSA, www.livinginegypt
    .org/portal/Publications/OasisMagazine/Articles/tabid/199/ID/4487/Helwan-les
    -Baines-Thermal-Spa.aspx (accessed November 28, 2017).

16. The description of stone tools and settlement at Helwan is taken from Hayes 1965,
    70–72, unless otherwise stated.

17. Burton 1878, 61.

18. Reil 1888, 10.

19. Reil 1874, 118–21.

20. For a full account of all private collections and finds made at Helwan during the
    late nineteenth and early twentieth centuries, see Debono and Mortensen 1990,
    8–12, and Schmidt 1996, 128.

21. Mook 1878, 142–45; Mook 1880, 1–28, tables 1–5, 12–14; Debono and Mortensen
    1990, 10; and Schmidt 1996, 128.

22. Mook 1880, 13.

23. Debono and Mortensen 1990, 10.

24. Mook 1880, 13.

25. Mook 1880, 13.

26. Mook 1880, 8, 14.

27. Mook 1880, 18.

28. Mook: "Die Anzahl der dortigen Funde eine so kolossale, dass auf einer kleinen
    Strecke, etwa so gross wie dieser Saal, sich Tausende von kleinen Messern fanden,"
    as quoted in Debono and Mortensen 1990, 10.

29. Mook 1880, 18.

30. Mook 1880, 20.

31. See Burton 1879, 307n.

32. Debono and Mortensen 1990, 10.

33. Debono and Mortensen 1990, tables 1–5, 12–13.

34. Debono and Mortensen 1990, 21–22.

35. Mook 1880, 21.

36. De Morgan 1896, 49.

37. Burton 1879, 291; Mook 1880, 5–8.

38. Schmidt 1996, 128.

39. Burton 1879, 291.

40. De Morgan 1896, 49. See also Schmidt 1996, 128–29.

41. Burton 1879, 291.
42. Burton 1879, 291.

CHAPTER 8. EGYPTIAN GENESIS

1. Mook 1880, tables 1–5, 12–13; Schmidt 1996, showing examples of the Debono collection, figs. 2–4.
2. Hayes 1965, 71.
3. Sharai 2010, ch. 8. This chapter of Sharai's book is available to download at: https://openaccess.leidenuniv.nl/bitstream/handle/1887/15339/Shirai%20Chapter%208.pdf?sequence=5 (accessed November 28, 2017).
4. Bar-Josef 1998, 166.
5. Browne 1878a.
6. Browne 1878a, 86.
7. Browne 1878a, 90, fig.1 of plate.
8. Browne 1878a, 90–91.
9. Hoffman 1979, 87–89; Wendorf and Schild 1976, 289–91; Clark 1982, 370.
10. Goring-Morris 2013, 571.
11. Stuiver and Reimer 1993, 215–30.
12. Bar-Josef 1998, 166; Goring-Morris 2013, 570, fig. 7f, 571, 574.
13. Hayes 1965, 71.
14. Hayes 1965, 71.
15. Schmidt 1996, 133.
16. Shea 2013, 204, 208; Goring-Morris 2013, 565, 566, fig. 3: 22–34.
17. Shea 2013, 204.
18. Schmidt 1996, 133.
19. Schmidt 1996, 133.
20. Goring-Morris 2013, 571.
21. Goring-Morris 2013, 577.
22. Goring-Morris 2013, 577.
23. Schmidt 1996, 133.
24. Goring-Morris 1991, 181–85.
25. Goring-Morris 1991, 184; Avner 2002, 81.
26. Email communication with Uzi Avner, July 2016. See also Avner 2002, 81.
27. Email communication with Uzi Avner, July 2016. See also Goring-Morris 1991, 180.
28. Thanks to Uzi Avner for supplying full details and recent images of Rosh Zin.
29. Goring-Morris 2013, 571.
30. Goring-Morris 2013, 571.
31. Moore 1978, 113–17.

32. Email communication between Uzi Avner and the author, July 2016.

33. Jeffreys 2005, s.v. "Helwan." In Bard 2005, 367–68.

34. Hoffman 1979, 90.

35. Hoffman 1979, 89–90.

36. Yeshurun, Bar-Oz, and Weinstein-Evron 2009.

CHAPTER 9. MYSTERY OF THE HELWAN POINT

1. Lombard and Phillipson 2010.

2. Derevianko 2016, 7.

3. Iovita 2011.

4. Mook 1880, 4–5, table 13.

5. De Morgan 1896, figs. 226, 228.

6. De Morgan 1896, 129. See also Mook 1880, 18, regarding Lombard's vast collection of stone tools found at Helwan.

7. Burton 1878, 57.

8. Debono and Mortensen 1990, 31–32, fig. 7.

9. Schmidt 1996, 128–29.

10. Browne 1878b.

11. Browne 1878a, 90, and fig. 3 of plate.

12. Gopher 1994, 194–95.

13. Kenyon 1979, pl. 18.

14. Gopher 1994, 252.

15. Schmidt 1994, 239–52.

16. Schmidt 2001, 51–52, 53, fig. 12.

17. Çelik 2000b, 5.

18. Çelik 2000b, 5.

19. Çelik 2000b, 5.

20. Gopher 1989, 91–106.

21. Mook 1880, 21.

22. Gopher 1994, 36.

23. Altın, Astruc, Binder, and Pelegrin 2012, 157–80.

24. Sørensen 2012, 255–56.

25. Darmark 2012, 269–71.

26. Zaliznyak 1999; Sørensen 2012, 255–56; Darmark 2012, 278.

27. Darmark 2012, 269–70.

28. See Collins 2014, ch. 19 and 20.

29. See Collins 2014, ch. 20 and 26.

30. Schmidt 2002, 10.

31. Roberts 2010, 276.
32. Roberts 2010, 21–22.
33. Gopher et al. 2014, 109, fig. 8c.

CHAPTER 10. VISIONS OF HELWAN

1. Schmidt 1996, 127–36.
2. Schmidt 1996, 128.
3. Schmidt 1996, fig. 2: points 1–8 and fragments 1–4.
4. Schmidt 1996, 133.
5. Schmidt 1996, 133.
6. See Peters and Schmidt 2004, 39, with regard to the discovery there of Helwan points.
7. Halvo, www.halvo.de, search word: "Nevali Cori."
8. Shirai 2002, 121–33.
9. Shirai 2002, 125.
10. Shirai 2002, 128.
11. Gopher 1994, 187; Simmons 2011, 88.
12. Gopher 1994, 185–86, 203–5.
13. Shirai 2002, 125.
14. Mellaart 1974, 43.
15. Todd 1976, 127.
16. Mellaart 1974, 37.
17. Shirai 2010, 326.
18. Personal observation of illustrations from Mook 1880 and Browne 1878a.

CHAPTER 11. A GRAND DESIGN AT GIZA

1. Agnew 1838, 5. Emphasis in the original.
2. For a good overview of the Giza pyramids and their builders, see Edwards 1993.
3. Agnew 1838; Ballard 1882; Legon 1979.
4. Goyon 1970, 91–92; Lehner 1985, 143, and Lehner 1997, 107; Quirke 2001.
5. Lehner 1985, 140–42; Dash 2011.
6. Collins 2009.
7. Hale and Collins 2016.
8. Flinders Petrie 1883.
9. See, for instance, Legon 1979.
10. Orofino and Bernardini 2016.
11. Goodman 2007; Goodman and Lehner 2007.

12. The GPMP grid map featured in this paper is available at www.andrewcollins.com /page/articles/GPMP.htm (accessed January 24, 2018). Its grid coordinates match the most recent map generated by AERA's GIS specialist Rebekah Miracle. See Lehner 2014, 68. For a full report on the history and development of the GPMP map, see Miracle 2011. For more information on how all calculations were made, see Collins and Hale 2016.

13. Aigner 1983.

14. Personal communication with Giza resident Hussein el-Mor in 2005.

15. See Lehner 2011.

16. Aigner 1983; Hawass and Lehner 1994.

17. Love 2006, 211.

18. Mortensen 1985; Sanussi and Jones 1997.

19. Mortensen 1985; Sanussi and Jones 1997.

20. Schoch 1992; Reader 1998.

21. See Collins 2009.

22. See Edwards 1986, 27–28; Pasquali 2007, 7–8; Pasquali 2008, 75–78.

CHAPTER 12. ORION VERSUS CYGNUS

1. Bauval 1989.

2. Bauval and Gilbert 1994.

3. Dash 2013, 8.

4. Collins 2006b, chs. 12–14.

5. See Collins 2006b and Collins 2007.

6. Collins 2009.

7. Collins 2009.

8. Orofino and Bernardini 2016

9. Lorenzis and Orofino 2015.

10. Orofino and Bernadini 2016.

11. Hale and Collins 2016.

12. Orofino and Bernadini 2016.

13. For earlier use of this term see Collins 2009; Collins 2011a, Collins 2011b.

14. Lehner 2013.

15. Hawass and Senussi 2008, 127.

16. Hawass and Senussi 2008, 128.

17. Lutley and Bunbury 2008.

18. Lutley & Bunbury 2008.

19. Hawass 1997.

20. Lehner 2014.

21. Lehner 2014.

22. For more on the subject of the Zaghloul Street Mound, see Collins 2011b.

CHAPTER 13. OSIRIS ARISEN

1. Bolshakov 1992.

2. Hirayama 2011.

3. For instance, Faulkner 1969 and Allen 2005.

4. Champollion 1836, 95.

5. See, for example, Bauval and Gilbert 1994; Bauval and Hancock 1996, Bauval 2006.

6. Pyramid Text (PT) 273, §408c. All Pyramid Text utterances from Mercer, 1952, unless otherwise stated.

7. PT 691, §2126a4, §2126b + 1.

8. PT 466, §883c.

9. PT 569, §1436c–§1436c.

10. PT 466, §882c.

11. PT 582, §1561a.

12. PT 437, §802c.

13. PT 610, §1717a.

14. For instance, Faulkner 1969 and Allen 2005.

15. PT 699, §2180c.

16. PT 219, §186a.

17. PT 691A, §2126b + 1.

18. PT 691A, §2126a-4.

19. PT 691A, §2126a-5.

20. Pogo 1932; Lull and Belmonte 2009, ch. 6.

CHAPTER 14. STARRY DESTINY

1. Allen 1994, 27.

2. PT 214, §138a; 372, §656c; 432, §782e, 468, §900d; 474, §940a; 481, §1000d.

3. Faulkner 1966, 153, 155–56.

4. Belmonte 2001, S18 note 18.

5. Faulkner 1969.

6. Faulkner 1966, 160. Emphasis added.

7. Faulkner 1966, 161.

8. Translation by Jan Summers Duffy for the author based on a reproduction of the pyramidion's inscriptions as seen in Maspero 1902, 207.

9. Allen 2005.

10. Allen 1994, 5.

11. Allen 2005, 11.

12. Allen 2005, 12.

13. Allen 2005, 8, 10, 11.

14. Allen 2005, 11.

15. Allen 2005, 11.

16. Allen 2005, 12.

17. Allen 2005, 12. Emphasis added.

18. Allen 2005, 12.

19. Allen 2005, 12. Emphasis added.

20. For a good exegesis of the King's Chamber's parallel role to that of the substructures of later pyramids containing Pyramid Texts, see "The Concept of the Pyramid," Pyramid of Man, www.pyramidofman.com/Concept.htm (accessed October 16, 2017).

21. Allen 2005, 12.

22. See, for instance, Conman 2013, 129, 174, 185.

23. PT 302, §2042c; 519, §1207a; 655, §1945b; 681, §2034c. The kite: PT 267, §366a–§366b; 302, §461c, §2042d.

24. PT 302, §463c.

25. PT 267, §§302, 470, 682.

26. PT 267, §302; 470, §682.

27. Allen 2005, 12. Emphasis in the original.

28. Eliade 1964, 37 n. 6, 272–73, 480–81.

29. Eliade 1964, 37 n. 6.

30. Eliade 1964, 278–89.

31. Eliade 1964, 278–89.

32. PT 519 (Faulkner translation).

33. Belmonte 2001, S6.

34. Belmonte 2001, S11.

35. Badaway 1964; Trimble 1964; Bauval and Gilbert 1994.

36. Belmonte 2001, S11.

37. See, for instance, Bauval and Hancock 1996.

38. Collins 2015c.

CHAPTER 15. WOMB OF THE STARS

1. PT 364, §616d–f (Allen translation).

2. Allen 1994, 25; Allen 2005, s.v. "Nut," 438.

3. PT 468, §902d; 483, §1016b; 513, §1169a.

4. PT 474, §939c–940a, §941a–941b.

5. PT 245, §250a, §251a.

6. Allen 1988.

7. PT517, §1188f.

8. PT 517, §1188e.

9. Allen 1989, 17.

10. Blasweiler 2014, 7.

11. Blasweiler 2014, 10.

12. Castel 2002, 27, cf. Westendorf 1977, s.v. "Himmelsvorstellungen," 1215–18; Westendorf 1982, s.v. "Panther," 664–65.

13. Lesko 1999, 25; Maravelia 2003a; Kozloff 1992 and 2007; Magli 2013, 48; Greco 2014, 183.

14. Wells 1992. See Kozloff 1992, 331–34.

15. Wells 1992.

16. Lankford 2007b, 181, 183, 189, 205.

17. Lankford 2007b, 193.

18. Lankford 2007b, 186, 208.

19. Lankford 2007b, 178.

20. See, for instance, Little 2016a, 2016b, and 2016c.

21. See, for example, Conman 2013, 203–7.

22. Diodorus 1.27.5.

23. Budge 1969, 107 n. 1.

24. Wilkinson 1841, 1:262; Poole 1851, 40–41.

25. "Papyrus of Ani," ch. 54, in Budge 1895, pl. 15.

26. Budge 1969, 107–8.

27. Budge 1969, 95–96.

28. Budge 1913a, 3:283.

29. Conman 2002.

30. Daressy 1912.

31. Róheim 1954, 63.

32. Zsuzsa 2009.

33. Poole 1851, 40–41.

34. Poole 1851, 42.

35. Massey 1883, 341.

36. Poole 1851, 42.

37. Poole 1851, 51.

38. Poole 1851, 51.

39. Allen 1899, s.v. "Cygnus, the Swan," 192–98.

40. Allen 1899, s.v. "Lyra, the Lyre or Harp," 280–88.

41. Richardson and Meniński 1829, s.v. *rukh,* 727.

42. Richardson and Meniński 1829, s.v. *rakham,* 728.

43. Hebrew and Aramaic Dictionary (Lexicon-Concordance) #H7350–H7399, http://lexiconcordance.com/hebrew/735.html (accessed October 22, 2017).

44. "Doing It in Hebrew," www.doitinhebrew.com/Translate/Default.aspx?kb=IL%20 Hebrew%20Phonetic&l1=iw&l2=en&txt=רחם&s= 1 (accessed October 22, 2017).

45. "Doing it in Hebrew," www.doitinhebrew.com/Translate/Default.aspx?kb=IL%20 Hebrew%20Phonetic&l1=iw&l2=en&txt=רחם&s= 1 (accessed October 22, 2017).

46. Allen 2005, 12.

47. Wells 1993, 315.

48. Suspected familial links after Dodson and Hilton 2004.

CHAPTER 16.
GIZA REVELATION

1. Orofino and Bernardini 2016.

2. Ward 2016.

3. Carville 2014, 4.

4. Balmer and Swisher 2012, 26.

5. Isler 2001, 271.

6. Isler 2001, 271.

CHAPTER 17.
THE HIDDEN KEY

1. Email communication from Rodney Hale to the author, March 20, 2016.

2. Reader 1998.

3. Reader 1998.

4. Hawass 1997, 245–48.

5. Lutley and Bunbury 2008.

6. Moussa, Dolphin, and Mokhtar 1977, section D4, fig. 36.

7. Moussa, Dolphin, and Mokhtar 1977, section D4, fig. 36.

8. Moussa, Dolphin, and Mokhtar 1977, section D4, fig. 36.

9. Collins 2009, chs. 16–19.

10. Klein 2012, 71. See also Clagett 1995, 2:465.

11. Barclay 1858, 247.

12. Cooper 1994, 358.

13. See Hutchinson 1893, 154; Smedley, Rose, and Rose 1845, 316.

14. Moyer 2006.

CHAPTER 18. COSMIC SYMMETRY

1. Legon 2007.
2. The earliest mention I can find of the Great Pyramid's measurements in terms of Hebrew reeds of 10.5 feet and long cubits of 21 inches is Gaunt 1993, 41–42, 75. I also acknowledge the extensive work done on this subject by Martin Doutré on his website Ancient Celtic New Zealand at www.celticnz.co.nz (accessed October 22, 2017). See, for instance, Doutré 2001.
3. Callataÿ 1996, 15, 256, based on Plato, *Timaeus,* 39b.
4. Graves 1972, 173.
5. After Diodorus 1.1.1. He gives the gods born on the five intercalary days as "Osiris, Isis, Typhon [i.e., Set], Apollo [Horus] and Venus [Nephtys]." See also Plutarch, "Isis and Osiris," ch. 13.
6. Plutarch, "Isis and Osiris," ch. 13.
7. Graves 1972, 173.
8. Harrell 2003, 369 and the references therein.
9. Harrell 2003, 368.
10. Harrell 2003, 378.

CHAPTER 19. HARMONIC CONVERGENCE

1. Berosus, in Hodges 1876, 60. See also Callataÿ 1996, 257.
2. After Volney 1819, 1:156.
3. Cajori 1991, 8.
4. For a good review of this subject, see Sokolowski, "Decoding Giza Pyramids: Part 1," World-Mysteries, Dec. 15, 2012, http://blog.world-mysteries.com/science/decoding-giza-pyramids-part-1/ (accessed November 28, 2017.)
5. See Prusinkiewicz and Lindenmayer 2012, 99–118, for a full review of the divergence angle of 137.5 degrees in the process of phyllotaxis.
6. See Adler 1998, who reviews the history of phyllotaxis and traces its roots back to Theophrastus.
7. Kappraff 2004, 335.
8. Kappraff 2004, 335, and also Adler 1998.

CHAPTER 20. MUSIC OF THE SPHERES

1. Collins 2009, ch. 10.
2. For Pythagoras's take on the music of the spheres, see, for instance, Pliny, *Natural*

History, 2:20, and for Plato's introduction to the subject see *Republic,* book 10, 614–21.

3. For a full introduction to this topic, see James 1993, 20–40.

4. Nicomachus, ch. 6. See Levin 1994, 83.

5. Nicomachus, ch. 6. See Levin 1994, 83–84.

6. Demetrius, 71:23–26.

7. Kamil 1988, 55.

CHAPTER 21. SECRETS OF THE GODS

1. Hornung 2001, 22.

2. Diogenes Laertius, 8.3.

3. Bunson 2014, s.v. "Pythagoras," 323.

4. Antonius Diogenes, quoted in Porphyry, *Vita Pythagorae,* ch. 11 (surviving fragment of original text).

5. Diogenes Laertius, 8.3.

6. Ogden 2002, 10.

7. Ogden 2002, 10.

8. Jenkyns 2013, 249.

9. Jenkyns 2013, 249.

10. Larson 2007, 70–71.

11. Larson 2007, 70–71.

12. Stroumsa 1996, 175.

13. Iamblichus, as quoted in O'Connor and Robertson 1999, npn.

14. Kilmer 1998, 13–15. See also Kilmer 1971.

15. Iamblichus, ch. 6; Diogenes Laertius, 8.13.

16. Iamblichus, ch. 28.

17. Plato, *Timaeus,* 34a–d. See Archer-Hind 1888, 103–4.

18. Plato, *Timaeus,* 35a–36b. See Archer-Hind 1888, 107, note to line 10; 108–18, note to lines 3, 8, 10. For a full exegesis of this subject see Padovan 2002, 105–7, and Brisson and Meyerstein 1995, 31–35.

19. Iamblichus, ch. 28.

20. Iamblichus, ch. 28.

21. Iamblichus, ch. 28.

22. Syrianus, *On Aristotle Metaphysics,* book 13, as quoted in Taylor 1818, 78, n. 1.

23. Iamblichus, ch. 28.

24. Taylor 1818, 33, n. 1.

25. Simplicius, *On Aristotle. On the Heavens,* bk. 2, as quoted in Taylor 1818, 33, n. 1.

26. See Collins 2016, chs. 1–2.

27. Plato, *Timaeus,* 39b.

28. Plato, *Timaeus,* 39b.

29. See Cornford 2014, 115, n. 4.

30. See, for instance, Callataÿ 1996, 15, 256.

CHAPTER 22. CELESTIAL SWAN SONG

1. See Reale and Catan 1990, 294.

2. Diodorus 4.25.3. See also Hornung 2001, 22, and Guthrie 1993, 198.

3. Plato, *Republic,* 620a: "'He saw the soul that had been Orpheus,' he said, select-ing the life of a swan, because from hatred of the tribe of women, owing to his death at their hands, it was unwilling to be conceived and born of a woman." See Greek Texts and Translations, February 2011, http://perseus.uchicago.edu/perseus -cgi/citequery3.pl?dbname=GreekTexts&query=Pl.%20Resp.%20619e&getid=1 (accessed November 28, 2017). Also Jowett 1888, 336, for his translation of the text, and Jodrell 1781, 44, on this same topic.

4. Hyginus 1960, 211.7, Lyre.

5. Allen 1899, s.v. "Cygnus, the Swan," 192–98.

6. King 1722, 86.

7. Ross 1648, 25.

8. Eschenbach, Estienne, Gesner, Hamberger, and Theophrastus 1764, 136, n. 1000 and 226, n. 33, 17. The proposal after Gesner is cited also in Mead 1965, 162.

9. See "History of the Harp," www.harp.com/history-of-the-harp.htm (accessed November 28, 2017).

10. Callimachus 4:375–79. In Nisetich 2001, 47.

11. Callimachus 4:375–82.

12. Harris 1925, 377.

13. Macrobius, 1:19, as quoted in Newton, and recorded in James 1993, 164.

14. Leland, *The Itinerary.* See Hearne 1769, vii.

15. Plato, *Phaedo* 84e.

16. For a full account of this anecdote, and its variations, see Riginos 1976, 21–24.

CHAPTER 23. SONIC TEMPLES

1. Collins 2014b, 45.

2. Collins 2014b, 62.

3. Email communication between the author and Rodney Hale dated April 2, 2016.

4. Srinivasan 1996, 26.

5. McBride 2014, 357–58.

CHAPTER 24. SHAPING SOUND

1. Marshall 2015, 43–56.
2. Marshall 2015, 45.
3. Marshall 2015, 45.
4. Piggott 1962, 15.
5. Marshall 2015, 46.
6. North 1996/2007, 80.
7. Marshall 2015, 47.
8. Marshall 2015, 47.
9. Marshall 2015, 52.
10. For Jerf al-Ahmar, see Stordeur et al. 1996, 1–2; for Tell es-Sultan/Jericho, see Gopher 1994, 194.
11. Schmidt 1996, 132–33.

CHAPTER 26. DIVISION OF THE TWO LANDS

1. Saad 1969, 5. See also Salleh 2004.
2. Jeffreys 2005, s.v. "Helwan." In Bard 2005, 367–68.
3. "The Memphite Theology," British Museum no. 498 (Shabaka Stone), ll. 7–9. See Lichtheim 1973, 52.
4. Khaled 2012. See Lichtheim 1980, 56; Brugsch 2015, 1:74; Lichtheim 1973, 57, n.6.
5. See s.v. "אהין AhYN," StudyLight, www.studylight.org/lexicons/hebrew/3284.html (accessed November 28, 2017). See Levine 2000, 118; Steingass 1963, s.v *ain,* 876. Cf. Hamari Web, http://hamariweb.com/names/muslim/boy/ayaan-meaning_7709 (accessed November 28, 2017).
6. Lichtheim 1973, 52.
7. Lichtheim 1973, 53.
8. Lichtheim 1973, 53. The restoration of the lacunae derives from the recurrence of this passage later in the text. See Lichtheim 1973, 55 and 56, n. 7.
9. Collins 2009, ch. 5–7.

CHAPTER 27. WHO STOLE IWNW?

1. Saad 1969, 5.
2. Saad 1969, 9.
3. Saad 1969, 10.
4. Debono and Mortensen 1990.
5. Saad 1969, 16.

6. For the etymology of Helwan's place-name, see Peterson 1893, 19. For the meaning of the root "Helwa," see Johnson 1852, s.v. "halw," 490.

7. Budge 1974, 99.

8. "Papyrus of Ani," ch. 54, in Budge 1895, pl. 15.

9. Budge 1969, 107–8.

10. Budge 1969, 95–96.

11. Jeffreys 2005, s.v. "Helwan." In Bard 2005, 367–68.

12. Conman 2002.

13. PT 214, §139a–139b.

14. PT 600, §1652a–1652b.

15. Burton 1879, 307n.

16. Burton 1879, 307n.

CHAPTER 28. PLACE OF THE BENNU

1. Wilkinson 1835.

2. Wilkinson 1837.

3. For a full treatment on Wilkinson's relationship with Thomas Young and Jean-François Champollion, and his learning of the Egyptian hieroglyphic system, see Thompson 2010, 71–78.

4. Wilkinson 1843, 2:9–11.

5. Wilkinson 1843, 2:9–11.

6. Wilkinson 1843, 10.

7. Wilkinson 1843, 10–11.

8. Wilkinson 1841, s.v. "Nehimeou? Nohemao" (pl. 66, part 3), V, 80–81.

9. Müller, s.v. "Nehem(t)-'auit," in Gray and Moore 1918, 12:141.

10. Wilkinson 1843, 2:2, 11.

11. Wilkinson 1843, 2:2, 11.

12. Wilkinson 1841, 2:262.

13. Wilkinson 1841, 2:262.

14. Wilkinson 1841, 2:263.

15. Wilkinson 1841, 2:225. In Wilkirson 1841, 1:342, he further states, "Osiris takes the character of the God Benno, with the head of a crane, peculiarised by a tuft of two long feathers."

CHAPTER 29. THE MOUNTAIN OF ANU

1. Necho II, stela 5. See Daressy 1911, 259–61.

2. Strabo 17:34. See Strabo 1932, 8:96–97.

3. "Helwan and Its Eastern Surroundings Surveyed by G. Schweinfurth 1895–1896." In May, Schweinfurth, and Sayce 1901 (contained in folder at the front of the book).

4. Jeffreys 2004, 838.

5. Jeffreys 2004, 838.

6. Allen 2014, 472, regarding hieroglyph D8.

7. Tallet and Marouard 2014, 10.

8. Strong 1894, s.v. "On," 370–71.

9. Budge 1913b, 1:25.

10. Budge 1913b, 25, n. 2.

11. See Budge 1913b, 24–25, for various quotes from the Pyramid Texts in the pyramids of Unas and Pepi I featuring Anu as the genesis point of the Ennead.

12. Wainwright 1932, 373–83.

13. Allen 1899, s.v. "Cygnus, the Swan," 192–98. See Berio 2014, 15; Lull and Belmonte 2009, ch. 6; Maravelia 2003b, 55–74; and Locher 1985, 152–53. The latter argues that the sky falcon was formed from stars making up the constellation of Ursa Minor.

14. Collins 2006a, ch. 12.

15. See Bauval 2007, and for responses to criticisms, see Collins 2006a and Collins 2008.

16. See, for instance, Zába 1953; Lauer 1960, 99–124 and pl. 13; and Stecchini 2001.

17. See, for example, Franci 2014, 48.

18. Berio 2014, 15.

19. PT 245, §250a–251a.

20. See, for instance, Sellers 1992, 94.

21. Debono and Mortensen 1990, 14, fig. 1.

22. May, Schweinfurth, and Sayce 1901, 6.

23. Debono and Mortensen 1990, 73, 77.

24. Debono 1902, 109.

CHAPTER 30. HOMELAND OF THE PRIMEVAL ONES: PART I

1. For a full review of the Shebtiw tradition, see Jelinkova 1962.

2. Reymond 1969, 107–8, 119.

3. Reymond 1969, 88–89, 101.

4. Reymond 1969, 118, 123, 125.

5. Reymond 1969, 68–70, 80, 84, 88.

6. Reymond 1969, 14–15, 23.

7. Reymond 1969, 94, 103.

8. Reymond 1969, 103.

9. Reymond 1969, 101–2.

10. Reymond 1969, 15, 94, 116.

11. Reymond 1969, 16, 305.

12. Reymond 1969, 110.

13. Reymond 1969, 18.

14. Reymond 1969, 169.

15. Reymond 1969, 169.

16. Reymond 1969, 169.

17. Reymond 1969, 111–12, 115–16.

18. Reymond 1969, 118.

19. Reymond 1969, 103.

20. Reymond 1969, 114.

21. Reymond 1969, 16, 133.

22. Reymond 1969, 115, 284.

23. Reymond 1969, 116, 120.

24. Reymond 1969, 28.

25. Reymond 1969, 30, 94, 96, 96n. 3, 102.

26. Reymond 1969, 142.

27. Wendorf and Malville 2001; Malville, Schild, Wendorf, and Brenmer 2007.

28. Hayes 1965, 121.

29. See, for instance, Bar-Yosef 1989, 60; and Flohr et al. 2015.

30. Reymond 1969, 27.

31. Reymond 1969, 110.

32. Reymond 1969, 14, 16, 91–92.

33. Reymond 1969, 110.

34. Reymond 1969, 179.

35. Reymond 1969, 16, 135–36, 165.

36. Reymond 1969, 30.

37. Reymond 1969, 121.

38. Reymond 1969, 15, 16.

39. Reymond 1969, 113.

40. Reymond 1969, 19, 148.

41. Reymond 1969, 113.

42. Reymond 1969, 113.

43. Reymond 1969, 113.

44. Reymond 1969, 114.

45. Reymond 1969, 80, 324.

46. Reymond 1969, 107–8.

47. Reymond 1969, 108, 110, 114.

48. Hawass 2007, 379–97.

49. See, for instance, Collins 2009, ch. 8.

50. See Collins 2014b.

51. See Clube and Napier 1982 for a full discussion of representations of comets as snakes and serpents in ancient art.

52. Personal communication between the author and Han Kloosterman in 2015.

53. Reymond 1969, 137.

54. Reymond 1969, 51, 77, 89, 117.

55. Reymond 1969, 118.

56. Reymond 1969, 268–69, 298, 312, 317.

57. Reymond 1969, 139.

CHAPTER 31. HOMELAND OF THE PRIMEVAL ONES: PART II

1. Reymond 1969, 18, 34, 138–39, 145.

2. Reymond 1969, 138–39.

3. Reymond 1969, 170.

4. Reymond 1969, 19.

5. Reymond 1969, 20.

6. Reymond 1969, 20, 142.

7. Reymond 1969, 20.

8. Reymond 1969, 23.

9. Reymond 1969, 194–95.

10. Reymond 1969, 35.

11. Reymond 1969, 20.

12. Reymond 1969, 95.

13. Reymond 1969, 57, 70–73, 83–84.

14. Reymond 1969, 262.

15. Reymond 1969, 227.

16. Reymond 1969, 262.

17. Reymond 1969, 262. Emphasis in the original.

18. Reymond 1969, 262.

19. Reymond 1969, 16, 25.

20. Reymond 1969, 26, 158.

21. Reymond 1969, 158.

22. Reymond 1969, 156.

23. Reymond 1969, 155.

24. Reymond 1969, 24–25.
25. Reymond 1969, 156.
26. Reymond 1969, 156.
27. Reymond 1969, 156.
28. Reymond 1969, 156.
29. For a full review of this subject, see Nigg 2016, 16.
30. Budge 1969, 95–96.
31. Reymond 1969, 227, 263.
32. Reymond 1969, 262. Emphasis in the original.
33. Reymond 1969, 263.
34. Reymond 1969, 264.
35. Reymond 1969, 264.
36. Reymond 1969, 264.
37. Reymond 1969, 264.
38. Rice 2004, 135–36. Emphasis added.
39. Rice 2004, 135–36. Emphasis added.
40. Schmidt 1996.
41. Reymond 1969, 317.
42. Reymond 1969, 316–17.
43. Reymond 1969, 317.
44. Reymond 1969, 317.

CHAPTER 32. HOMELAND OF THE PRIMEVAL ONES: PART III

1. Reymond 1969, 28, 329.
2. Reymond 1969, 220.
3. Reymond 1969, 316.
4. Reymond 1969, 45, 294–95.
5. Reymond 1969, 204.
6. Reymond 1969, 240, 335.
7. Reymond 1969, 240.
8. Reymond 1969, 223.

CHAPTER 33. BIRD ON A POLE

1. A radiocarbon date of 18,600 ± 190 years BP was obtained in 1998 from a fragment of a reindeer-antler baton found at the foot of the panel of the Shaft Scene. See Lawson 2012, 351.

2. Rappenglück 1999, 122.

3. Reymond 1969, 137.

4. Armstrong 1959, 14, 49.

5. Personal communication with Brian Wilkes in 2011.

6. Personal communication with Brian Wilkes in 2011.

7. Rogers 1995, 57.

8. Webb Hodge 1912, s.v. "John Ross," 396–97.

9. Lankford 2007b, 208, 211.

10. See, for instance, the entry for "Umay" on Türk Mitolojisi, http://erbuke.tumblr .com (accessed November 28, 2017).

11. Wilkinson 2009, 163.

12. Wilkinson 2009, 163.

13. In the case of the goose of Geb being Cygnus, see Conman 2002. For the Hamsa, the swan-goose, as Cygnus, see Collins 2006, 190, after P. K. Kunte of India's Space Physics Group and personal communications with him on the astronomical identity of the hamsa.

14. Shodoev 2012, 70.

15. Shodoev 2012, 78.

16. Shodoev 2012, 78.

17. Shodoev 2012, 76.

18. Shodoev 2012, 70.

19. Shodoev 2012, 52, 56.

20. Shodoev 2012, 87.

21. See, for instance, Stephany, 2008–09, Myths, Mysteries and Wonders, www.timothy stephany.com/constellations.html (accessed October 22, 2017).

22. Faulkes 1987, 18–19.

23. Stephany, 2008–09.

CHAPTER 34. SIBERIAN ROOTS

1. Shodoev 2012, 70.

2. Shodoev 2012, 61–64, 67.

3. Shodoev 2012, 64–65, 67.

4. Shodoev 2012, 63.

5. Shodoev 2012, 67.

6. Graves 1972, 173.

7. Harrell 2003, 369.

8. Harrell 2003, 368, 377–78.

9. Harrell 2003, 378.

10. Harrell 2003, 369.

11. Harrell 2003, 368.

12. Harrell 2003, 368.

13. Harrell 2003, 368.

14. Harrell 2003, 368.

15. Harrell 2003, 369.

16. See, for instance, Gypsy Goddess, "Calling of the White Tigress," July 1, 2008, http://gypsy-goddess.blogspot.co.uk/2008/07/calling-of-white-tigress.html (accessed January 25, 2018).

17. Werner 1958, 137.

18. Werner 1958, 137.

19. Werner 1958, 137–38.

20. Werner 1958, 136–37.

21. Dashu 2009.

22. For Hsi Wang Mu and Ursa Major, see Dashu 2009.

23. Harrell 1995, npn.

24. Harrell 1995, npn.

25. Harrell 1995, 370, 373.

26. "Heavenly Lake (Tianchi)," CITIC Trust Tour, www.toursxinjiang.com/attraction /heavenly-lake.html

27. Barber 1999, 24.

28. Barber 1999, 24, pl. 1.

29. Barber 1999, 47. See also Mair 1995, 30, for legendary accounts of similar-looking people entering China in mythical times.

30. Barber 1999, 104–5.

31. Hadingham 1994.

32. Mallory and Mair 2000, 236–37.

33. "Tarim Mummies in Xinjiang (West China)," Facts and Details, http:// factsanddetails.com/china/cat5/sub89/item166.html (accessed October 22, 2017).

34. Moose 2014.

35. Harrell 2003, 369.

36. For Akkadian as Uralic-Altaic, see Lenormant 1877, 265, and for Sumerian as Uralic, see Parpola 2010, 181–210, and Parpola 2012, 269–322.

37. Darmark 2012, 269–71.

38. Brunet 2012, 322–23.

39. For links between post-Swiderian cultures and Late Paleolithic societies of Siberia and the Urals, see Sørensen 2012, 255.

40. Sørensen 2012, 255–56.

CHAPTER 35. THE LAND OF DAWN

1. It is the topic also of his book, *The Ancient Wisdom,* Ashe 1977.
2. Ashe 1992, ch. 7.
3. Ashe 1992, ch. 7.
4. Ashe 1992, ch. 7.
5. Ashe 1992, ch. 16.
6. Ashe 1992, ch. 18.
7. Ashe 1992, 26–27.
8. Ashe 1992, 15–17.
9. Ashe 1992, 15–17.
10. For a full description of the Mal'ta plate, see Abramova, Page, and Chard 1967, 60, 79, pls. 1, no. 2; 1.1, no. 2.
11. For a full description of the Mal'ta plate, see Abramova, Page, and Chard 1967, 60, 79, pls. 1, no. 2, 1.1, no. 2, 60.
12. For a full description of the Mal'ta plate see Abramova, Page, and Chard 1967, 60, 79, pls. 1, no. 2, 1.1, no. 2, 56, 79.
13. Collins 2006a, 245–46.
14. Ashe 1992, chs. 13–14.
15. Ashe 1992, 172.
16. Ashe 1992, 216.
17. For a full account of Aristeas's encounter with the Issedones, see Phillips 1955, 161–71.
18. Ashe 1992, 174; Bolton 1962, 104–11; Ruck 1986, 226–27.
19. Ruck 1986, 227.
20. For Hecataeus of Abdera, cf. Aelian 11.1. Emphasis added.
21. Ashe 1992, 173.
22. Hamayon 1990, 310–11.
23. Jusha, n.d.
24. Chadwick and Zhirmunsky 2010, 299.
25. Go.Akim 2014.

CHAPTER 36. COUNTING TIME

1. Abramova, Page, and Chard 1967, 52–56, pls. 44–48, pl. 57, nos. 1–5.
2. Abramova, Page, and Chard 1967, 57–58, pl. 49, nos. 6–10, pl. 52, nos. 1–8, pl. 53, nos 1–3.
3. Abramova, Page, and Chard 1967, 63, pl. 57, no. 6.
4. Abramova, Page, and Chard 1967, 78.
5. Abramova, Page, and Chard 1967, 78.

6. Abramova, Page, and Chard 1967, 78.

7. Derevianko, Shimkin, and Powers 1998, 127, 135. See also Abramova, Page, and Chard 1967, 58 (Bird Figurines no. 11–15) for more on swan pendants.

8. Derevianko, Shimkin, and Powers 1998, 136.

9. Abramova, Page, and Chard 1967, 57, 58 (Bird Figurine no. 9).

10. Van Deusen 2004, 114.

11. Hatto 1961, 334–35, 351.

12. The findings of Vitaliy Larcihev with respect to the Mal'ta plate are spread across several publications. See, for instance, Larichev 1986 and Larichev 1989. A good précis in English of his work, written by Peter Zolin II, is "The Real Story of Russian Baikal Malta" (2010), which can be found at www.proza.ru/2010/12/22/1475 (accessed November 28, 2018).

13. Larichev 1989, 202.

14. Larichev 1989, 205–6.

15. See Larichev 1989, 210, and Zolin 2010.

16. Tacitus, *Annals,* 6.28. See also Hincks 1838, 25–26, after Censorinus.

17. Herodotus, *History,* 2.73; Tacitus, *Annals,* 6:28.

18. Larichev 1989, 212–13.

19. Larichev 1989, 220–21.

20. Chambers 1877, book 2, ch. 1, 174, note c.

21. Larichev 1989, 219.

22. Diodorus 2.31.7–9. A figure of 473,000 years is stated also by Epigenus, a Babylonian astrologer. See Barrett 1896, 263 fn.

23. Cicero 1.36.19.

24. Hales 1830, I, 41.

CHAPTER 37. REVOLUTION 432

1. Shodoev 2012, 67.

2. Shodoev 2012, 67.

3. Shodoev 2012, 61.

4. Shodoev 2012, 61.

5. Shodoev 2012, 61.

6. For a full exegesis on this subject, see Rothwangl 2009. He links a cycle of 216 years with the 19-year Meton cycle of the moon.

7. Plato, *Timaeus,* 39b.

8. Plato, *Republic* 546b–c.

9. See, for instance, Barton 1908, 212.

10. Shodoev 2012, 62.

11. Shodoev 2012, 62.

12. Shodoev 2012, 67.

13. Based on the yuga values outlined in Śrīmad-Bhāgavatam (Bhāgavata Purāna), verse SB 3.11.19. Other systems of yugas do exist within ancient Indian literature.

14. Purucker 1936, question 294.

15. Callataÿ 1996, 255.

16. Callataÿ 1996, 257.

CHAPTER 38. TIME TURNED TO STONE

1. For more on this subject, see Pattern and Spedicato 2002; and Hancock 1996, 9, 277; and also Hancock 2014 for a full exegesis of cosmic number symbolism.

2. Ashe 1992, ch. 18.

3. Ashe 1992, 63.

4. Ashe 1992, 62–63, 215.

5. Ashe 1992, 62–63, 215.

6. Ashe 1992, 217.

7. It is known as the Heart of Asia monument.

8. Van Deusen 2004, 50.

9. Shodoev 2012, 5, 29.

10. Shodoev 2012, 5.

11. Shodoev 2012, 29.

12. Shodoev 2012, 5, 24–25.

13. For a good introduction, see Jayaram 2016.

14. Mannikka 1996, 35–36.

15. Mannikka 1996, 18.

16. Mannikka 1996, 31, fig. 2.5.

17. Jayaram 2016.

CHAPTER 39. THE CYGNUS KEY

1. Rysdyk 2014, 48–49.

2. Cohn and Jingqing 1992, 175.

3. Mackenzie 1934, 4–5. See also McHardy 2003, especially ch. 6, for a full study of the origins and extent of the Nine Maidens legend.

4. Mackenzie 1934, 4–5.

5. For the Buryat story featuring nine swan maidens, see Wilkinson 2009, 173. For that of the Vaino in Finland featuring nine swan maidens, see Sherman 2015, 18–21.

6. Hatto 1961, 342.

7. Hatto 1961, 342.

8. Hatto 1961, 334–45, 351.

9. Hatto 1961, 335.

10. Hatto 1961, 352.

11. Hatto 1961, 351–52, quoting H. Findeisen.

12. Hatto 1961, 327–28, 340–42.

13. Hatto 1961, 331–33, 338–40.

14. Hatto 1961, 336 and 336, n. 1, quoting Uno Harva.

15. Wilkinson 2009, 173; Go.Akim 2014.

16. Hatto 1961, 336.

17. Brazil 2010, 56.

18. Hatto 1961, 352, quoting H. Findeisen.

19. See, for instance, "Big Dipper in Laoshan," CNTV/Qingdao, www.qingdaonese.com /big-dipper-in-laoshan (accessed October 22, 2017).

20. Rysdyk 2014, 49.

21. Wu and Wu 2014, 231. See also Needham 1962, 94

22. Wu and Wu 2014, 231.

23. De Kay 1898, 189, 198.

24. De Kay 1898, 189.

25. See Cohn and Jingqing 1992, 175.

26. "Ming Dynasty Unit of Measurement," Great Ming Military, Jan. 7, 2017, http:// greatmingmilitary.blogspot.com/p/ming-dynasty-unit-conversion.html (accessed November 28, 2017).

27. Cohn and Jingqing 1992, 175.

28. Harrell 2003, 369.

29. See Vermander 1999, 3, 10.

30. Van Deusen 2004, 35.

31. Hyder 2010.

32. Van Deusen 2004, 128.

33. Personal communication with Kira Van Deusen, March 2017.

34. Hamilton 2007.

35. Ashe 1992, 216.

CHAPTER 40. THE DENISOVAN LEGACY

1. Ashe 1992, 13.

2. The distal phalanx (Denisova 3) and molar (Denisova 4) were both found in Layer 11, and date to circa 50,000–40,000 BP. See Derevianko 2016, 13, and see Greshko 2015 for a background to these discoveries.

3. The older molar (Denisova 8) was found in Layer 12, beneath Layer 11. See Derevianko 2016, 13. The fourth fossil (Denisova 2) is a milk tooth, a molar, of a young girl aged 12-13, found in 2002 within Layer 22.1 of the main gallery. See Sion et al. 2017, 1.

4. Derevianko 2016, 12.

5. For an introduction to this subject, see Reich 2010a and Reich 2010b. For more information on the sequencing of the Denisovan genome see Meyer, 2012.

6. See Huerta-Sánchez 2014.

7. Estes 2013; Prfer 2014. See also Collins 2014c, and the references therein, available to read at www.andrewcollins.com/page/articles/denisovan.htm (accessed November 28, 2017).

8. Vasil'ev, Kuzmin, Orlova, and Dementiev 2002, 510.

9. Gibbons 2011, 1084.

10. "Sex in the Stone Age," National Geographic TV documentary, April 12, 2012, www.youtube.com/watch?v=k9IXPhTWusc (accessed November 28, 2017).

11. "Sex in the Stone Age," National Geographic TV documentary, April 12, 2012, www.youtube.com/watch?v=k9IXPhTWusc (accessed November 28, 2017).

12. Choi 2012.

13. "Denisovans," ER Services: The History of Our Tribe: Homini, https://courses .lumenlearning.com/suny-history-of-our-tribe/chapter/34-the-denisovans (accessed November 28, 2017).

14. Sion et al. 2017, 1.

15. Derevianko 2016, 11–12.

16. Bellwood 2015, 52–53. See also Callaway 2013.

17. Rogers, Bohlender, and Huff, 2017.

18. Rogers, Bohlender, and Huff, 2017.

19. Burger 2007.

20. See Collins 2014c.

21. Liesowska 2017; "Is This Stunning Bracelet Made by Paleolithic Man for His Favourite Woman Really 70,000 Years Old?" 2017.

22. Derevianko, Shunkov, and Volkov 2008.

23. Zubchuk 2016.

24. Hoffecker and Elias 2012, 90.

25. See, for instance, "Genome of Horse Linked to Extinct Human Species Decoded in Russia," UPI, July 31, 2013, www.upi.com/Genome-of-horse-linked-to-extinct -human-species-decoded-in-Russia/99001375311922 (accessed November 28, 2017); and "DNA Deciphered of Horse Used by Extinct Humans," July 31, 2013; https:// sputniknews.com/science/20130731182513837-DNA-Deciphered-of-Horse-Used-by -Extinct-Humans (accessed July 31, 2017).

26. "World's Oldest Needle Found in Siberian Cave that Stitches Together Human

History," *Siberian Times,* August 23, 2016; http://siberiantimes.com/science
/casestudy/news/n0711-worlds-oldest-needle-found-in-siberian-cave-that-stitches
-together-human-history (accessed November 28, 2017).

27. Buvit et al. 2015, 499–502, table 33.2–33.3.

28. Buvit et al. 2015, 502.

29. Gladyshev et al. 2012, 38.

30. Gladyshev et al. 2012, 41, 43–44.

31. Sørensen 2012, 255.

32. Sørensen 2012, 255–56.

33. Collins 2014a, chs. 19 and 20.

34. Guzman 2007, 762–63; Yi, Gao, Li, and Chen 2016.

35. Derevianko and Markin 1998, 93.

36. Hoffecker 2002, 169.

37. Lbova 2012, short book article, 227. (This has the reference to the beads found in both
the Denisova Cave and also at the Tolbor site.) See also Lbova 2012, full article on CD.

38. Zwyns et al. 2014, 61–62.

39. Zubchuk 2016.

40. Lbova 2010, 9, 12; Lbova 2012, CD-1123, CD-1127.

41. Lbova 2010, 11–12.

42. Lbova, Kozhevnikov, and Volkov 2012, CD-1902.

43. Kuzmin 2009, 100, table 1.

44. Lbova, Kozhevnikov, and Volkov 2012, CD-1900.

45. Lbova, Kozhevnikov, and Volkov 2012, CD-1903.

46. Lbova, Kozhevnikov, and Volkov 2012, CD-1902; Lbova 2010, 11–12.

47. Lbova, Kozhevnikov, and Volkov 2012, CD-1902.

48. Lbova 2010, 12.

49. Derevianko 2016, 13.

50. See Gibbons 2016.

51. See Gibbons 2016, 15.

52. Prüfer 2014; Sanders 2013. See also Wong 2010.

53. Gibbons 2016.

54. Gibbons 2016.

55. Callaway 2014.

56. Account from Go.Akim, "Ergune Khun, Realm of Refuge, Did It Tell A Fairy
Tale or Speak of History?" 2014, https://goakim.wordpress.com/author/goakim
(accessed November 28, 2017).

57. Account from Go.Akim, "Ergune Khun, Realm Of Refuge, Did It Tell A Fairy
Tale Or Speak Of History?" 2014, https://goakim.wordpress.com/author/goakim
(accessed November 28, 2017).

58. Gaster 1915, 249–55.

59. See Higham et al. 2012, 664–76.

60. Van Deusen 2004, 61, n. 2, 114.

61. "Face Music—Traditional Instruments—Khakas People," www.face-music.ch /instrum/khakassia/khakas_instrum.html (accessed October 22, 2017).

62. Van Deusen 2004, viii, x, xxiii.

63. Van Deusen 2004, 92.

64. Kazachinova and Van Deusen 2002, 28–29.

65. Kazachinova and Van Deusen 2002, 28. Emphasis in the original.

66. Choi 2012.

67. Ceram 1954, 316.

68. Chatelain 1988, 32, 34–35.

69. Chatelain 1988, 35.

70. Wilson 2011, 382–85.

71. Wilson 2011, 385.

72. Wilson 2011, 385–88.

73. Bogdashina 2016.

74. Pāvils 2010.

75. Winkelman 2002, 91.

CHAPTER 41.
GATEWAY OF THE GODS

1. Chadwick and Zhirmunsky 2010, 294.

2. Prior 2006, 15.

3. Prior 2006, 15, 90.

4. Jusha n.d.

5. Shelley 1945, 125; Deutsch and Yarmolinsky 1952, 17–27.

6. Shodoev 2012, 68.

7. Shodoev 2012, 68.

8. Shodoev 2012, 69.

9. Shodoev 2012, 69.

10. Halemba 2006, ch. 3, npn. See also "The Legend of Sartakpai," Altai Tour, www .altai-tour.ru/about_altai/legendy-altaya/legenda-o-sartakpae (accessed November 28, 2017). This has an account of Sartakpai's deeds, as well as a great picture of the giant riding on a mythical creature!

11. Deutsch and Yarmolinsky 1952, 24.

12. Butanayev and Butanayev 2007, 71–72.

13. Deutsch and Yarmolinsky 1952, 17; "Сартакпай ('Sartakpay')," Сказки ("Skazi"),

www.fairy-tales.su/narodnye/altajskie-skazki/3187-sartakpaj.html (accessed November 28, 2017).

14. "Fresh Discoveries of Ancient Man's Bone in Altai Mountains Cave," *The Siberian Times*, Aug. 14, 2015; http://siberiantimes.com/science/casestudy/news/n0356-fresh-discoveries-of-ancient-mans-bone-in-altai-mountains-cave/ (accessed November 28, 2017).

15. Holmberg 1927, 366; Jusha n.d.

16. See, for instance, David-Neel and Yongden 1933, 14–17, 45–48; Znamenski 2012, 25–27.

17. Van Deusen 1998, 59–60; "Face Music—Traditional Instruments—Khakas People." www.face-music.ch/instrum/khakassia/khakas_instrum.html (accessed October 22, 2017).

18. Agarkov 2016.

19. "Face Music—Traditional Instruments—Khakas People." www.face-music.ch/instrum/khakassia/khakas_instrum.html.

20. Gertcyk and Salnitskaya 2016.

21. Osadchiy, "Ergaki's Ridge of [*sic*],"

22. Osadchiy, "Ergaki's Ridge of [*sic*]."

23. "The Ergaki: Highland Riches," Siberian Corner, http://insiberia.com/en/article/the-ergaki-highland-riches (accessed October 22, 2017).

24. Osadchiy, "Ergaki's Ridge of [*sic*]."

25. Grachev, "Ergaki: Places of Power," To Discover Russia, http://todiscoverrussia.com/ergaki-places-of-power (accessed October 22, 2017).

26. Baklitskaya 2012.

27. "Ergak," White Stone Travel, www.belykamen.com/sights/item/47-ergak.html (accessed October 22, 2017).

28. Osadchiy, "Ergaki's Ridge of [*sic*]."

29. See "Ergaki," Sayan Ring, www.sayanring.com/guide/city/view/21 (accessed October 22, 2017).

30. Deutsch and Yarmolinsky 1952, 24–25; Kazachinova and Van Deusen 2002, 28.

31. Butanayev and Butanayev 2007, 71; Martinov 2013, ch. 3.

32. Archecotech, "Mysterious Sayan Mountains of Russia," Life in Russia, 2014, https://hague6185.wordpress.com/2014/10/18/mysterious-sayan-mountains-of-russia (accessed November 28, 2017).

33. Archecotech, "Mysterious Sayan Mountains of Russia," Life in Russia, 2014, https://hague6185.wordpress.com/2014/10/18/mysterious-sayan-mountains-of-russia (accessed November 28, 2017).

34. Osadchiy, "Ergaki's Ridge of [*sic*]."

35. Osadchiy, "Ergaki's Ridge of [*sic*]."

36. Kazachinova and Van Deusen 2002, 20–25; Butanayev and Butanayev 2007, 31–33.

37. Kazachinova and Van Deusen 2002, 20–21. See also Butanayev and Butanayev 2007, 31–32, who also refer to this subject.

38. Moseley 1879, 335.

39. Vernot 2016.

40. Kazachinova and Van Deusen 2002, 20.

41. Butanayev and Butanayev 2013; Butanayev and Butanayev 2007, 31.

42. Butanayev and Butanayev 2007, 31–33.

43. Kazachinova and Van Deusen 2002, iv, 20.

44. Kazachinova and Van Deusen 2002, iv, 21.

45. Van Deusen, 2004, 50.

46. Osadchiy, "Ergaki's Ridge of [sic]."

47. Osadchiy, "Ergaki's Ridge of [sic]."

48. Osadchiy, "Ergaki's Ridge of [sic]."

49. Gertcyk and Salnitskaya 2016.

50. Gertcyk and Salnitskaya 2016.

51. For more on the Denisovans and Neanderthals, and their impact on human civilization, see the lecture given by the author at the Origins 2014 conference in London titled "Lost World of the Human Hybrids," to be found at https://youtu .be/D9Pazv8baVI (accessed November 28, 2017).

BIBLIOGRAPHY

Key to Abbreviations: nd: no date given; np: no publisher given; npn: no page number given.

Abramova, Z. A., Catherine Page, and Chester S. Chard. 1967. "Paleolithic Art in the USSR." *Arctic Anthropology.* Vol. 4, no.2, 1–179.

Adachi, T. 1997. "Typological Analysis of the Arrowheads of the Neolithic Levant." *Aoyama Historical Review.* Vol. 15: 55–97.

Adler, Irving. 1998. "Generating Phyllotaxis Patterns on a Cylindrical Point Lattice." In Jean and Barabé, 249–79.

Aelian. 1959. *On the Characteristic of Animals.* Vol. 2 (books 6–9). Translated by A. F. Scholfield. Cambridge: Loeb Classical Library.

Agarkov, Anton. 2016. "The Swan People of Altai." *Russia Beyond,* December 9. https://www.rbth.com/arts/travel/2016/12/09/the-swan-people-of-altai_654963 (accessed January 25, 2018).

Agnew, H. C. 1838. *The Quadrature of the Circle in the Configuration of the Great Pyramids of Gizeh.* London: Longman, Orme, Brown, Green, and Longmans.

Aigner, Thomas. 1983. "A Pliocene Cliff-line around the Giza Pyramids Plateau, Egypt." *Palaeogeography, Palaeoclimatology, Palaeoecology.* Vol. 42, 313–22.

Allen, James P. 1988. *Genesis in Egypt: The Philosophy of Ancient Egyptian Creation Accounts: Yale Egyptological Studies.* Vol. 2. San Antonio, Texas: Van Siclen.

———. 1989. "The Cosmology of the Pyramid Texts." In Simpson, 1–28.

———. 1994. "Reading a Pyramid." In Berger, 5–28.

———. 2005. *The Ancient Egyptian Pyramid Texts.* Atlanta, Ga.: Society of Biblical Literature.

———. 2014. *Middle Egyptian: An Introduction to the Language and Culture of Hieroglyphs.* Cambridge: Cambridge University Press.

Allen, Richard Hinckley. 1963 [1899]. *Star Names: Their Lore and Meaning.* New York: Dover.

Altınbilek-Algul, Ç., L. Astruc, D. Binder, and J. Pelegrin. 2012. "Pressure Blade Production with a Lever in the Early and Late Neolithic of the Near East." In Desrosiers, 157–80.

Antonius Diogenes as quoted in Porphyry. 2005. See Berchman.

Archecotech. 2014. "Mysterious Sayan Mountains of Russia." *Life in Russia*, October 18, 2014. https://hague6185.wordpress.com/2014/10/18/mysterious-sayan-mountains -of-russia (accessed January 25, 2018).

Archer-Hind, R. D., ed. and trans. 1888. *The Timaeus of Plato*. London: Macmillan.

Armstrong, Edward A. 1959. *The Folklore of Birds*. Boston: Houghton Mifflin.

Ashe, Geoffrey. 1977. *The Ancient Wisdom*. London: Macmillan.

———. 1992. *Dawn behind the Dawn*. New York: Henry Holt.

Aurenche, O., and S. K. Kozlowski. 2011. "The Spatial Distribution of Arrowheads and Microliths in the Near East (10,200–8000 BC)." In Healey, Campbell, and Maeda, 449–56.

Avetisian, Haik. 1999/2000. "Urartian Ceramics from the Ararat Valley as a Cultural Phenomenon (A Tentative Representation)." *Iran and the Caucasus*. Vol. 3, no. 4, 293–314.

Avner, Uzi. 2002. *Studies in the Material and Spiritual Culture of the Negev and Sinai Populations, during 6th–3rd Millennia B.C.* Doctoral thesis. Submitted to Hebrew University, Jerusalem, December. www.stonewatch.de/media/download/sc%2003.pdf (accessed January 25, 2018).

Badawy, Alexander. 1964. "The Stellar Destiny of Pharaoh and the So-Called Air-Shafts of Cheop's Pyramid." *Mitteilungen des Instituts für Orientforschung*. Vol. 10, 189–206.

Baedeker, K. 1885. *Egypt: Handbook for Travellers: First Part: Lower Egypt, with the Fayûm and the Peninsula of Sinai*. Second revised edition. Leipzig, Germany: Baedeker.

Baklitskaya, Kate. 2012. "Siberian Secrets: The Majestic Yergaki National Park." *The Siberian Times*, November 1. http://siberiantimes.com/home/sent-to-siberia/siberian -secrets-the-majestic-yergaki-national-park/ (accessed January 25, 2018).

Ballard, Robert. 1882. *The Solution of the Pyramid Problem, or Pyramid Discoveries, with a New Theory as to Their Ancient Use*. New York: John Wiley.

Balmer, Jeffrey, and Michael T. Swisher. 2012. *Diagramming the Big Idea: Methods for Architectural Composition*. New York: Routledge.

Barber, Elizabeth Wayland. 1999. *The Mummies of Ürümchi*. London: Pan.

Barclay, James Turner. 1858. *The City of the Great King: Or, Jerusalem as It Was, as It Is, and as It Is to Be*. Philadelphia: J. B. Lippincott.

Barentine, John C. 2015. *The Lost Constellations: A History of Obsolete, Extinct, or Forgotten Star Lore*. New York: Springer.

Bard, Kathryn A. 2005. *Encyclopedia of the Archaeology of Ancient Egypt.* Abingdon, Oxfordshire, U.K.: Routledge.

Barrett, Francis. 1801/1896. *The Book of the Magi: A Complete System of Occult Philosophy, Consisting of Natural, Celestial, Cabalistic, and Ceremonial Magic; Invocations; Conjurations of Spirits, &c., &c.; Biographical Sketch of Seventeen Great Philosophers and Adepts.* Boston: W. W. Harmon.

Barron, T., and W. F. Hume. 1902. *Topography and Geology of the Eastern Desert of Egypt: Central Portion.* Cairo: National Printing Department.

Bárta, Miroslav, ed. 2006. *The Old Kingdom Art and Archaeology: Proceedings of the Conference, Prague,* May 31–June 4, 2004. Prague: Czech Institute of Archaeology.

Barton, George A. 1908. "On the Babylonian Origin of Plato's Nuptial Number." *Journal of the American Oriental Society.* Vol. 29, 210–19.

Bar-Yosef, Ofer. 1989. "The PPNA in the Levant: An Overview." *Paleorient.* Vol. 15, no. 1, 57–63.

———. 1998. "The Natufian Culture in the Levant, Threshold to the Origins of Agriculture." *Evolutionary Anthropology.* Vol. 6, no. 5, 159–177.

Bar-Yosef, Ofer, and François R. Valla, eds. 1991. *The Natufian Culture in the Levant.* Ann Arbor, Mich.: International Monographs in Prehistory.

———. 2013. *Natufian Foragers in the Levant: Terminal Pleistocene Social Changes in Western Asia.* Ann Arbor, Mich.: International Monographs in Prehistory.

Bauval, Robert. 1989. "A Master-Plan for the Three Pyramids of Giza Based on the Configuration of the Three Stars of the Belt of Orion." *Discussions in Egyptology.* Vol. 13, no. 7, 7–18.

———. 2006. *The Egypt Code.* London: Century.

———. 2007. "The Circumpolar Constellations in Ancient Egypt," http://robertbauval .co.uk/articles/articles/cciae.html (accessed January 25, 2018).

Bauval, Robert, and Adrian Gilbert. 1994. *The Orion Mystery: Unlocking the Secrets of the Pyramids.* London: Heinemann.

Bauval, Robert, and Graham Hancock. 1996. *Keeper of Genesis.* London: Heinemann.

Becker, Jörg, et al. 2014. "The 2012 and 2013 Excavation Seasons at Göbekli Tepe." *Göbekli Tepe Newsletter,* 4–7.

Bellwood, Peter. 2015. "Migration and the Origins of *Homo Sapiens.*" In Kaifu et al., 51–58.

Belmonte, Juan Antonio. 2001. "On the Orientations of the Old Kingdom Egyptian Pyramids." *Journal for the History of Astronomy: Archaeoastronomy.* Vol. 32, no. 26, S1–20.

———. 2010. "Finding Our Place in the Cosmos: The Role of Astronomy in Ancient Cultures." *Journal of Cosmology.* Vol. 9, 2052–62.

———. 2015. "Voyages of the Zodiac: An Impenitent Traveler across Lands and Ages." In Pimenta et al., 136–42.

Berchman, Robert M., ed. 2005. *Porphyry against the Christians*. Leiden: F.. J. Brill.

Berger, Catherine, ed.. 1994. *Hommages à Jean Leclant: I. Études Pharaoniques*. Cairo: Institut Francais d'Archéologie Orientale.

Berger, Catherine, and Bernard Mathieu, eds. 1997. *Études sur l'Ancien Empire et la nécropole de Saqqâra—dédiées à Jean-Philippe Lauer*. Vol. 1. *Orientalia Monspeliensia IX*. Montpellier, France: Université Paul Valéry.

Berio, Alessandro. 2014. *The Celestial River: Identifying the Ancient Egyptian Constellations. Sino-Platonic Papers*. Philadelphia: Department of East Asian Languages and Civilizations, University of Pennsylvania.

Berosus. 1876. *Of the Cosmogony and Causes of the Deluge*. In Hodges, 56–63. See also Volney, 1819.

Bickel, Susanne, and Antonio Loprieno, eds. 2003. *Basel Egyptology Prize 1: Junior Research in Egyptian History, Archaeology, and Philology*. Basel, Switzerland: Schwabe.

Bienkowski, Piotr, and Katharina Galor. 2006. *Crossing the Rift: Resources, Settlements Patterns and Interaction in the Wadi Arabah: Levant Supplementary*. Series 3. Oxford: Oxbow.

"Big Dipper in Laoshan." 2000. CNTV/Qingdao. www.qingdaonese.com/big-dipper-in -laoshan (accessed January 25, 2018).

Black, Jeremy, Andrew George, and Nicholas Postgate. *A Concise Dictionary of Akkadian*. Wiesbaden, Germany: Otto Harrassowitz Verlag.

Blasweiler, Joost. 2014. "The Ancestors Cult in Kanesh and the Goddess Išhara: Part II of the Stepgate and the Gate of God: The Royal Clan of Kanesh and the Power of the Cult." *Anatolia in the Bronze Age 8*. Leiden: Leiden University Press.

Bogdashina, Olga. 2016. "Synaesthesia in Autism." *Autism Network,* June 29. http:// network.autism.org.uk/good-practice/evidence-base/synaesthesia-autism (accessed January 25, 2018).

Bolshakov, Andrey O. 1992. "Princess Ḥm.t-Rʿ(w): The First Mention of Osiris?" *Chronique d'Egypte*. Vol. 67, 203–10.

Bolton, James David Pennington. 1962. *Aristeas of Proconnesus*. Oxford: Clarendon.

Borrell, Ferran, Juan José Ibáñez, and Miquel Molist, eds. 2014. *Stone Tools in Transition: From Hunter-Gatherers to Farming Societies in the Near East*. Barcelona: Servei de Publicacions de la Universitat Autónoma de Barcelona.

Brazil, Mark. 2010. *The Whooper Swan*. London: A. and C. Black.

Brisson, Luc F., and Walter Meyerstein. 1995. *Inventing the Universe: Plato's Timaeus, the Big Bang, and the Problem of Scientific Knowledge*. Albany: State University of New York Press.

Brown, Robert. 1899 and 1900. *Researches into the Origin of the Primitive Constellations of the Greeks, Phoenician,s and Babylonians*. 2 vols. London: Williams and Norgate.

Browne, A. J. Jukes. 1878a. "On the Flint Implements Found at Helwan near Cairo." *Cambridge Antiquarian Communications.* Vol. 4, part 2, no. 20, 85–95, plate and map.

———. 1878b. "On Some Flint Implements from Egypt." *The Journal of the Anthropological Institute of Great Britain and Ireland.* Vol. 7, 396–412.

Brugal, J.-P., A. Gardeisen, and A. Zucker. 2011. *Prédateurs dans tous leurs états: Évolution, biodiversité, interactions, mythes, symboles. XXXIe Rencontres Internationales d'Archéologie et d'Histoire d'Antibes.* Antibes, France: Éditions APDCA.

Brugsch, Heinrich Karl. 2015 [1879]. *A History of Egypt under the Pharaohs, Derived Entirely from the Monuments.* Vol. 1. Cambridge: Cambridge University Press.

Brunet, Frédérique. 2012. "The Technique of Pressure Knapping in Central Asia." In Desrosiers, 307–328.

Budge, E. A. Wallis. 1895. *The Book of the Dead: The Papyri of Ani in the British Museum.* London: Longmans.

———. 1913a. *The Book of the Dead: The Papyri of Ani.* 3 vols. New York: G. P. Putnam.

———. 1913b. *The Papyrus of Ani: A Reproduction in Fascimile Edited, with Hieroglyphic Transcript, Translation, and Introduction.* 3 vols. New York: G. P. Putnam.

———. 1969 [1904]. *The Gods of the Egyptians: Studies in Egyptian Mythology.* 2 vols. New York: Dover.

———. 1978 [1920]. *An Egyptian Hieroglyphic Dictionary.* 2 vols. New York: Dover.

———. 1988 [1934]. *From Fetish to God in Ancient Egypt.* New York: Dover.

Buitenhuis, H., A. M. Choyke, M. Mashkour, and A. H. al-Shiyab, eds. 2002. *Archaeozoology of the Near East.* Gröningen, The Netherlands: ARC-Publications.

Bunson, Margaret. 2014. *Encyclopedia of Ancient Egypt.* New York: Infobase.

Burger, Professor Lee. 2007. "Our Story: Human Ancestor Fossils." *The Naked Scientists: Science Interviews,* November 25. www.thenakedscientists.com/HTML/content/interviews/interview/833 (accessed January 25, 2018).

Burton, Richard F. 1878. *The Gold Mines of Midian and the Ruined Midianite Cities.* London: C. Kegan Paul.

———. 1879. "Stones and Bones from Egypt and Midian." *The Journal of the Anthropological Institute of Great Britain and Ireland.* Vol. 8, 290–319.

Butanayev, Victor, and İrina Butanayev. 2007. *Yenisei Kirgizlari Folklor Ve Tarih.* Istanbul: T. C. Kult Ötöken Nesriyat.

———. 2013. *Hongoraja,* at "Белоглазый Народ Ах-Харах ('Beloglazyi Nation Ak-Kharakh')." Askizon. http://askizon.ru/item/311-beloglazyj-narod-akh-kharakh (accessed January 25, 2018).

Buvit, Ian, Karisa Terry, Masami Izuho, and Mikhail V. Konstantinov. 2015. "The Emergence of Modern Behavior in the Trans-Baikal, Russia: Timing and Technology." In Kaifu et al, 490–505.

Cajori, Florian. 1991 [1919]. *A History of Mathematics*. Providence, R.I.: American Mathematical Society.

Callataÿ, Godefroid de. 1996. *Annus Platonicus: A Study of World Cycles in Greek, Latin, and Arabic Sources*. Publications de l'Institut Orientaliste de Louvain 47. Louvain-Paris: Peeters.

Callaway, Ewen. 2013. "Hominin DNA Baffles Experts: Analysis of Oldest Sequence from a Human Ancestor Suggests Link to Mystery Population." *Nature,* December 4. www.nature.com/news/hominin-dna-baffles-experts-1.14294 (accessed January 25, 2018).

——. 2014. "Oldest-Known Human Genome Sequenced." *Nature*. Vol. 514, October 23, 413. www.nature.com/news/oldest-known-human-genome-sequenced-1.16194 (accessed January 25, 2018).

Callimachus. 2001. "Poem Four: To Delos." In Nisetich.

Carville, D. J. 2014. "R. A. Schwaller and the Symbolist Key to Egypt." www.silverkeys .co.nz/uploads/7/1/7/6/7176604/08_r.a._schwaller__symbolist_egypt.pdf (accessed January 25, 2018).

Castel, Elisa. 2002. "Panthers, Leopards and Cheetahs: Notes on Identification." *Trabajos de Egiptología. Papers on Ancient Egypt*. Vol. 1, 17–28.

Çelik, Bahattin. 2000a. "A New Early-Neolithic Settlement: Karahan Tepe." *Neo-Lithics*. Vol. 2-3/00, 6–8. www.exoriente.org/docs/00019.pdf (accessed January 25, 2018).

——. 2000b. "An Early Neolithic Settlement in the Center of Şanlıurfa, Turkey." *Neo-Lithics*. Vol. 2–3/00, 4–6.

——. 2011. "Karahan Tepe: A New Cultural Centre in the Urfa Area in Turkey." *Documenta Praehistorica*. Vol. 38, 241–53. http://arheologija.ff.uni-lj.si/documenta /pdf38/38_19.pdf (accessed January 25, 2018).

Ceram, C. W., 1952/1954. *Gods, Graves and Scholars: The Story of Archaeology*. Translated by E. B. Garside. New York: Alfred K. Knopf.

Chadwick, Nora K., and Victor Zhirmunsky. 2010. *Oral Epics of Central Asia*. Cambridge: Cambridge University Press.

Chambers, George F. 1877. *A Handbook of Descriptive Astronomy*. Oxford: Clarendon.

Champollion, Jean-François. 1836. *Grammaire égyptienne*. Paris: Firmin-Didot Frères.

Chatelain, Maurice. 1987/1988. *Our Cosmic Ancestors*. Sedona, Ariz.: Temple Golden Publications.

Choi, Charles Q. 2012. "Genome of Mysterious Extinct Human Reveals Brown-Eyed Girl." *LiveScience,* August 30. www.livescience.com/22836-genome-extinct -humans-denisovans.html (accessed January 25, 2018).

Cicero, M. Tullius. 1923. *De Senectute de Amicitia de Divinatione*. Translated by William Armistead Falconer. Cambridge, Mass.: Harvard University Press.

Clagett, Marshall. 1995. *Ancient Egyptian Science, Vol. 2: Calendars, Clocks, and Astronomy*. Philadelphia: American Philosophical Society.

Clark, J. Desmond. 1982. *The Cambridge History of Africa, Vol. 1: From the Earliest Times to c.500 BC*. Cambridge: Cambridge University Press.

Clottes, J. (dir.). 2012. *L'art pléistocène dans le monde / Pleistocene art of the world / Arte pleistoceno en el mundo Actes du Congrès IFRAO, Tarascon-sur-Ariège, Septembre 2010 – Symposium "Datation et taphonomie de l'art pléistocène,"* LXV–LXVI, 2010–2011, CD and book. Tarascon-sur-Ariège, France: Société Préhistorique Ariège-Pyrénées.

Clube, Victor, and Bill Napier. 1982. *The Cosmic Serpent*. London: Faber and Faber.

Cohn, Don, and Zhang Jingqing. 1992. *Beijingwalks*. New York: Henry Holt.

Collins, Andrew. 1998. *From the Ashes of Angels*. Rochester, Vt.: Bear and Co.

———. 2000. *Gateway to Atlantis*. London: Headline.

———. 2004. "One Week in Kurdistan." www.andrewcollins.com/page/articles/kurdistan .htm (accessed January 25, 2018).

———. 2006a. *The Cygnus Mystery*. London: Watkins.

———. 2006b. "The Cygnus-Giza Correlation: The Facts and Alignments in Pictorial Form: A Reply to Critics by Andrew Collins." www.andrewcollins.com/page/articles /Cygnus_Orion_Giza.htm (accessed January 25, 2018).

———. 2007. "Cygnus versus Orion at Giza: A Response to Robert Bauval Queries by Andrew Collins." www.andrewcollins.com/page/articles/Bauval_Cygnus_Orion _Giza_020407.htm (accessed January 25, 2018).

———. 2008. "The Mystery of Dwn-'nwy and Its Identification and Role in Ancient Egyptian Astronomy." www.andrewcollins.com/page/articles/dwn_nwy.htm (accessed January 25, 2018).

———. 2009. *Beneath the Pyramids*. Virginia Beach, Va.: Fourth Dimension.

———. 2011a. "Giza's Cosmic Blueprint Revealed: Part One—Is Cygnus the Key to Unlocking the Pyramids' Grand Unified Plan?" www.andrewcollins.com/page /articles/cygnus_blueprint.htm (accessed January 25, 2018).

———. 2011b. "Giza's Cosmic Blueprint Revealed: Part Two: The Search for Egypt's Mound of Creation." www.andrewcollins.com/page/articles/cygnus_blueprint_2 .htm (accessed January 25, 2018).

———. 2014a. "Karahan Tepe: Göbekli Tepe's Sister Site: Another Temple of the Stars?" www.andrewcollins.com/page/articles/Karahan.htm (accessed January 25, 2018).

———. 2014b. *Göbekli Tepe: Genesis of the Gods*. Rochester, Vt.: Inner Traditions.

———. 2014c. "The Coming of the Giants: Rise of the Human Hybrids," In Little, 227–39. Also at www.andrewcollins.com/page/articles/denisovan.htm (accessed January 25, 2018).

———. 2015a. "First Pictorial Representation of Göbekli Tepe Found." www.ancient -origins.net/news-history-archaeology/first-pictorial-representation-gobekli-tepe

-found-003862. For the full-length article, see http://grahamhancock.com/collinsa4 (accessed January 25, 2018).

———. 2015b. "First Pictorial Representation of Göbekli Tepe T-Pillars Found on Tiny Bone Plaque." www.andrewcollins.com/page/articles/plaque.htm (accessed January 25, 2018).

———. 2015c. "Orion: The Eternal Rise of the Sky Hunter." www.andrewcollins.com /page/articles/Orion.htm (accessed January 25, 2018).

———. 2016. *Atlantis in the Caribbean*. Rochester, Vt.: Inner Traditions.

Collins, Andrew, and Rodney Hale. 2013. "Göbekli Tepe and the Rising of Sirius." www .academia.edu/5349935/GÖBEKLI_TEPE_AND_THE_RISING_OF_SIRIUS (accessed January 25, 2018).

Conman, Joanne. 2002. "The Round Zodiac Ceiling of the Temple of Hathor at Denderah." http://saturniancosmology.org/files/denderah/dendera.round.html.txt (accessed January 25, 2018).

———. 2013. *Ancient Egyptian Sky Lore*. London: Decan Wisdoms.

Cornford, Francis MacDonald. 2014 [1937]. *Plato's Cosmology: The Timaeus of Plato*. London: Routledge.

Cramer, John-Anthony. Engravings by J. Vincent. 1828. *Maps and Plans Illustrative of Herodotus Etc.* Oxford: J. Vincent.

D'Errico, Francesco. 2003. "Archaeological Evidence for the Emergence of Language, Symbolism, and Music: An Alternative Multidisciplinary Perspective." *Journal of World Prehistory*. Vol. 17, 1–70.

Daressy, M. Georges. 1911. "Inscriptions des carrières de Tourah et Mâsara." *Annales du Service des Antiquités de l'Égypte*. Vol. 11, 257–68.

———. 1915. "L'Égypte Céleste." *Bulletin de l'Institut Français d'Archéologie Orientale*. Vol. 12, 1–34.

Darmark, K. 2012. "Surface Pressure Flaking in Eurasia." In Desrosiers, 260–83.

Dash, Glen. 2011. "Solar Alignments of Giza." *AERAgram* Vol. 12, no. 2, (Fall), 3–8.

———. 2013. "How the Pyramid Builders May Have Found Their True North." *AERAgram*. Vol. 14, no.1 (Spring), 8–14.

Dashu, Max. 2009. "Xi Wangmu, the Shamanic Great Goddess of China." www.suppressed histories.net/goddess/xiwangmu.html (accessed January 25, 2018).

David-Neel, Alexandra, and Lama Yongden. 1933. *The Superhuman Life of Gesar of Ling: The Legendary Tibetan Hero, as Sung by the Bards of His Country*. London: Rider.

De Kay, Charles. 1898. *Bird Gods*. New York: A. S. Barnes.

Debono, Fernand, and Bodil Mortensen. 1990. *El Omari: A Neolithic Settlement and Other Sites in the Vicinity of Wadi Hof, Helwan*. Mainz am Rhein, Germany: Philipp von Zabern.

Demetrius. 1902. *On Style*. In Roberts, 1902.

Derevianko, A. P. 2016. "Paleoenvironment. The Stone Age." *Archaeology, Ethnology and Anthropology of Eurasia.* Vol. 44, no. 2, 3–18.

Derevianko, Anatoliy P., and S. Markin. 1998. "The Palaeolithic of the Altai." In Derevianko, Shimkin, and Powers, 84–105.

Derevianko, Anatoliy P., Demitri B. Shimkin, and W. Roger Powers, eds. 1998. *The Paleolithic of Siberia: New Discoveries and Interpretations.* Translated by Inna P. Laricheva. Champaign, Ill.: University of Illinois.

Derevianko, A. P., M. V. Shunkov, and P. V. Volkov. 2008. "A Paleolithic Bracelet from Denisova Cave." *Archaeology Ethnology and Anthropology of Eurasia.* Vol. 34, no. 2, 13–25.

Desrosiers, Pierre M. 2012. *The Emergence of Pressure Blade Making: From Origin to Modern Experimentation.* New York: Springer.

Deutsch, Babette, and Avrahm Yarmolinsky. 1952. *Tales of Faraway Folk.* New York: Harper.

Dietrich, Oliver. 2011. "Radiocarbon Dating the First Temples of Mankind. Comments on Fourteenth-Century Dates from Göbekli Tepe." *Zeitschrift für Orient-Archäologie.* Vol. 4, 12–25.

———. 2016a. "Out for a Beer at the Dawn of Agriculture." *The Tepe Telegrams,* April 24. https://tepetelegrams.wordpress.com/2016/04/24/out-for-a-beer-at-the-dawn -of-agriculture/ (accessed January 25, 2018).

———. 2016b. "How Old Is It? Dating Göbekli Tepe." *The Tepe Telegrams,* June 22. https://tepetelegrams.wordpress.com/2016/06/22/how-old-is-it-dating-gobekli -tepe/ (accessed January 25, 2018)

———. 2017a. "Two Foxes and a Bucranium: The First In Situ Porthole Stone from Göbekli Tepe." *Tepe Telegrams,* April 3. https://tepetelegrams.wordpress.com/2017/04/03 /two-foxes-and-a-bucranium-the-first-in-situ-porthole-stone-from-gobekli-tepe (accessed January 25, 2018).

———. 2017b. "A Decorated Bone Spatula, What's in That Picture? Iconology and Archaeology." *Tepe Telegrams,* March 15. https://tepetelegrams.wordpress .com/2017/03/15/iconology-and-archaeology-or-whats-in-that-picture (accessed January 25, 2018).

Dietrich, Oliver, Manfred Heun, Jens Notroff, Klaus Schmidt, and Martin Zarnkow. 2012. "The Role of Cult and Feasting in the Emergence of Neolithic Communities: New Evidence from Gobekli Tepe, South-Eastern Turkey." *Antiquity.* Vol. 86, 674–95.

Dietrich, Oliver, Jens Notroff, Lee Clare, Christian Hübner, Çigdem Köksal-Schmidt, and Klaus Schmidt. 2016 [2014]. "Göbekli Tepe, Anlage H: Ein Vorbericht beim Ausgrabungsstand von." In Yalçın, 53–69.

Dietrich, Oliver, Jens Notroff, and Klaus Schmidt. 2014. "Recent Research 2013–14: Insights into a New Enclosure at Göbekli Tepe." *Our Place: Our Place in the World.* John Templeton Foundation Newsletter (September): 5–6.

Diodorus Siculus. 1933. *Library of History: Volume 1* (books 1–2.34). Translated by C. H. Oldfather. Cambridge: Loeb Classical Library.

———. 1935. *Library of History: Volumes II* (books 2.35–4.58). Translated by C. H. Oldfather. Cambridge: Loeb Classical Library.

Diogenes Laertius. 1964. See Long.

Dionysius Periegetes. 1828. *The Periegesis of the Known World.* In Bernhardy.

"DNA Deciphered of Horse Used by Extinct Humans." 2013. *Sputnik,* July 31. https://sputniknews.com/science/20130731182513837-DNA-Deciphered-of-Horse-Used-by-Extinct-Humans/ (accessed January 25, 2018).

Dodds, Eric Robertson. 1986. *Euripides' Bacchae.* Oxford: Oxford University Press.

Dodge, Bayard. 1967. "The Sabians of Harran." In Sarrûf and Tamim, 59–85.

Dodson, Aidan, and Dyan Hilton. 2004. *The Complete Royal Families of Ancient Egypt.* London: Thames and Hudson.

Doutré, Martin. 2001. "The Dimensions of the Working Altar atop the Great Pyramid and the Size of the Earth." *Ancient Celtic New Zealand.* http://www.celticnz.co.nz/US3.html (accessed January 25, 2018).

Edwards, I. E. S. 1986. "The Shetayet of Rosetau." In Lesko, 27–36.

———. 1993. *The Pyramids of Egypt.* Rev. ed. London: Penguin.

Eliade, Mircea. 1964. *Shamanism: Archaic Techniques of Ecstasy.* London: Routledge and Kegan Paul.

Elman, Benjamin A. 2000. *A Cultural History of Civil Examinations in Late Imperial China.* Berkeley: University of California Press.

Eschenbach, Andreas Christian, Henri Estienne, Johann Matthias Gesner, George Cristoph Hamberger, and Theophrastus. 1764. *Otpheōs hapantas: Orphei Argonautica Hymni Libellus de lapidibus et fragmenta.* Leipzig: Sumtibus Caspari Fritsch.

Estes, Roberta. 2013. "Native Americans, Neanderthal and Denisova Admixture." DNA-Explained: Genetic Genealogy. December 26. http://dna-explained.com/2013/12/26/native-americans-neanderthal-and-denisova-admixture/ (accessed January 25, 2018).

Faulkes, Anthony, trans. 1987. *Snorri Sturluson: Edda.* Rutland Vt.: J. M. Dent and Charles E. Tuttle. Everyman's Library.

Faulkner, R. O. 1966. "The King and the Star-Religion in the Pyramid Texts." *Journal of Near Eastern Studies.* Vol. 25, 153–61.

———. 1969. *The Ancient Egyptian Pyramid Texts.* Warminster, Wiltshire, U.K.: Aris and Phillips.

Fix, William. 1978. *Pyramid Odyssey.* Toronto: Jonathan-James.

Flohr, Pascal, Bill Finlayson, Mohammad Najjar, and Steven Mithen. 2015. "Building WF16: Construction of a Pre-Pottery Neolithic A (PPNA) Pisé Structure in Southern Jordan." *Levant.* Vol. 47, no. 2, 144–63.

Franci, Massimiliano di. 2014. "La rappresentazione del cielo." *Egittologia.net Magazine.* Vol. 7, 44–50.

Frazer, Sir James George. 1939. *The Native Races of America.* Edited by Robert Angus Downie. London: Percy Lund Humphries.

"Fresh Discoveries of Ancient Man's Bone in Altai Mountains Cave." 2015. *The Siberian Times,* August 14. http://siberiantimes.com/science/casestudy/news/n0356-fresh-discoveries-of-ancient-mans-bone-in-altai-mountains-cave/ (accessed January 25, 2018).

Friesen, Courtney J. P. 2015. *Reading Dionysus: Euripides' Bacchae and the Cultural Contestations of Greeks, Jews, Romans, and Christians.* Tübingen, Germany: Mohr Siebeck.

Fung, Yu-lan. 1983. *History of Chinese Philosophy, Volume 2: The Period of Classical Learning from the Second Century B.C. to the Twentieth Century A.D.* Translated by Derk Bodde. Princeton, N.J.: Princeton University Press.

Gaster, Moses. 1915. *Rumanian Bird and Beast Stories, Rendered into English.* London: Sidgwick and Jackson.

Gaunt, Bonnie. 2003 [1993]. *Stonehenge and the Great Pyramid: Window on the Universe.* Kempton, Ill.: Adventures Unlimited.

Gebel, H. G., and S. K. Kozlowski. 1994. *Neolithic Chipped Stone Industries of the Fertile Crescent: Proceedings of the First Workshop on PPN Chipped Lithic Industries.* Berlin: Ex Oriente.

"Genome of Horse Linked to Extinct Human Species Decoded in Russia." 2013. UPI, July 31. www.upi.com/Genome-of-horse-linked-to-extinct-human-species-decoded-in-Russia/99001375311922/ (accessed January 25, 2018).

Gertcyk, Olga, and Vera Salnitskaya. 2016. "Hanging Rock 'Defies Gravity,' above a Thousand-Metre Abyss." *Siberian Times,* January 16. http://siberiantimes.com/other/others/features/f0200-hanging-rock-defies-gravity-above-a-1000-metre-abyss (accessed January 25, 2018).

Gibbons, Ann. 2011. "Who Were the Denisovans?" *Science.* Vol. 333 (August 26), 1084–87.

———. 2016. "Humans Mated with Neandertals Much Earlier and More Frequently than Thought." February 17. *Science-AAAS.* www.sciencemag.org/news/2016/02/humans-mated-neandertals-much-earlier-and-more-frequently-thought (accessed January 25, 2018).

Gladyshev, Sergei A., John W. Olsen, Andrei V. Tabarev, and Anthony J. T. Jull. 2012. "The Upper Paleolithic of Mongolia: Recent Finds and New Perspectives." *Quaternary International.* Vol. 281, 36–46.

Glanville, S. R. K., and Nora Macdonald Griffith. 1932. *Studies Presented to F. L. Griffith.* London: Egypt Exploration Society.

Go.Akim, Hatagin. 2014. "Ergune Khun, Realm of Refuge, Did It Tell a Fairy Tale or Speak of History?" https://goakim.wordpress.com/author/goakim (accessed January 25, 2018).

Göknil, Can. 1997. "Creation Myths from Central Asia to Anatolia." http://cangoknil.com /en/creation-myths-from-central-asia-to-anatolia (accessed January 25, 2018).

Goodman, David. 2007. "Survey: The GPMP Surveying and Mapping Control Datums." In Lehner and Wetterstrom, 95–101.

Goodman, David, and Mark Lehner. "The Survey: The Beginning." In Lehner and Wetterstrom, 2007, 97–98.

Gopher, Avi. 1989. "Diffusion Process in the Pre-Pottery Neolithic Levant: The Case of the Helwan Point." In Hershkovitz, 91–106.

———. 1994. *Arrowheads of the Neolithic Levant: A Seriation Analysis.* Winona Lake, Ind.: Eisenbrauns.

Gopher, Avi, Cristina Lemorini, Elisabetta Boaretto, Israel Carmi, Ran Barkai, and Heeli C. Schechter. 2014. "Qumran Cave 24, a Neolithic-Chalcolithic Site by the Dead Sea: A Short Report and Some Information on Lithics." In Borrell, Ibáñez, and Molist, 101–14.

Goring-Morris, A. Nigel. 1991. "The Harifian of the Southern Levant." In Bar-Yosef and Valla, 173–213.

Goring-Morris, A. Nigel, and Anna Belfer-Cohen. 2013. "Ruminations on the Role of Periphery and Centre in the Natufian." In Bar-Yosef and Valla, 562–83.

Gourichon, Lionel. 2002. "Bird Remains from Jerf el Ahmar: A PPNA Site in Northern Syria with Special Reference to the Griffon Vulture (*Gyps fulvus*)." In Buitenhuis et al., 138–52.

Goyon, G. 1970. "Nouvelles observations relatives a l'orientation de la Pyramide de Cheops." *Revue D'Egyptologie.* Vol. 22, 85–98.

Grachev, Andrey. nd. "Ergaki. Places of Power." TODISCOVERRUSSIA. http:// todiscoverrussia.com/ergaki-places-of-power.

Graf, Fritz, and Sarah Iles Johnston. 2013. *Ritual Texts for the Afterlife: Orpheus and the Bacchic Gold Tablets.* Abingdon, Oxfordshire, U.K.: Routledge.

Graves, Robert. 1972. *Difficult Questions, Easy Answers.* Garden City, N.Y.: Doubleday.

Gray, Louis Herbert, and George Foot Moore, eds. 1918. *The Mythology of All Races, Volume 12.* Boston: Marshall Jones.

Greco, Christian. 2014. "The Forgotten Tomb of Ramose." In Pischikova, Budka, and Griffin, 173–99.

Green, Tamara. 1992. *The City of the Moon God: The Religious Traditions of Harran.* Leiden: E. J. Brill.

Greshko, Michael. 2015. "DNA Reveals Mysterious Human Cousin with Huge Teeth." *National Geographic,* November 16. http://news.nationalgeographic.com/2015/11/151116 -denisovan-human-anthropology-ancient-dna (accessed January 25, 2018).

Griffiths, John Gywn. 1980. *The Origins of Osiris and His Cult*. Leiden: E. J. Brill.

Grube, G. M. A. 1977. *Plato's Phaedo*. Indianapolis, Ind.: Hackett.

Guthrie, W. K. C. 1993 [1935]. *Orpheus and Greek Religion: A Study of the Orphic Movement*. Princeton, N.J.: Princeton University Press.

Hadingham, Evan. 1994. "The Mummies of Xinjiang." *Archaeology*. Vol. 5, no. 4 (April), 68–77. Online at Discover. http://discovermagazine.com/1994/apr /themummiesofxinj359 (accessed January 25, 2018).

Hale, Rodney. 2015. "'Here I Stand.' A Possible Interpretation of an Image Inscribed on a Bone Plaque Found at Gobekli Tepe." www.academia.edu/18349700/_Here_I _stand_._A_possible_interpretation_of_an_image_inscribed_on_a_bone_plaque _found_at_G%C3%B6bekli_Tepe (accessed January 25, 2018).

Hale, R., and Andrew Collins. 2016. "A Study of the Simple Geometrical Relationship of the Main Monuments of Giza and a Possible Connection to Stars." *Archaeological Discovery*. Vol. 4, 87–102.

Halemba, Agnieszka. 2006. *The Telengits of Southern Siberia: Landscape, Religion, and Knowledge in Motion*. Abingdon, Oxfordshire, U.K.: Routledge.

Hales, Rev. William. 1830. *A New Analysis of Chronology and Geography, History and Prophecy etc*. Vol. 1. London: C. J. G. & F. Rivington.

Halloran, John A. 1999. "Sumerian Lexicon. Version 3.0." http://history-world.org /sumerian[1].pdf (accessed January 25, 2018).

Hamayon, Roberte. 1990. *La chasse à l'âme: Esquisse d'une théorie du chamanisme sibérien*. Paris: Société d'Ethnologie, University of Paris.

Hamilton, Dominic. 2007. "The Singing Shamen of Tuva." *Perceptive Travel*. www .perceptivetravel.com/issues/0107/hamilton.html (accessed January 25, 2018).

Hancock, Graham. 2001. *Fingerprints of the Gods*. London: Century.

———. 2015. *Magicians of the Gods: The Forgotten Wisdom of Earth's Lost Civilisation*. London: Coronet.

Harrell, Stevan. 1995a. "The History of the History of the Yi." In Harrell 1995b, 63–91.

———. ed. 1995b. *Cultural Encounters on China's Ethnic Frontiers*. Seattle: University of Washington Press.

Harrell, Stevan, and Li Yongxiang. 2003. "History of the Yi, Part II." *Modern China*. Vol. 29, no. 3 (July), 362–96.

Harris, J. Rendel. 1925. "Apollo's Birds." *Bulletin of the John Rylands Library*. Vol. 9, no. 2, 372–416.

Hatto, A. T. 1961. "The Swan Maiden: A Folk-Tale of North Eurasian Origin?" *Bulletin of the School of Oriental and African Studies*. Vol. 24, 326–52.

Hawass, Zahi. 1997. "The Discovery of the Harbors of Khufu and Khafre at Giza." In Berger and Mathieu, 245–56.

————. 2007. "The Discovery of the Osiris Shaft at Giza." In Hawass and Richards, 379–97.

Hawass, Zahi, and Mark Lehner. 1994. "The Sphinx: Who Built It and Why?" *Archaeology Magazine.* Vol. 47, no. 5 (September/October), 30–41.

Hawass, Zahi A., and Janet Richards, eds. 2007. "The Archaeology and Art of Ancient Egypt: Essays in Honor of David B. O'Connor." *Annales du Service des Antiquités de l'Égypte.* Vol. 1. Cairo: Conseil suprême des antiquités en Égypte.

Hawass, Zahi, and Ashraf Senussi. 2008. *Old Kingdom Pottery from Giza.* Cairo: American University in Cairo Press.

Hayes, William. 1965. *Most Ancient Egypt.* Chicago: University of Chicago Press.

Healey, E. S., and O. Maeda Campbell, eds. 2011. *The State of the Stone: Terminologies, Continuities, and Contexts in Near Eastern Lithics: Studies in Early Near Eastern Production, Subsistence, and Environment 13.* Berlin: Ex Oriente.

Hearne, Thomas. 1769. *The Itinerary of John Leland the Antiquary, Vol. the Fifth. Publish'd from the Original MS. In the Bodleian Library, etc.* Oxford: James Fletcher and Joseph Pote.

Hecataeus of Abdera. *On the Hyperboreans.* See Aelian.

Helck, Wolfgang. 1982. *Lexikon der Ägyptologie. Band 4: Megiddo: Pyramiden.* Wiesbaden, Germany: Harrassowitz.

Helck, Wolfgang, Eberhard Otto, and Wolfhart Westendorf. 1977. *Lexikon der Ägyptologie. Band 2: Erntefest—Hordjedef.* Wiesbaden, Germany: Harrassowitz.

Hendrickx, S., R. F. Friedman, K. M. Cialowicz, and M. Chlodnicki, eds. 2004 [2002]. *Egypt at Its Origins: Studies in Memory of Barbara Adams: Proceedings of the International Conference "Origin of the State, Predynastic, and Early Dynastic Egypt."* Krakow, Poland, August 28–September 1. Leuven, Belgium: Uitgeverij Peeters en Departement Oosterse Studies.

Herodotus. 1940 [1910]. *The History of Herodotus.* 2 vols. Translated by George Rawlinson. London: J. M. Dent.

Herouni, Paris M. 2004. *Armenians and Old Armenia: Archaeoastronomy, Linguistics, Oldest History.* Yerevan, Armenia: Tigran Metz.

Hershkovitz, Israel, ed. 1989. *People and Culture in Change: Proceedings of the Second Symposium on Upper Paleolithic, Mesolithic, and Neolithic Populations of Europe and the Mediterranean.* Oxford: British Archaeological Reports, International Series S508.

Heun, Manfred, Ralf Schäfer-Pregl, Dieter Klawan, Renato Castagna, Monica Accerbi, Basilio Borghi, and Francesco Salamini. 1997. "Site of Einkorn Wheat Domestication Identified by DNA Fingerprinting." *Science.* Vol. 278, no. 5341 (November 14), 1312–14.

Higham, Thomas, Laura Basell, Roger Jacobic, et al. 2012. "Testing Models for the Beginnings of the Aurignacian and the Advent of Figurative Art and Music: The

Radiocarbon Chronology of Geißenklösterle." *Journal of Human Evolution*. Vol. 62, no. 6, 664–76.

Hincks, Rev. Edward. 1838. *The Years and Cycles Used by the Ancient Egyptians*. Dublin: Royal Irish Academy.

Hirayama, Hiroshi. 2011. "Does the First Appearance of the Name Osiris Date Back to the End of the Fourth Dynasty? From Inscriptions of the Tombs of *nb-m-3ḥt*." *Bulletin of the Society for Near Eastern Studies in Japan*. Vol. 54, no. 2, 63–73.

Hodder, Ian. 2006. *The Leopard's Tale: Revealing the Mysteries of Çatalhöyük*. London: Thames and Hudson.

Hodges, E. Richmond. 1876. *Cory's Ancient Fragments of the Phoenician, Carthaginian, Babylonian, Egyptian, and Other Authors*. London: Reeves and Turner.

Hoffecker, John F. 2002. *Desolute Landscapes: Ice-Age Settlement in Eastern Europe*. Piscataway, N.J.: Rutgers University Press.

Hoffecker, John F., and Scott A. Elias. 2012. *Human Ecology of Beringia*. New York: Columbia University Press.

Hoffman, Michael A. 1979. *Egypt before the Pharaohs: The Prehistoric Foundations of Egyptian Civilization*. New York: Knopf Doubleday.

Holmberg, Uno. 1927. *The Mythology of All Races, Volume 4: Finno-Ugric, Siberian*. Edited by C. J. A. MacCulloch. Boston: Marshall Jones.

Hornung, Erik. 2001 [1999]. *The Secret Lore of Egypt: Its Impact on the West*. Ithaca, N.Y.: Cornell University Press.

Horowitz, Wayne. 1998. *Mesopotamian Cosmic Geography*. Winona Lake, Ind.: Eisenbrauns.

Hotz, Robert Lee. 2011. "Perhaps a Red, 4,100 B.C." *Wall Street Journal,* January 11. www .wsj.com/articles/SB10001424052748704458204576074141252276326 (accessed January 25, 2018).

Huerta-Sánchez, Emilia, et al. 2014. "Altitude Adaptation in Tibetans Caused by Introgression of Denisovan-like DNA." *Nature*. Vol. 512, no. 7513 (August 14), 194–97.

Hutchinson, P. O. 1893. "Roman Bricks and Tiles." *Lincolnshire Notes and Queries*. Vol. 3, 153–55.

Hyder, Ken. 2010."Siberian Shamans Come in from the Cold (Part 3)." *OpenDemocracy*. www.opendemocracy.net/ken-hyder/siberian-shamans-come-in-from-cold-part-3 (accessed January 25, 2018).

Hyginus. 1960. *Astronomica*. Book 2. Translated by Mary Grant. www.theoi.com/Text /HyginusAstronomica.html (accessed January 25, 2018).

Iamblichus. 1818. *Life of Pythagoras*. See Taylor.

Iovita, Radu. 2011. "Shape Variation in Aterian Tanged Tools and the Origins of Projectile Technology: A Morphometric Perspective on Stone Tool Function." *PLoS One*. Vol. 6,

no. 12 (December 27). http://journals.plos.org/plosone/article?id=10.1371/journal
.pone.0029029 (accessed January 25, 2018).

"Is This Stunning Bracelet Made by Paleolithic Man for His Favourite Woman Really
70,000 Years Old?" 2017. *The Siberian Times,* August 2. http://siberiantimes.com
/science/casestudy/features/could-this-stunning-bracelet-be-65000-to-70000-years-old
(accessed February 10, 2018).

Isler, Martin. 2001. *Sticks, Stones, and Shadows: Building the Egyptian Pyramids.*
Norman, Okla.: University of Oklahoma Press.

Jacobson-Tepfer, Esther. 2015. *The Hunter, the Stag, and the Mother of Animals: Image,
Monument, and Landscape in Ancient North Asia.* Oxford: Oxford University Press.

James, Jamie. 1993. *The Music of the Spheres.* New York: Springer.

Jayaram, V. 2016. "Symbolism of Ksheera Sagara Manthan," January 16. Hinduwebsite
.com. www.hinduwebsite.com/churning.asp (accessed January 25, 2018).

Jean, Roger V., and Denis Barabé, eds. 1998. *Symmetry of Plants.* Singapore: World Scientific.

Jeffreys, David. 2004. "Hierakonpolis and Memphis in Predynastic Tradition." In
Hendrickx et al., 837–45.

———. 2005. "Helwan." In Bard, 367–68.

Jelinkova, E. A. E. 1962. "The Shebtiw in the Temple of Edfu." *Zeitschrift für Ägyptische
Sprache und Altertumskunde.* Vol. 87, 41–54.

Jenkins, John Major. 1998. *Maya Cosmogenesis 2012.* Rochester, Vt.: Bear and Co.

Jenkyns, Richard. 2013. *God, Space, and City in the Roman Imagination.* Oxford:
Oxford University Press.

Jodrell, Richard Paul. 1781. *Illustrations of Euripides, on the Ion and the Bacchae Etc.*
Vol. 1. London: J. Nichols.

Jowett, Benjamin. *The Republic of Plato.* Oxford: Clarendon Press, 1888.

Jusha, Z. M. nd. "Myths, Legends, Historical Stories of Tuvinians Summary [*sic*]."
Translated by Edward J. Vajda. Institute of Philology of the Siberian Branch of
Russian Academy of Sciences. www.philology.nsc.ru/departments/folklor_en/t28
_summary.php (accessed October 23, 2017).

Kaifu, Yousuke, Masami Izuho, Ted Goebel, Hiroyuki Sato, and Akira Ono. 2015.
Emergence and Diversity of Modern Human Behavior in Paleolithic Asia. College
Station, Texas: Texas A&M University Press.

Kamil, Jill. 1988. *Coptic Egypt: History and Guide.* Cairo: American University in Cairo
Press.

Kappraff, Jay. 2004. "Growth in Plants: A Study in Number." *Forma.* Vol. 19, 335–54.

Kay, Charles de. 1898. *Bird Gods: With an Accompaniment of Decorations by George
Wharton Edwards.* New York: A. S. Barnes.

Kazachinova, Galina, and Kira Van Deusen. 2002. *Mountain Spirits: Khakass Stories.*
Vancouver: Udagan.

Kenyon, Kathleen M. 1979 [1960]. *Archaeology in the Holy Land.* New York: W. W. Norton.

Khaled, Rana. 2012. "Ain Helwan's Therapeutic Waters Are Squandered and Neglected." *Egypt Independent,* July 29. www.egyptindependent.com/news/ain-helwan-s -therapeutic-waters-are-squandered-and-neglected (accessed January 25, 2018).

Kilmer, Anne Draffkorn. 1971. "The Discovery of an Ancient Mesopotamian Theory of Music." *Proceedings of the American Philosophical Society.* Vol. 115, 131–49.

———. 1998. "The Musical Instruments from Ur and Ancient Mesopotamian Music." *Expedition Magazine.* Vol. 40, no. 2, 12–19. www.penn.museum/sites/expedition /the-musical-instruments-from-ur-and-ancient-mesopotamian-music (accessed January 25, 2018).

King, William. 1722. *An Historical Account of the Heathen Gods and Heroes, Necessary for the Understanding of the Ancient Poets: Being an Improvement of Whatever Has Been Hitherto Written by the Greek, Latin, French, and English Authors upon That Subject.* London: Bernard Lintot.

Klein, Herbert Arthur. 2012. *The Science of Measurement: A Historical Survey.* North Chelmsford, Mass.: Courier.

Kogan, Leonid, et al., eds. 2010. *Language in the Ancient Near East. Proceedings of the 53e Rencontre Assyriologique Internationale.* Vol. 1, part 2 (*Babel und Bibel 4/2*). Winona Lake, Ind.: Eisenbrauns.

Koster, Annelies. 2013. *The Late Roman Cemeteries of Nijmegen: Stray Finds and Excavations 1947–1983.* Steures D.C., The Netherlands: Museum Het Valkhof.

Kozloff, Arielle. 1992. "Ritual Implements and Related Statuettes." In Kozloff and Bryan, 331–48.

———. 2007. "Proof of the True Use of 'Cosmetic' Spoons as Funerary Ritual Spoons." Paper presented at the annual meeting of the fifty-eighth annual meeting of the American Research Center in Egypt, Toledo, Ohio, April 20. http://citation.allacademic .com/meta/p200754_index.html (accessed January 25, 2018).

Kozloff, Arielle, and Betsy M. Bryan. 1992. *Egypt's Dazzling Sun: Amenhotep III and His World.* Bloomington, Ind.: Cleveland Museum of Art and Indiana University Press.

Kozlowski, Stefan Karol, and Hans Georg K. Gebel, eds. 1996. *Neolithic Chipped Stone Industries of the Fertile Crescent, and Their Contemporaries in Adjacent Regions: Studies in Early Near Eastern Production, Subsistence, and Environment 3.* Berlin: Ex Oriente.

Kozlowski, Stefan Karol, and Jan Gurba. 1999. *Tanged Point Cultures in Europe.* Lublin, Poland: Maria Curie-Sklodowska University Press.

Kuzmin, Yaroslav V. 2007. "Chronological Framework of the Siberian Paleolithic: Recent Achievements and Future Directions." *Radiocarbon.* Vol. 49, no. 2, 757–66.

———. 2009. "The Middle to Upper Paleolithic Transition in Siberia: Chronological and Environmental Aspects." *Eurasian Prehistory.* Vol. 5, no. 2, 97–108.

Lankford, George E. 2007a. "The Great Serpent in Eastern North America." In Reilly and Garber, 107–35.

———. 2007b. "'The 'Path of Souls': Some Death Imagery in the Southeastern Ceremonial Complex." In Reilly and Garber, 174–212.

Larichev, Vitaliy. 1986. "Malta Plate from Mammoth Ivory." In Russian. Novosibirsk, Russia: Institute of Archaeology and Ethnography at the Russian Academy of Sciences.

———. 1989. *The Wisdom of Snakes: Primitive Man, Moon and Sun*. In Russian. Novosibirsk, Russia: Nauka.

Larson, Jennifer Lynn. 2007. *Ancient Greek Cults: A Guide*. Hove, East Sussex, U.K.: Psychology Press.

Lauer, Jean Philippe. 1960. *Observations sur les pyramides*. Cairo: Imprimerie de l'Institut Français d'Archéologie Orientale.

Lawson, Andrew J., 2012. *Painted Caves: Palaeolithic Rock Art in Western Europe*. Oxford: Oxford University Press.

Lbova, Liudmila. 2010. "Evidence of Modern Human Behavior in the Baikal Zone during the Early Upper Paleolithic Period." *Bulletin of the Indo-Pacific Prehistory Association*. Vol. 30, 9–13.

———. 2012. "The Chronological Context of Pleistocene Art in Siberia." In Clottes, CD-rom: CD, 198–99 and 1123–28; book, 226–27.

Lbova, Liudmila, Darya Kozhevnikov, and Pavel Volkov. 2012. "Musical Instruments in Siberia (Early Stage of the Upper Paleolithic)." In Clottes, CD, 1900–1904.

Legon, John A. R. 2000 [1979]. "The Plan of the Giza Pyramids." *Archaeological Reports of the Archaeology Society of Staten Island*. Vol. 10, no. 1. www.legon.demon.co.uk /gizaplan.htm (accessed January 25, 2018).

———. 2007. "The Design of the Great Pyramid." www.legon.demon.co.uk/greatpyr .htm (accessed January 25, 2018).

Lehner, Mark. 1985. "A Contextual Approach to the Giza Pyramids." *Archiv für Orientforschung*. Vol. 32, 136–58.

———. 1997. *The Complete Pyramids*. London: Thames and Hudson.

———. 2011. "Giza, Meter by Meter." AERA. www.aeraweb.org/gpmp-project /giza-meter-by-meter/ (accessed January 25, 2018).

———. 2013. "The Heit el-Ghurab Site Reveals a New Face: Lost Port City of the Pyramids." *AERAgram*. Vol. 14, no. 1 (Spring), 2–6.

———. 2013–14. "Giza Plateau Mapping Project: Introduction to 2014 Season." *Giza Plateau Mapping Project: 2013–2014 Annual Report*, 67–79. https://oi.uchicago .edu/sites/oi.uchicago.edu/files/uploads/shared/docs/ar/11-20/13-14/ar2013-14 _Giza-Plateau-Mapping.pdf (accessed January 25, 2018).

———. 2014. "On the Waterfront: Canals and Harbors in the Time of Giza Pyramid-Building." *AERAgram*. Vol. 15, no. 1 and 2 (Spring–Fall), 14–23.

Lehner, Mark, and Wilma Wetterstrom, eds. 2007. *Giza Reports: Giza Plateau Mapping Project. Volume 1: Project History, Survey, Ceramics, and Main Street and Gallery III.4 Operations.* Boston: AERA.

Leland, John. 1769. *The Itinerary.* In Hearne.

Lenormant, Francoise. 1877. *Chaldean Magic: Its Origin and Development.* London: Bagster and Sons.

Lesko, Barbara. 1999. *The Great Goddesses of Egypt.* Norman, Okla.: University of Oklahoma Press.

Lesko, L. H., ed. 1986. *Egyptological Studies in Honour of Richard A. Parker.* Hanover, N.H.: University Press of New England.

Levin, Flora R. 1994. *The Manual of Harmonics of Nicomachus the Pythagorean.* Grand Rapids, Mich.: Phanes Press.

Levine, Etan. 2000. *Heaven and Earth, Law and Love: Studies in Biblical Thought.* Berlin: Walter de Gruyter.

Lichtheim, Miriam. 1973. *Ancient Egyptian Literature, Vol. 1: The Old and Middle Kingdoms.* Berkeley: University of California Press.

———. 1980. *Ancient Egyptian Literature, Vol. 3: A Book of Readings.* Berkeley: University of California Press.

Liesowska, Anna. 2017. "Stone Bracelet Is Oldest Ever Found in the World." *The Siberian Times,* February 2. http://siberiantimes.com/science/casestudy/features/f0100-stone-bracelet-is-oldest-ever-found-in-the-world (accessed January 25, 2018).

"List of Rulers of Ancient Egypt and Nubia." 2000. See Metropolitan Museum.

Little, Greg. 2014. *Path of Souls: The Native American Death Journey.* With preface and afterward by Andrew Collins. Memphis, Tenn.: Eagle Wing.

———. 2016a. "Were the Portsmouth Earthworks a Portal to the Path of Souls? Cygnus, Orion, The Milky Way, and Scorpius Alignments at Portsmouth on the Winter Solstice in 2000 B.C." *Archaeotrek: Alternate Perceptions Magazine,* January. www.apmagazine.info/index.php?option=com_contentandview=articleandid=762 (accessed January 25, 2018).

———. 2016b. "Marietta, Ohio's Ancient Earthworks: Star Alignments as a Portal to the Path of Souls." *Archaeotrek: Alternate Perceptions Magazine,* February. www.apmagazine.info/index.php?option=com_contentandview=articleandid=767 (accessed January 25, 2018).

———. 2016c. "Star Portal Alignments at the Winterville, Mississippi Native American Indian Mound Complex." *Archaeotrek: Alternate Perceptions Magazine,* March. http://apmagazine.info/index.php?option=com_contentandview=articleandid=788 (accessed January 25, 2018).

Lloyd, Seton, and William Brice. 1951. "Harran." *Anatolian Studies.* Vol. 1, 77–111.

Locher, K. 1985. "Probable Identification of the Ancient Egyptian Circumpolar Constellations." *Archaeoastronomy* (supplement to *Journal for the History of Astronomy,* Vol. 16, no. 9, 152–53.

Lombard, Marlize, and Laurel Phillipson. 2010. "Indications of Bow and Stone-Tipped Arrow Use 64,000 Years Ago in KwaZulu-Natal, South Africa." *Antiquity.* Vol. 84, 635–48.

Long, H. S., ed. 1964. *Diogenis Laertii vitae philosophorum.* 2 vols. Oxford: Oxford University Press.

Lorenzis, Alessandro de, and Vincenzo Orofino. 2015. "New Possible Astronomic Alignments at the Megalithic Site of Göbekli Tepe, Turkey." *Archaeological Discovery.* Vol. 3, 40–50.

Love, Serena. 2006. "Stones, Ancestors and Pyramids: Investigating the Pre-Pyramid Landscape of Memphis." In Bárta, 209–18.

Lukan, Karl. 1979. *Herrgottsitz und Teufelsbett: Wanderungen in der Vorzeit.* Vienna: Jugend and Volk.

Lull, José, and Juan Antonio Belmonte. 2009. "The Constellations of Ancient Egypt." In Shaltout and Belmonte, 157–94.

Lutley, K., and J. M. Bunbury. 2008. "The Nile on the Move." *Egyptian Archaeology.* Vol. 32, 3–5.

Mackenzie, Donald A. 1934. *Teutonic Myth and Legend.* New York: William H. Wise.

Magli, Giulio. 2013. *Architecture, Astronomy, and Sacred Landscape in Ancient Egypt.* Cambridge: Cambridge University Press.

Mair, Victor H. 1995. "Mummies of the Tarim Basin." *Archaeology.* Vol. 48, no. 2 (March/April), 28–35.

Mallory, J. P., and Victor H. Mair. 2000. *The Tarim Mummies: Ancient China and the Mystery of the Earliest Peoples from the West.* London: Thames and Hudson.

Malville, J. McK., R. Schild, F. Wendorf, and R. Brenmer. 2007. "Astronomy of Nabta Playa." *African Sky.* Vol. 11, 2–7.

Manley, Deborah. 2008. *Traveling through Egypt: From 450 B.C. to the Twentieth Century.* Cairo: American University in Cairo Press.

Mannikka, Eleanor. 1996. *Angkor Wat: Time, Space and Kingship.* Honolulu: University of Hawai'i Press.

Maravelia, Amanda-Alice. 2003a. "Cosmic Space and Archetypal Time: Depictions of the Sky Goddess Nut in Three Royal Tombs of the New Kingdom and Her Relation to the Milky Way." *Göttinger Miszellen.* Vol. 197, 55–72.

———. 2003b. "The Stellar Horizon of Khufu." In Bickel and Loprieno, 55–74.

Marshall, Steve. 2016. "Acoustics of the West Kennet Long Barrow, Avebury, Wiltshire." *Time and Mind.* Vol. 9, no. 1, 43–56.

Martinov, Prof. A. İ. 2013. *Altay Kaya Resimleri Biçiktu-Boom.* Ankara, Turkey: Atatürk Kültür Merkezi.

Martzloff, Jean-Claude. 2016. *Astronomy and Calendars: The Other Chinese Mathematics.* Berlin: Springer.

Maspero, Gaston. 1902. "Sur le Pyramidion d'Amenemhat III, Dahchour." *Annales du Service des Antiquités de l'Égypte.* Vol. 3, 206–8.

Massey, Gerald. 1883. *A Natural Genesis.* 2 vols. London: Williams and Norgate.

Massoulard, Émile. 1949. *Préhistoire et protohistoire d'Égypte.* Paris: Institut d'Ethnologie.

May, W. Page, G. Schweinfurth, and A. H. Sayce. 1901. *Helwan and the Egyptian Desert: A Guide to the Health Resort of Egypt.* London: G. Allen.

McBride, Alexis. 2014. "The Acoustics of Archaeological Architecture in the Near Eastern Neolithic." *World Archaeology.* Vol. 46, no. 3, 349–61.

McClintock, John, and James Strong. 1894. *Cyclopaedia of Biblical, Theological, and Ecclesiastical Literature.* Vol. 7. New York: Harper.

McHardy, Stuart. 2003. *The Quest for the Nine Maidens.* Edinburgh: Luath.

Mead, G. R. S., 1965 [1896]. *Orpheus.* London: John M. Watkins.

Mellaart, James. 1967. *Çatal Hüyük: A Neolithic Town in Anatolia.* London: Thames and Hudson.

———. 1974 [1964]. *Earliest Civilizations of the Near East.* London: Thames and Hudson.

"The Memphite Theology," British Museum no. 498 (Shabaka Stone). In Lichtheim, 1973, 51–57.

Mercer, Samuel A. B., trans. 1952. *The Pyramid Texts in Translation I.* New York: Longmans, Green.

Metropolitan Museum, Department of Egyptian Art. 2000. "List of Rulers of Ancient Egypt and Nubia." In *Heilbrunn Timeline of Art History.* New York: Metropolitan Museum of Art. www.metmuseum.org/toah/hd/phar/hd_phar.htm (accessed January 25, 2018).

Meyer, Matthias, et al. 2012. "A High-Coverage Genome Sequence from an Archaic Denisovan Individual." *Science* vol. 338, no. 6104 (October 12), 222–26.

"Ming Dynasty Unit of Measurement." 2017. Great Ming Military, Jan. 7. http://greatming military.blogspot.com/p/ming-dynasty-unit-conversion.html (accessed January 25, 2018).

Miracle, Rebekah. 2011. "Something Old, Something New, Something Borrowed in Map View: GIS Brings It All Together." *AERAgram.* Vol. 12, no. 12 (Fall), 10–12.

Mkrtcyan, Karine. 2014. "Il Mistero di Qarahunj." *Akhtamar on line.* Vol. 9, no. 182 (July 15), 2.

Mook, Friedrich. 1878. "Steinzeit in Ägypten." *Correspondenz-Blatt der deutschen Gesellschaft für Anthropologie, Ethnologie, und Urgeschichte.* Vol. 11, 142–45.

———. 1880. *Aegyptens vormettalische Zeit.* Würzburg, Germany: Staudinger'sche Buchhandlung.

Moore, A. M. T. 1978. *The Neolithic of the Levant.* Oxford: Oxford University Press.

Moose, Margaret. 2014. "The Beauty of Loulan and the Tattooed Mummies of the Tarim Basin." *Ancient Origins,* January 16. www.ancient-origins.net/ancient -places-asia/beauty-loulan-and-tattooed-mummies-tarim-basin-001227?nopaging=1 (accessed January 25, 2018).

Morgan, J. de. 1896. *Recherches sur les origines de l'Égypte: l'age de la pierre et les métaux.* Paris: Ernest Leroux.

Mortensen, Bodil. 1985. "Four Jars from the Maadi Culture Found in Giza." *Mitteilungen des Deutschen Archäologischen Instituts.* Vol. 41, 145–47.

Moseley, Henry Nottidge. 1879. *Notes by a Naturalist on the Challenger etc.* London: Macmillan.

Moussa, Ali Helmi, Lambert T. Dolphin, and Gamal Mokhtar. 1977. *Applications of Modern Sensing Techniques to Egyptology: A Report of the 1977 Field Experiments by a Joint Team.* Cairo: Ain Shams University. www.ldolphin.org/egypt/egypt2 (accessed January 25, 2018).

Moyer, Ernest. 2006. "Egyptian Cubit Rods and Cubits C Part IV: Assessment: Total Rod Lengths." *Egypt Origins.* www.egyptorigins.org/cubitrodsd.htm (accessed January 25, 2018).

Müller, Max. 1918. "Egyptian [Mythology]." In Gray and Moore, 1–245.

Murray, Lucas. 2014. *Hölderlin's Dionysiac Poetry: The Terrifying-Exciting Mysteries.* New York: Springer.

Mustacich, Suzanne, 2012. "DNA Sleuth Hunts Wine Roots in Anatolia." *Wine-Searcher,* November 28. www.wine-searcher.com/m/2012/11/wine-roots-anatolia -turkey-origins (accessed January 25, 2018).

Najarian, Moses. 2016. Աստղային Երկինքն ու Աշխարհագրութիւնը ("Starry Heavens and Geography,") Ներդաշնակ Տուն (Harmony House). https://web .archive.org/web/20160913023740/http://www.nerdashnaktun.org/mn_article _nh; or via the author at: www.dropbox.com/s/2odoad3h3vbb2wm/Najarian 1 - Չիւ Քայլ՝ Իմաստասիրութեամբ | Ներդաշնակ Տուն.pdf?dl=0 (accessed January 25, 2018).

Needham, Joseph. 1962. "Astronomy in Classical China." *Quarterly Journal of the Royal Astronomical Society.* Vol. 3, 87–98.

Neguebauer, Otto, and Richard A. Parker. 1960. *Egyptian Astronomical Texts, Vol. 1: The Early Decans.* Providence, R.I.: Brown University Press.

Nicomachus, 1994. "The Manual of Harmonics." In Levin.

Nigg, Joseph. 2016. *The Phoenix: An Unnatural Biography of a Mythical Beast.* Chicago: University of Chicago Press.

Nisetich, Frank J., trans. 2001. *The Poems of Callimachus.* Oxford: Oxford University Press.

North, John. 1996/2007. *Stonehenge: Neolithic Man and the Cosmos.* New York: Simon and Schuster.

O'Connor, J. J., and E. F. Robertson. 1999. "Pythagoras of Samos." School of Mathematics and Statistics, University of St. Andrews, Scotland. www-groups.dcs .st-and.ac.uk/history/Biographies/Pythagoras.html (accessed January 25, 2018).

Ogden, Daniel. 2002. *Magic, Witchcraft, and Ghosts in the Greek and Roman Worlds: A Sourcebook.* Oxford: Oxford University Press.

Orofino, Vincenzo, and Paolo Bernardini. 2016. "Archaeoastronomical Study of the Main Pyramids of Giza, Egypt: Possible Correlations with the Stars?" *Archaeological Discovery.* Vol. 4, no. 1, 1–10.

Osadchiy, Vadim. "Ergaki's Ridge of [*sic*]." *Rus Articles Journal.* http://rusarticlesjournal .com/1/54804 (accessed January 25, 2018).

Padovan, Richard. 2002. *Science, Philosophy, Architecture.* New York: Taylor and Francis.

Parpola, Simo. 2010. "Sumerian: A Uralic Language (I)." In Kogan et al., 181–210.

——. 2012. "Sumerian: A Uralic Language (II)," *Babel und Bibel.* Vol. 6, 269–322.

Pasquali, Stéphane. 2007. "Des fouilles 'discrètes' à Ro-Sétaou en 1931?" *Göttinger Miszellen.* Vol. 215, 7–8.

——. 2008. "Les fouilles de S. Hassan à Gîza en 1938 et le temple d'Osiris de Ro-Sétaou au Nouvel Empire." *Göttinger Miszellen.* Vol. 216, 75–78.

Patten, Donald, and Emilio Spedicato. 2002. "On the Numbers 54 and 108." In Spedicato and Notarpietro, 130–42.

Pāvils, Gatis, 2010. "Denisova Cave—Abode of Denisova Hominins." *Wondermondo,* December 24. www.wondermondo.com/Countries/E/RUS/AltaiKrai/Denisova Cave.htm (accessed January 25, 2018).

Peters, Joris, and Klaus Schmidt. 2004. "Animals in the Symbolic World of Pre-Pottery Neolithic Göbekli Tepe, South-eastern Turkey: A Preliminary Assessment." *Anthropozoologica.* Vol. 39, no. 1, 179–218.

Peterson, Frederick. 1893. *Medical Notes in Egypt.* New York: M. J. Rooney.

Petrie, Flinders. 1883. *The Pyramids and Temples of Gizeh.* London: Field and Tuer.

Pettitt, Paul. 2013. *The Paleolithic Origins of Human Burial.* Abingdon-on-Thames, Oxfordshire, U.K.: Routledge.

Pflugradt-AbdelAziz, Elke. 1994. "La cité thermale d'Helwan en Égypte et son fondateur, Wilhelm Reil-Bey." *Revue du Monde Musulman et de la Méditerranée.* Vol. 73, no. 1, 259–79.

Phillips, E. D. 1955. "The Legend of Aristeas: Fact and Fancy in Early Greek Notions of East Russia, Siberia, and Inner Asia." *Artibus Asiae.* Vol. 18, no. 2, 161–77.

Piggott, Stuart. 1962. *The West Kennet Long Barrow: Excavations 1955–56.* London: Her Majesty's Stationery Office.

Pimenta, Fernando, N. Ribeiro, F. Silva, N. Campion, A., Joaquinito, and L. Tirapicos, eds. 2015. *Stars and Stones: Voyages in Archaeoastronomy: Proceedings of the SEAC 2011 Conference.* Oxford: Archaeopress.

Pinch, Geraldine. 2002. *Handbook of Egyptian Mythology.* Santa Barbara, Calif.: ABC-CLIO.

Pischikova, Elena, Julia Budka, and Kenneth Griffin. 2014. *Thebes in the First Millennium BC.* Cambridge: Cambridge Scholars Publishing.

Plato. 1973. *Phaedo.* In Grube.

———. 1984. *The Laws.* In Saunders.

———. 1888a. *The Republic.* In Jowett.

———. 1888b. *The Timaeus.* In Archer-Hind.

Pliny. 1938. *Natural History,* books 1–2. Translated by H. Rackham. Cambridge: Loeb Classical Library.

Plutarch, "Isis and Osiris." In Plutarch 1936, 7–49.

Plutarch. 1936. *Moralia.* Vol. 5. Cambridge: Loeb Classical Library.

Pogo, A. 1932. "Calendars on Coffin Lids from Asyut (Second Half of the Third Millennium)." *Isis.* Vol. 17, no. 1, 6–24.

Poole, Reginald Stuart. 1851. *Horæ Ægyptiacæ or The Chronology of Ancient Egypt.* London: John Murray.

Porphyry. 2005. *Vita Pythagorae.* In Berchman.

Prior, Daniel, ed. and trans. 2006. *The Semetey of Kenje Kara: A Kirghiz Epic Performance on Phonograph; with a Musical Score and a Compact Disc of the Phonogram.* Otto Wiesbaden, Germany: Harrassowitz Verlag.

Prüfer, Kay, et al. 2014. "The Complete Genome Sequence of a Neanderthal from the Altai Mountains." *Nature.* Vol. 505 (January 2), 43–49.

Prusinkiewicz, Przemyslaw, and Aristid Lindenmayer. 2012. *The Algorithmic Beauty of Plants.* New York: Springer.

Pseudo-Oppian. 2014. *Cynegetica.* In Weitzmann, 99–151.

Puglisi, Salvatore. 1939. "La stazione di Heluan nel Basso Egitto." *Bullettino di Palentologia Italiana,* n.s., 171–88, pls. 1–5.

Purucker, G. de. 1936. "The Theosophical Forum: Questions and Answers: 293–297." February. www.theosociety.org/pasadena/forum/f08n02p109_questions-and-answers.htm (accessed January 25, 2018).

Quirke, Stephen. 2001. *The Cult of Ra: Sun-Worship in Ancient Egypt.* London: Thames and Hudson.

Rappenglück, Michael A. 1999. *Eine Himmelskarte aus der Eiszeit?* Frankfurt am Main, Germany: Peter Lang.

Reader, Colin. 1999 [1997]. "Khufu Knew the Sphinx: A Reconciliation of the Geological and Archaeological Evidence for the Age of the Sphinx and a Revised Sequence

of Development for the Giza Necropolis." Unpublished. 1997. Revised 1999. www
.academia.edu/7046492/Khufu_Knew_the_Sphinx (accessed January 25, 2018).

Reale, Giovanni, and John R. Catan. 1990. *A History of Ancient Philosophy I: From the Origins to Socrates.* Albany: State University of New York Press.

Reich, David, et al. 2010a. "Genetic History of an Archaic Hominin Group from Denisova Cave in Siberia." *Nature.* Vol. 468, no. 7327 (December 23), 1053–60. www.nature.com/nature/journal/v468/n7327/abs/nature09710.html (accessed January 25, 2018).

———. 2010b. "Supplementary Information: Genetic History of an Archaic Hominin Group from Denisova Cave in Siberia." *Nature.* Vol. 368, no. 7327 (December 22). http://genetics.med.harvard.edu/reich/Reich_Lab/Publications_files/2010 _Nature_Denisova_Genome_Supplementary-1.pdf (accessed January 25, 2018).

Reil, Wilhelm. 1874. "Bearbeitete Feuersteine von Helwan (Ägypten)." *Verhandlungen der Berliner Anthropologischen Gesellschaft,* 118–21.

———. 1888. *Die Schefelthermen von Helouan bei Cairo in Egypten: Und Helouan als Sanatorium für Unflage.* Helwan, Egypt: Selbstverlage des Verfassers.

Reilly, F. Kent, and James F. Garber, eds. 2007. *Ancient Objects and Sacred Realms: Interpretations of Mississippian Iconography.* Austin: University of Texas Press.

Reymond, E. A. E. 1969. *The Mythical Origin of the Egyptian Temple.* Manchester, U.K.: Manchester University Press.

Rice, Michael. 2004 [1990]. *Egypt's Making: The Origins of Ancient Egypt 5000–2000 BC.* London: Routledge.

Richardson, John, and Franciszek Meniński. 1829. *A Dictionary, Persian, Arabic, and English: With a Dissertation on the Languages, Literature, and Manners of the Eastern Nations.* London: J. L. Cox.

Riginos, Alice Swirdt. 1976. *Platonica: The Anecdotes Concerning the Life and Writings of Plato.* Leiden: E. J. Brill.

Roberts, Alice. 2010 [2009]. *The Incredible Human Journey.* London: Bloomsbury.

Rogers, Alan R., Ryan J. Bohlender and Chad D. Huff. 2017. "Early History of Neanderthals and Denisovans," *Proceedings of the National Academy of Sciences.* Vol. 114, no. 37, September 12, 9859–9863.

Rogers, J. H. 1998. "Origins of the Ancient Constellations: I. The Mesopotamian Traditions." *Journal of the British Astronomical Association.* Vol. 108, no. 1, 9–28.

Rogers, Will. 1995. *The Papers of Will Rogers: The Early Years, November 1879–April 1904.* Norman, Okla.: University of Oklahoma Press.

Róheim, Géza. 1954. *Hungarian and Vogul Mythology: Monographs of the American Ethnological Society 23.* Locust Valley, N.Y.: J. J. Augustin.

Rosen, S. A. 1983. "The Microlithic Lunate: An Old-New Tool Type from the Negev, Israel." *Paléorient Année.* Vol. 9, no. 2, 81–83.

Ross, Alexander. 1648. *Mystagogus Poeticus or The Muses Interpreter Explaining the Historical Mysteries, and Mystical Histories of the Ancient Greek and Latine Poets.* London: Thomas Whitaker.

Rothwangl, Sepp. 2009. "One Day Every 216 Years, Three Days Each Decan: Rebirth Cycle of Pythagoras, Phoenix, Hazon Gabriel, and Christian Dogma of Resurrection Can Be Explained by the Metonic Cycle." In Rubiño-Martín et al., 487–93.

Rubiño-Martín, José Alberto, Juan Antonio Belmonte, Francisco Prada, and Antxon Alberdi, eds. 2009. *Cosmology across Cultures ASP Conference Series, Vol. 409: Proceedings of the Conference Held 8–12 September, 2008, at Parque de las Ciencias, Granada, Spain.* San Francisco: Astronomical Society of the Pacific.

Ruck, Carl A. P. 1986. "Poets, Philosophers, Priests: Entheogens in the Formation of the Classical Tradition." In Wasson et al., 151–257.

Rysdyk, Evelyn C. 2014. *A Spirit Walker's Guide to Shamanic Tools: How to Make and Use Drums, Masks, Rattles, and Other Sacred Implements.* New York: Weiser.

Saad, Zaki Y. 1969. *The Excavations at Helwan: Art and Civilization in the First and Second Egyptian Dynasties.* Norman, Okla.: University of Oklahoma Press.

Salleh, Anna. 2004. "Egyptian Tombs Reveal a Complex Society." *News in Science,* June 17. www.abc.net.au/science/news/stories/s1133289.htm (accessed January 25, 2018).

Sanders, Robert. 2013. "Neanderthal Genome Shows Evidence of Early Human Interbreeding, Inbreeding." UC Berkeley News Center, December 18. http://newscenter.berkeley.edu/2013/12/18/neanderthal-genome-shows-evidence-of-early-human-interbreeding-inbreeding/ (accessed January 25, 2018).

Santillana, Giorgio de, and Hertha von Dechend. 1969. *Hamlet's Mill: An Essay on Myth and the Frame of Time.* Boston: Gambit.

Sanussi, Ashraf el-, and Michael Jones. 1997. "A Site of the Maadi Culture near the Giza Pyramids."*Mitteilungen des Deutschen Archäologischen Instituts.* Vol. 53, 241–53.

Sarrûf, Fûad, and Suha Tamim, eds. 1967. *American University of Beirut Festival Book (Festschrift).* Beirut: American University of Beirut.

Saunders, T. J., trans. 1984. *The Laws by Plato.* Harmondsworth, Middlesex, U.K.: Penguin.

Schmidt, Klaus. 1994. "The Nevali Cori Industry." In Gebel and Kozlowski, 239–52.

———. 1996. "Helwan in Egypt: A PPN Site?" In Kozlowski and Gebel, 127–35.

———. 2001. "Göbekli Tepe, Southeastern Turkey: A Preliminary Report on the 1995–1999 Excavations." *Paleorient.* Vol. 26, no. 1, 45–54.

———. 2002. "Göbekli Tepe and the Early Sites of the Urfa Region: A Synopsis of New Results and Current Views." *Neo-Lithics.* Vol. 1, no. 1, 9–11.

———. 2012. *Göbekli Tepe: A Stone Age Sanctuary in South-eastern Anatolia.* Berlin: Ex Oriente.

Schmidt, Klaus, and Oliver Dietrich. 2010. "A Radiocarbon Date from the Wall Plaster of Enclosure D of Göbekli Tepe." *Neo-Lithics*. Vol. 2, no. 10, 82–83.

Schoch, Robert M. 1992. "Redating the Great Sphinx of Giza." *KMT: A Modern Journal of Ancient Egypt*. Vol. 3, no. 2 (Summer), 52–59, 66–70.

———. 2012. *Forgotten Civilization: The Role of Solar Outbursts in Our Past and Future*. Rochester, Vt.: Inner Traditions.

Schüz, E., and C. König. 1983. "Old Vultures and Man." In Wilbur and Jackson, 461–69.

Schweinfurth, G. 1901. "Helwan and Its Eastern Surroundings Surveyed by G. Schweinfurth 1895–96." In May, Schweinfurth, and Sayce (presented in a pocket at the front of the book).

Schwierz, Thomas. 2011. "Die Armen-Seelen-Löcher: Relikte einer entschwundenen Zeit." *Oberösterreichische Heimatblätter*. Vol. 65, 154–56.

Sellers, Jane B. 1992. *The Death of Gods in Ancient Egypt*. London: Penguin.

Shaltout, Mosalam, and Juan Antontio Belmonte. 2009. *In Search of Cosmic Order: Selected Essays on Egyptian Archaeoastronomy*. Cairo: Supreme Council of Antiquities.

Shaw, George. 1790. *Vivarium Naturæ or A Naturalist's Miscellany or Coloured Figures of Natural Objects Drawn and Described Immediately from Nature*. London: G. Shaw and F. P. Nodder.

Shea, John J. 2013. *Stone Tools in the Paleolithic and Neolithic Near East: A Guide*. Cambridge: Cambridge University Press.

Shelley, Gerard. 1945. *Folk Tales of the Peoples of the Soviet Union*. London: Herbert Jenkins.

Sherman, Josepha. 2015 [2009]. *World Folklore for Storytellers*. London: Routledge.

Shirai, Noriyuki. 2002. "Helwan Points in the Egyptian Neolithic." *Orient*. Vol. 37, 121–33.

———. 2010. *The Archaeology of the First Farmer-Herders in Egypt: New Insights into the Fayum EpiPaleolithic and Neolithic*. Leiden: Leiden University Press.

Shodoev, Nikolai. 2012. *Spiritual Wisdom from the Altai Mountains*. Alresford, Hants., U.K.: John Hunt.

Siikala, Anna-Leena. 1978. *The Rite Technique of the Siberian Shaman*. Helsinki: Suomalainen Tiedeakatemis.

Simmons, Alan H. 2011. *The Neolithic Revolution in the Near East: Transforming the Human Landscape*. Tucson: University of Arizona Press.

Simplicius. 1818. *On Aristotle. On the Heavens*. Book 2. In Taylor.

Simpson, William Kelly, ed. 1989. *Religion and Philosophy in Ancient Egypt*. New Haven, Conn.: Yale Egyptological Studies.

Sion, Viviane, et al. 2017. "A Fourth Denisovan Individual." *Science Advances*. Vol. 3, 1–8.

Smedley, Edward, James Rose, and Henry John Rose, eds. 1845. *Encyclopædia Metropolitana*. Vol. 5. London: B. Fellowes et al.

Sokolowski, A. 2012. "Decoding Giza Pyramids: Part 1." *World-Mysteries*. http://blog .world-mysteries.com/science/decoding-giza-pyramids-part-1/ (accessed January 25, 2018).

Solecki, Ralph S., Rose L. Solecki, and Anagnostis P. Agelarakis. 2004. *Proto-Neolithic Cemetery in Shanidar Cave*. College Station, Texas: Texas A & M University Press.

Solecki, Rose. 1977. "Predatory Bird Rituals at Zawi Chemi Shanidar." *Sumer*. Vol. 33, 42–47.

Solecki, Rose L., and Ralph S. Solecki. 2004. "The Zagros Proto-Neolithic and Cultural Developments in the Near East." In Solecki, Solecki, and Agelarakis, 114–58.

Sørensen, Mikkel. 2012. "The Arrival and Development of Pressure Blade Technology in Southern Scandinavia." In Desrosiers, 237–59.

Spedicato, Emilio, and Adalberto Notarpietro, eds. 2002. *Proceedings of the Conference: New Scenarios on the Evolution of the Solar System and Consequences on History of Earth and Man, Report Miscellanea 2002/2*. Bergamo, Italy: University of Bergamo.

Sperlich, Waltraud. 2000. "Die erste Siedlung der Altsteinzeit." *Bild der Wissenschaft*, August, 68–71.

Śrīmad-Bhāgavatam (Bhāgavata Purāna). Bhaktivedanta VedaBase. www.vedabase.com /sb/3/11/19 (accessed January 25, 2018).

Srinivasan, M. R. 1996. *Physics for Engineers*. New Delhi: New Age International.

Srsa, Daniel. 2003. *Prophet's Manual (Fractal Supersymmetry of Double Helix)*, Lincoln, Neb.: iUniverse.

Stecchini, Livio C. 2001. "The Dimensions of the Great Pyramid, a History of Measures: II: Units of Length." www.metrum.org/measures/dimensions.htm (accessed January 25, 2018).

Steingass, F. 1963 [1892]. *A Comprehensive Persian-English Dictionary: Including Arabic Words and Phrases to Be Met with in Persian Literature*. London: Routledge and Kegan Paul.

Stephany, Timothy J. 2008–09. "Norse Constellations." *Myths, Mysteries and Wonders*. www.timothystephany.com/constellations.html (accessed January 25, 2018).

Stordeur, D., B. Jammous, D. Helmer, and G. Willcox. 1996. "Jerf el-Ahmar: A New Mureybetian Site (PPNA)." *Neo-Lithics*. Vol. 2, no. 96, 1–2.

Strabo. 1917–1932. *Geography*. Translated by H. L. Jones. Cambridge: Loeb Classical Library.

Stroumsa, Guy G. 1996. *Hidden Wisdom: Esoteric Traditions and the Roots of Christian Mysticism*. Leiden: E. J. Brill.

Stuiver, M., and P. J. Reimer. 1993. "Extended 14C Database and Revised CALIB 3.0 14C Age Calibration Program." *Radiocarbon*. Vol. 35, 215–30.

Syrianus. 1818. *On Aristotle Metaphysics.* Book 13. In Taylor. *Iamblichus.* 78n.1. Tacitus. 1937. *The Annals of Tacitus.* Vol. 4. Translated by John Jackson. Loeb Classical Library.

Tallet, Pierre, and Gregory Marouard. 2014. "The Harbor of Khufu on the Red Sea Coast at Wadi al-Jarf, Egypt." *Near Eastern Archaeology.* Vol. 77, no. 1, 4–14.

Taylor, Thomas, trans. 1818. *Iamblichus' Life of Pythagoras, or Pythagoric Life.* London: Watkins.

Tedlock, Dennis. 1996. *Popol Vuh: The Mayan Book of the Dawn of Life.* New York: Touchstone.

Thapar, Romila. 2004. *Early India: From the Origins to A.D. 1300.* Berkeley: University of California Press.

"The Number 72 in Judaism, Confucianism, Taoism (and Buddhism?)." 2013. *Cultura Antiqua.* https://culturaantiqua.wordpress.com/2013/01/05/the-number-72-in -judaism-taoism-egyptian-religion (accessed January 25, 2018).

Thomas, Joseph. 1837. *The Gods of Homer and Virgil, or, Mythology for Children.* London: Joseph Thomas.

Thompson, Jason. 1992. *Sir Gardner Wilkinson and His Circle.* Austin: University of Texas Press.

Todd, Ian. 1976. *Çatal Hüyük in Perspective.* Menlo Park, Calif.: Cummings.

Torjussen, Stian Sundell. 2014. "Milk as a Symbol of Immortality in the 'Orphic' Gold Tablets." *Nordlit.* Vol. 33, 35–46.

Trimble, V. 1964. "Astronomical Investigation Concerning the So-called Air Shafts of Cheops' Pyramid." *Mitteilungen des Instituts für Orientforschung.* Vol. 10, 183–87.

Uyanik, Muvaffak. 1974. *Petroglyphs of South-Eastern Anatolia.* Graz, Austria: Akademishe Druck-u. Verlagsanstalt.

Vahradyan, Vachagan, and Marine Vahradyan. 2013. "About the Astronomical Role of 'Qarahunge' Monument." www.anunner.com/vachagan.vahradyan/About_the _Astronomical_Role_of_"Qarahunge"_Monument_by_Vachagan_Vahradyan, _Marine_Vahradyan.

Van Deusen, Kira. 1998. "New Legends in the Rebirth of Khakass Shamanic Culture." *The Anthropology of East Europe Review.* Vol. 16, no. 2, 55–61.

———. 2004. *Singing Story, Healing Drum: Shamans and Storytellers of Turkic Siberia.* Toronto: McGill-Queen's University Press.

Vasil'ev, Sergey A., Yaroslav V. Kuzmin, Lyubov A. Orlova, and Vyacheslav N. Dementiev. 2002. "Radiocarbon-Based Chronology of the Paleolithic in Siberia and Its Relevance to the Peopling of the New World." *Radiocarbon.* Vol. 44, no. 2, 503–30.

Vermander, Benoît. 1999. "The Religious System of the Yi of Liangshan." *China Perspectives.* Vol. 21 (January/February), 3–12.

Vernot, Benjamin, et al. 2016. "Excavating Neandertal and Denisovan DNA from the Genomes of Melanesian Individuals." *Science*. Vol. 352, no. 6282 (April 8), 235–39.

Volney, Constantin-François. 1819. Translated by Col. Corbet. *New Researches on Ancient History*. Vol. 1. London: W. Lewis.

Von Beckerath, Jürgen. 1997. *Chronologie des pharaonischen Ägypten: die Zeitbestimmung der ägyptischen Geschichte von der Vorzeit bis 332 v. Chr.* Darmstadt, Germany: Philipp von Zabern.

Vyse, Richard William Howard, and John Shea Perring. 1840. *Operations Carried On at the Pyramids of Gizeh in 1837: With an Account of a Voyage into Upper Egypt and an Appendix*. Vol. 3. London: James Fraser.

Wainwright, G. A. 1932. "A Pair of Constellations." In Glanville and Griffith, 373–83.

Ward, Richard. 2016. *Echoes from the Primal Grimoire*. New York: Von Zos.

Wasson, R. Gordon, Stella Kramrisch, Jonathan Ott, and Carl A. P. Ruck. 1986. *Persephone's Quest: Entheogens and the Origins of Religion*. New Haven, Conn.: Yale University Press.

Webb Hodge, Frederick, ed. 1912. *Handbook of American Indians North of Mexico*. vol. 3, N–S. Washington, D.C.: Government Printing Office.

Weitzmann, Kurt. 2014. *Greek Mythology in Byzantine Art*. Princeton, N.J.: Princeton University Press.

Wells, Ronald A. 1992. "The Mythology of Nut and the Birth of Ra." *Studien zur Altagyptischen Kultur*. Vol. 19, 305–21.

———. 1993. "Origin of the Hour and the Gates of the Duat." *Studien zur Altägyptischen Kultur*. Vol. 20, 305–26.

Wendorf, Fred, and J. McKim Malville. 2001. "The Megalith Alignments." In Wendorf, Schild, and Nelson, 489–502.

Wendorf, Fred, and Romuald Schild. 1976. *Prehistory of the Nile Valley*. New York: Academic Press.

Wendorf, Fred, Romuald Schild, and Kit Nelson. 2001. *Holocene Settlement of the Egyptian Sahara, Vol. 1: The Archaeology of Nabta Playa*. New York: Kluwer Academic/Plenum.

Werner, E. T. C. 1958 [1922]. *Myths and Legends of China*. London: Geo. G. Harrap.

Westendorf, W. 1977. "Himmelsvorstellungen." In Helck, Otto, and Westendorf, 1215–18.

———. 1982. "Panther." In Helck, 664–65.

White, Gavin. 2007. *Babylonian Star Lore*. London: Solaria.

Wilbur, S. R., and J. A. Jackson, eds. 1983. *Vulture Biology and Management*. Berkeley: University of California Press.

Wilkinson, Sir John Gardner. 1835. *The Topography of Thebes and General View of Egypt, Being a Short Account of the Principal Objects*. London: John Murray.

———. 1837. *Manners and Customs of the Ancient Egyptians.* 3 vols. London: John Murray.

———. 1841. *A Second Series of the Manners and Customs of the Ancient Egyptians: Including Their Religion, Agriculture, &c. Derived from a Comparison of the Paintings, Sculptures, and Monuments Still Existing, with the Accounts of Ancient Authors.* Vol. 2. London: John Murray.

———. 1843. *Modern Egypt and Thebes: Being a Description of Egypt, Including the Information Required for Travelers in That Country.* 2 vols. London: John Murray.

Wilkinson, Philip. 2009. *Myths and Legends.* London: Dorling Kindersley.

Wilkinson, Toby. 1999. *Early Dynastic Egypt.* London: Routledge.

Willerding, Margaret F. 1975. "The Pythagorean Legacy." *School Science and Mathematics.* Vol. 75, no. 2 (February), 145–54.

Wilson, Colin. 2007/2011. *From Atlantis to the Sphinx.* Revised edition. London: Virgin Books.

Winkelman, Michael. 2002. "Shamanism and Cognitive Evolution." *Cambridge Archaeological Journal.* Vol. 12, no. 1, 71–101.

Wong, Kate. 2010. "No Bones about It: Ancient DNA from Siberia Hints at Previously Unknown Human Relative." *Scientific American,* March 24. www.scientificamerican .com/article.cfm?id=new-hominin-species (accessed January 25, 2018).

"World's Oldest Needle Found in Siberian Cave that Stitches Together Human History." 2016. *Siberian Times,* August 23. http://siberiantimes.com/science/casestudy /news/n0711-worlds-oldest-needle-found-in-siberian-cave-that-stitches-together -human-history/ (accessed January 25, 2018).

Wu, Zhongxian, and Karin Taylor Wu. 2014. *Heavenly Stems and Earthly Branches: TianGan DiZhi: The Heart of Chinese Wisdom Traditions.* London: Singing Dragon.

Yalçın, Ünsal. 2016. *Anatolian Metal VII: Anatolien und seine Nachbarn vor 10.000 Jahren; Anatolia and Neighbours 10,000 Years Ago (Beiheft 31).* Bochum, Germany: Der Anschnitt.

Yang, Lihui, Deming An, and Jessica Anderson Turner. 2005. *Handbook of Chinese Mythology.* Santa Barbara, Calif.: ABC-CLIO.

Yardimci, Nurettin. 2008. *Mezopotamya'ya açilan kapi Harran.* Istanbul: Ege Yayın.

Yeshurun, R., G. Bar-Oz, and M. Weinstein-Evron. 2009. "The Role of Foxes in the Natufian Economy: A View from Mount Carmel, Israel." *Before Farming: The Archaeology and Anthropology of Hunter-Gatherers.* Vol. 3, 1–15.

Yi, Mingjie, Xing Gao, Feng Li, and Fuyou Chen. 2016. "Rethinking the Origin of Microblade Technology: A Chronological and Ecological Perspective." *Quaternary International.* Vol. 400, May 2, 130–39.

Zába, Zbyněk. 1953. *L'Orientation astronomique dans l'ancienne Égypte: Archiv Orientální Supplementa II.* Prague: Československá akademie.

Zaliznyak, L. L. 1999. "Tanged Point Cultures in the Western Part of Eastern Europe." In Koslowski, Gurba, and Zaliznyak, 202–18.

Zick, Michael. 2000. "Der älteste Tempel der Welt." *Bild der Wissenschaft* August, 60–66.

Zitman, Wim. 2006. "Egypt: 'Image of Heaven.'" www.zitman.org/websites/egypt-image-of-heaven/the-chapters/ (accessed January 25, 2018).

Znamenski, Andrei. 2012. *Red Shambhala: Magic, Prophecy, and Geopolitics in the Heart of Asia*. Wheaton, Ill.: Quest.

Zolin, Peter, II. 2010. "The Real Story of Russia Baikal Malta." www.proza.ru/2010/12/22/1475 (accessed January 25, 2018).

Zsuzsa, Tomory. 2009. "Magyar Creation: Part I." http://tomoryzsuzsa.weebly.com/magyar-creation.html (accessed January 25, 2018).

Zubchuk, Tamara. 2016. "Paleolithic Jewellery: Still Eye-Catching after 50,000 Years." *Siberian Times,* October 31. http://siberiantimes.com/other/others/news/n0789-paleolithic-jewellery-still-eye-catching-after-50000-years/ (accessed January 25, 2018).

Zwyns, Nicolas, et al. 2014. "The Open-Air Site of Tolbor 16 (Northern Mongolia): Preliminary Results and Perspectives." *Quaternary International*. Vol. 347 (June), 53–65.

INDEX

Numbers in *italics* preceded by *pl.* indicate color insert plate numbers.